AN UNCIVIL WAR

The Southern Backcountry
during the American Revolution

UNITED STATES CAPITOL HISTORICAL SOCIETY
Fred Schwengel, President

PERSPECTIVES ON THE AMERICAN REVOLUTION

Ronald Hoffman and Peter J. Albert, Editors

Diplomacy and Revolution: The Franco-American Alliance of 1778

Sovereign States in an Age of Uncertainty

Slavery and Freedom in the Age of the American Revolution

Arms and Independence: The Military Character of the American Revolution

An Uncivil War: The Southern Backcountry during the American Revolution

An Uncivil War

The Southern Backcountry
during the American Revolution

Edited by RONALD HOFFMAN,
THAD W. TATE
and PETER J. ALBERT

Published for the

UNITED STATES CAPITOL HISTORICAL SOCIETY

BY THE UNIVERSITY PRESS OF VIRGINIA

Charlottesville

THE UNIVERSITY PRESS OF VIRGINIA
Copyright © 1985 by the Rector and Visitors
of the University of Virginia

First Published 1985

Library of Congress Cataloging in Publication Data
Main entry under title:

An Uncivil war.

(Perspectives on the American Revolution)
Essays originally presented at a symposium in Washington, D.C., Mar. 18–19, 1982 under the sponsorship of the United States Capitol Historical Society and the Institute of Early American History and Culture.
Includes index.
1. Southern States—History—Revolution, 1775–1783—Social aspects—Congresses. I. Hoffman, Ronald, 1941–   II. Tate, Thad W. III. Albert, Peter J. IV. United States Capitol Historical Society. V. Institute of Early American History and Culture (Williamsburg, Va.)

VI. Series.
E230.5.S7U52 1985   974'.03   84-19632
ISBN 0-8139-1051-X

Printed in the United States of America

Contents

CONTENTS

MAPS

Preface

THE SUBJECT OF INTERNAL CONFLICT in the Revolution will perhaps seem to many a subject that has already received its due share of attention. Yet scholars have far too often confined their investigation to some of its simpler and more obvious manifestations, especially to political contests that centered in the older, seaboard regions of the colonies where social and economic divisions were presumably more long-standing and fully developed. Much of the past attention to conflicts in the South has concentrated on the Regulator movements of North and South Carolina—movements that in some respects anticipated the Revolution and arose from somewhat different, if perhaps ultimately related, circumstances. Given the focus of past work and the varied lines of research on the American Revolution now being pursued, the question of internal conflict and change, in fact, invites further and more searching investigation.

At the same time the issues involved appeared so broad and complex that in planning the symposium we decided to attempt to illuminate them by focusing on the four states of the Revolutionary South, from Virginia through the Carolinas to Georgia. That decision was prompted in part by our knowledge that an active group of scholars was at work on the era of the Revolution in each of the four, especially the Carolinas and Georgia. Many of these historians were only beginning to bring their work to completion, promising to have fresh conclusions to offer. An even more important consideration, however, was our sense that in the southern backcountry questions of diversity, internal struggle, and resolution of conflict were unusually intense and very likely too complicated to be comprehended within the traditional interpretation that had emphasized east-west political rivalry as the principal source of difficulty within these states.

Mindful at the same time of the warning that Jack P.

PREFACE

Greene issues in the first essay of this volume against the assumption that the four southern states necessarily exhibited similar patterns of development, economic circumstances, or social structure, we were nonetheless convinced that for a number of reasons the southern backcountry during the Revolution could provide a promising theme for study.

1. In each of these states the backcountry was a very recently settled area, society was less fully formed, the economy was weaker and less developed, and the inhabitants lived on an exposed Indian frontier. In every respect backcountry inhabitants were more directly in need of the British connection than their fellow colonists to the east. Yet even though there were predictably strong loyalist elements in the region, there was also powerful support for the patriot side. Hence the region offers a particularly good example of the way in which allegiances were formed in the Revolutionary conflict.

2. Given the above conditions, the social order was only beginning to define itself in the region and in some cases to do so with great difficulty, as the Regulator movement in the two Carolinas on the eve of the Revolution might suggest. In sum, the region affords an opportunity to look at the internal history of the Revolution in an area that was already undergoing some obvious stress.

3. Despite its remoteness, the area was one that was directly involved in the military phases of the Revolution. And, because of the extent of Indian and partisan warfare there, the conflict was particularly intense and violent, having more of the appearance of civil war about it than was true of the large-scale engagements fought in the east by Continental and British forces. The region therefore affords an opportunity to investigate the impact of the military conflict itself on a civilian population in a particularly dramatic way.

In addressing these themes and without losing sight of the distinct circumstances that prevailed in each of the four states, the essayists demonstrate that the southern backcountry has an important history in its own right but can also provide a particularly incisive illustration of the difficult process of change and adjustment within the American states during the Revolution.

THAD W. TATE

Acknowledgments

THE ESSAYS IN THIS VOLUME were originally presented at a symposium in Washington, D.C., on March 18–19, 1982, under the cosponsorship of the United States Capitol Historical Society and the Institute of Early American History and Culture. The cooperation of the Society and the Institute came about when the two institutions discovered that each was considering a conference on the backcountry South during the era of the Revolution. Rather than attempt to organize competing meetings that would inevitably draw on some of the same participants, it seemed far more constructive to join forces. The successful outcome of both the symposium and this study has, in the editors' judgment, amply justified that decision.

As both conference organizers and editors we have benefited greatly from the contributions made by a number of fine scholars and generous institutions. First and foremost, Fred Schwengel, the tireless president of the United States Capitol Historical Society, provided advice, encouragement, and all else that was asked of him. Two grants—one from the National Endowment for the Humanities and the other from the Historical Research Foundation—enabled the scope of this study to be broadened and deepened. During the symposium the comments delivered by Marvin L. Michael Kay, Pauline Maier, and Clarence L. Ver Steeg enriched the meeting; subsequently their observations served as valuable points of departure as the papers were converted into formal essays. The maps for the volume were prepared by Douglas Roesser of the Cartographic Services Laboratory at the University of Maryland, College Park. Finally, the skilled abilities of our typist, Eleanor Darcy, provided reassurance to the editors as the volume proceeded from manuscript to publication.

Introduction

WITH THE DECLARATION of their independence Americans embarked on the difficult task of defeating the British in military combat. But the Revolution's leaders faced another challenge as well, just as formidable as the challenge of arms: the necessity of uniting a people characterized by ethnic, religious, economic, and class diversity. Although internal conflict during the American Revolution was a complex and important phenomenon, the subject has seldom received, as the preface to this volume has suggested, its due share of scholarly attention. This is unfortunate since the civil tensions and divisions of the period 1775–83 tell us a good deal not only about the nature of the war years but also about the political, economic, and social realities of pre-Revolutionary society.

Historiographically, eighteenth-century colonial society has been interpreted from two dominant perspectives. At one extreme there are those historians who posit a harmonious golden age in which the upper class exercised power as a form of gracious stewardship that received the enthusiastic endorsement of the submissive and deferential populace. Conversely, other scholars portray a social system riddled with dissension and on the brink of violent upheaval as abused farmers and increasingly impoverished urban dwellers came to define themselves in class-conscious terms.

While both of these historiographical viewpoints are problematical, two facts about late colonial society should be stressed. First, strains and tensions unmistakably rent the fabric of pre-Revolutionary life. The record here is clear, whether one examines the more obvious manifestations such as the backcountry and tenant rebellions or the less overt antagonisms engendered by political, religious, and economic divisions. Second—and this dimension has been largely ignored—the colonial economy was generally prosperous in

xi

the decade before the Revolution, and the expansion in demand for the products of British North America created a context of genuine economic opportunity and social mobility within the colonies. Thus two conflicting realities were juxtaposed in pre-Revolutionary America: division, disorder, and resentment coexisted with the potential for economic improvement and social advancement. As egalitarian notions of social justice and equitable representation intensified during the 1760s and 1770s, the tensions generated by these adversely related forces grew increasingly abrasive. During the war, as I observed in an essay several years ago, they exploded as "the Revolution brought popular anger to a boil so that it took on the appearance of a spasmodic social convulsion essentially hostile to any rigid political direction."

There are no easy interpretive formulas to be applied here, but one general assumption seems warranted: in times of severe social stress, societies lay bare their essential structural elements. A basically cohesive community will remain reasonably united in a period of adversity while one containing divisive elements will fragment. Thus New England—although not without some serious internal tension during the fighting—remained largely unified despite having weathered less than favorable economic conditions during the prewar period. By contrast the southern backcountry, which had enjoyed substantial economic growth in the years preceding the war, endured such violent unrest between 1775 and 1783 that the survival of the patriot cause was placed in severe jeopardy. Any meaningful interpretation of the American experience during the Revolutionary War cannot, therefore, focus solely upon the admittedly shattering effects of wartime violence and upheaval but must take into account the complex range of political, economic, and social developments that strained colonial society during the third quarter of the eighteenth century. The studies presented here provide compelling evidence of the validity of this approach.

Jack P. Greene's provacative opening essay, which provides a general framework for understanding the experience of the southern backcountry during the Revolution, reflects a growing trend among historians to recognize the limitations of deference in maintaining social order and to emphasize

Introduction

the instability inherent in colonial society. While the other authors in the volume tend to underscore the contrast between the backcountry and the seaboard societies, Greene addresses the fundamental similarities and the shared values that linked the two. Moreover, he questions the extent to which the ruling elites dominated the southern states and emphasizes the fragile nature of the authority they exercised, a fragility obscured by such terms as *hierarchical society* or *deferential society*. This authority, he maintains, rested not on the power of the rulers but on the consent of the ruled. Far from enjoying unchallenged sovereignty, the state governments were sorely tested during the Revolution.

The next two essays, by Rachel N. Klein and Robert M. Weir, concentrate on the South Carolina backcountry. Klein examines the factors that led South Carolinians to align with the whigs or the tories, and argues that the whigs more consistently represented the broad class interests of backcountry slaveholders than did the tories. She outlines whig attempts to attract the support of men of influence in the backcountry by offering them access to political and military positions, and demonstrates that the constitution of 1776, which expanded the role of the backcountry in the legislature, and policies such as the offensive against the Cherokee in 1776, gained further backcountry adherents to the whig cause. Meanwhile, loyalists antagonized the backcountry by allying themselves with the Indians as well as the roving hunters and bandits who had aroused the Regulators in the 1760s. In sum, Klein argues that South Carolina's whigs attracted support in the backcountry during the Revolution by presenting themselves as protectors of the farmers who settled there, champions of the social order, and defenders of property; the tories and the British alienated potential support by attracting allies who did them more harm than good. Weir's essay studies South Carolina in the immediate postwar era. Confronting the question of how a state marked by disorder and violence during the war could evidence such a degree of social and political stability in the years following the conflict, he describes the process by which South Carolina's authorities reestablished public order and their own legitimacy, particularly their use of punitive legislation against tories

xiii

enacted in 1782 and 1783. Employing disfranchisement, amercement, confiscation, and banishment, this legislation met the popular demand for retributive justice, thereby legitimizing the authority of the government and establishing the legislature as the proper forum for dealing with the loyalists after the Revolution. Subsequently, however, the legislators considered petitions from those who were the targets of this legislation and often rescinded or lessened the penalties on a case-by-case basis, thus gaining the support of these disaffected members of the political community.

In the following two essays A. Roger Ekirch and Jeffrey J. Crow present two quite different analyses of the whig response to disaffection in the North Carolina backcountry. Ekirch describes it as a region where the defeat of the Regulators at Alamance had left a large segment of the population hostile or indifferent to the whigs during the early years of the Revolution and where the whig position was further eroded by the efforts of royal governor Josiah Martin. Nevertheless, the patriots made a determined effort to secure the allegiance of disaffected residents of the backcountry and had considerable success. Whig strategy during the course of the war—the attempt to recreate a semblance of law, discipline, and social stability through the military presence of cavalry units, the adoption of a moderate course of action toward penitent loyalists and harsher measures toward plunderers, and the activation of the local court system—met the demands of many of the settlers in western North Carolina and promoted the popular acceptance of the state's government once the war was over. Crow, on the other hand, is critical of whig activities in the backcountry where disaffection, already widespread when the Revolution began, hardened into loyalism after 1778 and erupted into a civil war in 1780. Resistance in the region was triggered, Crow argues, primarily by class tensions as poor and middling backcountry farmers resisted the exactions of the eastern elite that had crushed the Regulation. When whigs met backcountry disaffection with harsh penalties, test oaths, the confiscation of property, and the draft—measures which Crow describes as a "reign of terror"—the disaffected responded with verbal insolence, interference with civil officials, resistance to militia service and the draft, and, finally, open and armed insurgency. The end of the Revolution saw the triumph of the whig oligarchy, but this group failed to extinguish lower-class resentment of its impositions and dominance, and former loyalists in the backcountry remained objects of violence, social ostracism, and political discrimination.

Emory G. Evans and Richard R. Beeman then consider the Revolution in backcountry Virginia. Evans explores in close detail one area of the state—the southwest, particularly Montgomery County—where disaffection was rampant and persistent, appearing as early as 1776, worsening after 1777, and exploding into insurrection in 1779 and 1780. He estimates that by 1780, 40 percent of the population in Montgomery County were disaffected and that there was also significant disaffection in Bedford and Botetourt counties. Studying the Virginians who were prosecuted in the county court, he concludes that the disaffected formed no distinct economic or religious group in Montgomery County but were probably recent immigrants to the area who chafed at their exclusion from the power wielded by their longer-established neighbors. While Evans's essay focuses on a six-county area of southwest Virginia, Beeman's is broader in scope. Given what he describes to be essential similarities within the southern backcountry as a whole—rapid population increase as well as a substantial turnover in the population, great economic opportunity and social mobility, ethnic and religious diversity, and a commitment to subsistence agriculture—Beeman attempts to account for the contrast between the relative tranquility of Virginia's backcountry and the extensive disorder that pervaded North and South Carolina. The explanation, he argues, lies in the nature of politics and political leadership in Virginia as opposed to that found in the Carolinas. Virginians, he maintains, had built a tradition of political leadership that included the backcountry, both by representing its interests in the legislature and by meeting the judicial needs of its citizens in local courts. During the war Virginia's whig leadership was able to demonstrate to the backcountry that supporting the Revolution was in its interest. In the Carolinas, on the other hand, the backcountry was poorly represented in the legislature, and

local political institutions were limited at best. Despite constitutional changes, the backcountry felt little attachment to the
whig leadership or its cause, and this lack of a working political rapport between the seaboard and backcountry areas underlay the violent internal conflict that marked the area
during the Revolution.

The final three essays in the volume, those of Edward J.
Cashin, Harvey H. Jackson, and W. W. Abbot, explore the
Revolution in the Georgia backcountry. Cashin's narrative re-
capitulates the course of the war there and studies its consequences. The principal outcome of the conflict, he writes,
was to transfer the control of a vast frontier from the Indians—Creeks and Cherokee—and those associated with
them—loyalists, Indian traders, and elements of the royal
establishment—to whigs of all factions, particularly those settlers who had moved into Georgia after the cessions of 1763
and 1773 and the new men who emerged during the war to
lead them. Jackson, on the other hand, examines political developments in Georgia during the Revolution. The transformation was profound—from a royal colony governed by an
appointive governor and an assembly dominated by a coalition of Savannah and Christ Church Parish planters and
merchants to an independent state governed by a legislature
dominated by Augusta and the backcountry. He traces the
evolution of factional coalitions among the state's whigs and
describes the emergence of western leaders and the backcountry's assumption of a more important role in Georgia's
political balance. The adoption of the state's constitution in
1777, which lowered qualifications for voting and officeholding and reapportioned the state, guaranteed that western
members would shape Georgia's political future. In the volume's concluding essay, W. W. Abbot thoughtfully discusses
the standard political and military chronicles of Revolutionary Georgia by McCall, Stevens, Jones, and Coleman. He
points to the need for understanding Georgia as a newly
formed frontier society, and for pursuing within this context
such questions as the factional nature of politics in Revolutionary Georgia, the radical-conservative split in 1774–75,
and the upcountry-lowcountry struggle for control in the
1780s.

RONALD HOFFMAN

AN UNCIVIL WAR

The Southern Backcountry

during the American Revolution

JACK P. GREENE

Independence, Improvement, and Authority

Toward a Framework for Understanding the Histor*ies* of the Southern Backcountry during the Era of the American Revolution

THE TITLE OF this volume contains two large general concep-
tions: *southern backcountry* and *American Revolution*. As every-
body understands, the first refers to that vast inland region
stretching from the Potomac River south to Florida and from
the fall line west to the Appalachian Mountains. But the term
carries with it a cultural as well as a geographical connotation
and strongly implies a basic socioeconomic, even an ideological unity among the people who inhabited the area. The
concept has a distinguished ancestry: as used by the authors
of the essays in this volume, it coincides almost exactly with
the southern portions of Frederick Jackson Turner's "Old
West." Although it was divided into several parts, each of
which was tied politically to one of the seaboard societies of
the southern colonies, this area, according to Turner, was "a
new continuous social and economic area, which cut across
the artificial colonial boundary lines." More like Pennsyl-

3

vania, an area from which it drew substantial numbers of settlers, than like the lowcountry South, this "new Pennsylvania," as Turner called it, existed in an uneasy relationship with older settled areas to the east and was defined primarily by its differences from those areas. To the extent that it was an extension of the older societies of the colonial South, it was, according to Turner, certainly a "new South," one that was altogether less dependent on slave labor, less devoted to a staple agriculture, less tied to foreign markets and foreign culture, and more self-sufficient and self-contained. It was not the first frontier in British America. But it was the British Americans' first frontier, and its very distance from the Old World combined with conditions of life on the frontier to make it the most purely *American* area up to that time. In terms of "its society, its institutions, and [its] mental attitudes," the southern backcountry, according to Turner, was a harbinger of what America was to become, and it was much more individualistic, egalitarian, democratic, and antagonistic to privilege, aristocracy, and religious and civil establishments than were the older, more European societies along the seaboard.[1]

Most later scholars have affirmed the essential socioeconomic and cultural unity of the southern backcountry and have continued to contrast it with the seaboard areas.[2] Indeed, according to Carl Bridenbaugh, the backcountry was, along with the Chesapeake and lowcountry South Carolina and Georgia, one of three distinctive "souths" at the time of the Revolution, though he followed Turner in linking the southern backcountry more closely to Pennsylvania than to the eastern souths, referring to it as *"Greater Pennsylvania."* As in so many other respects, Bridenbaugh in this formula-

[1] Frederick Jackson Turner, *The Frontier in American History* (New York, 1947), pp. 67–125. The quotations are from pp. 68, 99–100.

[2] See, in particular, Carl Bridenbaugh, *Myths and Realities: Societies of the Colonial South* (Baton Rouge, 1952), pp. 119–96; Jack M. Sosin, *The Revolutionary Frontier, 1763–1783* (New York, 1967), esp. pp. 61–81, 161–92, 197–98, 207–10; and Rowland Berthoff, *An Unsettled People: Social Order and Disorder in American History* (New York, 1971), pp. 81–134, 484–86.

tion anticipated one of the most powerful recent trends in early American historiography, the trend toward *regionalization*. As scholars have moved strongly away from political to social and economic history during the 1960s and 1970s, they have come to think of British America less as a congeries of separate colonies than as a group of socioeconomic regions. New England, the Caribbean, the Chesapeake, the middle colonies, the lower South—these have become the organizing categories, the overarching frames of reference, for much recent work. The underlying assumption behind this movement has been, of course, that distinctions revolving around the nature of socioeconomic life and not formal—in Turner's language, artificial—political designations constitute the most appropriate units of study within the broad culture area of colonial British America.[3]

Of course, this regionalization of colonial America has turned out to be but a preliminary stage in a second powerful historiographical trend that may be termed the *deconstruction* of early America. Especially during the past decade, the rapid proliferation of scholars working on early America has produced a series of studies that have broken regions down into increasingly smaller temporal, spatial, and social units. With specific reference to the southern backcountry, Bridenbaugh had again anticipated this development when he cautioned historians about the limitations of a broad regional characterization. Despite overall similarities in geographic, demographic, and economic conditions throughout the backcountry and despite a strong cultural similarity among various parts of the backcountry when they were compared to the seaboard societies to which they were attached, the area "did not," Bridenbaugh insisted, "compose a uniform society." He called attention to the two important variables that distinguished one part of the backcountry from another. One was time of settlement and stage of socioeconomic de-

---

[3] Bridenbaugh, *Myths and Realities*, p. 127. A powerful argument in behalf of this regional approach to early American history is to be found in Part Two of John J. McCusker and Russell R. Menard, *The Economy of British America, 1607–1789: Needs and Opportunities for Study*, Institute of Early American History and Culture, forthcoming.

5

velopment; the other was the nature of political relationships with provincial and local governments in the east.[4]

If Bridenbaugh's cautions suggested the continuing relevance of political relations to backcountry behavior and development, the validity of his suggestion is dramatically underlined by the essays in this volume. While its title strongly emphasizes the existence of a single grand socioeconomic unit, *the southern backcountry,* the essays demonstrate that, whatever similarities may have existed among them, there were at least five different backcountries in the South at the time of the American Revolution. Furthermore, as Richard R. Beeman has made explicit and as most of the authors imply, the nature of relations with the established seaboard political societies of which they were a part was an enormously important, probably the single most important, variable in distinguishing among these several backcountries and their distinctive histories.[5] Moreover, the logic of most of the essays and specific evidence in some of them strongly suggest that there was not just one Virginia and one South Carolina backcountry but several, distinguished one from another according to a great many variables, including ethnic composition and the nature of local leadership.[6] This suggestion strongly underscores the need for still further deconstruction into still smaller and smaller units of analysis if we are ever going to understand the rich complexity of either the southern backcountry during the late eighteenth century or its Revolutionary experience.

If the logic of scholarly inquiry into the social history of early America has pushed most scholars toward regional

[4] *Myths and Realities,* pp. 122, 156–63.

[5] Richard R. Beeman, "The Political Response to Social Conflict in the Southern Backcountry: A Comparative View of Virginia and the Carolinas during the Revolution," infra. (Citations to the essays in this volume do not include specific page references.)

[6] In this regard see especially Emory G. Evans, "Trouble in the Backcountry: Disaffection in Southwest Virginia during the American Revolution," Jeffrey J. Crow, "Liberty Men and Loyalists: Disorder and Disaffection in the North Carolina Backcountry," and Rachel N. Klein, "Frontier Planters and the American Revolution: The South Carolina Backcountry, 1775–1782," all infra.

analysis and deconstruction, the study of the second general subject, the *American Revolution*, continues to suffer from a failure to achieve a consensus over precisely what perspective is most useful in understanding it. At least since the end of the last century, there have been two quite distinct and not always complementary approaches to the study of the Revolution. The first has seen the Revolution as a culmination of the colonial experience, as a contingent and highly problematic outcome of that experience. Hence, the classic questions for people writing from this *colonial perspective* on the American Revolution have been why the Revolution happened at all and how it related to—that is, grew out of, reflected, altered, transformed, or rejected—the colonial experience. More particularly, they have wanted to know, not how the Revolution prefigured or contained early manifestations of later and as yet only vaguely defined socioeconomic and political developments or qualities that were characteristic of later United States history, but how it affected—that is, resolved, interacted with, or exacerbated—tensions already present in pre-Revolutionary America. Knowing where British-American society had been, they have been concerned to point out how the colonial experience informed the War for Independence, the creation and mobilization of the first independent political societies in the thirteen states and their respective localities, and the subsequent creation of a national political system and a national political society. For that reason, I think it is fair to say, they have generally tried to situate the Revolution in its contemporary context and tended to be far more impressed by the continuities than by the discontinuities between the colonial and Revolutionary periods. This is the perspective from which I have always tried to approach the American Revolution.[7]

By contrast, a second, *national approach* to the study of the Revolution has tended to look at it from the vantage point of later American developments. Knowing where the United States was going, those who have taken this approach have wanted to search the Revolutionary landscape for early indi-

[7] See Jack P. Greene, "The Social Origins of the American Revolution: An Evaluation and an Interpretation," *Political Science Quarterly* 88 (1973):1–22.

cations of the democratic and egalitarian impulses and the sociopolitical divisions and conflicts that became so prominent in Jeffersonian and Jacksonian America. Relatively uninterested in relating the Revolutionary to the colonial experience, they have emphasized both the discontinuities between the Revolutionary era and a supposedly much more rigidly structured and stable colonial past, and the continuities between the Revolution and subsequent United States history. By applying to the Revolution terminology, concepts, categories, and units of analysis derived—and densely packed with layers of meanings—from later periods, this national approach has too often led in the direction of the sort of anachronistic results that are difficult to avoid when, in Marc Bloch's words, the "idol of origins," rather than the contemporary context, dictates the questions, concerns, and language we bring to the analysis of the past.[8]

Not all of the essays in this volume have entirely avoided the problems associated with this national perspective on the American Revolution. Nor, in focusing on their particular

---

[8] Marc Bloch, *The Historian's Craft* (New York, 1959), pp. 29–35. No doubt the transitional character of the Revolution has contributed to these divergent approaches. Like the era in which it occurred, the Revolution was both an early modern and a modern event, one that both looks backward to the recreation of an earlier, golden era and forward to a new and better era. Not yet fully articulated, much less accepted, the idea of progress had not yet become the guiding assumption of revolutionaries that it would become during and after the French Revolution. See J. H. Elliott, "Revolution and Continuity in Early Modern Europe," *Past and Present* no. 42 (1969):35–56, and Jack P. Greene, "Paine, America, and the 'Modernization' of Political Consciousness," *Political Science Quarterly* 93 (1978): 73–92.

Historiographers have conventionally attributed this divergence in perspective to the sociopolitical perspectives of historians. My own feeling is that the point of view of intellectual mentors and the subject matter of initial research experiences are probably much more important.

A prime example of anachronistic language is the use of the terms *radical* and *conservative*. Neither acquired political connotations until the nineteenth century, the former in 1802 and the latter in 1830. Though some scholars of the Revolution have made a valiant effort to use these terms in a neutral way, they are laden with emotional connotations deriving from nineteenth- and twentieth-century western European and United States history.

areas of investigation, have the authors much concerned themselves with some of the problems inherent in their essentially deconstructionist approach. While deconstruction is invariably enriching, all too often it is also confusing for it produces such an abundance of special cases as to make it difficult to comprehend the whole; it may even call into question the very existence of that whole. If we now know as a result of these nine papers that there were several southern backcountr*ies*, each with its own peculiar Revolutionary experience, we are no longer so sure that those peculiar experiences had enough in common for it to make much sense for us to talk about *the* Revolutionary experience of *the* southern backcountry. To strengthen an as yet weak impulse toward still a third historiographical trend that, I hope, will gain momentum over the next few years, a trend that may be referred to as *reconstruction*, I would like in this essay, from the perspective of a *colonial* historian, to propose a general framework that may help us make sense of, or at least put into clearer perspective, the various histories of the southern backcountries during the American Revolution.

One place to begin is with the explicit contrast—present in most of the essays included here—between backcountries and lowcountries. In general the authors follow Turner in making a sharp distinction between the loose frontier settlements in the backcountries and the "tradition-bound, stable" communities of the seaboard. The latter are said to have been characterized by "elaborately structured, hierarchical social systems" with authoritative institutional centers and "clearly defined hierarchies of power, prestige, and personal authority." Strong "lines of patronage and preferment . . . ran from the top down," and cohesive elites—"oligarchies" united by a common ideology, similar economic interests, close kinship ties, and a genteel life-style—presided over a deferential political order. In this order, the bulk of the white population, sharing with the elite a common fear of and separation from the large numbers of blacks in their midst, almost always deferred to their betters. By contrast, backcountry societies were composed of new, rapidly expanding, highly mobile, and ethnically and religiously diverse popula-

9

tions. They had weaker local traditions and commitments to place, less economic specialization and social differentiation, and inchoate or fragile institutions of authority. With ruling elites deficient in personal prestige, affluence, and gentility, political hierarchies in the backcountries lacked clear definition, and politics there was less deferential and more egalitarian, democratic, contentious, and disorderly.[9]

My contention is that this contrast has been considerably overdrawn. It rests upon both an overemphasis on the coherence and rigidity of older societies of the lowcountry and a misperception of the underlying nature and thrust of backcountry development and aspirations. Just as there were powerful continuities between the colonial and the Revolutionary eras, so there were fundamental continuities between the southern backcountries and the seaboard societies to which they were connected. Turner to the contrary notwithstanding, in several fundamental ways the southern backcountries were every bit as much a reflection of the older

[9] In addition to the essays included in this volume, see Richard R. Beeman, "Social Change and Cultural Conflict in Virginia: Lunenburg County, 1746 to 1774," *William and Mary Quarterly*, 3d ser. 35 (1978):455–76; idem, "Robert Munford and the Political Culture of Frontier Virginia," *Journal of American Studies* 12 (1978):169–83; Beeman and Rhys Isaac, "Cultural Conflict and Social Change in the Revolutionary South: Lunenburg County, Virginia," *Journal of Southern History* 46 (1980):525–50; A. Roger Ekirch, *"Poor Carolina": Politics and Society in Colonial North Carolina, 1729–1776* (Chapel Hill, 1981), pp. 19–47, 161–202, 236–45, 266–79; Marvin L. Michael Kay and William S. Price, Jr., "'To Ride the Wood Mare': Road Building and Militia Service in Colonial North Carolina, 1740–1775," *North Carolina Historical Review* 57 (1980):361–409; Richard Maxwell Brown, *The South Carolina Regulators* (Cambridge, Mass., 1963); Robert M. Weir, "'The Harmony We Were Famous For': An Interpretation of Pre-Revolutionary South Carolina Politics," *William and Mary Quarterly*, 3d ser. 26 (1969):479–89; David R. Chestnutt, "'Greedy Party Work': The South Carolina Election of 1768," in Patricia U. Bonomi, ed., *Party and Political Opposition in Revolutionary America* (Tarrytown, N.Y., 1980), pp. 70–86, 136–39; and Ronald Hoffman, "The 'Disaffected' in the Revolutionary South," in Alfred F. Young, ed., *The American Revolution: Explorations in the History of American Radicalism* (DeKalb, Ill., 1976), pp. 273–316. The quotations are from Beeman, "Social Change and Cultural Conflict," pp. 457, 468, 475.

colonial British-American world as they were a prefigurement of the new American order.

Among recent literature, Robert D. Mitchell's impressive work on the Shenandoah Valley, the oldest and longest settled of the southern backcountries, most fully anticipates this line of argument. It clearly reveals a strong tendency over time toward assimilation to seaboard norms. As the Shenandoah acquired better transportation facilities and more credit, as its population became more settled and less equal, as its elite became more affluent and more coherent, and as its institutions and social structure became more sharply articulated, it became more and more like the eastern Chesapeake. It moved from subsistence to a more specialized and commercial agriculture employing tenants and slaves, from ethnic spatial separation to ethnic mixing, and from relative isolation to much closer social and economic integration with the east. Similarly, in his work on Lunenburg County in southside Virginia, Richard Beeman has noted a tendency over time toward a closer conformity to the colony's traditional political and social systems.[10]

If, with the increasing articulation of its socioeconomic and political structures, the oldest areas of the Virginia backcountry were thus becoming not less but more like the east, then the much-emphasized differences between backcountry and seaboard areas would seem to have been as much temporal as spatial phenomena, differences not in kind that would persist over time but in stages of development that would decline over time. At the time of the Revolution, this

[10] Robert D. Mitchell, "The Shenandoah Frontier," *Annals of the Association of American Geographers* 62 (1972):461–86; idem, "Content and Context: Tidewater Characteristics in the Early Shenandoah Valley," *The Maryland Historian* 5 (1974):79–92; idem, *Commercialism and Frontier: Perspectives on the Early Shenandoah Valley* (Charlottesville, Va., 1977); Beeman, "Social Change and Cultural Conflict," p. 463. See also Thomas Perkins Abernethy, *Three Virginia Frontiers* (Baton Rouge, 1940); Harry Roy Merrens, *Colonial North Carolina in the Eighteenth Century: A Study in Historical Geography* (Chapel Hill, 1964); and Daniel Thorp, "Wilkes County, North Carolina: The Articulation and Stabilization of a Late Eighteenth-Century Frontier Society," unpublished seminar paper, The Johns Hopkins University, 1978.

assimilative process was probably strongest in areas where the relationship with the east was most fully developed—in the lower Shenandoah Valley and in the oldest settled areas of the South Carolina backcountry—and weakest in Georgia, which, as the three papers on Georgia included here all strongly suggest, was, lowcountry and backcountry together, all a new society. But there is no reason to doubt that this assimilative process was at work throughout the southern backcountries and was supported and stimulated by shared values and aspirations. The remainder of this essay will explore the nature and emphasize the primacy of the two values referred to in my title—*independence* and *improvement*. It will also explore the relationship between these values and the fragile *authority* structures that characterized the societies of colonial British America in the eighteenth century. Finally, it will speculate tentatively and briefly about the profound ways those values and aspirations affected the Revolutionary experiences of the southern backcountries.

Perhaps the most powerful drive in the British-American colonizing process from the seventeenth century through much of the nineteenth century, and from the eastern to the western coasts of North America, was the drive for personal *independence*. Quite simply, *independence* meant freedom from the will of others. It was the opposite of *dependence*, which was subordination or subjection to the discretion of others. Independence implied a sovereignty of self in all private and public relations, while dependence connoted the very opposite, the absolute "contrary of sovereignty." Indeed, the social categories *independents* and *dependents* historically had been the single most basic division in English social life. Among independent people there was a further distinction between those whose circumstances were merely "sufficient" and who therefore usually had to work with their hands, and a much smaller group whose means were so substantial that they no longer needed to work with their hands and could therefore live like gentlemen. If independence did not require great affluence, it did imply, to quote Samuel Johnson's *Dictionary*, "a fortune . . . equal to the conveniences of life." Independence was also associated with competence, virility, and manhood and entitled people to respect from their inferiors, superiors, and themselves. Though it did not guarantee a man "plenary satisfaction," a modest independence did insure that he and his family—his *dependents*—could live "at ease" rather than in anxiety, in contentment rather than want, in respectability rather than meanness, and, most importantly, in freedom from rather than thralldom to the dictates of others.[11]

In Britain the proportion of independents in the total male population was small. But in the American colonies the opportunity to acquire land or an independent trade was so widespread that the achievement of independence lay within the grasp of most able-bodied, active, and enterprising free men. The prospect for "a very comfortable and independent subsistence," held out by promotional writers, land developers, and governmental authorities, acted as a powerful, perhaps the single most powerful, magnet in attracting settlers to new colonies and newly opening areas. Moreover, although the achievement of genuine affluence and a gentle status was confined to a very small number of people, as it had been in Britain, the comparatively widespread realization of independence by people whose beginnings were small, a realization achieved merely by the disciplined application of industry to the mastery of the soil, contributed to an equally broad diffusion of an expansive sense of self-worth through the independent, mostly landowning population in each new area of settlement.[12]

Even in America, however, the boundary line between independence and dependence was not so great that people who had once gained an independent status might not slip

[11] The definitions in this and later paragraphs are derived from Samuel Johnson, *A Dictionary of the English Language*, 8th ed., 2 vols. (London, 1799). In stressing the importance to eighteenth-century Americans of the quest for personal independence, I emphatically do not, as the above paragraph makes clear, associate that quest with a drive for profit maximization.

[12] See, among many examples, the less familiar but extraordinarily thoughtful and full contemporary development of these themes in Samuel Williams, *The Natural and Civil History of Vermont*, 2 vols. (Walpole, N.H., 1794), 2:352–435. The quotation is from p. 354.

back into dependence. As Richard Beeman notes, "Only good fortune—or the avoidance of misfortune—separated the great mass of farmers from a return to dependence."[13] As well as pride in their own achievements and in their newly gained independence, the fear of a return to dependence was thus a powerful animating force among those who had only recently risen out of, or were not yet very far removed from, dependence. Among such people anxiety over the loss and an intense jealousy of recently gained or narrowly held independent status was probably never far below the surface of consciousness and could easily be activated. Certainly one reason why Americans from all sections appeared to be so tenacious of their liberty was that liberty was an essential attribute of their status as independent men.[14]

The comparative ease of obtaining independence in the relatively open and new societies of colonial British America meant, of course, that failure to achieve or maintain an independent status bore a much greater social stigma than it did in contemporary Britain or continental Europe. Presumably such failure could correspondingly produce a much deeper sense of personal unworthiness. With no social excuse, the onus of failure fell directly and fully upon the failed individual. As Turner long ago emphasized, the presence of new places with new opportunities provided the failed with a new opportunity for redefinition. What part of the high mobility rates in the southern backcountry noted by several scholars was composed of failures is a subject that requires considerably more attention.[15] But much evidence presented

[13] Beeman, "Political Response to Social Conflict."

[14] For citations to some of the many contemporary attributions of an unusually tenacious sense of liberty among colonial and Revolutionary Americans and a discussion of the social meanings of *liberty* in the late eighteenth-century South, see Jack P. Greene, "'Slavery or Independence': Some Reflections on the Relationship among Liberty, Black Bondage, and Equality in Revolutionary South Carolina," *South Carolina Historical Magazine* 80 (1979):193–214.

[15] See Beeman and Isaac, "Cultural Conflict and Social Change," p. 544; Mitchell, *Commercialism and Frontier*, pp. 45–58; Robert W. Ramsey, *Carolina Cradle: Settlement of the Northwest Carolina Frontier, 1747–1762* (Chapel Hill, 1964); Merrens, *Colonial North Carolina*, pp. 53–81.

in the essays published in this volume suggests that the surge of population into the southern backcountry during the last half of the eighteenth century contained not only the active and the enterprising, the character types conventionally associated with American frontiers, but also the failed. It indicates as well that the failed was a category comprised of two distinct, if also overlapping, groups: first, those in search of a new start in a new place as well as the individual redefinition that such a situation might make possible, and, second, those who had either given up all hopes of success or rejected contemporary definitions of success in favor of a hand-to-mouth existence as hunters, vagabonds, or plunderers and thereby, in their own ways, sought to put themselves beyond dependence.[16]

Individuals came to the new societies of colonial British America not merely in quest of personal independence but also with the complementary hope of transforming those new societies into *improved* societies that could both guarantee the independence or, for the fortunate few, affluence they expected to achieve and enable them to enjoy the fruits of that independence or affluence to the fullest possible extent. Such demands and aspirations for *improvement* were nearly as prominent among settlers in new places as were those for independence and affluence. Ubiquitous in the economic writings of early modern Britain, the language of improvement referred primarily to schemes, devices, or projects through which the economic position of the nation might be advanced, the estates or fortunes of individuals might be bettered, or existing resources might be made more productive.[17] In the new societies of colonial British America,

[16] The character and importance of independence and dependence in colonial and Revolutionary America are explored more fully in Jack P. Greene, *All Men Are Created Equal: Some Reflections on the Character of the American Revolution* (Oxford, 1976).

[17] See especially Joan Thirsk, *Economic Policy and Projects: The Development of a Consumer Society in Early Modern England* (Oxford, 1978). Seventeenth-century English literature on improvement is analyzed from another perspective by Joyce Oldham Appleby, *Economic Thought and Ideology in Seventeenth-Century England* (Princeton, 1978).

the term *improvement* carried similar connotations. Settlers sought to improve their situation by securing the necessary capital and labor to develop their lands and fortunes; towns that would provide them with local markets in which they could exchange the produce of their lands for finished goods; bounties that would encourage them to experiment with new crops; and roads, bridges, and ferries that would provide them with better access to wider markets and link them more closely to economic and administrative centers. To gain access to or to protect the broadly, though by no means equally, diffused benefits conferred by such improvements, men were even willing to perform or to permit their dependents to perform such burdensome obligations as road and militia service.[18]

In the new and relatively undeveloped societies of colonial British America, however, the term *improvement* also acquired a much wider meaning: it was used to describe a state of society that was far removed from the savagery associated with the native Indians. An *improved* society was one defined by a series of positive and negative juxtapositions. Not wild, barbaric, irregular, rustic, or crude, it was settled, cultivated, civilized, orderly, developed, and polite.[19] The model for an improved society in both colonial and Revolutionary America was emphatically not the egalitarian yeoman societies of the Old Northwest that were later glorified by Turner. The massive rustication of European life produced by the settlement of America had not, by the time of the Revolution, yet led to the development of new, distinctly American, paradigms of the improved society. The celebration of a rural life by people like Robert Beverley, William Byrd of Westover,

[18] The pressure of such demands in the southern backcountries and how they affected development can be seen in Mitchell, *Commercialism and Frontier*, pp. 133–240; Merrens, *Colonial North Carolina*, pp. 85–172; Ekirch, *"Poor Carolina,"* pp. 161–202; Brown, *South Carolina Regulators*, pp. 13–37; and Kay and Price, *"'To Ride the Wood Mare.'"*

[19] Among earlier studies that have emphasized this dichotomy between the barbarous and the civilized are Roy Harvey Pearce, *The Savages of America: A Study of the Indian and the Idea of Civilization* (Baltimore, 1953) and Louis B. Wright, *Culture on the Moving Frontier* (Bloomington, Ind., 1955), pp. 11–45.

and other southern colonial writers earlier in the eighteenth century seems to have owed more to contemporary literary trends in Augustan England than to America and, unlike Jefferson's post-Revolutionary celebration of the virtues of rural life, served more as mock celebrations of, even apologies for, the still unimproved state of seaboard America.[20]

For prior to the American Revolution, settlers throughout the new societies of colonial British America seemed to have aspired to the creation of a settled society on the distant model of the Old World and on the closer models of older-settled regions of colonial British America. During the last half of the eighteenth century, as during earlier phases of English colonization, the new societies of colonial British America, including those of the southern backcountry, saw the older societies to which they were attached not as negative but as positive points of reference. Insofar as those older societies were more improved, settled, orderly, and coherent, the newer societies in the west hoped to imitate them by themselves acquiring all those attributes of *improvement*. Recreation, not innovation, was their aim. They aspired to a fully developed market society with credit, commercial agriculture, slavery, and a brisk circulation of money and goods. They wanted a more settled and hierarchical social structure with social distinctions ranging from the genteel down to the vulgar, a term that in contemporary usage meant simply "the common people." In particular, they wanted a social structure in which successful, independent, and affluent people would have the opportunity, in conformity with the long-standing traditions of western civilization (and probably all other highly developed civilizations), to exploit dependent

[20] See Leo Marx, *The Machine in the Garden: Technology and the Pastoral Ideal in America* (New York, 1964), pp. 75–144; Kenneth S. Lynn, *Mark Twain and Southwestern Humor* (Boston, 1959), pp. 3–22; Richard Beale Davis, *Intellectual Life in the Colonial South, 1585–1763*, 3 vols. (Knoxville, 1978), 1:84–91. Celebrations of the rural life in the literature of Augustan England are analyzed by Maren-Sofie Røstvig, *The Happy Man: Studies in the Metamorphoses of a Classical Ideal*, 2 vols. (New York, 1962–71), vol. 2; Maynard Mack, *The Garden and the City: Retirement and Politics in the Later Poetry of Pope, 1731–1743* (Toronto, 1969); and Raymond Williams, *The Country and the City* (New York, 1973), pp. 1–68.

people, albeit they wanted, in imitation of seaboard America rather than of Britain, a ranked social order that would be based upon achievement and performance rather than upon ascription, legal privilege, or family charisma. They desired authoritative, if not very obtrusive, political institutions that could facilitate their socioeconomic and cultural development and would be presided over by the "best [that is, the most successful] part of the community," men whose very success testified to their evident capacity for and legitimate claims to political leadership. They wanted vital traditional social institutions that would contribute to and stand as visible symbols of their improvement, including churches, schools, and towns. And they aspired to eventual political parity with older regions, a parity that would itself constitute recognition of their improved state.[21]

The concept of improvement thus enabled people in new colonial British-American societies to think of those societies in developmental terms. They assumed and hoped that the simplifications of traditional social forms that were so obvious during the first phases of settlement would sooner or later be followed by a process of social articulation. They also assumed that that process, in turn, would ultimately lead in the direction of an ever-greater assimilation to traditional paradigms derived from the socioeconomic and political order of older colonial societies on the seaboard. Indeed, despite the continuing tendency of many scholars to emphasize the egalitarianism of backcountry societies, no societies that put so much emphasis upon achievement and improvement, especially improvement in the way they defined it, could give a high priority or maintain an enduring commitment to egal-

[21] Although in the case of the southern backcountries these aspirations for improvement may in the first instance have been articulated by those strategic, mostly elite segments of the population that have traditionally given definition to societies, my hypothesis is that they were widely diffused among the vast majority of independent men in the area. The quotation is from George R. Lamplugh, "'To Check and Discourage the Wicked and Designing': John Wereat and the Revolution in Georgia," *Georgia Historical Quarterly* 61 (1977):304. For a general consideration of the power of English models in shaping early American social aspirations, see Jack P. Greene, "Search for Identity: An Interpretation of the Meaning of Selected Patterns of Social Response in Eighteenth-Century America," *Journal of Social History* 3 (1970):189–220.

itarianism, if that term in any way implies equality of social condition. In the early days of the southern backcountry such an equality of condition may very well have been a fact of life. But it was probably never a goal for more than a very few, not even the Separate Baptists. No less than their lowcountry predecessors, backcountry people showed no disposition to forego exploitation of their fellowmen, no unwillingness to build their own independence and affluence at the cost of the dependence of other people, including white servants, laborers, and tenants as well as black slaves. Indeed, no less than in contemporary Europe, the status of independent men was *defined* to a significant degree by their capacity—their liberty—to have dependents and by the numbers of those dependents.

As long as the goals of achievement of independence and improvement continued to animate settlers, there could hardly be any rejection of class distinctions or any significant decline of "old hierarchic ideals" in favor of "a new egalitarianism."[22] The absence of legally privileged orders in the truncated societies of colonial British America certainly required some modifications in those older ideals, modifications that all but a tiny minority of Americans seem to have thought represented a distinct improvement upon their English inheritance. But if few people lamented the lack of a hereditary aristocracy in America, most contemporaries appreciated that the pursuit of happiness by people of ability and merit would, in the race of life—that metaphor of individual development that was so powerful among British-American social theorists during the late eighteenth century—invariably produce not equality but inequality.[23] Despite the subsequent idealization of equality in American life,

[22] Rowland Berthoff and John M. Murrin, "Feudalism, Communalism, and the Yeoman Freeholder: The American Revolution Considered as a Social Accident," in Stephen G. Kurtz and James H. Hutson, *Essays on the American Revolution* (Chapel Hill, 1973), p. 281.

[23] See Williams, *History of Vermont*, 2:374–76, 392–94, for a penetrating contemporary discussion of the limited nature of the American commitment to equality. More generally, see also Greene, *All Men Are Created Equal*; idem, "'Slavery or Independence,'" pp. 205–13; and Isaac Kramnick, "Equal Opportunity and 'The Race of Life': Some Historical Reflections on Liberal Ideology," *Dissent* 28 (1981):181–87.

few early Americans would have had it any other way. Like the continued presence of hunters and robbers among them, the persistence of an undifferentiated society was an unwelcome reminder of how far away they were from a fully improved social existence. The more settled, cultivated, slave, commercial, urban, and differentiated they became, the more successful—that is, the more improved—these new societies were thought to be. The obvious differences between backcountries and lowcountries in the 1760s and 1770s, differences that were largely a function of different stages in the colonizing process, have thus tended to obscure the existence in the backcountries of aspirations and expectations that were leading those societies strongly in the direction of those in the east. Only to the extent that they fell short of achieving those aspirations did those societies become an unintended forerunner or an early example of the democratic and egalitarian order of the new west idealized by Frederick Jackson Turner.[24]

Stressing the extent to which independent men in the southern backcountries aspired to recreate the social and political hierarchies of the east does not necessarily imply that those hierarchies were anywhere near so coherent, strong, and rigid as scholars have conventionally assumed. Certainly recent analysts have been correct in pointing out that degree to which colonial British-American seaboard societies were endeavoring to replicate and, to a growing extent, succeeding in assimilating to the "Old Society" of England as it has been defined, for example, by Harold J. Perkin.[25] In all prob-

[24] Among the essays included in this volume, such aspirations are most evident in W. W. Abbot, "Lowcountry, Backcountry: A View of Georgia in the American Revolution," A. Roger Ekirch, "Whig Authority and Public Order in Backcountry North Carolina, 1776–1783," Harvey H. Jackson, "The Rise of the Western Members: Revolutionary Politics and the Georgia Backcountry," and Klein, "Frontier Planters." But see also Mitchell, "Content and Context," pp. 79–92; Ekirch, *Poor Carolina,* pp. 161–202; and Rachel N. Klein, "Ordering the Backcountry: The South Carolina Regulation," *William and Mary Quarterly,* 3d ser. 38 (1981):661–80.

[25] Harold J. Perkin, *The Origins of Modern English Society, 1780–1880* (London, 1969), pp. 17–62. For a perceptive discussion of the extent to

ability, however, these scholars have considerably exaggerated the degree to which, even in long-settled areas such as tidewater Virginia and certainly in more recently developing places like lowcountry South Carolina, North Carolina, and Georgia, those aspirations for assimilation had by the 1750s and 1760s been achieved. In the process, perhaps, they have tended to confound aspiration for reality.

A conspicuous way in which the hierarchies of colonial British America fell short of assimilating to the metropolitan model was in their inability fully to solidify their authority. As here used, *authority* must be carefully distinguished from *power.* In contemporary usage, *power* was a synonym for strength, force, and might. Although it was a neutral term, it sometimes connoted an illegitimate exertion of strength for corrupt purposes: might as opposed to right. For this reason, among others, early modern British Americans, as Bernard Bailyn has shown, were extremely wary of power.[26] At the same time, however, they yearned for authority. *Authority,* which as Sir William Temple noted in his late seventeenth-century tract on that subject, was "the foundation of all ease, safety, and order, in the Governments of the World," was a term that implied legitimacy and was associated with justice and right. Though power invariably "follow[ed] Authority in all Civil Bodies," authority, unlike power, was rooted not only in strength but, much more importantly, in respect, in "trust and opinion." It derived from popular regard, "strengthened and confirmed ... by custom" and habit, for the "Wisdom . . .[and] Goodness" of the persons and institutions to which it was accorded. Whereas power might compel people to submit to it, authority thus always commanded "the willing obedience of the people."[27]

That authority in the new societies of the southern back-

---

which tidewater Virginia conceived of itself in terms of the English model described by Perkin, see Rhys Isaac, *The Transformation of Virginia, 1740–1790* (Chapel Hill, 1982), pp. 18–129.

[26] Bernard Bailyn, *The Ideological Origins of the American Revolution* (Cambridge, Mass., 1967), pp. 55–93.

[27] Sir William Temple, "An Essay upon the Original and Nature of Government," *Miscellanea* (London, 1680), pp. 55–59, 72–74, 82.

country was fragile seems to be widely accepted among scholars of all persuasions. Institutions were still weak and open to challenge, and local elites, yet new and divided, had only tenuous claims to personal authority and little patronage or other utilitarian resources with which to attach the rest of the community to them. But the many open challenges to the authority of eastern elites both before and during the war raise the question of just how firm and entrenched authority was even within longer-settled localities. In North Carolina and Georgia, where elites had only modest wealth, were mostly new, were divided, and, in North Carolina, were also corrupt and irresponsible, the authority of existing political establishments—that is, the institutions and offices of government and the elites who presided over them—seems to have been little more secure than that of emerging elites in the backcountry. To be sure, where they were affluent, well established, and relatively cohesive, as in tidewater Virginia and lowcountry South Carolina, such establishments seem to have commanded considerable respect and exerted substantial influence. Where they had proved responsive to the interests, needs, and aspirations of new areas, had proved willing to devolve responsibility for local governance upon new local political units, had moved swiftly to incorporate those units fully into the existing political system, and had established strong personal, social, and economic links with the new areas, as in Virginia, these establishments were able, to a palpable degree, to extend their authority over the whole province.[28]

But not even the most respected, cohesive, and responsible of these older colonial political establishments seems to have been as secure in its authority as modern historical concepts such as *hierarchical society* and *deferential order* have come to imply. To understand the course and character of events in the southern backcountries during the Revolution, it is important to comprehend precisely how fragile the authority

[28] See Bridenbaugh, *Myths and Realities*, pp. 157–63; Beeman, "Political Response to Social Conflict"; Brown, *South Carolina Regulators*; Klein, "Ordering the Backcountry," pp. 661–80; Ekirch, *"Poor Carolina,"* pp. 161–202, 236–45; Abbot, "Lowcountry, Backcountry."

of these establishments actually was throughout colonial British America—in older as well as the newer areas.

Characteristic of every colonial British-American society during the seventeenth and eighteenth centuries, with the possible exceptions of those of the orthodox Puritan colonies of Massachusetts and Connecticut during their first two generations of settlement, the fragile nature of authority was evident in virtually every area of colonial life through the middle decades of the eighteenth century: in the successful challenges to religious establishments growing out of the Great Awakening;[29] in the massive popular uprisings against unresponsive or ineffective and corrupt political systems in several colonies;[30] in the difficulties governmental authorities had in containing these and other forms of civil strife, particularly those that occurred along disputed boundaries between political jurisdictions;[31] in the enervation of the militia, which, in the absence of effective constabularies, was the only significant source of coercive power available to civil officials and "the ultimate sanction of political authority" in colonial America; in the difficulties authorities experienced in trying to send the militia to places or on missions to which its members did not want to go;[32] in the laxity of law enforcement in

[29] See especially Richard L. Bushman, *From Puritan to Yankee: Character and the Social Order in Connecticut, 1690–1765* (Cambridge, Mass., 1967), pp. 147–232; Isaac, *Transformation of Virginia*, pp. 143–295.

[30] See Ekirch, *"Poor Carolina,"* pp. 161–202; Richard Maxwell Brown, "Violence and the American Revolution," in Kurtz and Hutson, eds., *Essays on the American Revolution*, pp. 81–120; idem, *South Carolina Regulators*, pp. 53–95; and John Crowley, "The Paxton Disturbance and Ideas of Order in Pennsylvania Politics," *Pennsylvania History* 37 (1970):317–39.

[31] Sung Bok Kim, *Landlord and Tenant in Colonial New York: Manorial Society, 1664–1775* (Chapel Hill, 1978), pp. 281–415; Thomas L. Purvis, "The New Jersey Assembly, 1722–1776," Ph.D. diss., The Johns Hopkins University, 1979, pp. 189–235; Frank W. Porter III, "From Backcountry to County: The Delayed Settlement of Western Maryland," *Maryland Historical Magazine* 70 (1975):329–49.

[32] John Shy, "A New Look at Colonial Militia," *William and Mary Quarterly*, 3d ser. 20 (1963):173–85; idem, "The American Revolution: The Military Conflict Considered as a Revolutionary War," in Kurtz and Hutson, eds., *Essays on the American Revolution*, pp. 149, 154; Clyde R. Fergu-

many localities;[33] in the weakness of parental controls over their children;[34] in the insubordination of slaves toward their masters and overseers;[35] in the widespread fear, especially among less cohesive elites and in the uncertain times beginning with the Stamp Act crisis, of social revolt by the lower orders;[36] and, perhaps most of all, by widespread lack of re-

son, "Carolina and Georgia Patriot and Loyalist Militia in Action, 1778–1783," in Jeffrey J. Crow and Larry E. Tise, eds., *The Southern Experience in the American Revolution* (Chapel Hill, 1978), pp. 174–99; idem, "Functions of the Partisan-Militia in the South during the American Revolution: An Interpretation," in W. Robert Higgins, ed., *The Revolutionary War in the South: Power, Conflict, and Leadership: Essays in Honor of John Richard Alden* (Durham, N.C., 1979), pp. 239–58; Kay and Price, "'To Ride the Wood Mare,'" pp. 384–85.

[33] See Douglas Greenberg, *Crime and Law Enforcement in the Colony of New York, 1691–1776* (Ithaca, 1976), pp. 154–236; Beeman, "Social Change and Cultural Conflict," p. 468; Gwenda Morgan, "The Hegemony of the Law: Richmond County, 1692–1776," Ph.D. diss., The Johns Hopkins University, 1980, pp. 183–284; Michael Stephen Hindus, *Prison and Plantation: Crime, Justice, and Authority in Massachusetts and South Carolina, 1767–1878* (Chapel Hill, 1980), pp. 1–84.

[34] See Philip J. Greven, Jr., *Four Generations: Population, Land, and Family in Colonial Andover, Massachusetts* (Ithaca, 1970), pp. 222–58; idem, *The Protestant Temperament: Patterns of Child-Rearing, Religious Experience, and the Self in Early America* (New York, 1977), pp. 21–61, 151–91, 265–331; Stephanie Grauman Wolf, *Urban Village: Population, Community, and Family Structure in Germantown, Pennsylvania, 1683–1800* (Princeton, 1976), pp. 287–326; Daniel Blake Smith, *Inside the Great House: Planter Family Life in Eighteenth-Century Chesapeake Society* (Ithaca, 1980), pp. 25–54, 82–125; Michael Zuckerman, "Penmanship Exercises for Saucy Sons: Some Thoughts on the Colonial Southern Family" (Paper presented at the Sixtieth Annual Meeting of the Canadian Historical Association, Halifax, Nova Scotia, June 1981).

[35] Gerald W. Mullin, *Flight and Rebellion: Slave Resistance in Eighteenth-Century Virginia* (New York, 1972), pp. 35–82; Morgan, "Hegemony of the Law," pp. 136–82; Hindus, *Prison and Plantation*, pp. 129–61; Daniel C. Littlefield, *Rice and Slaves: Ethnicity and the Slave Trade in Colonial South Carolina* (Baton Rouge, 1981), pp. 115–73; Jeffrey J. Crow, "Slave Rebelliousness and Social Conflict in North Carolina, 1775 to 1802," *William and Mary Quarterly*, 3d ser. 37 (1980):79–102.

[36] See Jack P. Greene, "Social Context and the Causal Pattern of the American Revolution: A Preliminary Consideration of New York, Virginia

spect or deference of inferiors to their social betters and political officials, a lack of respect vividly expressed in the reference to the Continental Congress as "a passell of Rackoon Dogs."[37]

Historians have often regarded these and other examples of the tenuousness of authority in the older seaboard societies of colonial British America in the decades immediately before the American Revolution as evidence that those societies were suddenly coming apart, as formerly authoritative establishments came under challenge from new popular or "democratic" forces. But this interpretation is based upon a profound misunderstanding of the direction of social development in colonial British America. In the old Puritan colonies of Massachusetts and Connecticut authority was strong in the beginning and declined over time. As in so many respects, however, those colonies deviated sharply from British-American norms. Unlike the old Puritan societies, the rest of the British-American colonies moved not from order to disorder but from a state of profound unsettledness and uncertain and extremely weak authority to ever-greater social and political coherence. As a consequence of this development, provincial and local establishments, as well as the institutions and leaders of which those establishments were composed, had by the late colonial period acquired greater authority than they had ever had before. But that authority was still tenuous, and the many manifestations of its fragility listed above ought to be viewed as merely the most recent symptoms of a problem that had been endemic to these societies from their several beginnings.

The social sources of this continuing fragility of authority—often perceived as an absence of "all ideas [and habits]

and Massachusetts," in *La Révolution Américaine et L'Europe* (Paris, 1979), pp. 55–63; Marvin L. Michael Kay, "The North Carolina Regulation, 1766–1776: A Class Conflict," in Young, ed., *American Revolution*, pp. 71–123; Kay and Lorin Lee Cary, "Class, Mobility, and Conflict in North Carolina on the Eve of the Revolution," in Crow and Tise, eds., *Southern Experience*, pp. 109–51.

[37]Crow, "Liberty Men and Loyalists"; Hoffman, "'Disaffected' in the Revolutionary South," pp. 290–311.

of subordination and dependence"—have never been explored in depth and can be only briefly considered here.[38] Throughout the first century and a half of English colonization in America, of course, independent Englishmen had taken jealous pride in their celebrated devotion to the preservation of the liberty that was thought to be the primary emblem of their status as independent men. In America this inherited regard for liberty and independence seems to have been extended significantly by the much broader diffusion of property and independence through the society as a whole. Simultaneously, in the southern colonies it appears to have been even further enhanced by the presence of so many permanent dependents in the persons of black slaves, who served as omnipresent reminders to independent men of precisely how valuable their independence was.[39] The very extent and depth of this jealousy of their independent status among the property holders of colonial British America thus seems to have served as a powerful preventive to their giving unreserved deference to people and institutions in authority. At the same time, truncated social structures with correspondingly narrower distances between elites and other independent men along with the newness and precariousness of elite status meant that not even the oldest and most settled elites could command either the patronage or the respect accorded to their much more ancient and affluent counterparts in Britain. With few coercive resources at their disposal, political institutions suffered from a similar lack of regard.

Whatever the sources of the fragility of authority in colonial British America, the weakness of traditions and habits of subordination meant that authority, wherever it was reasonably well established, most assuredly did not depend, as has so often been asserted, upon power, upon tight elite control "exercised on the basis of class prerogative or rightful privi-

[38] The quotation is from Jack P. Greene, ed., "William Knox's Explanation for the American Revolution," *William and Mary Quarterly*, 3d ser. 30 (1973):299.

[39] A fuller explanation of the relationship between slavery and the weakness of habits of subordination and deference among independent men may be found in Greene, "'Slavery or Independence,'" pp. 193–214.

lege." If, Temple insisted, "Authority arising from opinion" resided "in those that Govern, who are few," "Power arising from Strength" was "always in those that are governed, who are many." "The ground upon which all Government stands," the foundation for all genuine authority, was thus, according to Temple, "the consent of the people, or the greatest or strongest part of them." Temple's observations seem to apply with special force to the loose societies of colonial British America. With weak police powers and such a large proportion of independent men, their governments derived power almost entirely from "public opinion," from the consent and acquiesence of those constituent elements of political society who held residual power.[40]

"Authority to govern" in colonial British America thus rested, it cannot be emphasized too strongly, upon "a popular base," upon "the consent of ordinary property owners."[41] Not even among the most thoroughly entrenched elite groups did superior rank and the supposedly greater wisdom it carried with it seem to have been sufficient to command automatic deference from inferiors or to have enabled superiors to ignore, much less to go against, the wishes of the people. "Alienating the affections, losing the opinions, and crossing the interests of the people" were certain routes toward loss of authority. No doubt, some elite figures, especially those new to or insecure in their status, presented themselves as proud, haughty, "hectoring [and] domineering" tyrants and claimed political office on the basis of superior rank and social position.[42] But the usual approach of officials and representatives to their constituents seems to have been one that, to employ the language of the day, was characterized by affability, familiarity, complaisance, and

[40] Hoffman, "'Disaffected' in the Revolutionary South," p. 312; Temple, "Essay upon the Original and Nature of Government," pp. 54, 84; Williams, *History of Vermont*, 2:394.

[41] Jackson, "Rise of the Western Members"; Edmund S. Morgan, "Conflict and Consensus in the American Revolution," in Kurtz and Hutson, eds., *Essays on the American Revolution*, p. 304.

[42] Temple, "Essay upon the Original and Nature of Government," pp. 84–85; Crow, "Liberty Men and Loyalists."

condescension—*condescension* meaning at that time a departure "from the privileges of superiority by a *voluntary* submission," a *willing* descent "to equal terms with inferiors," a soothing "by familiarity." Deference of inferiors to superiors was thus most easily elicited by a corresponding deference of superiors to inferiors. "Influence with the People" in America, one British official noted in the 1770s, could "only be obtained by following the humor or disposition of the People. To be the greatest was to be the servant of all. Withholding Grants or opposing Taxes . . . was the ready road to . . . favor, . . . as it flattered the People's pride by reducing those who assumed a higher rank than they, to become their dependants and supplicants." Such behavior, this official implied, not only "never failed" but was absolutely necessary "to attract [the people's] . . . regard and confidence."[43]

Indeed, from this perspective on the deferential systems of colonial British America, the preoccupation of the population with the pursuit of independence, affluence, and the improvements that would both guarantee and enhance their economic achievements suggests still another reason for the failure of the middle and lower orders of political society to play a more conspicuous role in political life. For the vast majority in those societies, the pursuit of happiness did not involve the pursuit of public office or even the active occupation of a public space. Although the sense of civic responsibility varied in strength from one political society to the next according to many different considerations, the primary concerns of most of these independent Americans were private rather than public. Their allegiances were to themselves rather than to their society. To quote one traveler, they were mostly "too much engaged in their respective occupations for the enticements" of public life.[44]

They or their ancestors had, in any case, left Britain or Europe not only to escape want and to gain independence but also, as contemporaries were fond of pointing out, to get

---

[43] Greene, ed., "William Knox's Explanation," p. 300.

[44] François Alexandre Frédéric, duc de La Rochefoucauld-Liancourt, *Travels through the United States of North America*, 2 vols. (London, 1799), 2:679.

away from excessive political intrusions into their private lives, intrusions in the form of high taxes, rapacious civil and religious establishments, obligations to military or naval service, and war. While they wanted enough government to secure peace and to maintain a just civil order, and this desire sometimes meant, as with the South and North Carolina Regulators, that they demanded more government than they had, they were usually, to quote one contemporary, in favor of just "so much government as will do justice, protect property, and defend the country."[45] As long as government performed these functions and did nothing to diminish their independence or to impede the improvement of their societies, Americans could be—and were—relatively indifferent to politics. Quite as much as deference to superiors, then, indifference to public affairs would seem to have accounted for the widely noted depoliticization of most older colonial societies through the middle decades of the eighteenth century as well as for the political prominence of elites. A greater concern for other interests, *private* interests, and, in time, habit on the part of the constituency, thus lay behind the minimal levels of popular involvement in the political systems of late colonial British America, and elite predominance seems to have been as much or more the result of passive as of active endorsement. In societies where most men were absorbed by private concerns, elites governed by default—and without necessarily ever obtaining much authority, defined as public respect.

But the failure of the broader public to take a more active public role did not mean that it had lost its capacity to do so. In a society in which political institutions did not have a monopoly of force, where authority was fragile, and where traditions of subordination were not only weak but were deemed inappropriate for independent men, even long-standing habits of civil order and political inactivity could be rapidly transformed into public involvement characterized by widespread political mobilization, conflict, competition,

[45] See Brown, *South Carolina Regulators*, pp. 38–111; Ekirch, *"Poor Carolina,"* pp. 161–211; idem, "Whig Authority and Public Order"; Williams, *History of Vermont*, 2:358, 424.

and, ultimately, even open contempt for and active challenges to constituted authority. Such a transformation could be produced by any number of events or conditions that impinged upon the ability of individuals to pursue their traditionally private goals. These included the failure of existing institutions to provide a just order, to guarantee security of property, or to take routine measures designed to facilitate the socioeconomic or political interests of the population, including roads, new governmental units, courts, and schools. They also included fear of loss of the essential components of private welfare and independence through taxes, disorder, corruption, crime, murder, or military service, and resentment against treatment that seemed to deny status and rewards thought appropriate to people in an independent and improved situation, including especially denial of the liberty and autonomy thought to pertain to that situation.

In a society with such a pronounced private orientation, public mobilization produced by these or other conditions and events could not, however, be easily sustained. Once the demands that had mobilized the polity had been secured and the people had once again been left at liberty, to borrow a contemporary cliché, to sit in safety and without fear under their own vines and fig trees enjoying the fruits of their labor—and that of their dependents—public concern with politics invariably receded, as it did following the Regulator movements in both Carolinas, and public life once again came to be dominated by elites.

An underlying assumption of this essay has been that prior social conditions determine much that happens in large-scale political events such as the American Revolution.[46] The argument has been that a fuller understanding of the aspirations for independence and improvement and of the fragility of authority in colonial British America, themselves all-important components of those prior conditions, can help

---

[46] This point has been argued more fully in Greene, "Social Origins of the American Revolution," pp. 1–22. See also Hoffman, "'Disaffected' in the Revolutionary South," p. 277.

put the sources and nature of conflict and other aspects of the Revolutionary experience of the southern backcountries into a clearer—and less anachronistic—focus.

A full comprehension of the strong orientation of the vast majority of the free population toward the pursuit and preservation of individual independence and their relative disinterest and lack of concern with government and public life makes it much easier to understand why the Revolution with its heavy demands presented so many problems for them. Even where society was already seriously divided and elites were the least cohesive and most insecure in their province-wide authority, as, to varying degrees, seems to have been the case in both Carolinas and Georgia, the challenge presented by the Coercive Acts and the initial stages of their military enforcement in 1774–76 could, as Gordon S. Wood and David Ammerman have shown, produce a contagion of "self-sacrifice and patriotism" that was surprisingly extensive, if by no means universal.[47] Like the Regulator movements in both Carolinas a few years before, this contagion seems even to have produced among those who were swept up in it a powerful and remarkably widely shared sense of group solidarity that in these profoundly private societies of militantly independent men may very well have appealed to and have been sustained by a deep, if in ordinary times usually sublimated, yearning for fraternity and communal dependence. But this early flush of public spiritedness proved impossible to sustain among a population whose most basic drives were individual rather than collective, private rather than public. Wanting most of all to be left alone, they quickly found themselves confronted with many new and burdensome public intrusions into their private lives, including high taxes, military service, supply levies, demands for declarations of allegiance, and, eventually in many areas, military action. All of these intrusions threatened both to undermine the order and se-

---

[47] Gordon S. Wood, *The Creation of the American Republic, 1776–1787* (Chapel Hill, 1969), pp. 413–25; David Ammerman, *In the Common Cause: American Response to the Coercive Acts of 1774* (Charlottesville, Va., 1974), pp. 89–101.

curity to which they aspired and to disrupt the progress they were making toward independence and improvement.[48]

In societies so strongly oriented toward private ends and with such weak authority structures, it is not at all surprising that people tended to pursue private, local, or regional interests at the expense of the larger public welfare wherever there was not a shared and broadly internalized consensus, a strong majority consensus, about precisely what constituted that larger public welfare. Where such a majority consensus existed, it could act as a powerful sanction—the sanction of opinion, the main ingredient in authority. Where it did not exist, however, those who sought to impose their definitions of the public welfare upon the rest of the population were unable to do so without the exertion of coercive resources that were considerably more powerful and dependable than those they had at their disposal. In modern societies consensual sanctions are usually achieved, or at least facilitated, through well-developed infrastructures, such as political parties. On the eve of the Revolution, however, none of the southern colonies had a well-developed party system that could serve as a colonywide organization to promote such a consensus, though in 1774–76 the committee system organized to resist the Coercive Acts began to serve that function.[49]

With a reasonably undivided, authoritative, and responsive central elite, with new economic opportunities presented by the war for people in the backcountry to increase their independence by supplying foodstuffs and other items for the army, and with a fair amount of sectional integration already established before the Revolution, the state government of Virginia was reasonably successful in achieving a

[48] For similar assessments of the basically private orientations of the populace in the southern backcountries, see Ferguson, "Functions of the Partisan-Militia," p. 245; Hoffman, "'Disaffected' in the Revolutionary South," pp. 278, 289, 300; Shy, "American Revolution," pp. 147–52; Sosin, *Revolutionary Frontier*, p. 98.

[49] See Pauline Maier, "The Beginnings of American Republicanism, 1765–1776," in *The Development of a Revolutionary Mentality* (Washington, D.C., 1972), pp. 99–117.

consensus on the question of what constituted the public welfare, at least until a competing authority turned up with the
invasion of the British army in 1780–81. Indeed, as Richard
Beeman and Rhys Isaac have shown, this consensus about
war aims in Virginia was strong enough to have a dampening
effect upon long-standing and bitter internal contentions between Evangelicals and Anglicans.[50]

By contrast, where prior conditions were not especially
conducive to the realization of such a consensus, and this
seems to have been the situation in both Carolinas and Georgia, the Revolution provided powerful new incentives for
people at the center to try through concessions and patronage to build such a consensus, which, given the weakness of
their coercive resources, was absolutely necessary to the extension of central authority to the peripheries. Where local
leadership in the peripheries was still uncertain and had not
coalesced into cohesive local or regionwide elites, as, again,
was the case in both Carolinas and Georgia, such efforts
risked failure because rivalries were so intense that concessions or patronage to one group could—and did—alienate
other groups. Here the effort to achieve a statewide consensus produced instead much local disunity among leaders.
When, as in the Carolinas and Georgia, local leadership was
divided, the rest of the population, not surprisingly, also divided. The great uncertainties inherent in so radical a tran-
sition as that from colony to state, from dependence to
independence, and the prior existence of significant distrust
or resistance to people in power at the center further increased the potential for such divisions. In such situations,
people, again unsurprisingly, seem to have chosen sides on
the basis of which of the contending local leaders they were
most closely attached to or which side seemed most likely to
guarantee order, security, and independence.[51] In this con-

[50] Mitchell, "Shenandoah Frontier," p. 478; Beeman and Isaac, "Cultural Conflict and Social Change," pp. 536–37; Morgan, "Conflict and
Consensus," p. 291.

[51] Ferguson, "Functions of the Partisan-Militia," p. 243; Klein, "Ordering the Backcountry," p. 679; Ekirch, *"Poor Carolina,"* pp. 145, 171, 178,
212; James P. Whittenburg, "Planters, Merchants, and Lawyers: Social

text it may not make much sense to organize historical analyses around such traditional concepts as allegiance, loyalty, or even neutrality, concepts that imply a degree of certainty about and levels of long-term commitment to public positions that were uncommon in the developing societies of the southern backcountries.

Where internal divisions and a lack of majority consensus characterized the situation, as in both Carolinas and Georgia as well as in the areas of western Virginia described by Emory G. Evans, coercion through force was the only way for centers to maintain their authority, to suppress political dissent and resistance to legal authority, at least before the appearance of a sizable regular American army in 1779. The militia seems to have functioned reasonably well in this regard until the British army came, albeit in divided areas only through methods that produced a deepening of divisions and of resentments that would, at the first opportunity, send people scurrying to the British in the hope of settling old scores.[52]

Notwithstanding the success of the militia in maintaining a semblance of central political power, authority remained fragile in all states during the Revolution and at the center as well as on the peripheries. This fragility contributed to a powerful chain of developments that led in dialectical fashion strongly in the direction of conflict and challenge to authority. Because authority was weak, people in authority were

---

Change and the Origins of the North Carolina Regulation," *William and Mary Quarterly*, 3d ser. 34 (1977):215–38; Klein, "Frontier Planters"; Jackson, "Rise of the Western Members."

[52] See Ferguson, "Carolina and Georgia Militia," pp. 175–76, 191, 194; idem, "Functions of the Partisan-Militia," pp. 240–43; Shy, "American Revolution," p. 145; Crow, "Liberty Men and Loyalists"; idem, "Tory Plots and Anglican Loyalty: The Llewelyn Conspiracy of 1777," *North Carolina Historical Review* 55 (1978):1–17; Abbot, "Lowcountry, Backcountry"; Edward J. Cashin, "'The Famous Colonel Wells': Factionalism in Revolutionary Georgia," *Georgia Historical Quarterly* 58 (1974):137–56; idem, "'But Brothers, It Is Our Land We Are Talking About': Winners and Losers in the Georgia Backcountry," infra; Harvey H. Jackson, "Consensus and Conflict: Factional Politics in Revolutionary Georgia, 1774–1777," *Georgia Historical Quarterly* 59 (1975):388–401; Evans, "Trouble in the Backcountry."

insecure. Because they were insecure, they were touchy about their authority and fearful that it would be challenged by competitors or would not be acknowledged by the rest of the population. Because of such fears and their justifiable doubts about the strength of their coercive resources, people in authority hesitated to exert their authority, a condition that, perhaps above all else, accounted for the looseness of sociopolitical controls over all of colonial British America during the late eighteenth century. Because authority was not consistently exerted and did not therefore consistently provide regular and predictable justice and protection, it was not especially respected. Because it was not respected, it was the more easily defied. When it was defied, those in authority tended to seek to establish it by overexerting it. Overexertion then invited overresistance in an escalating process that led to internecine strife, the breakdown of order, the loss or threat of loss of property, independence, and life itself, and the subordination to a spirit of savagery of all aspirations for improvement.

Such a situation could be retrieved only by retreating to a pattern of minimal retribution, moderation, and accommodation, an eventuality that in a society with few coercive resources was merely a function of political wisdom and a recognition both that authority was fragile and that fragile authority had to be applied leniently if it was going to retain the respect of the public at large. Once elites had come to this recognition and begun acting upon it, and the end of the war made it no longer necessary for them to make heavy demands upon the public, they had little difficulty in retaining their authority.[53] As long as government facilitated, rather than impeded, the drives for individual independence and social improvement that were so powerfully evident in and constituted the primary goals of all the new societies of colonial and Revolutionary British America, constituents were content to pursue those drives and, with their customary indifference to politics, to leave matters of governance to

[53] See especially Robert M. Weir, "'The Violent Spirit,' the Reestablishment of Order, and the Continuity of Leadership in Post-Revolutionary South Carolina," infra; Klein, "Frontier Planters."

those few largely elite or would-be elite figures who aspired to a public role. If democracy implies a "leveling tendency in political life," the Revolution had clearly failed to make Americans "addicted to democracy."[54]

This was not a lesson American leaders learned only as a result of the Revolution. It was something they had known—and practiced—for a long time, albeit some political societies had done so much more adroitly and successfully than others. But if older and successful elites like those in tidewater Virginia had managed to build their authority upon an acute awareness of its fragility, the Revolution certainly contributed to reinforce that awareness and to bring it home even more powerfully to their newer counterparts in the Carolinas and Georgia. Given the fragility of authority of the political establishments all over colonial British America and their awareness of that fragility, what needs to be explained, then, is not why the Revolution produced contention and conflict. That could hardly have been avoided. The wonder is that those establishments had the nerve to undertake revolution in the first place. In any effort to explain that wonder considerable emphasis needs to be given to the deeply rooted aspirations for independence and improvement and the ways they contributed to and interacted with the fragile authority structures that characterized colonial British America, including especially newly settled areas like the southern backcountries, before and during the Revolution.

[54] Sosin, *Revolutionary Frontier*, pp. 170–71; Hoffman, "'Disaffected' in the Revolutionary South," p. 290.

RACHEL N. KLEIN

Frontier Planters and the American Revolution

The South Carolina Backcountry, 1775–1782

NEARLY A YEAR before the colonies declared their independence from Great Britain, the South Carolina backcountry was already embroiled in a violent conflict between whigs and loyalists. Estimates of loyalist strength varied throughout the war, but several observers believed that the inhabitants of Ninety-Six District were about evenly divided and that tories may have outnumbered whigs in the fork between the Broad and Saluda rivers.[1] As early as 1774 coastal radicals were con-

I would like to thank Peter J. Albert, Steven H. Hahn, Ronald Hoffman, Edmund S. Morgan, Philip D. Morgan, George C. Rogers, Jr., Thad W. Tate, and Robert S. Westman for their helpful suggestions and encouragement. I am also grateful to Don Higginbotham, Pauline Maier, and Robert M. Weir for their comments on versions of this paper presented at the 1980 convention of the Southern Historical Association and at the 1982 symposium of the United States Capitol Historical Society.

[1] Contemporaries and subsequent historians have generally agreed that loyalists outnumbered whigs only in the fork between the Broad and Saluda rivers. The British campaign suffered in part because British commanders exaggerated reports of loyalist strength. David Ramsay, *The History of South Carolina from Its First Settlement in 1670 to the Year 1808*, 2 vols. (1809; reprint ed., Newberry, S.C., 1858), 1:144; "Colonel Robert Gray's Observations on the War in Carolina," *South Carolina Historical Magazine* 11 (1910):140; Robert W. Barnwell, Jr., "Loyalism in South Carolina, 1765–1785," Ph.D. diss., Duke University, 1941, pp. 131–34; Don Higginbotham, *The War of American Independence: Military Attitudes, Policies, and*

cerned about inland allegiances and struggled, with only mixed success, to win frontier support. In September 1775 the British governor William Campbell could write with confidence that "the loyalty of those poor, honest, industrious people in the back part of this and neighboring provinces discontents them [the Charleston whigs] greatly." By November of that year the two sides had come to blows, and not until winter did whig forces finally gain a temporary ascendancy by rounding up the "most leading and active" tories whom they carried to jail in Charleston. Sporadic fighting persisted through the later 1770s, and in 1780, with the arrival of the British, the frontier exploded into a virtual civil war.[2]

Historians have generally recognized a connection between frontier loyalism and sectional hostilities. On the eve of the Revolution the backcountry had only three seats allotted in the colonial assembly even though the region contained about three-fourths of the colony's white population. Before hundreds—perhaps thousands—of self-proclaimed Regulators drew attention to backcountry grievances, inland settlers had lacked local courts and jails. During the 1760s the growing colonial struggle had drawn legislative attention away from the backcountry, giving South Carolina frontiersmen added cause to resent coastal whigs. Finally, backcoun-

Practice, 1763–1789 (New York, 1971), pp. 133–39; Ronald Hoffman, "The 'Disaffected' in the Revolutionary South," in Alfred F. Young, ed., *The American Revolution: Explorations in the History of American Radicalism* (DeKalb, Ill., 1976), pp. 273–316. South Carolina's eighteenth-century backcountry is discussed in Rachel N. Klein, "The Rise of the Planters in the South Carolina Backcountry, 1765–1808," Ph.D. diss., Yale University, 1979.

[2] Edward McCrady, *The History of South Carolina in the Revolution, 1775–1780* (New York, 1901), pp. 33–858; David Duncan Wallace, *South Carolina: A Short History* (Columbia, S.C., 1961), pp. 243–331; Lewis P. Jones, *The South Carolina Civil War of 1775* (Lexington, Ky., 1975); Campbell to the Lords of Trade, Sept. 19, 1775, P.R.O. Transcripts, vol. 35, pp. 252–53, South Carolina Department of Archives and History, Columbia. For a more general account of the process by which backcountry areas were drawn into the Revolutionary struggle, see David Ammerman, *In the Common Cause: The American Response to the Coercive Acts of 1774* (Charlottesville, Va., 1974).

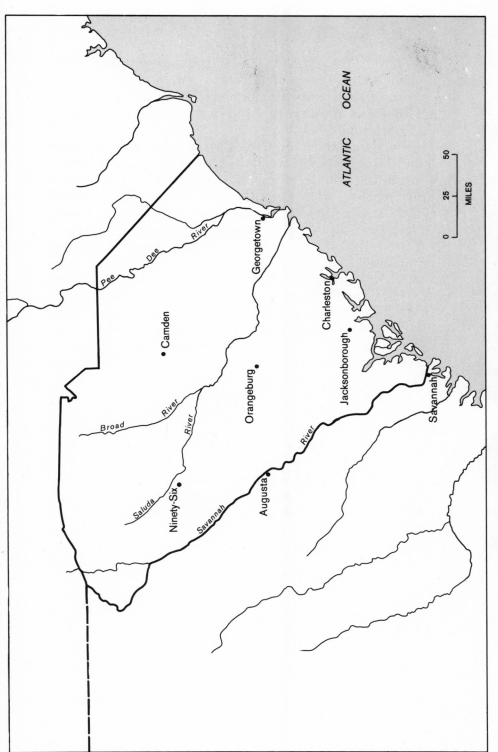

South Carolina during the Revolution

try settlers, particularly those in the western piedmont, complained that lowcountry leaders had provided insufficient protection against the Indians. When the Revolution came, they had ample reason to resent requests for support from Charleston rebels.[3]

This sectional interpretation of backcountry loyalism provides an insufficient explanation of frontier allegiances during the Revolution because it cannot account for the many frontier settlers who supported the Americans. Richard Maxwell Brown's discovery that only 6 of the 120 known Regulators actively supported the loyalists, while 55 joined the Americans, compounded the problem. Brown's research demonstrated that the most outspoken proponents of frontier demands for courts, schools, churches, and legislative representation tended to join the whig cause. Regulators resented the neglectful assembly, but their concern for the protection of property, their growing involvement in slavery, and their increasing interest in commercial agriculture tied them in fundamental ways to the wealthier planters and merchants of the coast. We can thus understand how Regulators managed to overcome their sectional animosity and join with lowcountry whigs, but the loyalty to the crown of many other inland settlers remains a mystery.[4]

Nor is there evidence to suggest that ideology distinguished backcountry whigs from loyalists. Charles Woodmason, the Anglican minister who became the Regulators' leading spokesman, demonstrated how easily republican rhetoric could be turned against Charleston radicals. Woodmason was one of the few former Regulators who remained a staunch loyalist, and he admonished lowcountry rebels who made "such a noise about Liberty! Liberty! Freedom! Property! Rights! Privileges! and what not; And at the same time keep half their fellow subjects in a State of Slavery." Wood-

[3] Wallace, *South Carolina*, p. 263; McCrady, *History of South Carolina, 1775–1780*, pp. 33–35; Richard J. Hooker, ed., *The South Carolina Backcountry on the Eve of the Revolution: The Journal and Other Writings of Charles Woodmason, Anglican Itinerant* (Chapel Hill, 1953), pp. 118–19.

[4] Richard Maxwell Brown, *The South Carolina Regulators* (Cambridge, Mass., 1963), pp. 123–25.

mason was not referring to black slaves but to the thousands of white frontiersmen who remained all but unrepresented in the South Carolina assembly. Inland and coastal leaders spoke the same political language, but on the frontier republican rhetoric could accommodate the loyalist as well as the whig position.[5]

Finally, ethnic and simplistic economic interpretations can provide little additional help in distinguishing frontier whigs from tories. Wallace Brown, in his analysis of South Carolina's 320 loyalist claimants, found that foreign-born were more likely than native-born colonists to have sided with the loyalists, and contemporaries believed that the German origin of many settlers at the lower Broad and Saluda fork was largely responsible for loyalism in that region. But many Irish, English-born, and German South Carolinians joined the rebels. Similarly, Camden-area Quakers and New Light Baptists of latter-day Union County inclined to loyalism, and Regular Baptists of Charleston and Cheraw supported the Americans, but Presbyterians and Anglicans, who formed the majority of the inland population, were divided. Neither wealth nor occupation provides additional clues as to divisions on the frontier. Storekeepers, planters, slaveholders, and nonslaveholders were found in both rebel and loyalist camps.[6]

If, however, the Revolutionary backcountry failed to divide along clearly defined class lines, the frontier struggle did

[5] Hooker, ed., *South Carolina Backcountry*, p. 220. A Regulator sympathizer at Pee Dee urged the institution of county and circuit courts so that backcountry settlers could "enjoy by that means, the rights and privileges of British subjects, which they think themselves now deprived of." He also observed that "as the jurisdiction of courts in Charleston extends all over the province, government is not a protection but an oppression; that they [backcountrymen] are not tried by their Peers" (*South Carolina and American General Gazette*, Sept. 2, 1768).

[6] Wallace Brown, *The King's Friends: The Composition and Motives of the American Loyalist Claimants* (Providence, 1965), pp. 213–28; McCrady, *History of South Carolina, 1775–1780*, pp. 32–52; Barnwell, "Loyalism in South Carolina," p. 2; Floyd Mulkey, "Rev. Philip Mulkey, Pioneer Baptist Preacher in South Carolina," South Carolina Historical Association *Proceedings* (1945):3–14.

have an important class dimension. Although ambitious planters and merchants chose one side or the other for a variety of reasons, the whigs more consistently represented the broad class interests of rising backcountry slaveholders. Those inland leaders who joined the whig side extended a process begun during the 1760s and gradually became the vanguard of an emerging planter class.

During the decade preceding the outbreak of the Revolution, South Carolina's backcountry had erupted into violence as Regulators struggled to suppress the bandit gangs that had been robbing and torturing frontier settlers and attracting slave runaways into their ranks. Leading Regulators were ambitious entrepreneurs. They were millowners, surveyors, distillers, and storekeepers who were in the process of acquiring slaves for the production of cash crops and were contributing to a growing backcountry demand for black labor. Their primary concern was to make the frontier safe for property holders, and they were especially concerned about property in slaves.[7]

Regulators were also angered by those frontier hunters whose hunting practices, tendency to pilfer from planters, and inclination to support the more aggressive bandits ran counter to the interests of the more settled population. Referred to by their contemporaries as "white Indians," some of these hunters were squatters or even landowners, but they were simply unable or unwilling to plant enough for a subsistence. Regulators demanded various measures designed to restrict this hunting population.[8]

Impelled to action by the immediate threat to their lives and property, Regulators took the opportunity to enumerate a series of smoldering backcountry grievances. In addition to calling for local courts, jails, schools, churches, and a va-

[7] Brown, *South Carolina Regulators*; Rachel N. Klein, "Ordering the Backcountry: The South Carolina Regulation," *William and Mary Quarterly*, 3d ser. 38 (1981):661–80.

[8] Klein, "Ordering the Backcountry," pp. 668–76.

grancy act, they expressed outrage that the backcountry had only two representatives in the assembly.[9]

As the Regulator uprising progressed, a number of prosperous frontiersmen became alarmed by the violence of Regulator methods and urged the council to authorize an all-out offensive against the insurgents. They chose a man named Joseph Scoffel (also spelled "Scophol," "Scovil," or "Coffel") to lead the anti-Regulator forces. Apparently they saw Scoffel as a man who would attract precisely those people who had fallen victim to Regulator attacks. Scoffel himself was later convicted of hog stealing, and Gen. William Moultrie recalled him as "a man of some influence in the backcountry, but a stupid, ignorant blockhead."[10]

Scoffel, assuming the title of "Colonel," succeeded very well in attracting followers who, not surprisingly, began to behave like bandits. According to one correspondent, Scoffel had "many returned horsethieves and banditti in his midst." Another insisted that Scoffel's party were impressing "provisions and horses" wherever they went, "leaving whole families destitute of both." These and other reports prompted the council to withdraw all support. Violence between the Regulators and Scoffel's people was narrowly averted.[11]

With the passage of the South Carolina Circuit Court Act in 1769, the Regulators finally dispersed, but resentment persisted. Although Regulators had, by marching to places of election in 1768, elected six of their candidates to the assembly, the backcountry remained grossly underrepresented. Regulators had prompted coastal leaders to pass a law restricting hunters, but as the assembly became increasingly preoccupied by the broader colonial struggle, it failed

[9] Ibid.; Brown, *South Carolina Regulators*.

[10] Brown, *South Carolina Regulators*, ch. 6; Moultrie, *Memoirs of the American Revolution So Far As It Related to the States of North and South Carolina and Georgia*, 2 vols. (New York, 1802), 1:109.

[11] *South Carolina Gazette*, Mar. 23, Apr. 6, 1769; South Carolina Council Journal, Mar. 22, 1769, S.C. Dept. Arch. and Hist.; Brown, *South Carolina Regulators*, pp. 83–95.

to follow through on a proposed vagrancy act. The grievances and social divisions that had erupted in the Regulator
uprising would influence the configuration and outcome of
the longer struggle on the Revolutionary frontier.[12]

As the Revolution approached, coastal whigs rightly feared
that sectional animosities would incline South Carolina frontiersmen to support the loyalists. They sought to offset the
loyalist threat not only by increasing backcountry legislative
representation but by dispatching a three-man committee on
a stump-speaking tour through loyalist strongholds. The
committee, consisting of the Baptist minister Oliver Hart, the
Presbyterian minister William Tennent, and the Charleston
radical William Henry Drayton, struggled to win the support
of certain prominent "men of influence." They recognized
that the primary divisions within the Carolina backcountry
were by neighborhoods or communities that tended to coa-
lesce around such key individuals. The committee had only
mixed success, but the record of their mission serves as a
window onto the process by which backcountry settlers chose
one side or the other during the first phase of the Revolution.[13]

The committee concentrated its efforts on Thomas Fletchall, a militia colonel in the area between the Broad and Saluda rivers. Though he appears not to have joined the
Regulation, Fletchall had publicly supported several Regulator demands. His defection to the loyalist side caused considerable alarm among lowcountry whigs. As one observer later
wrote, Fletchall's position as colonel "of course gave him
great influence in that part of the country." At a stump meeting held near Fletchall's home at Fairforest Creek, Oliver

[12] Brown, *South Carolina Regulators*, pp. 60–82; *South Carolina Gazette*,
Oct. 10, 1768; *South Carolina and American General Gazette*, Sept. 28–30,
1768; Thomas Cooper and David J. McCord, eds., *The Statutes at Large of
South Carolina*, 10 vols. (Columbia, 1836–41), 4:298–302.

[13] Glenwood Clayton and Loulie Latimer Owens, eds., "Oliver Hart's
Diary of the Journey to the Backcountry," *Journal of the South Carolina Bap-
tist Historical Society* 1 (1975):18–30; "Fragment of a Journal Kept by the
Reverend William Tennent," in Robert Wilson Gibbes, ed., *A Documentary
History of the American Revolution*, 3 vols. (Columbia, S.C., and New York,
1853–57), 1:225–38.

Hart observed "with Sorrow . . . that Col. Fletchall has all those people at his beck, and reigns amongst them like a little King." Not surprisingly, those areas in which Drayton, Tennent, and Hart enjoyed greatest success were neighborhoods in which militia captains were sympathetic to the whig cause.[14]

There were other such loyalist men of influence who helped to make that region a persistent problem for South Carolina whigs. Among these were two former Regulators, Moses Kirkland and Robert Cunningham. The American militia general Andrew Pickens later testified to Cunningham's local prestige when he insisted that "there would not have been so virulent an opposition to our cause in this country" had Cunningham joined the rebels. Evan McLaurin, a prosperous storeowner at the lower Broad and Saluda fork, was also successful in attracting surrounding settlers to the loyalist cause. When Drayton visited the area in August 1775, he found that McLaurin was able to throw such "a damp on the people" that no one signed the Continental Association. McLaurin managed to put a stop to one meeting "only by his presence."[15]

The very term *man of influence*, so frequently used by contemporaries, is revealing. In communities where settlers depended upon stores and mills for a variety of services, it is not surprising that merchants and millers, many of whom were also magistrates or militia officers, should have wielded extensive political influence. Drayton recognized the power of such men when, in the course of his journey, he declared that "no miller who was a subscriber [to the Continental Association] should grind wheat for a non-subscriber." It is no coincidence that such prominent backcountry loyalists as Cunningham, McLaurin, and Kirkland were all involved in

[14] John Drayton, *Memoirs of the American Revolution*, 2 vols. (Charleston, 1821), 1:312; Clayton and Owens, eds., "Oliver Hart's Diary," pp. 21, 18–30; "Fragment of a Journal," 1:225–38; Barnwell, "Loyalism in South Carolina," p. 141.

[15] Pickens to Maj. Gen. Henry Lee, Aug. 28, 1811, Andrew Pickens Papers, South Caroliniana Library, University of South Carolina, Columbia; Drayton, *Memoirs*, 1:364; Drayton to Council of Safety, Aug. 16, 1775, Gibbes, ed., *Documentary History*, 1:141.

local trade and that Fletchall owned and operated large grist-mills.[16]

Influence could and apparently did work two ways. Thomas Fletchall lived on lands adjoining those of the pacifist and tory minister Philip Mulkey and presumably serviced the Mulkey community with his mills. One cannot help but wonder to what extent Mulkey and Mulkey's followers influenced Fletchall. Similarly, Evan McLaurin operated his store in the lower Broad and Saluda fork, where Germans predominated. According to contemporary reports, these "Dutch" settlers became tories because they feared that coastal rebels would retract all royal land grants. McLaurin's proximity to the German settlement may have encouraged him to remain loyal.[17]

Whatever the interaction between various inland areas and their leading men, it worked to divide the Revolutionary backcountry by neighborhood. When persuasion failed, communities had ways of enforcing or trying to enforce unanimity. One loyalist refugee from the Camden area admitted to having taken the "Rebel Oath," but insisted that "the millers and blacksmiths would not work for any one who did not take the oath." That families and common ethnic groups often lived on adjoining lands only reinforced the tendency for clusters of population to act as whig or tory units. Follow-

[16] Drayton to Council of Safety, Aug. 16, 1775, Gibbes, ed., *Documentary History*, 1:141. McLaurin operated a large store at Dutch Fork and had a partner in Charleston. Cunningham operated a ferry on the Saluda River. His claim to £1,000 due in book accounts and notes indicates that he was involved in trade. Fletchall claimed compensation for fourteen slaves, over 1,000 acres, gristmills at Fairforest Creek, and £165 in debts due (Audit Office, Transcripts of the Manuscript Books and Papers of the Commission of Enquiry into the Losses and Services of American Loyalists in the Public Record Office [London], vol. 53, p. 320, vol. 54, pp. 317–26, vol. 56, pp. 223–39, New York Public Library, New York City [hereafter cited as Loyalist Claims, Transcripts]; Drayton to Council of Safety, Aug. 21, 1775, Gibbes, ed., *Documentary History*, 1:150).

[17] Bob Compton, "The Fairforest Church," *Journal of the South Carolina Baptist Society* 1 (1975):49; Drayton to Council of Safety, Aug. 21, 1775, William Tennent to Henry Laurens, Aug. 20, 1775, Gibbes, ed., *Documentary History*, 1:151, 141; Drayton, *Memoirs*, 1:311–12, 325–26; Drayton to Council of Safety, Aug. 16, 1775, Gibbes, ed., *Documentary History*, 1:141.

ing the British occupation, one loyalist officer could observe that "the whole province resembled a piece of patch work, the inhabitants of every settlement when united in sentiment being in arms for the side they liked best and making continual inroads into one another's settlements."[18]

Not surprisingly, the storeowners, millers, magistrates, and officers most likely to wield local influence were also those most likely to entertain statewide political and military ambitions. For some, the decisive consideration in choosing sides was status. In January 1775 both Robert Cunningham and Moses Kirkland were, by all appearances, sympathetic to the American cause. Yet by the following summer, the two were among the staunchest opponents of the provincial government.[19] Many years later Andrew Pickens offered what seems a plausible explanation. When the Council of Safety established a backcountry regiment, the candidates for colonel were Cunningham, Kirkland, and James Mayson—all former Regulators. The position went to Mayson which, according to Pickens, "so exasperated the others that they immediately took the other side of the Question." Pickens was not concerned with bad-mouthing tory leaders, for he also pointed out that he "never had any doubt but that . . .[Cunningham] . . . would have made the best officer." Henry Laurens, president of the Council of Safety, suspected that Thomas Fletchall had been motivated by similar concerns.

[18] "Gray's Observations on the War," p. 153; Loyalist Claims, Transcripts, vol. 52, pp. 461–71. Claims filed by loyalists from Ninety-Six District confirm the officers' picture of a region divided by neighborhood. Of more than fifty claimants, most lived in the region of Long Cane, Hard Labor, and Cuffeytown creeks. Many had been neighbors or friends before the Revolution. All appear to have served in a militia regiment officered by Col. John Hamilton (Loyalist Claims, Transcripts, vol. 26).

[19] Kirkland and Cunningham were among those appointed to the committee responsible for circulating the Continental Association (*South Carolina Gazette*, Jan. 30, 1775). Kirkland was also a member of the grand jury of Ninety-Six when that body protested the exercise of parliamentary power "to tax and bind the Americans in all Cases whatsoever" (ibid., Dec. 12, 1774). In June 1775 he accepted a commission as captain from the whig government in Charleston. See McCrady, *History of South Carolina, 1775–1780*, pp. 14, 37–38; Barnwell, "Loyalism in South Carolina," pp. 98–103; Drayton, *Memoirs*, 1:321.

"It has been said," wrote Laurens in a letter to Fletchall, "that you were in some measure disposed to unite with the friends of America, but that you were deterred partly . . . by the dread of losing your commission of Colonel and your rank of Justice of the Peace."[20]

Recognizing both the ambition and the local authority of backcountry men of influence, lowcountry whigs sought to win support by offering access to political and military positions. In July 1775 Henry Laurens was eager to prevent the defection of a Captain Whitfield to the loyalists. It occurred to Laurens "that Captn. Whitfield however chearfully he may shew an inclination to serve the colony by resignation, may not be content with a subcommand," and he suggested that the captain petition the council for a higher rank. Also in 1775 the provincial congress established three regular regiments, one of which was to consist of backcountry mounted rangers. As the Revolutionary general William Moultrie later recalled, "It was thought not only useful, but political to raise them, because the most influential gentlemen in the backcountry were appointed officers which interested them in the cause."[21]

As the Revolution progressed—as people lost friends and family in the fighting—the war assumed greater meaning for many of those involved. Some undoubtedly fought to preserve liberty as they conceived it. As one frontier officer wrote to his son from headquarters at Ninety-Six: "I feel myself distracted on both hands by this thought, that in my old age I should be obliged to take field in defense of my rights and liberties, and that of my children. God only knows that it is not by choice, but of necessity, and from the consideration that I had rather suffer anything than lose my birthright

---

[20] Pickens to Lee, Aug. 28, 1811, Pickens Papers; William Thomson to Laurens, July 22, 1775, in A. S. Salley, Jr., *The History of Orangeburg County, South Carolina, from Its First Settlement to the Close of the Revolutionary War* (Orangeburg, S.C., 1898), p. 406; Laurens to Fletchall, July 14, 1775, "Journal of the Council of Safety for the Province of South Carolina, 1775," South Carolina Historical Society *Collections* 2 (1858):24.

[21] Laurens to Fletchall, July 15, 1775, Salley, *History of Orangeburg County*, pp. 402–3; Moultrie, *Memoirs*, 1:64.

and that of my children." Experience on the frontier may well have made some such men particularly sensitive to colonial complaints about Parliament.[22]

But during the early phase of the struggle most backcountry settlers were less concerned about Britain than their own local grievances and personal aspirations. Coastal whigs were able to win inland support precisely because they recognized and helped fulfill the political and military ambition of leading frontiersmen. In so doing, they extended the statewide political power of backcountry settlers and thereby furthered the political goals expressed by Regulators during the preceding decade. Following roughly the system of apportionment established for the provincial congress, the state constitution of 1776 allowed the backcountry 76 out of 202 seats in the assembly. Although the new constitution did not establish anything approximating proportional representation of the white population, it greatly increased the political influence of frontier settlers. For Moses Kirkland and Robert Cunningham, the whig offer was not good enough; but for others with similar ambitions, opportunities opened by the Revolution must have been very welcome.[23]

Like their whig counterparts, many backcountry loyalists were ambitious slaveholders, storekeepers, millowners, and rising planters, but in their effort to attract followers they played on widespread resentments against the wealthier planters and merchants of the coast. Writing of his unsuccessful labors between the Broad and Saluda rivers, William Tennent complained that leading loyalists "blind the people and fill them with bitterness against the gentlemen as they are called." Settlers believed that "no man that comes from below, and that no paper printed there can speak the truth." At a meeting held near Fairforest Creek, Colonel Fletchall addressed the nonslaveholding population by intimating that "the people below wanted them to go down and assist them

[22] James Williams to his son, June 12, 1779, Gibbes, ed., *Documentary History*, 2:115–16.

[23] Cooper and McCord, eds., *Statutes at Large*, 1:131–46; Wallace, *South Carolina*, pp. 271–82; William A. Schaper, *Sectionalism and Representation in South Carolina* (Washington, D.C., 1901), pp. 367–69.

against the Negroes." Only a "Fool," suggested Fletchall, would agree to go.[24]

Another loyalist leader addressed a meeting in the same upper piedmont region by reading a "ministerial piece," similarly designed to tap sectional animosities. "It is hard," observed the author, "that the charge of our intending to enslave you, should come oftenest from the mouths of lawyers who in your Southern Provinces at least, have long made you slaves to themselves." After the reading Oliver Hart observed "with sorrow" that there were "Marks of approbation set almost on every Countenance." Many, wrote David Ramsay, were "induced to believe that the whole was an artful deception imposed upon them for interested purposes, by the gentlemen of fortune and ambition on the seacoast."[25]

Whig leaders struggled against these sectional and class hostilities. When the Regular Baptist minister Richard Furman wrote an open letter to settlers living between the Broad and Saluda rivers, he attempted to counter their suspicions by insisting that in war "the Great Men are the Chief Losers." Not only were their coastal houses most vulnerable to bombs and cannon, but "as they have the most in their Hands, the Taxes must be Heavier upon them." A circular letter to the backcountry used the same peculiar logic. Suggesting that poor people had suffered most from the Stamp Act, the author observed that "the Rich men of America" nonetheless made "such a resistence that the cruel act was repealed." The letter admonished those "ill disposed persons" who claimed that "this duty upon tea could not hurt the poor people who did not drink it."[26]

Although resentment against lowcountry planters proved a powerful weapon in the hands of backcountry loyalists, it

[24] Tennent to Laurens, Aug. 20, 1775, Gibbes, ed., *Documentary History*, 1:145; Clayton and Owens, eds., "Oliver Hart's Diary," pp. 21–22; Drayton, *Memoirs*, 1:411.

[25] Clayton and Owens, eds., "Oliver Hart's Diary," pp. 21–22; Peter Force, ed., *American Archives*, 4th ser. 6 vols. (Washington, D.C., 1837–46), 1:1431; Ramsay is quoted in Salley, *History of Orangeburg County*, p. 337.

[26] Nov. 1775, Richard Furman Papers, S.C. Library; *South Carolina Gazette*, Sept. 7 and 11, 1775.

also involved them in the first of a series of inconsistencies. Such prominent tories as Evan McLaurin, Moses Kirkland, and Robert Cunningham had various business connections with the coastal elite and, as slaveowners, had fundamental interests in common with them. They also had statewide political ambitions. By fueling antagonism toward the "gentlemen of fortune and ambition on the seacoast," loyalist leaders worked against the broad class interests of wealthy inland settlers who were seeking greater participation in statewide political and economic affairs. Although many backcountry whigs also felt personally suspicious of seacoast gentlemen, their participation in the American cause helped to accelerate a pre-Revolutionary trend toward growing political and economic association between the elites of both sections.

A far greater advantage for South Carolina whigs was their own inability to win support from the western Indians, a failure that actually strengthened the whig position among frontier settlers who lived in constant fear of Cherokee attack. As inland men of influence were drawing their local communities toward one side or the other during the first months of the Revolutionary conflict, many settlers were unwilling to become actively involved on either side. They were suspicious of coastal whigs, but apart from those areas in which loyalist men of influence held sway, they tended not to join the tories. Some of these previously uninvolved people—particularly those living in the western piedmont—became sympathetic to the American cause only after the broader colonial struggle became identified with a frontier war against the Indians.[27]

During the summer and fall of 1775, many inland families had their attention focused not on the growing colonial crisis but on the growing threat from the western Indians. Both loyalists and whigs attempted to capitalize on the situation by accusing each other of trying to foment a Cherokee war. The

---

[27] Many backcountry settlers were disaffected but not actively loyal. The subject is discussed in Hoffman, "'Disaffected' in the Revolutionary South."

accusations were probably groundless on both sides, but the ensuing rumors caused great alarm among western settlers, who had borne the brunt of the Indian conflicts of the 1760s. Writing from the backcountry in July 1775, the American officer Andrew Williamson told of "considerable confusion . . . on account of the expected danger from the Cherokees."[28]

Although neither side wanted to instigate an Indian war, both whigs and tories were trying to win the allegiance of the Cherokee to prevent the Indians from joining the opposition. The British sent the deputy Indian agent, Alexander Cameron, to negotiate with the Cherokee, while the Council of Safety, in a last effort at conciliation, agreed to send a gift of ammunition. On November 3, 1775, a band of loyalists intercepted the shipment of powder and used it as evidence that the whigs were, in fact, attempting to provoke a conflict. Andrew Williamson's militiamen were able to retake the ammunition, but in late November two thousand loyalist troops laid siege to Fort Ninety-Six, where the powder was held. That Williamson had fewer than six hundred recruits for defense of the fort is itself testimony to the unpopularity of whig efforts at appeasement.[29]

Recognizing the seriousness of the situation, the provincial congress tried to defend its actions by issuing a declaration claiming that "nothing could in the least degree satisfy them [the Cherokee] but a promise of some ammunition." Although the gift was "the only probable means of preserving the frontiers from the inroads of the Indians," it had been "by some non-associators made an instrument for the most diabolical purposes." The whigs, by their very efforts to win the allegiance of the western Indians, were alienating back-

[28] Gary D. Olson, "Loyalists and the American Revolution: Thomas Brown and the South Carolina Backcountry, 1775–1776," *South Carolina Historical Magazine* 68 (1967):201–19, and 69 (1968):44–58; James H. O'Donnell III, *Southern Indians in the American Revolution* (Knoxville, 1973), pp. 17–29; Williamson to Council of Safety, July 1775, "Journal of the Council of Safety," 2:55; Drayton, *Memoirs*, 1:383.

[29] Major Mayson to Colonel Thomson, Nov. 24, 1775, Gibbes, ed., *Documentary History*, 1:215; Drayton, *Memoirs*, 2:64–65.

country settlers, particularly those in the vulnerable area of Ninety-Six District.[30]

What finally decided the question of Cherokee allegiance and brought on an Indian war had little to do with whig or loyalist efforts. The Cherokee had good reason to be less suspicious of British officials than of the rebel government because the former had at least tried to restrict western migration onto Indian lands. By spring of 1776 the Cherokee were on the brink of war with South Carolina settlers over the familiar problem, and in April they attacked a community in latter-day York County.[31]

With the Cherokee veering toward the British side, whig leaders abandoned their policy of conciliation and called for an all-out offensive against the Indians. This time Williamson had no problem in raising troops. By July 1776 he had approximately one thousand militiamen from Ninety-Six District who virtually burned their way through the Cherokee nation. William Henry Drayton, who had negotiated the gift of ammunition less than a year before, now called for the total destruction of the western Indians. "It is expected," wrote Drayton to a backcountry officer, "that you make smooth work as you go—that is, you cut up every Indian corn-field and burn every Indian town."[32]

Though the whigs adopted an aggressive policy only after failing at conciliation, their new strategy was far more consistent with the experience and aspirations of backcountry settlers. Many, particularly in Ninety-Six District, had lost friends and relatives during the Cherokee War and other clashes of the 1760s. The threat of Indian attack had been a perpetual source of terror. By their all-out anti-Cherokee campaign, whig forces inevitably won some support from previously neutral settlers. That several active loyalists ad-

[30] "Declaration by Authority of Congress," Nov. 19, 1775, Gibbes, ed., *Documentary History*, 1:211–12.

[31] O'Donnell, *Southern Indians*, pp. 6–15; Wade Hampton's Recollection, 1819, Lyman C. Draper Collection, 6VV193, State Historical Society of Wisconsin, Madison.

[32] Rev. James Creswell to Drayton, July 27, 1776, and Drayton to Francis Salvadore, July 24, 1776, Gibbes, ed., *Documentary History*, 2:29 and 31.

mitted to having served under Williamson during the summer of 1776 suggests the broad consensus that underlay the newly aggressive whig strategy.[33]

Although greed for land was not an immediate motive behind Williamson's Cherokee campaign, the connection between land hunger and Indian war was obvious. Land hunger had been the source of the initial conflict. Even while Williamson was raising his troops, Drayton urged that the Cherokee nation "be extirpated, the lands become the property of the public." He promised never to support a treaty with the Indians "upon any other terms than their removal beyond the mountains." As it turned out, Drayton had his way. In the ensuing treaty, the Cherokee ceded the entire area of latter-day Pendleton County. From those lands South Carolina's militia and Continental soldiers would receive their bounty payments after the war.[34]

Evan McLaurin, who eventually became a loyalist officer, inadvertently identified the tory dilemma. "The Indians," he wrote, "God knows they are good for Little." McLaurin believed that they could be used only as a "Bug Bear" to annoy whig settlements and interrupt communications. For that purpose he proposed the building of a frontier fort in order to protect the Indians' northern townships. But in return for a negligible military advantage, McLaurin found himself advocating a measure that could only have antagonized western settlers.[35] All in all, the Indians did the Americans far more good as enemies than they could have done as allies. It was whigs, rather than loyalists, who found themselves in a position to continue the struggle for land and security begun during the preceding decade.

Loyalists attracted others as allies who, like the Indians, did them more harm than good. If, as seems to have been the

[33] See, for example, Loyalist Claims, Transcripts, vol. 26, pp. 67–70 and 133–38, and Wade Hampton's Recollection.

[34] Drayton to Salvadore, July 24, 1776, Gibbes, ed., *Documentary History*, 2:29; Wallace, *South Carolina*, p. 278.

[35] McLaurin to Colonel Balfour, Aug. 7, 1780, Emmet Collection, N.Y. Public Library.

case, the whigs had best success in winning allegiance from former Regulators, loyalists attracted the hunters and bandits who had inspired Regulator wrath. With the outbreak of Revolution, Joseph Scoffel, formerly the leader of anti-Regulator forces, reappeared in the backcountry, this time as a British supporter. The Council of Safety was alarmed in July 1775 by the appearance of "one Coffel" at Fort Charlotte, and Henry Laurens ordered that the fort be immediately taken. Later that year the council received information that "the Scoffol Lights were coming down from the backcountry in great force" to take public records and ammunition being held by whig forces at Dorchester. According to South Carolina's first historian, David Ramsay, "The names of scovilites and regulators were insensibly exchanged for the appellation of tories and whigs, or the friends of the old and new order of things." Many, he thought, had actually followed Scoffel, though the name "was applied to others as a term of reproach on the alleged similarity of their principles."[36]

By the close of the war, South Carolinians were using the term *scoffelite* in order to designate and denigrate all former loyalists, but some early commentators made important distinctions between loyalists in general and the type of people who had followed Joseph Scoffel. One writer noted that frontiersmen who had "been marshalled by scovel under the authority of the royal governor, most of them joined the tories." And David Ramsay was willing to distinguish between lowcountry tories, some of whom were "gentlemen of honor, principle and humanity," and backcountry tories, who included "a great proportion of . . . ignorant unprincipled banditti; to whom idleness, licentiousness and deeds of violence were familiar. Horse thieves and others whose crimes had exiled them from society attached themselves to the British." Even the loyalist Woodmason wrote that "the Rogues . . . called themselves Friends of Government."[37]

[36] Laurens to Colonel Thomson, July 16, 1775, "Journal of the Council of Safety," 2:44–45; Moultrie, *Memoirs*, 1:109; Ramsay, *History of South Carolina*, 1:122–24.

[37] Ramsay, *History of South Carolina*, 1:259; Joseph Johnson, *Traditions*

It is possible to trace more precise links between the scof-felites and the tories. In the winter of 1775, when whig forces rounded up the leading loyalists of Ninety-Six District, they designated 6 of the 136 prisoners as "scopholite." The American general Richard Richardson termed 5 of the 6 men "scopholite Captain"—a title that set them apart from the others whom he referred to simply as "militia captain." Like followers of Joseph Scoffel, the group was interracial. Of the 5 scoffelite captains, 2 were nonwhite. "Capt. Jones of Ninety Six" was a "Colored Powderman," and William Hunt was listed as "mulatto." That Richardson distinguished the 6 from other prisoners is itself an indication that individuals who had followed Scoffel in 1769 subsequently joined the tories.[38]

Evidence of close cooperation between scoffelites and Indians is a further indication of continuity between hunters and bandits of the 1760s and tories during the Revolution. The very term *white Indian* suggests that hunters had, or appeared to have, more in common with Indians than with the more settled backcountry population. Not coincidentally, the prominent Cherokee trader Richard Pearis appeared on Richardson's list of prisoners as one of the five scoffelite captains. Like other frontier traders, Pearis maintained ties not only with Indians but with white hunters as well. During the summer of 1776 a whig officer referred to Pearis's home as a "rendeavous for Indians and Scopholites."[39]

During the early years of the Revolution, whigs captured a number of white men who had joined with the Cherokee in attacking backcountry settlements. In July 1776 a backcoun-

---

and Reminiscences Chiefly of the American Revolution in the South (Charleston, 1851), p. 46; Charles Woodmason, "Memorandum," Sermon Book IV, p. 12, New-York Historical Society, New York City. See also Aedanus Burke to Arthur Middleton, July 25, 1782, in Joseph W. Barnwell, ed., "The Correspondence of Hon. Arthur Middleton, Signer of the Declaration of Independence," *South Carolina Historical and Genealogical Magazine* 26 (1925):205; *Memoirs of General William Butler* (Atlanta, 1885), p. 10.

[38] Richardson to Council of Safety, Jan. 2, 1776, Gibbes, ed., *Documentary History*, 1:249–53.

[39] Salvadore to Drayton, July 18, 1776, Gibbes, ed., *Documentary History*, 2:25.

try militia unit defeated a party consisting of "about ninety Indians, and 120 white men." According to one writer, "Ten of the white Indians were made prisoners, nine of which were painted." At a trial of tory prisoners held near Augusta in 1779, a man named Edmond Lyceums confessed "that he was with the Indians in arms against the United States." Years later Andrew Pickens wrote that "some of the worst tories went to the Cherokees & were almost continually harassing & murdering the frontier inhabitants." He personally led an expedition against a "powerful tribe of Indians, aided by a banditti of desperadoes."[40]

The term *scoffelite* referred broadly to the type of people whom Regulators had struggled to suppress, but individual bandits of the 1760s also attached themselves to the British. Included on the list of Richardson's prisoners was James Burgess of Ninety-Six District, described as "an old man, but bloody minded." Burgess was not a particularly common name, and James may well have been related to the bandits Joseph and Benjamin. The latter was a hunter in the loyalist-leaning region between the Broad and Saluda rivers where James was probably captured. Several years later a whig captain heard of a party of tories hiding out near Orangeburg. He set out to surprise them and captured a "disaffected man named Hutto." Two members of the Orangeburg Hutto family had been well-known bandits during the preceding decade.[41]

Most intriguing is the association between the loyalist leader William Cunningham and the bandit William Lee. The latter had been sentenced to death for horse and cattle stealing in 1763 but was subsequently reprieved on grounds

[40] Ramsay, *History of South Carolina*, 1:123, 159, 258; Rev. James Creswell to Drayton, July 27, 1776, and Andrew Williamson to [?], July 22, 1776, Gibbes, ed., *Documentary History*, 2:27, 31; Proceedings of a Court Held in 1779 by Order of General Williamson, Matthew Singleton Papers, S.C. Library; John Linn to his wife, Apr. 1, 1779, Draper Coll., 6VV62; Pickens to Lee, Aug. 28, 1811.

[41] "Prisoners Sent to Charles Town by Col. Richardson," Gibbes, ed., *Documentary History*, 2:249–53; Johnson, *Traditions and Reminiscences*, p. 548; Miscellaneous Records, VVV, p. 164, S.C. Dept. Arch. and Hist.; *South Carolina and American General Gazette*, May 6, 1768.

of insanity. Among the most widely feared of backcountry tories, William ("Bloody Bill") Cunningham was related to Robert, David, and Patrick Cunningham, all of whom were officers in the loyalist militia. William had begun his Revolutionary career as a whig but switched sides after participating in Williamson's Cherokee campaign. According to tradition, Cunningham had helped the whig captain John Caldwell to organize a militia company on condition that Caldwell promote him to lieutenant and allow his early retirement from the company. The captain not only reneged on his promise but had Cunningham court-martialed for insubordination. Despite his acquittal, Cunningham enlisted in the royal militia, rose to the rank of major, and sought revenge against his former allies.[42]

By 1783 William Lee was a member of Cunningham's gang. When, in the spring of that year, the Senate created a special company of rangers to "capture such notorious offenders who disturb the peace, tranquility and harmony of the country," both Lee and Cunningham received special mention. Like the bandits of the 1760s, Cunningham's party enjoyed "great connection . . . with a number of people," such that it was almost "impossible either to have him taken or drove off." The Senate offered a reward for Cunningham, Lee, and several others, dead or alive. Lee was still active in 1785 when the Senate offered another reward for his capture and termed him one of the "Most noted of the banditti who have so long infested the district of Ninety-Six." Cunningham had fled to East Florida where he continued his pillaging raids.[43]

Scoffel's own activities are difficult to trace, but according to General Moultrie he recruited a band of South Carolina

[42] Misc. Records, MM, p. 21; Edward McCrady, *The History of South Carolina in the Revolution, 1780–1783* (New York, 1902), pp. 467–70; John A. Chapman, *History of Edgefield County from Its Earliest Settlements to 1897* (Newberry, S.C., 1897), pp. 70–71; Lorenzo Sabine, *Biographical Sketches of Loyalists of the American Revolution with an Historical Essay* (Boston, 1864), 1:349; Ramsay, *History of South Carolina*, 1:257.

[43] South Carolina Senate Journal, Mar. 6, 1783, South Carolina House of Representatives Journal, Mar. 7, 1785, S.C. Dept. Arch. and Hist.; Joseph B. Lockey, ed., *East Florida, 1783–85* (Berkeley, 1949), pp. 114–17.

loyalists during the spring of 1776 with whom he joined loyalist exiles in East Florida. From there, under the leadership of Thomas Brown, British and loyalist forces engaged in a series of pillaging raids into backcountry Georgia and South Carolina. Apparently the British hoped to harness Scoffel and his followers into an antiwhig force. During the summer of 1778 the *South Carolina Gazette* referred to the campaign of the American general Robert Howe into East Florida as an "expedition lately undertaken to put a stop to the ravages, murders and thefts, of late so frequently committed upon the frontiers of Georgia and this state, by the East Florida Rangers." Brown's forces, added the article, consisted of "about 40 vagabond creeks, about 150 of the most infamous horse thieves and other banditti and various others." Clearly not all East Florida loyalists had been followers of Scoffel, but they were, with encouragement from British commanders, behaving like bandits of the preceding decade.[44]

Not coincidentally, contemporaries used the term *scoffelite* specifically to designate those tories who fled to East Florida during and after 1775. Thomas Pinckney, while serving in General Howe's unsuccessful expedition against the East Florida loyalists, spoke to a captured "lieutenant of Scoffieldites" who informed him "that Brown whose Party amounts to 150 men has been reinforced by 200 Regulars under a Major Bovost [Prevost] and 200 Scoffieldites." Another member of the same expedition received news that Brown had about three hundred men at Fort Tonyn (East Florida) and about "500 Scophilites & a few Red Coats" between the fort and St. Johns. Rumors circulated among the whig forces that Gen. Augustine Prevost intended to march through the middle settlements of Georgia where he would be joined "by a number of Scopholites supposed to amount to 1000 or 2000 disaffected Insurgents from the back parts of South Carolina, North Carolina and Georgia."[45]

---

[44]Moultrie, *Memoirs*, 1:109, 203–4; *South Carolina Gazette*, July 15, 1778, in Draper Coll., 3VV33.

[45]Pinckney to his brother, July 1, 1778, in Jack L. Cross, ed., "Letters of Thomas Pinckney, 1775–1780," *South Carolina Historical Magazine* 59 (1958):157; John F. Grimké, "Journal of the Campaign to the Southward:

The exceptional career of Daniel McGirt suggests how various lawless or alienated segments of the inland population gravitated to the loosely organized East Florida tories. The son of a prosperous merchant from the Camden area, he became a loyalist after a whig officer placed him on trial and had him punished on trumped-up charges. (The officer had wanted McGirt's prize mare.) McGirt escaped to East Florida, where he joined Brown's loyalist Rangers. Perhaps this experience of injustice helped make him sensitive to others with grievances against the settled backcountry population, but whatever his motives McGirt had emerged by 1779 as a bandit leader whose "corps" resembled the gangs of the 1760s.[46]

Like his predecessors', McGirt's relationship to the black population was ambiguous. One backcountry woman reported that the gang would "only take . . . clothes and negroes," and on at least one occasion McGirt sold two slaves to a backcountry settler. Nevertheless, the gang was interracial, and despite accusations that it "stole" slaves, black Carolinians apparently also joined the group voluntarily.[47] An article in the *South Carolina Gazette* told of "a large body of the most infamous banditti and horsethieves that perhaps were ever collected together anywhere under the direction of McGirt (dignified with the title of colonel) a corps of Indians, with

---

May 9th to July 14th, 1778," *South Carolina Historical and Genealogical Magazine* 12 (1911):63, 128. See also Pinckney to Harriott Pinckney, Apr. 7, 1778, in Cross, ed., "Letters of Pinckney," pp. 148–49.

[46] Wilber Henry Seibert, ed., *Loyalists in East Florida, 1774–1785: The Most Important Documents Related Thereto, Edited with an Accompanying Narrative*, 2 vols. (De Land, Fla., 1929), 2:328–30; Thomas J. Kirkland and Robert M. Kennedy, *Historic Camden*, 2 vols. (Columbia, S.C., 1905–26), 1:114–15, 297–304; Johnson, *Traditions and Reminiscences*, pp. 172–74.

[47] Backcountry woman quoted in Alexander Garden, *Anecdotes of the American Revolution*, 3 vols. (1828; reprint ed., Brooklyn, N.Y., 1865), 2:xxv; Loyalist Claims, Transcripts, vol. 26, p. 40. Contemporaries accused McGirt of "stealing" slaves. See James Hume to Arthur Middleton, June 9 and Aug. 12, 1783, "Signers," Dreer Collection, Historical Society of Pennsylvania, Philadelphia; Patrick Tonyn to Vincente Manuel de Zespedes, Sept. 24, 1784, Lockey, ed., *East Florida*, p. 360.

negro and white savages disguised like them, and about
1,500 of the most savage disaffected poor people, seduced
from the back settlements of this state and North Carolina."
McGirt was still associated with the British in April 1780
when General Prevost considered using a corps of "McGirt's
people" to attack whigs in Georgia.[48]

Association with bandits proved risky for British and loyalist leaders. During the confused period of joint British and
Spanish rule in Florida, McGirt, Cunningham, and others
took advantage of the situation by plundering numerous
wealthy loyalists. It was the British governor of East Florida
who, in 1784, proclaimed McGirt "an outlaw, the Head and
support of a desperate Gang of High Way Robbers."[49]

By associating with well-known bandits, the British gave
their opponents a moral advantage among backcountry settlers. In fighting the Revolution, whigs were also continuing
the struggle against South Carolina's bandit and wandering
population. They were better able than loyalists to present
themselves as protectors of inland farmers. Thus William
Thomson ordered another whig officer to "keep the inhabitants secure from the depredations of such unlawful banditty
as may cross Savannah River . . . and protect those citizens
who are well affected in their Persons and Properties." A
whig militia colonel near Peedee requested aid for his regiment which was trying to protect neighboring settlements
from "every murder, plundering, every cruelty, that could be
perpetrated by a banditti of the most desperate villains and
mulattoes, immediately bordering in our settlements." In
characteristic fashion David Ramsay was able to pinpoint the
British and loyalist dilemma. Referring to "horse thieves"
and other "banditti" who attached themselves to parties of
the British, he observed that "the necessity which their indiscriminate plundering imposed on all good men of defending
themselves, did infinitely more damage to the royal cause

[48] *South Carolina Gazette*, July 7, 1779, quoted in Kirkland and Kennedy,
Historic Camden, 1:300; Seibert, ed., *Loyalists in East Florida*, 2:330.

[49] Seibert, ed., *Loyalists in East Florida*, 2:44, 48, 230, 237; Tonyn to
Zespedes, July 5, 1785, Lockey, ed., *East Florida*, 214.

than was compensated by all the advantages resulting from their friendship."[50]

The British made matters worse by participating themselves in plundering raids, thereby failing to conciliate settlers who otherwise might have been willing to accept British protection. The British officer Banastre Tarleton, whose "Loyal Legion" moved into the backcountry during the spring of 1780, became infamous among back settlers for his pillaging raids. Writing to his cousin in 1782, a settler from Ninety-Six District described his personal experience of the British occupation in the following terms: "Our own true Colonels & head officers fled into the North State & a grat many of the young men went also. We being left like sheep among wolves, were obliged to give up to them our Arms & take purtection. But no sooner we had yielded to them but set to Rob us taking all our livings, horses, Cows, Sheep, Clothing, of all Sorts, money pewter, tins, knives, in fine Everything that sooted them. Untill we were Script Naked."[51] Even a loyalist officer saw that "the abuses of the [British] Army in taking peoples Horses, Cattle & provisions in many cases without paying for them, abuses perhaps inseparable from a Military Government, disgusted the inhabitants." A wealthy Georgetown planter made essentially the same observation when he wrote that "the British Commanders, & Officers in South Carolina, who with every wish, (I may safely do them that justice) of promoting the entire reduction of the Country, have done every thing, that could keep it ours. . . . The horror of war should have been softened, &

[50] Thomson to Isaac Huger, Oct. 3, 1778, in Salley, *History of Orangeburg County*, pp. 457–58; Col. Lamb Benton to Gov. John Mathews, Aug. 20, 1782, Gibbes, ed., *Documentary History*, 2:207–8; Ramsay, *History of South Carolina*, 1:259. For excellent accounts of the British southern strategy, see John Shy, "British Strategy for Pacifying the Southern Colonies, 1778–1781," and Clyde R. Ferguson, "Carolina and Georgia Patriot and Loyalist Militia in Action, 1778–1783," in Jeffrey J. Crow and Larry E. Tise, eds., *The Southern Experience in the American Revolution* (Chapel Hill, 1978), pp. 155–99.

[51] George Park to Arthur Park, July 23, 1782, Private Papers, Gift Box 1, S.C. Dept. Arch. and Hist.

the returning beams of Royal Government would have gladdened the heart of many a now determined foe."[52]

Despite complaints of plundered backcountrymen, the British general Cornwallis was less than sympathetic to the problems of frontier settlers. Writing from a backcountry post in November 1780, he observed that "if those who say they are our friends will not stir, I cannot defend every man's house from being plundered; and I must say that when I see a whole settlement running away from twenty or thirty robbers, I think they deserve to be robbed." By the following month Nathanael Greene could write that many tories were giving themselves up to the whigs, "being tired of such a wretched life & not finding the Support, Respect or attention which they expected from the British army."[53]

Torn between policies of terrorizing and attracting the backcountry population, the British were never able to make the most of loyalist sympathies. They compounded their problems by issuing a series of orders that further alienated active whigs. Gen. Henry Clinton's proclamation of June 3, 1780, stated that all paroled prisoners, excepting those who had been in Charleston or Fort Moultrie at the time the city surrendered, were subject to British military service. In Camden the British Lord Rawdon attempted to enforce the order by imprisoning about 160 people, including John Chesnut and Joseph Kershaw, for refusing to join the royal militia. The result of this rigid policy was that many whig officers resumed active opposition to the invading army. To make matters worse, in August 1780 Lord Cornwallis ordered that the property of anyone refusing to take up arms with the British be confiscated. According to one prominent South Carolinian, it was "notorious that he [Cornwallis] has no abil-

[52] "Gray's Observations on the War," p. 141; Francis Kinloch to Thomas Boone, Oct. 1, 1782, in Felix Gilbert, ed., "Letters of Francis Kinloch to Thomas Boone, 1782–1788," *Journal of Southern History* 8 (1942):91.

[53] Cornwallis to Lieutenant Colonel Kirkland, Nov. 13, 1780, Charles Ross, ed., *Correspondence of Charles, First Marquis Cornwallis* (London, 1859), p. 69; Greene to the President of Congress, Dec. 28, 1780, Nathanael Greene Papers, Library of Congress.

ities as a politician, or he would have endeavored to conciliate the affections of those he had subdued."[54]

Plundering and banditry were not, of course, the exclusive province of British and loyalist forces. By the later years of the Revolution, South Carolina rebels and tories were, with considerable justification, accusing each other of behaving like bandits. Parties from both sides were plundering their opponents (and sometimes their allies) with impunity. Thomas Sumter, who solemnly urged the American general Francis Marion to "suppress every species of plundering," personally took the entire library of a wealthy backcountry loyalist. Officers who were genuinely concerned that at least whig settlements be protected still had considerable difficulty controlling their men. A chronic shortage of supplies exacerbated the problem. Through their repeated injunctions against plundering, Nathanael Greene, his generals, and even Gov. John Rutledge suggest that the practice was widespread.[55]

But if whigs engaged in plunder along with their opponents, the behavior and policy of the two sides was far from identical. Whigs escaped the stigma of association with Scoffel's people, and their commanders were far more consistent in refusing to sanction plundering raids. General Greene understood what the British would never quite grasp: that the country would be "inevitably ruined" and the inhabitants "universally disgusted, if, instead of protection, they are exposed to the ravages of every party." Finally, it was whigs, rather than loyalists, who found themselves in a position to reestablish order. As rebel militiamen retook posts once held

[54] Ramsay, *History of South Carolina*, 1:193–94, 210–11; McCrady, *History of South Carolina, 1775–1780*, pp. 618–19, 706–10. C. C. Pinckney to the delegates from South Carolina in Philadelphia, Jan. 5, 1782, *South Carolina Historical Magazine* 27(1926):58. The contradictions of British strategy are brilliantly analyzed in Shy, "British Strategy."

[55] Sumter to Marion, Feb. 20, 1781, Gibbes, ed., *Documentary History*, 3:23; Loyalist Claims, Transcripts, vol. 26, pp. 75–81; Draper Coll., 7VV162; Pickens to William Butler, Aug. 21, 1782, Gibbes, ed., *Documentary History*, 2:210–11; Rutledge to Sumter, Jan. 1781, Draper Coll., 7VV178–79. See also Sumter to Marion, Mar. 28, 1781, Gibbes, ed., *Documentary History*, 3:43–46.

by the British, they, along with the government in Charleston, set about trying to suppress plundering parties. During the spring of 1781, Governor Rutledge issued a proclamation ordering an end to plunder and appointing magistrates in all parts of the state recovered from the British. In August 1782 Andrew Pickens requested twenty-five horsemen to suppress "such parties of men, as lost to every sense of justice or principle of honesty or humanity, make it their sole study to ruin and distress . . . every man who shews the least attachment to honesty, regular order and civil government." Also in 1782 the legislature passed a militia law establishing severe penalties for officers and men found guilty of plundering. It was whigs who, like the Regulators before them, became the champions of social order and defenders of private property.[56]

The British attracted other allies who, like Indians, hunters, and bandits, did them more harm than good. In June 1780 General Clinton issued a proclamation promising freedom to all rebel-owned slaves on the condition that they agree to serve the British throughout the war. Thousands of slaves followed Clinton's troops in the belief that the invading army was an army of liberation. Many died in disease-ridden camps or were shipped to the West Indies for sale. But some made their way to East Florida and others became foragers, spies, workmen, or even soldiers for the British. Toward the close of the war, the whig major Henry Hampton attacked a black British regiment in the backcountry, and in 1782 British commanders created a black cavalry unit.[57]

The problem for British and loyalist forces was obvious. By using slaves as soldiers with the promise of freedom in payment, they simultaneously threatened the slave system

[56] Greene to Sumter, Aug. 1, 1781, Thomas Sumter Papers, Library of Congress; Ramsay, *History of South Carolina*, 1:156; Pickens to Butler, Aug. 21, 1782, Gibbes, ed., *Documentary History*, 2:210; S.C. Senate Journal, Feb. 10, 1782; S.C. House of Representatives Journal, Mar. 4, 1785.

[57] Benjamin Quarles, *The Negro in the American Revolution* (Chapel Hill, 1961), pp. 138, 149; Draper Coll., 2VV341; McCrady, *History of South Carolina, 1775–1780*, pp. 313–14; Ira Berlin, "The Revolution in Black Life," in Young, ed., *American Revolution*, pp. 352–54.

and evoked the specter of insurrection. In so doing, the British could only have alienated people from whose support they might have benefited. Writing to General Marion from a backcountry whig encampment, Sumter observed that "the Enemy oblige the negroes they have to make frequent sallies. This circumstance alone is sufficient to rouse and fix the resentment and detestation of every American who possesses common feeling."[58]

Had the British been a true army of liberation for South Carolina's slave population, they might have gained considerable military advantage from their natural allies. The irony was that British leaders could not wholeheartedly embrace the notion of having large numbers of armed slave recruits. The prominent South Carolina loyalist William Bull was alarmed even by the formation of the small black cavalry unit that, he insisted, was committing the sort of "outrages" to which "their savage nature prompts them." In 1781 British commanders rejected or ignored proposals calling for the creation of two black regiments. Instead they followed a halfhearted policy. Clinton encouraged slaves to follow his armies, and he used some runaways as soldiers. But, ultimately, leading loyalists were as dependent on slavery as their whig opponents. They could not, without having threatened their own interests, exploit the potential military strength of the thousands of slaves who flocked to their camps.[59]

By contrast, whig policies were consistent with the interests and attitudes of both actual and aspiring slave owners. Despite a serious problem in raising recruits, South Carolina's leadership continually resisted attempts to employ slaves as soldiers. In 1779 the legislature decisively rejected a proposal by Congress to recruit slave troops. According to David Ramsay, the plan was "received with horror by the planters [in the House], who figured to themselves terrible consequences." Subsequent efforts by Nathanael Greene and others to use slaves as soldiers fared no better in the legislature. Instead,

[58] Sumter to Marion, Feb. 20, 1781, Gibbes, ed., *Documentary History*, 3:23.

[59] Quarles, *Negro in the American Revolution*, pp. 111–57. William Bull is quoted, p. 149.

the whig government chose to deal with the recruitment problem by appealing to the burgeoning backcountry demand for slaves.[60]

That greed for slaves could become a motive for Revolutionary service was apparent as early as 1776 when Andrew Williamson asked the legislature whether he might tell his men that "such of those Indians as should be taken Prisoners would become slaves and the Property of the Captors." According to Governor Rutledge, that expectation already "prevailed in his [Williamson's] Camp insomuch that an Indian woman who had been taken prisoner was sold as a slave." William Drayton probably helped to encourage the notion by suggesting that "every Indian taken shall be the slave and property of the taker." The assembly refused to grant Williamson's request, insisting that Indians should be regarded as prisoners of war because enslavement might "give the Indians a precedent which may be fatal to our own people who may unfortunately fall into their Hands." Williamson's troops had to settle for indents issued in return for Indian scalps.[61]

When it came to black slaves, South Carolina's legislature had no such reservations. Members sanctioned efforts by militia generals to raise recruits by providing a bounty payment not only in land, but in slaves taken from tory estates. Thomas Sumter set a precedent for other generals when, in April 1781, he sought to raise six regiments by offering a slave bonus to each militiaman who would serve for ten months. Even privates were to receive "one grown negro,"

[60] Ramsay to Drayton, Sept. 1, 1779, Gibbes, ed., *Documentary History*, 2:212; M. Foster Farley, "The South Carolina Negro in the American Revolution, 1775–1783," *South Carolina Historical Magazine* 79 (1978): 80–82; Quarles, *Negro in the American Revolution*, pp. 60–67; McCrady, *History of South Carolina, 1775–1780*, pp. 312–14; Greene to Rutledge, Jan. 21, 1782, Greene Papers. Revolutionary leaders in the upper South were somewhat less wary of using black recruits. See Ira Berlin, *Slaves without Masters: The Free Negro in the Antebellum South* (New York, 1974), pp. 16–19, and idem, "Revolution in Black Life," pp. 354–55.

[61] South Carolina Assembly Journal, Dec. 25, Sept. 27, 1776, S.C. Dept. Arch. and Hist.; Drayton to Salvadore, July 24, 1776, Gibbes, ed., *Documentary History*, 2:29.

and the numbers increased with rank. Sumter promised each lieutenant colonel "three large and one small negro." Other militia generals followed suit, with slight variations in their pay scales. The legislature also established a slave bonus for Continental troops.[62]

So great was the demand for slaves among backcountry troops that Greene and others had considerable difficulty preventing soldiers and officers from taking slaves, without discrimination, from whigs and loyalists alike. After the war, numerous petitions requested that slaves taken by Sumter's troops be returned or that compensation be provided by the state.[63]

Once again the British managed to act in opposition to the broad class interest of South Carolina's planters without incurring to themselves any significant military advantage. By serving as a magnet for runaway slaves, and by using such slaves as armed fighters, the British could hardly have endeared themselves to South Carolina's slave-owning population. Meanwhile, whigs not only avoided the contradictions of British policy, they also exploited and encouraged a growing backcountry demand for slaves.

The Revolution in South Carolina's backcountry cannot be called a class struggle in any simple sense. Rather than wealth or occupation, it was neighborhood affiliation reinforced by ethnic, religious, and familial ties that influenced the initial division between whigs and loyalists. Considerations of status more than ideological disagreements moved many leading men to choose one side or the other during the early phase of Revolutionary conflict. But if whig and loyalist forces failed to divide along clear-cut class lines, the British did attract groups that had fundamental grievances against the elites of both sections. The Cherokee, hunters, bandits, and

[62] S.C. House of Representatives Journal, Feb. 13, 1782; Richard Hampton to John Hampton, Apr. 2, 1781, Draper Coll., 6VV22–23; Quarles, *Negro in the American Revolution*, pp. 108–9; S.C. Senate Journal, Mar. 6, Mar. 8, 1783.

[63] S.C. Senate Journal, Feb. 8, Mar. 13, 1783, Mar. 11, 1784, Nov. 30, Dec. 12, 1792, Dec. 12, 1793, Dec. 8, 1797; S.C. House of Representatives Journal, Mar. 4, 1785.

slaves all gravitated to the British in opposition to an emerging social order more clearly represented by the whigs. Had the British been able fully to accept their "disaffected" allies, those groups might have done them considerable military service. As it was, leading loyalists were involved in a series of contradictions. By their various associations they alienated potential supporters and sealed the fate of the British war effort in the South.

It was finally the whigs who were best able to represent the interests and aspirations of those rising planters and merchants previously represented in the Regulator movement. The Revolution had forced lowcountry whigs to make political concessions to their inland counterparts. By joining the whig cause, leading frontiersmen could pursue their struggle for greater access into statewide political affairs. In fighting the war, whigs were also continuing a pre-Revolutionary struggle for Indian lands and security from Indian attack. By opposing backcountry loyalists, they were simultaneously working to suppress the bandits and "low" population previously opposed by the Regulators. And while South Carolina whigs may not have fought for anything so abstract as American slavery in general, many did, particularly in the backcountry, fight the Revolution for slaves.

ROBERT M. WEIR

"The Violent Spirit," the Reestablishment of Order, and the Continuity of Leadership in Post-Revolutionary South Carolina

AMONG THE MANY intriguing questions concerning the American Revolution one of the most puzzling, to quote historian John Shy, is "how a national polity so successful, and a society so relatively peaceful, could emerge from a war so full of bad behavior, including perhaps a fifth of the population actively treasonous (that is, loyal to Crown)." What makes the question difficult, of course, is that common sense suggests a direct correlation between the amount of disorder and violence, on the one hand, and postwar social and political instability, on the other. And if the aftermath of the Revolution in the other parts of the nation appears puzzling, the situation in South Carolina seems to be almost inexplicable. For that state, in the words of one scholar, had "seethed in the early 1780's with the irregular campaigns" of partisan leaders, but then soon returned "to stability and internal unity almost unparalleled even among the relatively tranquil histories of the states of the American Union." Indeed, it was perhaps the prime example of an area in which, to use the words of another historian, Ronald Hoffman, "a rather unpopular Whig elite managed to emerge from a near anarchic revolutionary situation with much of its authority still intact."[1] South Carolina in this period thus seems to have been a historical paradox. Although present knowledge is still too limited to permit an accurate assessment of the uniqueness of South Carolina's experience, the degree to which it contradicts conventional assumptions about revolutionary wars and their aftermath gives general significance to an understanding of how local authorities reestablished public order and their own legitimacy.

Perhaps the most expeditious way of approaching the problem is to begin by questioning the putative correlation between social disruption and change, which in a sense was Shy's strategy in noting that "the character of the war itself" made Americans aware of "their own political peril" and channeled their energies into combating the specter of anarchy.[2] But precisely how Americans went about this has perhaps never been adequately spelled out, certainly not for South Carolina. Some of their efforts are, of course, obvious or have been described; others, if pursued, would extend far beyond the confines of what is feasible here. Accordingly, this essay will focus on some of the most misunderstood and consequently neglected aspects of the process.

As many historians have recognized, South Carolina was the scene of some of the most vicious fighting in the war. "The lower South," historian Don Higginbotham has noted, "was ravaged by the war as no other section of the country. Its governmental processes had collapsed, and its society had disintegrated to the point that it approached John Locke's savage state of nature." As Hoffman observed, "No more chaotic a situation can be imagined than that of the lower South in the years from 1780 to 1783." It is all too easy to

---

[1] John Shy, *A People Numerous and Armed: Reflections on the Military Struggle for American Independence* (London, 1976), p. 15; Russell F. Weigley, *The Partisan War: The South Carolina Campaign of 1780–1782* (Columbia, S.C., 1970), p. 73; Ronald Hoffman, "The 'Disaffected' in the Revolutionary South," in Alfred F. Young, ed., *The American Revolution: Explorations in the History of American Radicalism* (DeKalb, Ill., 1976), p. 293.

[2] Shy, *A People Numerous and Armed*, p. 17.

find evidence for their generalizations. The earliest American historians perpetuated many accounts of British atrocities so their wartime outrages are consequently well known. One of the most notorious incidents occurred shortly after the British captured Charleston in the spring of 1780 when Banastre Tarleton's Legion overtook a fleeing unit of Virginians near the border of the two Carolinas. Exactly what happened cannot be learned from the contradictory reports, but it seems that Tarleton's men slaughtered the Americans while they tried to surrender. "This barbarous massacre," according to David Ramsay, who wrote about the fighting in South Carolina shortly after it ended, "gave a more sanguinary turn to the war," as Americans soon retaliated with cries of "Tarleton's Quarter."[3] Bloody enough already, the struggle reached some sort of a climax, at least in local legend, when a tory later known as Bloody Bill Cunningham led a raid through the western part of the state during the autumn of 1781. At Cloud's Creek he and his men surprised thirty whigs and hacked twenty-eight of them to death after they capitulated; across the Saluda River at Hayes's Station the tory raiders dispatched eight more men in similar fashion.[4]

Whig atrocities have been less well publicized, but even regular army officers such as Light Horse Harry Lee sometimes let violence get out of hand, as when he sanctioned the summary execution of prisoners captured at Fort Motte in the spring of 1781. Francis Marion put an end to those executions, but despite his popularity Marion had trouble restraining his men who, it was reported, whipped prisoners "almost to death." In fact, some tories who fell into their hands fared even worse. A John Stilwell was thrown from his

[3] Don Higginbotham, *The War of American Independence: Military Attitudes, Policies, and Practice, 1763–1789* (New York, 1971), pp. 361, 375; Hoffman, "'Disaffected' in the Revolutionary South," p. 292; David Ramsay, *The History of the Revolution of South-Carolina, From a British Province to an Independent State*, 2 vols. (Trenton, 1785), 2:110. For a graphic account of one such massacre of prisoners by Americans, see John C. Dann, ed., *The Revolution Remembered: Eyewitness Accounts of the War for Independence* (Chicago, 1980), p. 202.

[4] Richard Maxwell Brown, *Strain of Violence: Historical Studies of American Violence and Vigilantism* (New York, 1975), p. 81.

horse in an engagement and, according to his commanding officer, was then "desired to surrender, which he did; he was asked for his pistol, he delivered it up and was instantly shot through the body with it; he complained of this behaviour," and, the account continued, "he was abused and ordered to deliver his sword, he did and was cut through the skull in five or six places with his own sword, and when a [British] party brought him home . . . his brains, that is part of them, were two inches issued from his head. He preserved his senses perfect for two days, and told regularly the same story, then died."[5] Not without reason, a British officer reported that the enemy "uniformly murdered in cold blood, all our Militia whom they have been able to get at." Late in the war some of the survivors compiled a list of more than three hundred of their fellows who, they claimed, had been "massacred" in South Carolina. Some of these alleged murders involved court proceedings, and others, like the hangings that were supposed to have occurred in Charleston immediately after the British evacuation, may have been figments of the loyalists' imagination. Nevertheless, the compilers of the list claimed to have specific information about the enumerated men, such as Robert Love and another individual who were "killed asleep." Furthermore, they were certain that "at least thrice the number have been Butchered" in similar manner.[6] Americans later implicitly corroborated many of these charges when they acknowledged that an order to send a prisoner "to Halifax" (North Carolina) or to grant him a "Georgia parole" was the equivalent of a "thrust with the bayonet." There is no better capsule description of the society in

[5] Charles Royster, *Light-Horse Harry Lee and the Legacy of the American Revolution* (New York, 1981), p. 37; Levi Smith's Account, [Charleston] *Royal Gazette*, Apr. 17, 1782, in Catherine S. Crary, ed., *The Price of Loyalty: Tory Writings from the Revolutionary Era* (New York, 1973), p. 290; Col. John Watson to Francis Marion, Mar. 15, 1781, Robert Wilson Gibbes, ed., *A Documentary History of the American Revolution*, 3 vols. (1853–57; reprint ed., Spartanburg, S.C., 1972), 3:39.

[6] Nisbet Balfour to Lord Cornwallis, May 21, 1781, Cornwallis Papers, P.R.O. 30/11/6, and Thomas Fletchall and Others to the King, Apr. 19, 1782, CO5/82 (microfilm), South Carolina Department of Archives and History, Columbia.

which such practices flourished than the incident related by a British major, George Hanger, who had become convinced that the backcountrymen of the Carolinas were "more Savage than the Indians." According to Hanger, one of "this distinguished race of men" tracked an enemy for two hundred miles through the woods, shot him down before his own door, and rode away to boast of the exploit.[7]

Whether the killer in this case was whig or tory is immaterial; he could have been either. Both sides were guilty of atrocities, especially during 1781 when neither could really control the countryside, and sorting out the various charges and countercharges in an attempt to assign blame is neither feasible nor useful. Nevertheless, a pattern does emerge from the last three years of the war. At first, Gen. Henry Clinton and other British commanders were interested in conciliating as much of the populace as possible. Mindful of the counterproductive looting and burning on Gen. Augustine Prevost's march through lower South Carolina in 1779, Clinton reminded subordinates the following year, "For God's sake no irregularities." But the approach of Horatio Gates's army toward Camden in August 1780 "seemed," as one loyalist observed, "to be a signal for a general revolt in the disaffected parts of the back Country," and British officers soon adopted a policy of calculated severity. Thus, for example, Maj. James Wemyss burned some fifty houses in a swath more than seventy miles long through the northeastern part of the state. Further experience with a war in which, according to one loyalist, "every man is a soldier" and distinguishing friend from foe was often impossible, tended to make the British less restrained and less discriminating in their use of violence.[8]

---

[7] Joseph Johnson, *Traditions and Reminiscences Chiefly of the American Revolution in the South* (1851; reprint ed., Spartanburg, S.C., 1972), p. 567; Ramsay, *Revolution of South-Carolina*, 2:365; *The Life, Adventures, and Opinions of Col. George Hanger [Baron Coleraine] Written by Himself*, 2 vols. (London, 1801), 2:404–5.

[8] Sir Henry Clinton to Alexander Innes, Feb. 19, 1780, Historical Manuscripts Commission, *Report on American Manuscripts in the Royal Institution of Great Britain*, 4 vols. (London, 1904–9), 2:93; "Colonel Robert Gray's Observations on the War in Carolina," *South Carolina Historical and Genea-*

As the conflict swung in their favor American authorities, on the other hand, become increasingly aware of the need to curb irregularities in order to restore order. Thus, in August 1781 Gov. John Rutledge issued a proclamation against plundering, and the commander of the southern army, Nathanael Greene, threatened to impose the death penalty on men caught marauding.[9] But partisan operations almost inevitably encouraged the kind of thing Rutledge and Greene were trying to control, and before the war was over the legislature was forced to sanction legalized plunder to support troops.

As many men realized, condoning such behavior was risky. In 1776 Charles Lee, a whig general who understood the utility of partisan operations, sought to mount an expedition against the British in St. Augustine by recruiting men with the promise of plunder. This idea disturbed Arthur Middleton, who was then one of the delegates to the Continental Congress from South Carolina. Believing Lee to be "an odd fish," Middleton was shocked at "the predatory intention" of his plan. "Instead of that noble Spirit which should animate the Soldiers of a free State," Middleton cautioned, "let us beware of encouraging a Spirit of a different kind & of converting them into a Band of Robbers egg'd on by avaricious Views; when that is the Case, adieu to all Liberty, peace & happiness." Others shared Middleton's fears. Greene, too, later became alarmed that the vicious civil war would undermine the stability of postwar institutions. There was good reason to believe that these forebodings would prove accurate. Judge Aedanus Burke, for example, was certain at the end of the war that South Carolinians had become so habit-

logical Magazine 11 (1910):141, 157; George C. Rogers, Jr., *The History of Georgetown County, South Carolina* (Columbia, 1970), p. 129; Jerome J. Nadelhaft, *The Disorders of War: The Revolution in South Carolina* (Orono, Maine, 1981), p. 57.

[9] William Moultrie, *Memoirs of the American Revolution So Far As It Related to the States of North and South Carolina and Georgia,* 2 vols. (1802; reprint ed., 2 vols. in 1, New York, 1968), 2:407–9; Clyde R. Ferguson, "Carolina and Georgia Patriot and Loyalist Militia in Action, 1778–1783," in Jeffrey J. Crow and Larry E. Tise, eds., *The Southern Experience in the American Revolution* (Chapel Hill, 1978), p. 192.

uated to killing the British that they had "reconciled their minds to the killing of each other." Another politician, Pierce Butler, remarked at the outbreak of the French Revolution that had the French "felt as much of the Miseries of Civil War" as he and other Carolinians, "they would enter on the business with Caution. When Once the Dogs of Civil War are let loose it is no easy matter to Call them back."[10]

Evidence of physical destruction and social disruption had been all around Butler. Considering the relatively limited technology available to eighteenth-century armies, one is amazed at the damage to the countryside. Free to rejoin the American army after an exchange of prisoners, Gen. William Moultrie, accompanied by a small guard, made the ride of about a hundred miles from the Georgetown area to Greene's camp southwest of the Ashley River in 1782. It was, he recalled, the "most dull, melancholy, dreary ride that any one could possibly take." A countryside that had once been filled with "live-stock and wild fowl of every kind, was now destitute of all. It had been so completely checquered by the different parties, that not one part of it had been left unexplored; consequently, not the vestiges of horses, cattle, hogs, or deer, &c. was to be found. The squirrels and birds of every kind were totally destroyed." The dragoons with him told him that "on their scouts, no living creature was to be seen, except now and then a few camp scavengers [vultures], picking the bones of some unfortunate fellows, who had been shot or cut down, and left in the woods above ground." Whigs and tories, in the words of one of the latter, "dared not sleep in their Houses, but concealed themselves in swamps," for fear of being murdered. Indeed, shortly after

[10] Arthur Middleton to William Henry Drayton, Sept. 14, 1776, Joseph W. Barnwell, ed., "Correspondence of Hon. Arthur Middleton, Signer of the Declaration of Independence," *South Carolina Historical and Genealogical Magazine* 27 (1926):143–44; Higginbotham, *War of American Independence*, p. 375; Aedanus Burke to the Grand Jury of Charleston, June 9, 1783, John Almon, *American Remembrancer* 16 (1783):286–87, quoted in Jerome J. Nadelhaft, "The Revolutionary Era in South Carolina, 1775–1788," Ph.D. diss., University of Wisconsin, 1965, p. 151; Pierce Butler to Rev. [Weeden] Butler, Mar. 15, 1789, Letters of Pierce Butler, 1784–1799, Add. Ms. 16603, folio 57, British Library, London.

hostilities had ostensibly ended, a Scottish minister who had left the area around Beaufort and later returned found that "all was desolation. . . . Every field, every plantation, showed marks of ruin and devastation. Not a person was to be met with in the roads. All was gloomy." All society, he continued, "seems to be at an end. Every person keeps close on his own plantation. Robberies and murders are often committed on the public roads. The people that remain have been peeled, pillaged, and plundered. Poverty, want, and hardship appear in almost every countenance. A dark melancholy gloom appears everywhere, and the morals of the people are almost entirely extirpated."[11]

Given what Gov. Benjamin Guerard termed this "uncommonly Cruel War," the bitterness of South Carolinians toward the British and the tories is understandable. Even generally merciful whigs who advocated leniency toward most former loyalists revealed a barely controlled rage. "I detest the British Army, and despise from my Soul the mass of unfeeling men which compose its Officers," Aedanus Burke remarked after the British surrender at Yorktown. Later, looking back on the British occupation of South Carolina, he observed that "their treatment was so extravagantly outrageous, that no description will ever give a just idea of it; and to myself who was a witness and a sufferer, it appears like a dream, and almost incredible to me."[12] Christopher Gadsden, a member of the legislature who had been imprisoned at St. Augustine by the British, would later prove to be remarkably fair to loyalists. Yet in December 1781, soon after his return to South Carolina, he encountered two Carolinians who had congratulated the British commanders after

[11] Moultrie, *Memoirs*, 2:352–55; "Gray's Observations on the War in Carolina," p. 154; Account of Rev. Archibald Simpson, 1783–1784, in Katherine M. Jones, ed., *Port Royal under Six Flags* (Indianapolis, 1960), pp. 138–39.

[12] Theodora J. Thompson and Rosa S. Lumpkin, eds., *Journals of the House of Representatives, 1783–1784*, July 31, 1783 (Columbia, S.C., 1977), p. 317; Burke to Middleton, Oct. 16, 1781, Barnwell, ed., "Correspondence of Middleton," 26:187; Aedanus Burke, *An Address to the Freemen of the State of South-Carolina . . . By Cassius* (Charleston, 1783), p. 27.

their victories at Charleston and Camden. They extended their hands in greeting, whereupon Gadsden told them that he did not shake hands with "Rascals." As a bystander later described the incident, one of the loyalists then asked, "What do you think will be done to us? Done to you says G; why hang'd to be sure." Six months later Edward Rutledge declared that he "would as soon have an Alliance with a Band of Robbers as with the People of Great Britain." Even Francis Kinloch, who remained on affectionate terms with the man who had been his guardian and a governor of South Carolina, informed his old friend that "such scenes have been perpetrated by Officers whom I could Name, & whose families are amongst the first in Great Britain, as would make you, and every worthy Englishman blush for the degeneracy of the Nation. The consequences of such bad policy, & of such conduct has been that South Carolina is again in the hands of the Americans." Kinloch added that "the lower sort of People, who were in many parts, particularly in South Carolina, originally attached to the British Government, have suffered so severely, & been so frequently deceived, that Great Britain has now a hundred enemies, where it had one before."[13]

Accordingly, when the first legislature to meet since the British had overrun the state in the spring of 1780 assembled at the small town of Jacksonborough in January 1782 (because the enemy still occupied Charleston), "passions," in the words of one contemporary, ran "very high." The governor's opening speech appeared to reflect the general feeling. In the last two years, John Rutledge reminded the legislators, "the good People of this state have not only felt the Common Calamities of War, but from the Wanton and Savage manner in which it has been prosecuted they have experienced such severities as are unpractisd and will Scarcely be Credited by Civilized Nations." There followed a catalog of horrors including prison ships, the exile of families "without the means

[13] Edward Rutledge to Middleton, Dec. 12, 1781, Feb. 26, June 23, 1782, Barnwell, ed., "Correspondence of Middleton," 26:208, 27:8–9, 17–18; Francis Kinloch to Thomas Boone, Oct. 1, 1782, Felix Gilbert, ed., "Letters of Francis Kinloch to Thomas Boone, 1782–1788," *Journal of Southern History* 8 (1942):91–92.

of support," and the treatment of prisoners of war—some murdered in "Cold Blood" and others "delivered up to Savages and put to tortures under which they expired." Adding that the British used "Indians, Slaves, and desperate Banditti of the most profligate characters" to accomplish "their infamous purposes," Rutledge maintained that "neither the Tears of Mothers, nor the Cries of Infants could excite in their Breasts, pity or Compassion, not only the peaceful Habitations of the Widow, the aged and infirm, but the Holy Temples of the most high were consumed in flames kindled by their Sacreligious hands." He then observed that the state had been lenient with the loyalists but that it was time for the legislature "to determine, whether the forfeiture and appropriation of their Property should now take place."[14] Given such antagonism, most tories might have considered themselves lucky to be left any property at all.

Considering what might have happened, the loyalists came off rather well. The Jacksonborough Assembly passed a series of acts disfranchising all who had not met specific conditions, amercing—or imposing a capital tax on the estates of—a number of individuals and, most important, banishing approximately 375 men whose property was to be confiscated. In 1783 the next legislature followed up these measures with another act confiscating the estates of all loyalists who had left the state with the British. Ultimately, the militia commanders of the various districts returned the names of nearly seven hundred individuals who belonged in this category.[15] But at the same time as the legislature added this later act vastly increasing the number of men penalized, it began considering petitions from those named in the first acts and, in many cases, lessening or entirely remitting their penalties.

[14] Rutledge to Middleton, Feb. 2, 1782, Barnwell, ed., "Correspondence of Middleton," 27:3; A. S. Salley, Jr., ed., *Journal of the House of Representatives of South Carolina, January 8, 1782, to February 26, 1782,* Jan. 18, 1782 (Columbia, 1916), pp. 9, 10, 13.

[15] Thomas Cooper and David J. McCord, eds., *The Statutes at Large of South Carolina,* 10 vols. (Columbia, 1836–41), 4:510–11, 516–25, 568–70; Nadelhaft, *Disorders of War,* p. 83; Robert W. Barnwell, Jr., ed., "Reports on Loyalist Exiles from South Carolina, 1783," South Carolina Historical Association *Proceedings* (1937):43–46.

There are several ways of accounting for these measures. The simplest perhaps is Moultrie's explanation. "When it comes to be considered," he observed, that "the very men who composed that legislature were yet in the field, and many of them had been fighting during the whole war; and some of them perhaps with their wounds still bleeding; and others just returned from captivity and banishment, it is not to be wondered at, that they should be in an ill humour, and displeased with their countrymen" who had been tories. Yet, he continued, "when they had got possession of their country again, and peace was restored, they were softened with pity, and had compassion for their fellow citizens." Moultrie himself was a member of the 1783 legislature and therefore in a position to know. As far as his analysis went he was undoubtedly correct. Some members of the Jacksonborough legislature, like the one who had killed "his fourteen" or his colleague who had twenty-five notches on the barrel of his pistol, probably intended to make politics a continuation of war. "'Twould make you laugh were you to attend this Committee" (which reported the confiscation acts), Burke observed to Arthur Middleton, "tho' the Subject is a melancholy one. Every one gives in a List of his own and the State's enemies." And at one time, if Burke's figures are accurate, nearly a thousand names were on tentative but official lists.[16] Similar assumptions about the essential nature of the punitive legislation account for much contemporary criticism of the acts. According to a perhaps apocryphal story, when the measures were being discussed, one proponent noted "that there was a voice in his ears crying, 'slay, slay, utterly slay the Amalekites'"—at which another member observed that he too heard "a voice in his ears, but it was like unto the voice of a long eared animal." In similar fashion Kinloch condemned "the violent spirit of injustice which prevails in councils," comparing it to "the same cruel joy" that "animates a child to torment some helpless insect." For a while he refused to take part in politics partly because of it.[17]

[16]Moultrie, *Memoirs*, 2:325–26; Burke to Middleton, Jan. 25, 1782, Barnwell, ed., "Correspondence of Middleton," 26:192–93.

[17]John Belton O'Neall, *Biographical Sketches of the Bench and Bar of South*

One cannot ignore the emotional element behind this legislation, but it would be myopic to see nothing more. Many of the men at Jacksonborough were experienced politicians and, as such, were subject to imperatives that should have constrained their behavior. "Private men," Gadsden observed, "are thrown frequently into passions and extravagences . . . but the representatives of a State, when met on a public duty, are supposed to be without passion." That such an astute politician as John Rutledge needed to be reminded that intelligent politics involved more than emotional reflexes is inconceivable. If that had been the case, however, he could scarcely have escaped repeated reminders, since he worked closely with Greene who espoused leniency and who cautioned southern governors that "legislatures should follow policy not their own private resentments. A man in his Legislative capacity is not at liberty to consult his own private feelings in determining upon measures, but how they will affect the interests of his Country."[18] Furthermore, Rutledge was scarcely a demagogue but was rather one of the most consistently conservative local whigs, a man who had long been reluctant to sever the British connection. His inflammatory call for confiscation therefore demands explanation.

One answer is that he was applying the stick while offering a carrot to the loyalists. About three months earlier, on September 27, 1781, Rutledge had issued a proclamation offering pardon to most tories who would surrender themselves within thirty days and agree to serve six months in the whig militia. Continuing the same policy, the Jacksonborough legislature passed an act confirming and extending the terms of the governor's amnesty. Although the proclamation and the act applied only to men who had given themselves up before the meeting of the legislature, such concessions conveyed a

---

Carolina, 2 vols. (1859; reprint ed., Spartanburg, S.C., 1975), 1:24; Kinloch to Boone, June 27, Sept. 1, 1783, Gilbert, ed., "Letters of Kinloch," pp. 95–97.

[18] To Marion, Nov. 17, 1782, Richard Walsh, ed., *The Writings of Christopher Gadsden* (Columbia, S.C., 1966), pp. 196–97; Nathanael Greene to Gov. John Martin, Mar. 12, 1782, Nathanael Greene Papers, Library of Congress.

message of "better late than never" to tardy loyalists. More-over, it scarcely seems coincidental that the chairman of the house committee that enumerated those to be penalized, John Laurens, supervised much of the intelligence-gathering operation for Greene.[19] The pressure was effective. Doubt-less some of the leaks about the proceedings at Jacksonbor-ough were deliberate. Certainly the loyalists still with the enemy in Charleston were well aware of what was going on, and, as one observer noted, the prospect of confiscation made them frantic. Many deserted to the Americans. While the legislature was still in session, Burke reported that "above one hundred of their adherents (the inhabts. of Chas. Town & the Country) have deserted over to us, and more are daily coming over their Lines." Some six months later "the Crowds of repenting, & returning Sinners" were large enough to make Edward Rutledge suspect that the British were about to evacuate the city.[20] Many of the repentant found their penance appropriately reduced. Even the man who has come down in history as the "Arnold of the South," Andrew Wil-liamson, supplied information to the Americans, and Gen-eral Greene in turn later interceded with the legislature in his behalf. As a result, his estate was amerced rather than confiscated.[21]

In addition, Rutledge and others hoped that confiscated property could be used to help finance the war. For all that anyone knew at the time, it might be necessary to lay siege to Charleston to dislodge the British, and the Continental Con-gress had called upon South Carolina to provide more troops. Paying them presented a problem, however, for it was

[19] Gibbes, ed., *Documentary History*, 3:175–78; Cooper and McCord, eds., *Statutes at Large*, 4:526–28; Salley, ed., *Journal of the House*, Jan. 22, 23, 1782, pp. 21–22; Greene to John Mathews, Dec. 22, 1782, Nathanael Greene Papers, Clements Library, University of Michigan, Ann Arbor.

[20] Raymond G. Starr, "The Conservative Revolution: South Carolina Public Affairs, 1775–1790," Ph.D. diss., University of Texas, 1964, p. 127; Burke to Middleton, Jan. 25, 1782, Rutledge to Middleton, Aug. 1782, Barnwell, ed., "Correspondence of Middleton," 26:191, 27:21.

[21] Johnson, *Traditions and Reminiscences*, p. 148; Thompson and Lumpkin, eds., *Journals of the House*, Jan. 24, 25, Mar. 2, 1783, Mar. 14, 18, 1784, pp. 32–33, 42, 205, 553, 569.

neither politically expedient nor feasible to levy taxes in 1782. The obvious solution lay in the use of confiscated property. Congress had recommended that course to the states as early as 1777, and most of them had already taken it. Burke noted that deliberations in the committee considering the subject frequently concerned less what a man had done than "what Estate he has." When a rich man became the topic, it was said that a cry went up, "a fat sheep; a fat sheep—prick him! prick him!"[22] Accordingly, the legislature decided to pay troops with confiscated slaves. Perhaps another reason for supporting the legislation lay in the fact that a number of prominent politicians—including Edward Rutledge and Benjamin Guerard—eventually purchased confiscated property. Certainly the tories professed to see sordid motives at work, and one, writing in the *Royal Gazette*, claimed that confiscation was designed at least partly "to gratify the Back-countrymen with a share of the plunder, and keep them in good humour."[23]

Yet a closer look at the proceedings suggests that if private plunder and public revenue were the primary objects of the punitive acts, the matter was conducted very strangely indeed. In the first place, remission of the penalties began well before the state had made much if any progress toward reducing its debt. Secondly, the original confiscation and amercement acts were not designed to maximize the proceeds. In fact, as Edward Rutledge observed, almost everyone in whose behalf something could be said escaped confiscation, and, like others, Rutledge worked hard to keep

[22] To Middleton, Jan. 25, 1782, Rutledge to Middleton, Jan. 28, 1782, Barnwell, ed., "Correspondence of Middleton," 26:193, 212; James W. Thompson, "Anti-Loyalist Legislation during the Revolution," *Illinois Law Review* 3 (1908):81–90, 147–71; Alexander Garden, *Anecdotes of the Revolutionary War in America, With Sketches of Character of Persons . . .* (Charleston, 1822), p. 196.

[23] Cooper and McCord, eds., *Statutes at Large*, 4:520; Walter B. Edgar and Louise N. Bailey, eds., *Biographical Directory of the South Carolina House of Representatives: The Commons House of Assembly, 1692–1775* (Columbia, 1977), p. 573; "Sales at Jacksonburgh the 15th of August 1782 . . . ," Commissioners of Forfeited Estates Account of Sales Book, 1782–1783, S.C. Dept. Arch. and Hist.; [Charleston] *Royal Gazette*, Feb. 16, 1782.

friends and relatives off the list. Obviously, the whole business was, as he repeatedly stated, extremely "painful" to him. Thus his intention was to compile a list of prominent individuals (not, as he said, "insignificant Characters") and to do it as quickly as possible.[24] Given these criteria, it is scarcely surprising that many of those whose property was confiscated had signed the addresses congratulating Sir Henry Clinton and Lord Cornwallis on their victories in South Carolina; published in loyalist newspapers, these addresses provided convenient lists of conspicuous offenders. Nowhere, it should be added, did Rutledge sound like a man who was enjoying his revenge or reveling in the prospect of large returns. Nevertheless, he not only supported the principle of confiscation but drafted the basic act.[25] That he was courting popularity by bowing to the pressure to punish tories, as some of his political opponents implied, is a possibility, but one should not hastily conclude that this was the case without carefully examining the opposition to these acts.

The most vocal critics of the punitive legislation were Christopher Gadsden and Aedanus Burke. Before the Jacksonborough legislature met, Gadsden hoped that Carolinians would "pursue every prudent, reasonable, humble and truly political step, devoid of passions and vindictive resolutions." Revenge, he believed, was "below a brave man; vengence belongeth to the Almighty; He has claimed it expressly as His right, wisely foreseeing the shocking havoc man would make with such a weapon left to his discretion." While the bill was under consideration, Gadsden "fought it through," he later observed, "inch by inch, as unjust, impolitic, cruel, premature," and unfair to innocent families and men who had acted under duress. Believing that it might stiffen the ene-

[24] To Middleton, Feb. 2, 14, 1782, Barnwell, ed., "Correspondence of Middleton," 27:3, 5, 8–9.

[25] Robert W. Barnwell, Jr., ed., "Addressers of Clinton and Arbuthnot," South Carolina Historical Association *Proceedings* (1939):44; Ella Pettit Levett, "Loyalism in Charleston, 1761–1784," ibid. (1936):6–9; Rutledge to Middleton, Feb. 26, 1782, Barnwell, ed., "Correspondence of Middleton," 27:7.

my's resistance, he tried to have passage of the act postponed until Charleston was recovered from the British, reminding his fellow members of the legislature "of the proverb not to sell the bear-skin before they had catched the bear." During the last part of the debate, he even held up his hands and declared that "before I would give my vote for such a Bill I would suffer them to [be] cut off." But, as he conceded, his efforts were "all to no purpose." For his part, Burke posed "one political Question. Can Property be secure under a numerous democratic Assembly which undertakes to dispose of the property of the Citizen? The men of property in our house join heartily in this measure, but they do not reflect the time may come when the Precedent will be execrated by their posterity." Burke, however, went further than most opponents of confiscation in also condemning the amercement acts, which he feared would permanently stigmatize loyalists. Taking his argument to the public in the form of a pamphlet addressed "To the Freemen of the State of South-Carolina," written under the pen name of Cassius, he argued that "the experience of all countries has shewn, that where a community splits into a faction, and has recourse to arms, and one finally gets the better; a law to bury in *oblivion* past transactions is absolutely necessary to restore tranquility." In short, he added, "my idea of managing internal enemies, or seditious revolters, is this, either to drive them out of the State altogether; at least the leaders of them, or make them our Friends by Pardoning."[26]

Without doubt, a number of men agreed with him and objected to the confiscation acts as written, but to conclude that most of them opposed all punishment of tories is to overlook their own statements. Middleton wanted banishment of the individuals in question and lifetime deprivation of the use of their property. Gadsden admitted that "a just retaliation, upon an abandoned and cruel enemy, may be sometime absolutely necessary and unavoidable," and Burke

---

[26]Gadsden to Morton Wilkinson, Sept. [1781], Gadsden to Marion, Nov. 17, 1782, Walsh, ed., *Writings of Gadsden*, pp. 174, 195; Burke to Middleton, Jan. 25, May 14, 1782, Barnwell, ed., "Correspondence of Middleton," 26:193, 200; Burke, *Address to the Freemen*, pp. 42, 48.

wanted "an act of amnesty and oblivion, with as few exceptions as possible" who would be entitled to a hearing.[27] Ad-
vocates of the punitive acts such as Edward Rutledge, who
wished to keep them limited, repeatedly made similar statements. At least among articulate members of the old lowcountry elite, considerable agreement existed that there
should be some confiscation and punishment of tories; the
disagreement arose over the question of how much. At this
point one has to ask, Why bother with confiscation at all if
many who favored it wished to keep it as minimal as possible?
Aside from pressuring loyalists to jump the British ship,
there is one obvious answer, and Burke himself gave it. He
expected a measure "calculated to make people friends, and
reconcile to each other men whose fate it was to live together," and he assumed it would take the form of a general
amnesty, "with some exceptions to satisfy publick justice" as,
in his words, "you would throw a Tub to a whale to satisfy the
vengeance of those who had suffered. This," he admitted,
"was necessary, I believe."[28]

Few public figures who had any acquaintance with the recent
history of the state would have disagreed with him. Deference to established leaders may have been the rule under
normal conditions, but crises involving crucial issues and
powerful emotions might make common men very assertive,
especially when the credentials of their leaders were open to
question. Take, for example, the unusually revealing incident that occurred after the first battle of Ninety-Six in November 1775 when loyalist and whig officers negotiated a
truce permitting the besieged whigs to keep their small cannon—whereupon, the whig commander later reported,
"their people to the number of between three and four
hundred surrounded the house where we were and swore if
the swivels were not given up they would abide by no ar-

[27] Middleton to Burke, Apr. 7, 1782, Barnwell, ed., "Correspondence of
Middleton," 27:29; Gadsden to Wilkinson, Sept. [1781], Walsh, ed., *Writings of Gadsden*, p. 174; Burke, *Address to the Freemen*, p. 54.

[28] To Middleton, Jan. 28, 1782, Burke to Middleton, May 14, 1782,
Barnwell, ed., "Correspondence of Middleton," 26:212, 200.

ticles." As a result, "the gentlemen of the opposite party declared upon their honor that if we" agreed in writing to surrender the guns "they would return them, which they have done."[29] Memories of the Regulator movement nearly a decade earlier probably helped the leaders on both sides see the utility of a charade designed at least in part to maintain their authority. Certainly that upheaval had provided object lessons in popular initiative and the perils of insensitive leadership.

More specifically, the Regulator movement appeared to establish an axiom that was to be repeatedly demonstrated during the Revolutionary period: nothing was so apt to render established leaders irrelevant as their failure to punish those whom the populace considered to be wrongdoers. In 1766 a rash of crime in the backcountry led to the arrest and conviction of a number of outlaws. When the governor pardoned them, backcountrymen organized themselves and administered vigilante justice. In 1778, when the president of the state, Rawlins Lowndes, sought to postpone the deadline for taking an oath of allegiance prescribed by the legislature, those who objected to such apparent leniency toward tories almost rioted, and Lowndes found himself in danger of being impeached. Not wishing to make the same mistake again, the local leadership later executed two loyalists who were suspected of arson, largely, as Moultrie admitted, "to appease the people." Marion worked harder to protect his prisoners but his ability to command obedience was limited. One loyalist militia officer who sought his protection discovered that "his life was threatened even if found in the Generals Tent"; Marion himself had to spirit another man away to save him.[30]

[29] Andrew Williamson to Drayton, Nov. 25, 1775, Gibbes, ed., *Documentary History*, 1:218.

[30] Richard Maxwell Brown, *The South Carolina Regulators* (Cambridge, Mass., 1963); Robert M. Weir, *Colonial South Carolina—A History* (Millwood, N.Y., 1983), pp. 212–13, 275; Carl Vipperman, *The Rise of Rawlins Lowndes, 1721–1800* (Columbia, S.C., 1978), pp. 211–13; Moultrie, *Memoirs*, 1:331; Thompson and Lumpkin, eds., *Journals of the House*, Jan. 22, 1783, p. 17; Jerome J. Nadelhaft, "The 'Havoc of War' and Its Aftermath in Revolutionary South Carolina," *Histoire Sociale* 12 (1979):108.

British commanders had similar difficulties. As one official observed after the fall of Charleston, the loyalists, "elated with their present Triumph, and resentful for their past Injuries, . . . are clamourous for retributive Justice, and affirm that the Province will never be settled in Peace until those People whose persecuting spirit hath caused such calamities to their fellow subjects shall receive the punishment their Iniquities deserve. Indeed, I am convinced there are some who are deservedly so obnoxious that whatever measures may be adopted by Government, it will be impossible for them to escape the Effects of private Resentment." He was correct, and once again treatment that seemed excessively lenient produced popular disturbances. Thus, a tory mob broke windows in the house of a local merchant who sought and received permission to go to England rather than serve in the British militia.[31]

The meaning was clear to contemporaries. Being too soft on offenders—whether criminal, whig, or tory—invited the populace to take care of the matter in its own way and risked a popular challenge to duly constituted authorities. Where, in the words of a contemporary, "the lower and rougher class . . . breathed nothing but the bitterness of vengeance" while the older elite was struggling to maintain its political footing in a ravaged land full of hatred, it would have been both futile and foolhardy for a Revolutionary government, which sought to establish order and its own legitimacy, to have ignored the popular demand for retributive justice. Controlling popular disturbances by force was scarcely feasible, especially in the backcountry where the militia was often as much a part of the problem as a solution. Scarcely six months before the Jacksonborough legislature met, for example, a party of Col. LeRoy Hammond's unit had been engaged, according to reports Greene received, in plundering "without mercy" and murdering "the defenseless people just as private peak prejudice or personal resentments shall dictate."

[31] "James Simpson Reports to Sir Henry Clinton on the Disposition of the Charleston Inhabitants toward the Crown," May 15, 1780, Crary, ed., *Price of Loyalty*, p. 277; Thompson and Lumpkin, eds., *Journals of the House*, Feb. 17, 1783, p. 149.

Given such realities, Lt. Gov. William Bull's assessment of the situation during the Regulator movement of the 1760s still applied: repression was impossible and flexibility on the part of the authorities was the "surest and only method of quieting the minds" of the populace. Furthermore, joining their constituents in punishing tories enabled local leaders to distance themselves from the enemy and thereby demonstrate their patriotism. Thus, throwing "a Tub to a whale" in the closing days of the war was not merely a matter of bowing to political pressure in the ordinary sense of the word. As Gov. Benjamin Guerard told members of the legislature in 1784, "Our political life and death" were at stake.[32]

In short, one of the most useful perspectives from which to view the confiscation acts is provided by Pauline Maier's observation about the pre-Revolutionary period, namely, that "revolutionary institutions . . . curtailed the recourse to violence; embryonic popular government and mob pressure remained alternative expressions of community convictions and hostilities." Appropriately modified to suit the altered context, that insight applies equally well to the postwar period. That the legislature clearly understood the situation is revealed by the confiscation act itself, which stated that the law was enacted in part because "the peace and safety of this State require that proper examples should be made of such atrocious offenders." That the observtion was accurate is demonstrated by Burke's difficulties in attempting to hold court. "Several members [of the legislature] & others of the Back Country warned me," he observed, "agt. admitting Lawyers to plead for the Tories, and as to myself, that I should be cautious how I adjudged any point in their favor." Fearing that legal proceedings in this atmosphere would make him "a tool to gratify the fierce revenge of the people," Burke reluctantly set out on the circuit, and the results con-

---

[32] Johann David Schoepf, *Travels in the Confederation*, Alfred J. Morrison, trans. and ed. (1911; reprint ed., New York, 1968), p. 204; Greene to Andrew Pickens, June 5, 1781, quoted in Ferguson, "Carolina and Georgia Militia," p. 192; William Bull to Lord Hillsborough, Sept. 10, 1768, P.R.O. Transcripts, vol. 32, p. 40, S.C. Dept. Arch. and Hist.; Thompson and Lumpkin, eds., *Journals of the House*, Feb. 2, 1784, pp. 405–6.

firmed his judgment.[33] American dragoons impressed his horses and the enemy overtook one of his colleagues on the bench, Henry Pendleton. Repeatedly searching the house in which the judge was hiding, they eventually found Pendleton rolled up in a rug. As a result of such harassment, most courts failed to meet during the spring of 1782. Burke was relieved, though somewhat prematurely, for on a later circuit he discovered how limited his own authority still was. The crucial test came at Ninety-Six, where Matthew Love was on trial for participating in Cunningham's massacres. Burke ordered him discharged on the grounds that killing in war could not be considered murder. Whereupon, after a decorous delay during which the judge left the courtroom, a number of local men took the prisoner out and hanged him.[34]

This episode suggests that the benefits of punitive legislation were greater than most members of the legislature initially envisaged. Men like Edward Rutledge wished to be as merciful as possible toward loyalists, yet they also wanted to open the courts immediately, apparently because they regarded these institutions as alternatives to mob violence and symbols of reestablished governmental authority. Burke, who had more experience on the circuit than most of the lowcountry gentry, realized that the results were apt to be quite different—that the courts would either become instruments of vengeance or provoke a serious challenge to a government that could ill afford it. What neither supporters nor

[33] "The Charleston Mob and the Evolution of Popular Politics in Revolutionary South Carolina, 1765–1784," *Perspectives in American History* 4 (1970):185; Cooper and McCord, eds., *Statutes at Large*, 4:519; Burke to Middleton, May 14, July 6, 1782, Barnwell, ed., "Correspondence of Middleton," 26:201–2, 205.

[34] Charles Cotesworth Pinckney to Middleton, Apr. 24, 1782, Burke to Middleton, May 14, 1782, Barnwell, ed., "Correspondence of Middleton," 27:62, 26:202; JoAnne McCormick, "Civil Procedure in the Camden Circuit Court, 1772–1790," in Herbert A. Johnson, ed., *South Carolina Legal History* (Columbia, 1980), p. 252; William L. McDowell, Jr., "Colonial and Early State Court Records in the South Carolina Archives," ibid., p. 272; Burke to Benjamin Guerard, Dec. 14, 1784, enclosed in Guerard to House of Representatives, Jan. 24, 1785, Governors' Messages, Records of the General Assembly, S.C. Dept. Arch. and Hist.

opponents of the acts seem to have recognized at first is that punitive legislation represented a temporary alternative to court action that could provide a reasonably satisfactory solution to these problems. Partly because many believed that the legislature had done its duty in punishing the loyalists and thereby obviated the need for private initiative in the matter, the governor could inform the house in February 1784 that "the utmost decorum and tranquility" prevailed. No state, he continued, had exceeded South Carolina "in moderation, quiet, good order and prudence since the recovery of our Country." Unfortunately, he exaggerated; scattered popular responses to official attempts at mercy throughout 1783 and 1784 gave an indication of what, in the absence of the confiscation acts, would probably have occurred on a much wider scale. In Charleston, rioters warned some recipients of legislative clemency to leave the state; near Camden a group of whigs apparently led by Thomas Sumter attempted to intimidate a William Reese with a beating that resembled Regulator rituals; and on Fishing Creek neighbors may have killed eight tories who failed to leave.[35] And this, it should be noted, was after the government had more than two years in which to reestablish its authority and restore order.

Despite the scattered violence, by 1783 and 1784 the legislature was in a better position to run the risks associated with showing mercy to the loyalists, and there were good reasons for doing so. In the first place, the punitive legislation had created numerous problems. In 1783 alone the House of Representatives received more than 250 petitions dealing with the confiscation and amercement acts. In some instances, whigs claimed they had purchased slaves and other

[35] Thompson and Lumpkin, eds., *Journals of the House,* Feb. 2, 1784, p. 403; Adele S. Edwards, ed., *Journals of the Privy Council, 1783–1789,* July 8, 1784 (Columbia, S.C., 1971), p. 117; "To the Public," [Charleston] *Gazette of the State of South Carolina,* May 6, 1784, in Walsh, ed., *Writings of Gadsden,* pp. 201–2; Anne K. Gregorie, *Thomas Sumter* (Columbia, S.C., 1931), pp. 207–9. For the possibility that reports of the incident on Fishing Creek involved some calculated exaggeration intended to intimidate tories, see Nadelhaft, "'Havoc of War,'" p. 120.

property from tories only to find that the seller could not convey title because his property had been confiscated; in other cases, it turned out that ardent whigs were the heirs of loyalists whose entire estates were declared forfeit; in still other instances, individuals maintained that they had mistakenly been put on the confiscation lists. Most commonly, however, a woman like Florence Cook, who was the wife of a carpenter, might petition, noting that the confiscation of her husband's property "deprived [her] of her rights of dower, and her daughter (whome she has always endeavourd to inculcate in the love of the Liberty of this her Native Country) [of] the future Claim of the Inheritance of her Father." Minty Musgrove, the widow of John, did "not attempt to Excuse her late husbands conduct but as he is now no more," she sought relief. A legatee of Jeremiah Savage, whose estate had been confiscated, succinctly observed that the loyalist in question was "politically dead" and prayed to be allowed the inheritance.[36]

A host of cases alleged to involve extenuating circumstances of one kind or another presented more difficult questions. David Bruce, a printer who had "resided 24 Years in Charles Town, and ... maintained an honest Character," claimed that he had "never taken up Arms, or Acted in any Post" against the whigs, but that he had "been much distressed Since the Fall of Charles Town, for printing in favour of America." Other petitioners maintained that they had taken protection from the British to avoid being sent to prison ships, or to protect their families, and some militia officers claimed that they had taken commissions to prevent them from falling into the hands of individuals less acceptable to their neighbors. One man even noted that because his health was bad he had been given the option of becoming a militia officer so that he would be exempt from duty as a sentinel, which suggests something about the condition of the British militia. Indeed, if all of these petitions were truthful, one might wonder about some of the other British adherents. Elizabeth Mitchell, for example, observed that "for

[36] Thompson and Lumpkin, eds., *Journals of the House*, Jan. 23, 27, 28, 30, Feb. 5, 13, 20, 1783, pp. ix, 22, 47, 54, 65–66, 95, 134, 171.

many Years preceeding his death" her husband was "a man of very distracted Mind and if he has been Guilty of any Acts to Occasion the displeasure of the Legislature, Such misconduct must have been the result of insanity only." And Eleanor, the wife of a cooper, James Mackey, believed "that if he incautiously made himself in any degree conspicuous for an adherence and attachment to the British Government it was because his simplicity and timidity made him a miserable Dupe to the Suggestions & persuasions of more artfull designing and malignant Men." In exile and having been "pursued by a series of unlucky Accidents, and now sinking under the pressure of accumulated misfortunes," he could hope for no relief, she observed, but "from the humane & forgiving temper of this honorable house."[37] And so the petitions went, seemingly without end.

As Edward Rutledge had noted earlier, "The Difficulty of knowing what is best to be done" in such cases was sufficient to be "a very considerable Drawback" to his joy at the British evacuation of Charleston. Other members of the legislature took their responsibilities in dealing with the petitioners equally seriously. At first, committees of both the house and senate, usually composed of individuals from the areas in which the petitioners resided, considered pleas for relief. Soon, however, the number of petitions prompted the appointment of a large joint committee including members from each parish and district. Frequently meeting at night, the committee members held hearings at which the petitioners and members of the public could present evidence;[38] as early as February 1783 the committees were recommending leniency in some cases. Joseph Seabrook, the committee dis-

---

[37] Ibid., Jan. 22, 23, 30, Feb. 10, 15, 1783, Jan. 29, Feb. 3, 1784, pp. 12, 23, 25–26, 66, 113–14, 144, 387, 409.

[38] To Middleton, Aug. 1782, Barnwell, ed., "Correspondence of Middleton," 27:21; Thompson and Lumpkin, eds., *Journals of the House*, Jan. 22, 23, 1783, Feb. 2, 3, 1784, pp. 18, 27, 407, 410; South Carolina Senate Journals, Jan. 24, 1783, pp. 10–11, Feb. 2, 1784, pp. 28–29, S.C. Dept. Arch. and Hist.; Edwards, ed., *Journals of the Privy Council*, Feb. 13, 1784, p. 4; Legislative Committee Minutes: Committee on the Confiscation Act, 1783–84, Examination of Persons on the Confiscation Bill, 1783, S.C. Dept. Arch. and Hist.

covered, "bore a British Commission of Captain of Militia on Edisto Island, yet it was not of his own seeking but by the unanimous choice of the Inhabitants for the purpose of preserving Order & preventing of Plunder, & that in the execution of his Office he did not oppress the people in other respects." Accordingly, the committee recommended that his estate be amerced 12 percent rather than confiscated and that he be permitted to remain in the state. Mitchell, the committee found, "was generally thought to be a man not in his perfect senses for some time past"; the committee recommended that his estate be restored to his widow and children. John Walter Gibbes, the committee felt, appeared "to be a Character beneath the attention or Resentment of this House; his turn for Buffoonery seems to have been a principal inducement for his being taken notice of by the British Officers to whom he was attached no longer than whilst they remained Masters of the Town." Believing "that he would not be a dangerous Person, to the Government, if suffered to reside among us," the committee recommended that his estate be amerced rather than confiscated. David Bruce, "having formerly been active in promoting the Interest of America, particularly by printing the Pamphlet intitled *Common Sense* rendered him self very obnoxious to the British, and hoping to avoid persecution was prevailed upon by his fears & the insinuations of Artful Persons to sign the [loyalist] Address. But your Committee are of opinion, that if permitted to reside among us he will in future demean himself as a good citizen & endeavour to make amends for past misconduct."[39]

Attempting to deal with such cases on their own merits alone would have imposed a heavy workload, but the legislature did not operate in a vacuum, and the remission of penalties, like their original imposition, inevitably became an exercise in statecraft. On February 4, 1783, for example, the "inhabitants of the upper part of Prince George's Parish" being "greatly allarmed from a report which Prevails through the Country . . . that petitions are makeing out for

[39] Thompson and Lumpkin, eds., *Journals of the House*, Feb. 12, Mar. 4, 5, 1783, pp. 131, 210, 219, 220.

Pardoning the most atrocious offenders against the State," ardently prayed that the legislature would "never be Induced to Pass any Resolve, act, or Law, so as to rank the worthy Cytizens of this, or any other of the united States, with such a set of Miscriants as those their adhereants & abetters, who have Joined their Enemy to Massacree" Americans. Three days later another petition, signed by about 150 inhabitants of Prince Frederick's Parish protested—in terms similar enough to suggest collaboration with the petitioners from Prince George—against the "almost or Genl. Amnesty" which, it was rumored, "is to take place this Sessions. May God forbid such an Unanimity [*sic*]." Clearly, to pass a general act of amnesty was to risk real trouble. On the other hand, withholding mercy also had its pitfalls. Such conduct often seemed unfair and, as Arthur Middleton observed about the confiscation act itself, "abhorrent to the dignified Spirit of pure & genuine republicanism." Moreover, recent history demonstrated that such behavior on the part of the British had undermined their authority. Finally, the text of the preliminary treaty of peace with Great Britain was made public by the end of April 1783. As Kinloch noted, it required "that Congress should recommend restitution to the different States, but," he also observed, "the recommendations of Congress are more like the pastoral Letters of a Bishop, than anything else I can think of" and had little chance of being obeyed.[40] Whatever might be the case with some Americans, however, South Carolinians were still too dependent on British trade and credit to ignore these provisions of the treaty.

Thus, it is scarcely surprising to find that the legislature considered the possibility of a general amnesty, even before the text of the peace treaty arrived. Interestingly enough, Col. John Baxter, a representative from Prince Frederick's Parish who had served with Marion, made the motion; Gadsden seconded it, and the house promptly voted it down. The legislators continued to reject the measure as late as 1787. In

[40] Ibid., Feb. 4, 7, 1783, pp. 92, 103–4; Middleton to Burke, Apr. 7, 1782, Barnwell, ed., "Correspondence of Middleton," 27:29; Edwards, ed., *Journals of the Privy Council*, May 15, 1783, p. 32; Kinloch to Boone, June 27, 1783, Gilbert, ed., "Letters of Kinloch," p. 95.

the interim, however, they rescinded or lessened the penalties individually for most of those who petitioned. No doubt a majority of the legislature was reluctant to have undeserving loyalists escape punishment; many members, with good cause, feared the popular reaction to a general amnesty. Furthermore, at least one historian has argued that the act of 1783 confiscating the property of those who left the state with the British—most of whom were from the backcountry—appeased western representatives and thereby divided the opposition to individual acts of clemency. The lack of a comparable concession in 1787, he implies, helps to account for the relatively solid vote of backcountry representatives against a general repeal.[41] Perhaps, but it is also worth noting that the issues were really quite different.

To have passed a general act of amnesty would have removed the legislature from the center of the stage. Had the punitive legislation done nothing else, it served an immensely useful role in making the legislature the focal point of the debate over one of the key issues of public policy during the postwar period. The acts moved the question indoors, from the streets and countryside to the legislative chambers. Even those who petitioned against leniency in effect accepted the idea that the legislature was the proper forum for deciding such questions. Accordingly, the time-consuming process of considering each case individually helped to legitimate the authority of the Revolutionary legislature, much in the same way that Lance Banning has suggested that the party battles of the 1790s helped to legitimate the United States Constitution. The document and the political body became—each in its own way—the fixed point of reference to which appeal was made.[42]

[41] Thompson and Lumpkin, eds., *Journals of the House*, Mar. 5, 1783, p. 218; Nadelhaft, "The Revolutionary Era," pp. 123–25. It should be noted that this interpretation has been modified in the author's more recent book (*Disorders of War*, pp. 79, 97).

[42] Lance Banning, "Republican Ideology and the Triumph of the Constitution, 1789–1793," *William and Mary Quarterly*, 3d ser. 31 (1974):167–88.

Furthermore, a blanket repeal of the punitive legislation would have forfeited another benefit accruing from the piecemeal method. It can be glimpsed in the petition of Jacob Valk, who addressed the house in the hope that "your Honours will think him an object worthy of your Clemency and take off the Proscription, whereby His Children a son and daughter American Born may one day or other remember with gratitude Your act of Benevolence." If the acts themselves demonstrated that the state could wield the instruments of vengeance and thereby struck terror, their repeal showed that the representatives of the people could also be merciful and thereby prompted gratitude. The process was not unlike that by which a "bloody penal code" and liberal use of the pardoning power supported the ruling classes in Britain during the eighteenth century. There, Douglas Hay has recently argued, the courts schooled a people "in the lessons of Justice, Terror and Mercy."[43] In South Carolina the legislature and the confiscation acts schooled former loyalists in the power of the new state and the benevolence of its leaders. No blanket repeal of the punitive acts could convey these lessons with the force of an individual hearing and the equivalent of a personal reprieve.

On the one hand, the notion that the end justifies the means is an abhorrent doctrine; yet, on the other, it is apparent that, at least in South Carolina, "the violent spirit" in the legislature not only operated to contain the violent spirit out of doors but also helped in a number of ways to generate popular support for the new government and its leaders on the part of both former loyalists and whigs. Obviously, the whole process did not work perfectly; the initial harsh laws did not completely preempt private vengeance, and subsequent leniency prompted some resentment against the legislature itself. Moreover, Burke and the other opponents of the confiscation acts were right; bills of attainder were odious

---

[43] Thompson and Lumpkin, eds., *Journals of the House*, Jan. 27, 1783, p. 46; Douglas Hay, "Property, Authority and the Criminal Law," in Douglas Hay et al., *Albion's Fatal Tree: Crime and Society in Eighteenth-Century England* (New York, 1975), p. 63.

and risky, and to assure themselves—as well as their British trading partners—that they would not have recourse to such measures again, the Founding Fathers made them unconstitutional. No doubt the resulting stigma is one reason that so many historians have been quick to condemn the punitive legislation as arbitrary and "impolitic." One also has to admire and sympathize with a man like Burke who was deeply "shocked at the very idea of trying & condemning to death after so singular, so complicated & so suspicious a Revolution."[44] But given the kind of Revolution he so accurately described, as well as a concomitantly weak and embyronic state, one has to ask what was going to substitute for lynch law or the bloody assizes, and how were men whose fate it was to have to live together to be reconciled. Despite Burke's fears and reasonable reservations, it is highly doubtful that contemporaries had any other options that would have worked better than the ones ultimately adopted. Whether the same was true in other states is for other historians to decide. But if it was, we are confronted with a paradox in which one answer to the question of "how a national polity so successful, and a society so relatively peaceful, could emerge from a war so full of bad behavior" seems to be, in part, more ostensibly bad behavior.

[44] Edward McCrady, *The History of South Carolina in the Revolution, 1780–1783* (New York, 1902), p. 583; Burke to Middleton, July 6, 1782, Barnwell, ed., "Correspondence of Middleton," 26:205.

A. ROGER EKIRCH

Whig Authority and Public Order in Backcountry North Carolina, 1776–1783

ALMOST NOWHERE IN British North America did whigs go to war with less support than in North Carolina. Just as Carolina during the colonial era had experienced severe, at times paralyzing, factionalism in its public realm, serious divisions continued to plague the state during the Revolution. As early as February 1776 the battle of Moore's Creek Bridge pointed to the presence of a sizable loyalist element in the upper Cape Fear valley. A year later the danger arising from another loyalist effort, the so-called Llewelyn conspiracy, was narrowly averted in several northeastern counties; if successful, the conspirators would have captured a magazine in the town of Halifax, taken Gov. Richard Caswell prisoner, and ultimately rendezvoused with a large British force arriving from the north.[1]

Still, the greatest opposition to whig control arose in the

I am very grateful to Robert J. Brugger, Philip D. Morgan, Arthur A. Ekirch, Sung Bok Kim, the American Studies Seminar at Cambridge University, and the American History Seminar at Oxford University for assistance in the preparation of this paper. A Small Project Grant from Virginia Polytechnic Institute and State University supplied the resources for its completion.

[1] Carole Watterson Troxler, *The Loyalist Experience in North Carolina* (Raleigh, 1976), pp. 5, 7, 12–17; Jeffrey J. Crow, "Tory Plots and Anglican Loyalty: The Llewelyn Conspiracy of 1777," *North Carolina Historical Review* 55 (1978):1–17. For political developments in colonial North Carolina, see A. Roger Ekirch, *"Poor Carolina": Politics and Society in Colonial North Carolina, 1729–1776* (Chapel Hill, 1981).

state's vast backcountry, which by 1776 encompassed upwards of twelve counties extending from the central piedmont west to the Appalachians. Before the Revolution, the
backcountry had experienced repeated outbursts of violence
during the Regulator riots. Defeat of the Regulators in 1771
by a provincial army at the battle of Alamance had left a
large embittered population that remained openly hostile or
at least indifferent to the state's whig elite during the early
years of the Revolution. Indeed, according to John Adams,
"the back part of North Carolina" afforded the chief instance
of people rising "in large bodies" against whig authority,
which Adams attributed to "particular" causes and the "hatred" former Regulators felt "towards their fellow-citizens."
"It is the particular misfortune of North Carolina," affirmed
Joseph Hewes, one of the colony's delegates to the Continental Congress, "that in a very populous part of that Province
there is seated a body of Men who . . . refuse to become active
in support of those rights and privileges which belong to
them."[2]

These backcountry divisions had a significant impact upon
North Carolina's whig leaders who, during the Revolution,
had to cope with varying degrees of western disaffection
ranging from tacit neutrality to overt loyalism. Especially by
the later stages of the war, whig supremacy faced a major
threat that could not be defused solely through military force
or legislative action. At issue in the backcountry were basic
questions involving government authority and the preservation of public order. Legitimacy for the patriot cause lay in
achieving a semblance of stability in the midst of endemic
conflict. It was, by all accounts, an imposing task.

On the eve of the Revolution, North Carolina whigs faced a
troubling world. Not only was Great Britain pursuing a
course that had already antagonized large numbers of
people up and down the eastern seaboard, but internal problems seemed equally foreboding. In the Regulator riots, pro-

---

[2] Adams quoted in Charles Francis Adams, ed., *The Works of John Adams*,
10 vols. (Boston, 1850–56), 7:282–84; Joseph Hewes et al. to [?], Dec. 8,
1775, Hayes Collection, typescripts, Archives, North Carolina Division of
Archives and History, Raleigh. For the Regulators see Ekirch, *"Poor Carolina,"* pp. 161–202.

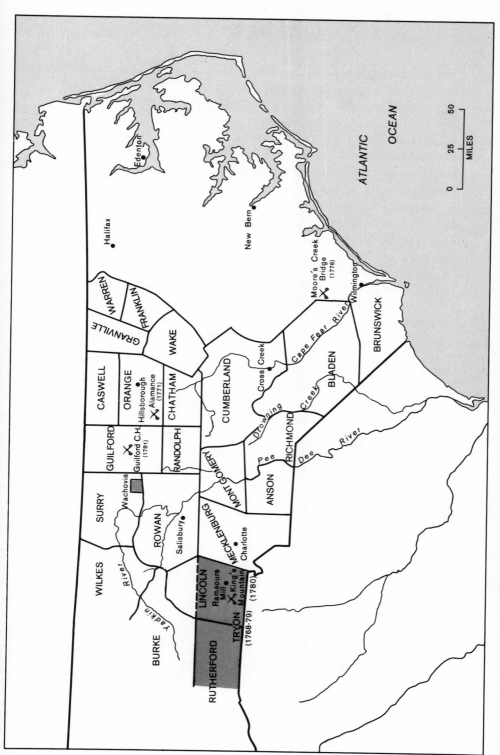

Western North Carolina during the Revolution

vincial leaders had faced the greatest assault upon their power and prestige in the eighteenth century. For four years thousands of backcountry settlers had defied their authority and vigorously protested their public conduct. Victory at Alamance, the largest single instance of collective violence in early American history, had brought a formal end to the Regulators, but it also left a strong undercurrent of popular resentment.

Worse still, North Carolina received in 1771 a new governor who was openly sympathetic to Regulator grievances. Gov. Josiah Martin, an ardent champion of imperial authority, held no brief for provincial insurgents, but he became steadily convinced after his arrival that local and provincial authorities had indeed committed serious abuses of power. Like the Regulators, Martin was particularly disturbed by widespread instances of corruption, ranging from the embezzlement of public taxes to the collection of extortionate court fees. A visit he made to the backcountry in the summer of 1772 effectively removed any remaining doubts he might have had about the validity of Regulator grievances. From June to September he resided in the small village of Hillsborough, visiting nearby counties and talking to scores of settlers, including former Regulator leaders like James Hunter.[3] The trip confirmed Martin's worst suspicions about county officials. "My progress through this Country," he wrote, "hath opened my eyes exceedingly with respect to the commotions and discontents that have lately prevailed in it. . . . They have been provoked by insolence and cruel advantages taken of the peoples ignorance by mercenary tricking Attornies, Clerks and other little Officers who have practiced upon them every sort of rapine and extortion."[4]

British officials in America typically denigrated the politi-

[3] Upper House Journals, Nov. 19, 1771, William L. Saunders, ed., *The Colonial Records of North Carolina*, 10 vols. (Raleigh, 1886–90), 9:102; Josiah Martin to the earl of Hillsborough, Jan. 30, Mar. 1, 7, Apr. 12, June 5, 1772, ibid., pp. 235, 258–59, 266, 279, 300; James Hunter to William Butler, Nov. 6, 1772, William S. Powell et al., eds., *The Regulators in North Carolina: A Documentary History, 1759–1776* (Raleigh, 1971), pp. 537–38.

[4] Martin to Hillsborough, Aug. 30, 1772, Saunders, ed., *Colonial Records*, 9:330. See also Martin to Samuel Martin, Oct. 23, 1772, Add. Ms. 41361, 245, British Library, London.

cal qualifications of colonial elites, but Martin became especially disdainful of North Carolina's ruling group. Genuine
sympathy for former Regulators, combined with traditional
notions of British superiority and a rather tactless temperament, made him outwardly contemptuous of provincial leaders, whom he generally thought incapable of public service.
"I think he has determined to purge the country of them,"
James Hunter wrote a compatriot in the wake of Martin's
backcountry visit.[5]

The policies Martin subsequently devised in an attempt to
restructure North Carolina's government seriously alienated
leading provincials from royal authority. Any understanding
of the Revolution in North Carolina cannot ignore the explo-
sive impact of his attempts to remodel the all-important office of sheriff, the provincial tax system, and the entire
county court structure.[6] Equally important, Governor Martin, in thoroughly antagonizing leading provincials, made
firm friends with many former Regulators. Western settlers
now had a British governor who was openly sympathetic to
their interests, thereby winning him, in one observer's words,
"their highest confidence and esteem."[7]

Whig leaders were well aware of their lack of strong backcountry support. Not only had Martin struck a responsive
chord, but many former Regulators were loath to break the
royal oath of allegiance they had been compelled to take
upon their defeat at Alamance. And, of course, just as dis-
tasteful to backcountry settlers was the fact that joining the
patriot cause meant embracing many of their former enemies. For all these reasons, Martin could write with confidence, "I have no doubt that the people in the Western
Counties of this Province . . . will generally unite in support
of Government"[8]

5 Hunter to Butler, Nov. 6, 1772, Powell et al., eds., *Regulators in North
Carolina*, p. 537.

6 See Ekirch, *"Poor Carolina,"* pp. 206–9.

7 Alexander Schaw to the earl of Dartmouth, Oct. 30, 1775, Evangeline
W. and Charles M. Andrews, eds., *Journal of a Lady of Quality; Being the
Narrative of a Journey from Scotland to the West Indies, North Carolina, and
Portugal, in the Years 1774 to 1776* (New Haven, 1923), p. 281.

8 Martin to Thomas Gage, Mar. 16, Martin to Dartmouth, Apr. 20, 1775,

But western support was well worth a contest. By the eve of the Revolution, roughly 50 percent of the colony's total population resided in the backcountry, and the backcountry proportion of the white population was even higher. Western settlers also constituted a significant element in the provincial economy, providing sizable quantities of wheat, corn, and other foodstuffs for export through eastern ports.[9]

Whig leaders were not entirely without grounds for hope. During the Regulator riots, westerners had not infrequently voiced opposition to British policies. In their mind, the crimes of their own county officers had borne a close resemblance to the abuses of imperial officials. One set of Regulators even declared, "Every one of our Enemies here are utter Enemies to WILKES, and the Cause of Liberty."[10] And in the years following Alamance, customary Regulator grievances were occasionally voiced side by side with protests against crown rule. In the instructions sent Orange County representatives in 1773, for example, western residents not only expressed long-standing fears regarding the embezzlement of public taxes, they also protested special prerogative courts that Governor Martin had recently authorized. Clearly Martin was unable to achieve for the crown the level of popularity that he himself enjoyed among westerners.[11]

Saunders, ed., *Colonial Records*, 9:1167, 1228. See also William Lenoir to Archibald Murphey, Aug. 1821, William Henry Hoyt, ed., *The Papers of Archibald D. Murphey*, 2 vols. (Raleigh, 1914), 1:225.

[9] Ekirch, *"Poor Carolina,"* pp. 8–9; Harry Roy Merrens, *Colonial North Carolina in the Eighteenth Century: A Study in Historical Geography* (Chapel Hill, 1964), pp. 112–19, 156, 159–60; Charles Christopher Crittenden, *The Commerce of North Carolina, 1763–1789* (New Haven, 1936), pp. 93–95.

[10] Regulators' Letter [1770?], Archibald Henderson, ed., "Hermon Husband's Continuation of the Impartial Relation," *North Carolina Historical Review* 18 (1941):81. See also Regulators' Advertisements, Aug. 1766, Powell et al., eds., *Regulators in North Carolina*, pp. 35–36.

[11] Instructions for Ralph McNair and Thomas Hart, [1773], Saunders, ed., *Colonial Records*, 9:704–6. See also Instructions for Mecklenburg County Representatives, [1775], and Instructions for Provincial Congress Delegates from Mecklenburg and Orange Counties, Nov. 1776, ibid., 10:239–42, 870a–70h.

Hoping to woo backcountry support, leading whigs adopted, in part, a conciliatory strategy. In August 1775 the third provincial congress, meeting in Hillsborough, sought to arrange a conference with disgruntled former Regulators. Three months later the Continental Congress made a similar attempt by voting to send two representatives to the back-country. As one of the delegates in Philadelphia explained to North Carolina's lawyer-politician Samuel Johnston, Jr., "They are to endeavour to prevail on those people by reason and argument to become active in support of those rights and privileges which belong to them in common with the rest of America." Attempts were also made to distribute pamph-lets to strengthen pro-whig sentiment still further, and in 1776 a few former Regulator demands, including elections by secret ballot and a reformed public treasury, were incor-porated into the North Carolina constitution.[12]

Besides appealing to former Regulators, whigs took more severe measures. They disarmed large numbers of back-country settlers and stationed military patrols on principal roadways to apprehend emissaries from Governor Martin—in August 1775 patrols intercepted several messages sent by Martin to bolster crown support. Forced by whigs to take ref-uge aboard a British vessel that July, Martin complained to the earl of Dartmouth, "The difficulty of communication which becomes daily greater and greater, will totally cut me off from all intercourse with the Interior parts of it [North Carolina] hereafter until I am able by force to lay it open."[13]

Martin took the offensive in early 1776, but on February 27 a force of a thousand patriots routed his army of fourteen hundred Scottish Highlanders and perhaps two hundred

[12][Hewes?] to [Samuel Johnston, Jr.], Jan. 6, 1776, Hayes Coll.; Pro-ceedings of the Provincial Congress, Aug. 21, 1775, Extracts from the Pro-ceedings of the Continental Congress, Nov. 28, 1775, Proceedings of the North Carolina Provincial Council, Dec. 24, 1775, Saunders, ed., *Colonial Records*, 10:169, 338, 360; Marvin L. Michael Kay, "The North Carolina Regulation, 1766–1776: A Class Conflict," in Alfred F. Young, ed., *The American Revolution: Explorations in the History of American Radicalism* (De-Kalb, Ill., 1976), p. 107.

[13]Martin to Dartmouth, July 16, Aug. 28, 1775, Jan. 12, 1776, Saun-ders, ed., *Colonial Records*, 10:97, 231–32, 408.

former Regulators at the battle of Moore's Creek Bridge. The engagement gave whig morale a considerable boost. Not only had whigs won a smashing victory, but the comparatively small number of former Regulators at Moore's Creek Bridge was a pleasant surprise. "I believe," Samuel Johnston, Jr., later exulted, "there will be no danger of any injury from these people for some time." Another North Carolinian wrote, "This, we think, will effectually put a stop to Toryism in North Carolina," whereas William Hooper, the Cape Fear political leader, declared, "From within ourselves, . . . little is to be feared."[14]

Yet flash fires of loyalist activity continued to burn in the backcountry for the next several years. Tory marauders on horseback, rumored insurrections in Burke and Tryon counties, and outlaw bands that robbed "the Friends of America," all dampened the euphoria of Moore's Creek Bridge. In Guilford County, a stronghold of former Regulator activity, dissidents in 1777 convened a public meeting at which they "drank the King's health," and vowed "damnation to all that would not join them." According to a whig lieutenant they "seemed ripe for something daring and desperate."[15] For the time being, however, these and other manifestations of disaffection remained manageable. For the most part, backcountry violence was sporadic and uncoordinated. Nothing on the scale of Moore's Creek Bridge occurred again, and whig authorities could generally rely upon small, fast-moving cavalry units to pursue loyalist detachments when they threatened.

[14] Johnston to Hewes, Mar. 10, 1776, Hayes Coll.; *Pennsylvania Evening Post*, Mar. 23, 1776, Walter Clark, ed., *The State Records of North Carolina*, 16 vols., numbered 11–26 (Winston and Goldsboro, 1895–1907), 11:290; William Hooper to [?], Nov. 16, 1776, Saunders, ed., *Colonial Records*, 10:905; Troxler, *Loyalist Experience*, pp. 5, 7; Robert O. DeMond, *The Loyalists in North Carolina during the Revolution* (1940; reprint ed., Hamden, Conn., 1964), pp. 94–96.

[15] Council Journals, July 3, 1779, John Williams to Richard Caswell, July 23, 1777, Clark, ed., *State Records*, 14:321, 11:527; Richard Henderson to Williams, Aug. 18, 1778, John Williams Papers, N.C. Div. Arch. and Hist.; House of Commons Journals, Feb. 12, 1779, Clark, ed., *State Records*, 13:734b.

The gravest threat arose during the summer of 1777 when a large mob of western settlers marched to the inland trading town of Cross Creek in the upper Cape Fear valley. Probably they only intended to demand much-needed supplies of salt, but Gov. Richard Caswell, fearing an attack on a military magazine located downriver in Wilmington, called out nearby militia companies. Whatever the mob's real objective, Caswell's display of force insured that the settlers retreated northward after receiving their supplies.[16]

Backcountry hostilities, however, abruptly escalated in 1780. With the fall of Charleston that spring and Cornwallis's advance toward North Carolina, loyalist attacks increased in frequency and boldness. Toward the end of the year, with opposing forces under Cornwallis and Nathanael Greene in the vicinity, western North Carolina became a battle zone in which many civilities of eighteenth-century warfare were quickly discarded. Both sides committed brutal assassinations, tortured prisoners, abused civilians, and freely engaged in plundering. On one occasion British or tory troops near Hillsborough assaulted a handful of young girls in the presence of their distraught parents. Whigs meanwhile earned a reputation for whipping enemy suspects and burning their farms.[17] "The whole Country," Nathanael Greene wrote, "is in Danger of being laid waste by the Whigs and Tories who pursue each other with as much relentless Fury

[16] DeMond, *Loyalists in North Carolina*, pp. 106–7; Williams to Caswell, July 23, 1777, Caswell to David Smith, July 25, 1777, John Ashe to Caswell, July 28, 1777, Caswell to Cornelius Harnett, Sept. 2, 1777, Clark, ed., *State Records*, 11:527, 533, 546, 603–4.

[17] See, for example, Rev. Friedrich W. Marshall to Henry XXVIII, Jan. 2, 1781, Salem Diary, entry of Mar. 12, 1782, Adelaide L. Fries et al., eds., *Records of the Moravians in North Carolina*, 11 vols. (Raleigh, 1922–69), 4:1906, 1790; Jean Blair to Hannah Iredell, May 10, 1781, Don Higginbotham, ed., *The Papers of James Iredell*, 2 vols. to date (Raleigh, 1976–), 2:239; Thomas Burke to James Craig, June 27, 1781, Burke to the General Assembly, July 14, 1781, Herndon Ramsey et al. to Burke, July 22, 1781, John Butler to Burke, Aug. 10, 1781, Joseph Rosser to [Roger Griffith?], Feb. 28, 1782, Griffith to [John] Butler, Mar. 2, 1782, Matthew Ramsey to Burke, Mar. 18, 1782, Thomas Brown to Alexander Lillington, Mar. 24, 1782, Clark, ed., *State Records*, 22:1027, 1042, 550–51, 557, 16:210–11, 212–13, 236, 245.

as Beasts of Prey." "For near twelve months past," reported several patriot leaders in January 1781, "the western country has been the theatre of the most wasteful ravage, committed reciprocally by irregular bands of whigs and tories."[18]

Militia companies were the most common offenders. Lacking the discipline of regular troops and less than enthusiastic about military service, whig and loyalist militia earned a notorious reputation for plundering. The worst excesses, wrote a Moravian settler, "did not take place by order of those in authority nor of the army officers, but by mob violence of a released hungry militia." Greene complained in early 1781, "The militia have ravaged their quarter in such a manner, that it will be with the greatest difficulty we shall be subsisted."[19]

Much of the violence lacked any clear, partisan purpose. Outlaw gangs, which had plagued the backcountry before the Revolution, operated with near impunity. Most felt only faint political loyalties. Seeking to exploit western turbulence, they launched repeated attacks against outlying settlements. A whig officer wrote of one force operating west of Hillsborough, "I do not learn that they are connected with any party, but . . .[are] an independent company for the Special purpose of stealing and plundering."[20]

[18]Nathanael Greene to Samuel Huntington, Dec. 28, 1780, Nathanael Greene Papers, Library of Congress; Burke et al. to John Laurens, Jan. 16, 1781, Samuel Johnston, Jr., Papers, N.C. Div. Arch. and Hist.

[19]Marshall to a member of the Unity's Elders Conference, June 21, 1781, Fries et al., eds., *Records of Moravians*, 4:1910; Greene to George Washington, [Jan. 19?], 1781, Greene Papers. See also Archibald Maclaine to Alexander Martin, Dec. 19, 1781, Thomas Burke Papers, Southern Historical Collection, University of North Carolina, Chapel Hill; Extracts from Wachovia Congregations, 1781, Salem Diary, entry of Jan. 6, 1782, Fries et al., eds., *Records of Moravians*, 4:1882–83, 1787; Greene to chevalier de La Luzerne, Jan. 9, 1781, Greene Papers.

[20]Andrew Armstrong to Burke, Aug. 28, 1781, Clark, ed., *State Records*, 22:1047. See also Williams to James Iredell, Oct. 6, 1781, James Iredell to Hannah Iredell, Oct. 9, 1782, Higginbotham, ed., *Papers of Iredell*, 2:305, 354; Thomas Robeson to Burke, July 10, 1781, Robert Rowan to Burke, July 13, 1781, Burke to Greene, Mar. 28, 1782, Clark, ed., *State Records*, 22:543, 545, 16:565; Bethania Diary, entries of Feb. 25, Mar. 16, 1781, Apr. 1, 1782, Friedberg Diary, entries of Apr. 27, 28, 1781, Mar. 28, 1782,

Backcountry unrest had disastrous consequences. Not only was whig control of a populous part of North Carolina jeopardized, but the entire state felt the reverberating effects of western violence. Trade through eastern ports was disrupted, public taxes went uncollected, coastal counties faced heavy requisitions for men and supplies, and whig authorities frequently found themselves on the run. From 1780 to 1782, the assembly often could not convene because of the threat of tory raiders. "There are great Parties prevailing in this State," Greene wrote in late 1780, "and its Policy is much distracted by it, . . . nothing can be more pernicious, as it greatly weakens the Power of Government."[21]

Civil war is the term historians have used to describe backcountry hostilities between 1780 and 1783.[22] This label aptly suggests the ferocity of the contest, but it exaggerates the extent to which most backcountry residents were committed to one side or the other. Despite the region's sizable population, both sides faced severe shortages of manpower. Whig officers often complained of the lack of troops, while Cornwallis's failure to arouse loyalist support was even more renowned. As Ira Gruber has written, "The loyalists were an almost worthless ally, too few and too frightened to be of any real assistance." Even the numbers that assembled to meet Cornwallis at Charlotte in the fall of 1780 included many who feared they might be hanged for not appearing.[23]

Extracts relating to Friedland and Hope, Dec. 27, 1781, Salem Diary, entries of Sept. 30, Dec. 7, 1782, Fries et al., eds., *Records of Moravians,* 4:1767, 1768, 1819, 1777, 1829, 1782, 1797, 1798.

[21]Greene to Robert Howe, Dec. 29, 1780, Greene Papers; Burke et al. to Laurens, Jan. 16, 1781, Johnston Papers; House of Commons Journals, June 29, 1781, May 17, 1782, Alexander Martin to Robert Morris, June 22, 1782, Clark, ed., *State Records,* 17:910, 16:174, 340.

[22]See, for example, DeMond, *Loyalists in North Carolina,* p. 139. Wallace Brown, *The King's Friends: The Composition and Motives of the American Loyalist Claimants* (Providence, 1965), pp. 197–98; Troxler, *Loyalist Experience,* p. 22.

[23]Gruber, "Britain's Southern Strategy," in W. Robert Higgins, ed., *The Revolutionary War in the South: Power, Conflict, and Leadership: Essays in Honor of John Richard Alden* (Durham, N.C., 1979), p. 230; Penelope Sue Smith, "Creation of an American State: Politics in North Carolina, 1765–1789,"

In all likelihood, a substantial majority of backcountry settlers were not strongly attached to either side. Because of the Regulator riots, many westerners were ambivalent in their allegiances at the outbreak of independence. Though committed to the principles of Revolutionary protest, they shared more immediate grievances that happened to be supported by North Carolina's fugitive royal governor. The war itself had an even more immobilizing impact on backcountry sentiment. Certainly by 1781 the typical settler, whatever his initial loyalties, felt a profound need for order and regularity in his daily affairs. For some, the savagery of war begot more savagery, but for most it fueled contrary yearnings for peace and stability. "I cannot help thinking," complained an American officer, "that those at home who give the provocation to begin this war and those here who was too easily provoked deserves a damned threshing either in this World or the Next." Wrote another: "If some means is not fallen upon to support the Civil Law . . . the peaceable Inhabitants must be under the necessity of removing themselves very speedily."[24]

As early as 1781 large numbers of settlers began moving away from the fighting and the disorder it spawned. A patriot officer wrote in August, "It seems . . . to be the general opinion of those yet at liberty to withdraw themselves to places of safety." Greene noted that though settlers below the Pee Dee River were "nearly equally divided in their attachments," they all seemed "to wish to find safety and repose by flight."[25]

Ph.D. diss., Rice University, 1980, pp. 390–91, 418, 457; Hugh F. Rankin, *Greene and Cornwallis: The Campaign in the Carolinas* (Raleigh, 1976), pp. 17, 53, 58–59, 76, 78; Petition of [195] Rowan County Inhabitants to Alexander Martin and the Assembly, Dec. 30, 1781, Legislative Papers, N.C. Div. Arch. and Hist. See also Lord Rawdon to Sir Henry Clinton, Oct. 29, 1780, Clark, ed., *State Records*, 15:288; DeMond, *Loyalists in North Carolina*, pp. 136–37; Robert M. Calhoon, *The Loyalists in Revolutionary America, 1760–1781* (New York, 1973), p. 497.

[24] Armstrong to Burke, Aug. 22, 1781 [1780], Rowan to Burke, July 13, 1781, Clark, ed., *State Records*, 15:616, 22:545.

[25] John Ramsay to Burke, Aug. 15, 1781, Burke Papers; Greene to La Luzerne, Jan. 9, 1781, Greene Papers. See also Armstrong to Burke, Aug. 22, 1781 [1780], Clark, ed., *State Records*, 15:616; Petition of Rowan County Inhabitants, Dec. 30, 1781, Legislative Papers.

Petitions to whig authorities in 1781 and 1782 reveal many of the fears and frustrations of backcountry inhabitants. Signed by hundreds of settlers, the petitions share a number of similarities. Virtually all condemned the harsh measures pursued by whig forces in the backcountry. Leading grievances included widespread plundering, arbitrary impressments, murders committed under the cloak of authority, and the extensive use of torture. "Numbers of persons such as Women and Children," Rowan County petitioners protested, "have been tortured, hung up and strangled, cut down, and hung up again, sometimes branded with brands or other hot irons in order to extract Confessions from them."[26]

Not only had such measures created a wave of terror, but they had also seriously disrupted the local economy. For settlers who had originally migrated to the backcountry with strong expectations of profit, this was a doubly crushing blow. Thus, petitioners in the newly created county of Franklin complained of the "loss of their Crops," while others bemoaned the damage done to western "commerce."[27]

Most backcountry petitioners denied that they had loyalist sympathies and proclaimed at least token allegiance to the whig banner, though clearly many were also victims of patriot abuse and were onetime loyalists. Otherwise, their declarations voiced very few protests of an ideological or overtly partisan nature. Remarkably few bore any resemblance to past Regulator grievances, except for the plea that government authorities take greater care in their handling of public funds.[28] Nor did distinctly lower-class demands or rhetoric find more than fleeting expression in these petitions. If one searches long enough, there is little doubt that outbursts of class hostility can be found during this period, but certainly

---

[26] Petition of Rowan County Inhabitants, Dec. 30, 1781, Legislative Papers. See also Petitions of [397] Salisbury District Inhabitants to the Speaker and Members of General Assembly, Dec. 1781, Petition of Franklin County Committee to County Representatives, June 18, 1781, Petition of Surry County Inhabitants to General Assembly, [1781?], Petition of [81] Salisbury Area Inhabitants, [Apr. 19, 1782], ibid.

[27] Petition of Franklin County Committee to County Representatives, June 18, 1781, Petitions of Salisbury District Inhabitants, Dec. 1781, ibid.

[28] Petitions of Salisbury District Inhabitants, Dec. 1781, ibid.

they did not form the principal element in western protests.

What petitioners did urge, with great vehemence, was the reestablishment of civil order. As a set of Surry County residents protested, "We find we are yet not within the Protection of the Laws of the State." In particular, petitioners pleaded that courts and other institutions of government convene more regularly to help maintain law and order. "There is Scarce the Shadow of civil government exercised in the State," protested hundreds of backcountry settlers in December 1781. They asserted that not only had county and superior courts not met but the state legislature had also failed to assemble. Petitioners in Franklin County complained, "There is no Sufficient Law to Compell Representatives to meet in General Assembly at the times Appointed."[29]

In nearly every respect settlers wished to see government assume a more assertive role. Among other demands they urged that officials make greater efforts to boost revenues (presumably through taxation), promulgate laws more speedily, court-martial negligent military officers, and station a regular army instead of the militia in the field. They also bemoaned the lack of "public encouragement given to Learning and literature." Still other settlers, in Franklin County, criticized the want of "sufficient fines provided by Law to Suppress Immorallity." In addition, they urged the imposition of a poll tax to support local clergymen. The lack of ministers, they complained, had helped to fuel the backcountry's "unnatural Warrs and Divisions."[30]

Recent literature has argued that backcountry settlers, in refusing to embrace the whig cause, evinced a deep strain of antiauthoritarianism rooted in sharp class differences.[31] This

[29] Petition of Surry County Inhabitants, [May 4, 1782?], Petitions of Salisbury District Inhabitants, Dec. 1781, Petition of Franklin County Committee, June 18, 1781, Petition of Rowan County Inhabitants, Dec. 30, 1781, ibid.

[30] Petitions of Salisbury District Inhabitants, Dec. 1781, Petition of Franklin County Committee, June 18, 1781, ibid.

[31] Ronald Hoffman, "The 'Disaffected' in the Revolutionary South," pp. 291–92, 300.

interpretation, however, rests upon a misreading of both western society and the North Carolina Regulator riots. The riots embodied a variety of conservative elements that defy recent attempts to find evidence of significant class conflict where there was none.[32] Moreover, even those few Regulator demands that carried the potential for a more democratic polity did not find expression in later backcountry petitions. These petitions that residents addressed to state officials were themselves not so much sets of instructions but pleas for government action—quite a surprising happenstance since some backcountry settlers in the mid-1770s had occasionally instructed their assemblymen, thereby carrying out one of the original demands of the Regulators.

But in the midst of war backcountry residents felt a more pressing imperative, the effective maintenance of public order by existing government authorities. Far from unleashing tides of antiauthoritarianism, the war in its later stages spurred a strong backlash in favor of peace and stability. Some backcountry protests might be called antiauthoritarian, such as the proposal that government officials conduct an audit of public funds and the complaint that too many officials were neglecting their public duties. But these and other pleas reflected a much more fundamental desire to see government assume a more authoritative role. For the aver-

[32] Ekirch, *"Poor Carolina,"* pp. 161–202. Cf. Elisha P. Douglass, *Rebels and Democrats: The Struggle for Equal Rights and Majority Rule during the American Revolution* (Chapel Hill, 1955), pp. 71–100; Marvin L. Michael Kay, "The Institutional Background to the Regulation in Colonial North Carolina," Ph.D. diss., University of Minnesota, 1962; idem, "An Analysis of a British Colony in Late Eighteenth Century America in the Light of Current American Historiographical Controversy," *Australian Journal of Politics and History* 11 (1965):170–84; idem, "North Carolina Regulation," in Young, ed., *American Revolution*, pp. 84–103; Kay and Lorin Lee Cary, "Class, Mobility, and Conflict in North Carolina on the Eve of the Revolution," in Jeffrey J. Crow and Larry E. Tise, eds., *The Southern Experience in the American Revolution* (Chapel Hill, 1978), pp. 109–51; James P. Whittenburg, "Backwoods Revolutionaries: Social Context and Constitutional Theories of the North Carolina Regulators, 1765–1771," Ph.D. diss., University of Georgia, 1974. See also idem, "Planters, Merchants, and Lawyers: Social Change and the Origins of the North Carolina Regulation," *William and Mary Quarterly*, 3d ser. 34 (1977):215–38.

age backcountry settler, civil order had collapsed at least in part because the public treasury was exhausted, officials were neglecting their duties, basic institutions were not functioning, and government was not pursuing an aggressive role in preserving public and private morals. Hardly opposed to the existing structure of political power, backcountry residents wished to see that structure operate more effectively.

Not surprisingly, whigs did not feel buffetted by rising waves of class animosity. The wartime correspondence that has survived reflects little if any awareness of lower-class hostility. Whigs felt no necessity either to modify elitist pretensions or to succumb to nonexistent lower-class demands. If the problem had been that clear-cut, more than one official would have found it cheering news indeed. Instead, whigs after 1780 faced a steadily deteriorating situation for which solutions were few.

To combat backcountry chaos, state authorities devised several policies. To begin with, they sought to maintain a strong military presence. Manpower shortages and pressing demands elsewhere prevented stationing a permanent body of troops in the backcountry, so cavalry units were usually dispatched to the scene of tory assaults. These, of course, could not forestall enemy attacks, but, with some luck, they could pursue and engage slower-moving loyalist bands. Mobilizing the light horse was also thought good for whig morale. As Gov. Abner Nash wrote the feisty militia commander Gen. John Butler in the fall of 1780, "I wish you to move as soon as you can, as it will give spirits to our Western Friends."[33]

Some military officers favored more drastic steps. Only a concerted display of force, both on and off the battlefield, they believed, could sufficiently awe the disaffected into submission. At least a few would have agreed with one whig colonel's belief that "there was no resting place for a tory's foot upon the Earth," or with Gen. Allen Jones's prescription for

[33] Board of War Proceedings, Sept. 29, 1780, Clark, ed., *State Records*, 14:399. See also, for example, Board of War Proceedings, Sept. 18, Oct. 17, 1780, John Butler to Burke, Aug. 10, 1781, Burke to Butler, Feb. 5, 1782, John Collier to Burke, Feb. 25, 1782, ibid., pp. 381–82, 427, 22:557, 16:500, 204.

the Llewelyn conspirators. "I make no doubt," wrote this prominent Halifax County resident in 1777, "but hanging, about a dozen, will have exceedingly good effect, in this State, and give stability to our new government."[34]

Of backcountry officers, Gen. Griffith Rutherford early on established a reputation for wartime brutality. A planter-politician from Rowan County, Rutherford eagerly applied his skills as a veteran Indian fighter to countering local loyalists. With some justice, Cornwallis called him a "violent and cruel Incendiary." A "blood thirsty old scoundrel" is how a Carolina whig put it.[35]

Yet few state leaders entirely concurred with harsh measures. In both their public and private correspondence, most urged more moderate steps. Ronald Hoffman has recently described Nathanael Greene's opposition to backcountry excesses; Greene's views, however, were reasonably typical of those of other patriot officials, at least in North Carolina. If whigs were alarmed by backcountry antiauthoritarianism, it was the reckless actions of their own militia, not lower-class disaffection, that they found so disturbing. Patriot militia seemed oblivious to established legal procedures. "The depredations committed by the Western Militia upon friend and foe," complained a whig in Wilmington, "are scarcely to be paralleled."[36]

Plundering was especially widespread, and officers were specifically ordered to punish all offenders. "Great care must be taken," state authorities typically warned Col. Thomas Taylor, an Orange County commander, "not to let the Soldiers plunder." Upon complaints made in late 1780 against

[34] "A Journal of Col. David Fanning's Transactions . . . ," June 24, 1790, Allen Jones to Burke, Aug. 6, 1777, ibid., 22:220, 11:562.

[35] Cornwallis to Clinton, Aug. 29, 1780, Maclaine to George Hooper, June 12, 1783, ibid., 15:276, 16:966. See also "Report of the Brn. Bagge and Bluhm . . . ," [1778], Fries et al., eds., *Records of Moravians*, 3:1376.

[36] Maclaine to Alexander Martin, Dec. 19, 1781, Burke Papers. See also, for example, Board of War Proceedings, Sept. 18, 21, 1780, House of Commons Journals, May 5, 1782, Clark, ed., *State Records*, 14:382, 385, 16:107; Greene to Henry Knox, Dec. 7, 1780, Greene to Howe, Dec. 29, 1780, Greene to La Luzerne, Jan. 9, 1781, Greene to Washington, [Jan. 19?], 1781, Greene Papers.

Rowan County officers and their companies, North Carolina's Board of War immediately ordered their apprehension and court-martial. The state legislature also passed laws in 1780 and 1781 to restrain wartime excesses. The 1780 statute threatened jail terms and fines amounting to three times the value of plundered goods. A legislative committee in May 1782 urged still stiffer penalties. "Let not rapine and licentiousness, under the garb of Liberty," affirmed Gov. Alexander Martin, "stalk around and triumph amongst us with impunity."[37]

Patriot officials also struck a moderate course toward penitent loyalists. Numbers of loyalist estates were confiscated, but authorities issued proclamations on several occasions offering conditional pardons to all who agreed to lay down their arms. Loyalists normally had the choice of two alternatives: taking an oath of allegiance and enlisting in the militia for twelve or eighteen months or remaining prisoners of war until returned to British lines in a mutual exchange of prisoners. The principal exceptions applied to enemy soldiers charged with particularly heinous offenses, such as murder, robbery, and arson.[38] For example, during a session in January 1782 a Hillsborough circuit court convicted four men of high treason, but only two, Thomas Dark and Thomas Ricketts, were later executed. Dark bore the nickname of "young Tarleton" for reportedly "hacking" his prisoners, whereas Ricketts had committed numerous offenses ranging from ar-

---

[37] Board of War Proceedings, Sept. 21, 1780, Martin to General Assembly, Apr. 22, 1782, Board of War Proceedings, Nov. 25, 1780, Laws, 1780, House of Commons Journals, May 5, 1782, Clark, ed., *State Records*, 14:385, 16:297, 14:468–69, 24:350–51, 376–78, 16:107. See also Burke to Thomas Hogg, Mar. 13, 1782, State Military Orders, Apr. 7, 1782, ibid., 16:231, 264.

[38] Caswell to Abner Nash, July 31, 1780, Senate Journals, Feb. 3, Council Journals, July 25, Armstrong to Burke, Aug. 28, 1781, ibid., 15:11, 17:668, 19:861–62, 22:1048; Burke to William Moore, Sept. 9, 1781, Burke Papers; Burke to Major Hogg, Mar. 13, Burke to Greene, Mar. 28, House of Commons Journals, Apr. 16, Alexander Martin to Lillington, May, to John Matthews, June 9, to Maclaine, Oct., to Anne Hooper et al., June 1782, House of Commons Journals, Apr. 19, 1783, Clark, ed., *State Records*, 16:229–31, 565–68, 9, 686–87, 690, 417–18, 337, 19:242.

son to murder. More fortunate were Meredith Edwards and Thomas Eastridge, who received pardons from the governor on condition of enlisting in the military. Though tories, both were known for their humane treatment of enemy prisoners. "Except [for] the very mischievous and atrocious," Gov. Thomas Burke had earlier instructed a subordinate, "I wish to see very few submitted to the Executioner."[39]

Both Burke and Martin also formulated plans for the relocation of loyalist families. Each, while governor in the early 1780s, proposed sending behind British lines the families of loyalists in order to deny the enemy additional means of support. Martin freely admitted, "In times of Peace such a measure may be violative of the Constitution . . . yet in the tumult of War, the Civil operations of Law . . . must cease for a moment till the Government be restored to calmness." On the other hand, no evidence exists to suggest that large numbers of loyalist families were ever transported. Furthermore, by early 1782 Burke at least was having serious misgivings. "If finally, it must be executed," he instructed a subordinate, "I am every way disposed to make it as easy as possible in the execution."[40]

For whig measures to succeed in the backcountry, local courts and other institutions had to assume an aggressive role. Once the fighting began to intensify after 1779, county officials faced obvious difficulties in maintaining regular court sessions. Surviving records suggest, however, that their efforts were remarkably successful. In more tranquil times county courts normally convened four times a year. Between 1779 and 1783 courts in Rowan and Surry counties at most failed to meet only once, both in February 1781. In Wake and Orange and in the newer counties of Caswell and Ruth-

[39] Burke to Hogg, Mar. 13, Williams to Martin, June [Jan.] 27, Burke to Jethro Sumner, Feb. 26, 1782, Clark, ed., *State Records*, 16:230, 345–46, 522. See also State Military Orders, Apr. 21, 1782, ibid., pp. 266–69; Burke to [Joel?] Lewis, Apr. 6, 1782, Burke Papers; House of Commons Journals, Apr. 21, 1783, Clark, ed., *State Records*, 19:245–46.

[40] Council Journals, Oct. 5, 1781, Burke to Hogg, Mar. 13, 1782, Council Journals, July 25, 1781, Clark, ed., *State Records*, 19:871, 16:231, 19:861–62; Burke to marquis de Lafayette, Aug. 30, 1781, Burke Papers.

erford, courts never failed to convene, though two of these counties experienced abbreviated sessions: Rutherford in July and October 1780, Orange in February and May 1781. Court minutes are less revealing but indicate no significant differences for the counties of Mecklenburg and Lincoln.[41] Meanwhile, the legislature authorized the governor to create special courts of oyer and terminer to supplement the state's superior court system. Under an act passed in June 1781 the governor could commission judges to hear cases of treason and misprision of treason.[42]

Soon afterwards efforts to preserve local order received further encouragement from Thomas Burke. A native Irishman, Burke had settled in North Carolina in 1772 and quickly became an influential Orange County politician. During the first years of the Revolution he spoke forcefully against the dangers of centralized authority, but by the early 1780s became more and more persuaded by the need for government action. Upon being elected governor in June 1781 he proposed a series of steps to bolster government authority in the backcountry and other strife-torn areas. Besides supporting the pardoning of former loyalists, the immediate creation of oyer and terminer courts, and the repair of local jails, Burke favored "the exact and rigorous execution of the Laws" against all acts of "arbitrary violence," including offenses committed by whig forces and their officers. As such, when two soldiers in Greene's army were indicted for murdering an enemy prisoner, Burke immediately urged they be sent to Salisbury for trial "according to the Laws of the State."[43]

He also proposed that superior and county court judges,

[41] This section is based on inferior court minutes in the N.C. Div. Arch. and Hist. for the counties of Rowan, Surry, Caswell, Wake, Rutherford, Orange, Mecklenburg, and Lincoln.

[42] Laws, 1781, Clark, ed., *State Records*, 24:396–98.

[43] Council Journals, July 25, 1781, ibid., 19:861–62; Burke to Greene, Aug. 31, 1781, Burke Papers; Proclamation by Burke, July 28, 1781, Clark, ed., *State Records*, 15:579; Elisha P. Douglass, "Thomas Burke, Disillusioned Democrat," *North Carolina Historical Review* 26 (1949):150–86.

as well as other civil officers, execute their normal duties "on pain of being punished agreeably to law." "The great remissness in the discharge of public duties," Burke wrote county sheriffs in July, "has been productive of many disorders and Enormities dangerous to the public peace and good order, and disgraceful to the dignity of the State. I hope the Vigilance and Vigor wherewith the Judges, Justices and Civil Officers will hereafter discharge their respective duties, and the Support which it may be in my power to give them will restore Internal peace and good order."[44]

It was partly in an attempt to lend his personal encouragement to such efforts that Burke traveled to the backcountry in early September, where he was captured in Hillsborough during a daring raid by the notorious loyalist David Fanning and a force of nearly a thousand men. Several trying months of British detention ensued before he broke parole on James Island, South Carolina, and fled to whig lines. Burke's precipitous return, in violation of his promise not to escape, severely damaged his reputation and all but destroyed his political career. Though he resumed his duties as governor, he left office in May 1782 under a heavy cloud of doubt and suspicion. By defying the canons of military law, he became another casualty of North Carolina's wartime turbulence.[45]

Whig policy toward the backcountry reflected a multitude of concerns. Some steps were taken partly in response to sudden exigencies. With the capture of whig armies in South Carolina in 1780, exchanging tory prisoners, rather than imposing more severe penalties, immediately became more appealing. From then until 1783 state authorities proved open to military exchanges. At the same time, enlisting prisoners in patriot forces provided additional recruits for severely undermanned regiments. As Burke explained to Greene in early 1782, "I . . . propose to declare all who shall not choose

[44]Council Journals, July 25, Burke to Sheriffs, July 28, 1781, House of Commons Journals, Apr. 16, 1782, Clark, ed., *State Records*, 19:859, 15:579–80, 16:11.

[45]Douglass, "Thomas Burke," pp. 177–86.

to enter into Our Service, of such who have been in Arms against us, as Prisoners of war; all who do shall be regarded as restored Citizens. From these Measures you will probably derive some recruits, and we shall obtain an Equivalent to give for our citizens who are Languishing in Captivity." Affirmed a whig officer, "It is certainly as easy to reduce the number of our enemies by pardoning than by killing them and much better suited to our present condition."[46]

A humanitarian element probably also played a role. Burke for one at least paid lip service to it.[47] But still more important in shaping policy was the whig desire to conciliate wavering loyalists. If they could not always be converted into ardent whigs, extending pardons and restraining whig excesses could at least help to neutralize pro-British sympathies. "Strike at the root of the evil by removing the British," wrote Greene in August 1781, "and offer these poor deluded Wretches some hopes of forgiveness, and you will feel little injury from this class of People." Burke, though he favored expelling the "incorrigible by force of arms," similarly believed that reconciling "all that are reclaimable" both the "most humane as well as the most prudent Counsel." "The minds of the Men," asserted a patriot general in July 1781, "never wanted conciliating measures to be used more than Now."[48]

In addition, adopting a moderate tack conformed to long-standing attitudes toward loyalists. For years whig leaders had portrayed their internal foes as frail beings acting out of fear and deluded expectations. In making conciliatory ges-

[46] Burke to Greene, Feb. 15, 1782, Armstrong to Burke, Aug. 28, 1781, Clark, ed., *State Records*, 16:511, 22:1048. See also James Iredell to Hannah Iredell, Sept. 3, 1781, Higginbotham, ed., *Papers of Iredell*, 2:288; Senate Journals, May 11, Alexander Martin to Alexander Leslie, May 12, 1782, Clark, ed., *State Records*, 19:98–99, 16:685.

[47] House of Commons Journals, June 29, 1781, Burke to Hogg, Mar. 13, 1782, Clark, ed., *State Records*, 17:913, 16:231. See also Francis Marion to Horatio Gates, Oct. 4, 1780, ibid., 14:666.

[48] Greene to Burke, Aug. 12, House of Commons Journals, June 29, Stephen Drayton to Burke, July 6, 1781, ibid., 15:605, 17:913, 15:513. See also William Davidson to Nash, Oct. 22, 1780, ibid., p. 127.

tures, whigs normally saw them not as irredeemable enemies but what Atty. Gen. James Iredell described as the victims of "fear" and the "distraction of the times." "The Leaders," predicted Iredell, "will then probably be left to suffer deservedly by themselves." Declared Gov. Alexander Martin to the state legislature, "Our late revolted Citizens who, through ignorance and delusion, have forfeited their lives but are endeavouring to expiate their crimes by new proofs of fidelity, have fresh claims to your Clemency."[49] Repatriation, in addition to offering practical advantages, reaffirmed the original righteousness of the whig cause. Accepting a pardon meant confessing one's transgressions, swearing an oath of allegiance, and endorsing the virtues of American independence.

Backcountry loyalism, however, was not the only object of whig policy. Also troublesome was the large body of noncombatants who felt aggrieved by both sides. As whig authorities recognized, the support of these North Carolinians was essential if loyalists were to be denied places of refuge, provisions, and recruits. "We must endeavour to keep up a Partizan War," wrote Greene in late 1780, "and preserve the Tide of Sentiment among the People as much as possible in our Favour."[50]

Whigs understood that the best means of broadening their support lay in creating a semblance of law, discipline, and order, however trying the circumstances. By the early 1780s a majority of settlers were inclined to support whichever side could ensure a modicum of stability. Burke thought it "essential" to "peace, good order and sound policy" that the "laws have a free, vigorous and impartial operation upon all." According to Samuel Strudwick, a wealthy western planter,

[49] James Iredell to Hannah Iredell, Sept. 3, 1781, Higginbotham, ed., *Papers of Iredell*, 2:288; House of Commons Journals, Apr. 19, 1783, Clark, ed., *State Records*, 19:241. See also Davidson to Nash, Oct. 22, 1780, House of Commons Journals, June 29, Maclaine to Burke, June 30, 1781, Burke to Greene, Mar. 28, 1782, Clark, ed., *State Records*, 15:127, 17:913, 22:538, 16:566.

[50] Greene to Marion, Dec. 4, 1780, Greene Papers. See also Greene to Nash, Dec. 6, Greene to Knox, Dec. 7, 1780, Greene to Thomas Sumter, Jan. 8, 1781, ibid.

backcountry inhabitants would "chearfully" submit to their legal obligations "if Ravage and plunder were not superaded." "By prudence and good conduct," asserted Governor Martin, "civil government will be restored to its former power."[51]

Establishing an orderly course of proceedings, in addition to curtailing wartime excesses, would enable whigs to create a vital measure of legitimacy for their cause. Like the British, they fully realized that restoring civil government would bolster their claim to representing lawful authority. If whigs could provide a means by which settlers recorded deeds, adjudicated disputes, licensed taverns, punished lawbreakers, and tended to all their normal affairs, backcountry support would correspondingly grow. As early as 1778 William Hooper wrote of his fear that "Tories make observations that are painful to men who love [our] cause. Our Laws they say are a caput mortuum; that they are such that they cannot be executed or that we are afraid to execute them." "The justice of this country, which has long been offended with impunity," Martin wrote in June 1782, "should at this time receive some reparation, to convince our enemies we have a Government, and will support it against all opposers whatsoever."[52] More compelling, in short, than reconciliation was the larger need to establish a degree of public order.

Of course, this meant that whig measures could be severe as well as lenient. Partly for this reason, loyalist attacks did not go unanswered and enemy prisoners convicted of committing atrocities were normally executed. As Burke wrote Greene in early 1782, "It is vain to think of Executing the Laws on our friends while those barbarians are to be exempted. . . . The Consequences is [sic] plainly an utter Ex-

[51] Burke to Jones, July 31, 1781, Burke Papers; Samuel Strudwick to Burke, July, Council Journals, Dec. 20, 1781, Clark, ed., State Records, 15:503, 19:876.

[52] William Hooper to James Iredell, Nov. 17, 1778, Alexander Martin to James Iredell, June 24, 1782, Higginbotham, ed., Papers of Iredell, 2:55–56, 346. See also House of Commons Journals, June 29, 1781, Clark, ed., State Records, 17:913; Burke to Caswell, Sept. 11, 1781, Burke Papers; Alexander Martin to Lillington, Oct. 28, 1782, Clark, ed., State Records, 16:662–63.

tinction of Government and an abandoning the Country to blood and Anarchy."[53]

It was this need to establish legitimacy that probably most influenced whig policy. Largely as a consequence, authorities attempted to restrain plundering and other excesses, make legal distinctions between enemy prisoners, and strengthen local institutions of government. Ironically, because of the disorder caused by backcountry fighting, North Carolina's political elite had a better opportunity to establish its authority among westerners than at any time since the beginning of the Regulator riots. Scores of settlers at that time had hoped to enlist provincial leaders in backcountry efforts to cleanse local government of corruption. Authorities had so soundly rebuffed their appeals that later attempts to spread the whig gospel could not eradicate the Regulator riots' bitter legacy. Only the war itself and the chaos that it unleashed now afforded such an opportunity. Increasingly, backcountry settlers became concerned less with the specific nature of government authority than with the more basic need for government intervention.

How successful whigs were in trying to capitalize on this turn of events is less certain. They faced a number of difficulties, ranging from roving loyalists and Cornwallis's regular troops to their own militiamen. In addition, not all officials felt the same imperatives. A few urged sterner measures, while others were slow to honor official responsibilities and enforce state orders. The consequences for both the state and backcountry were devastating. "The Country everywhere," wrote Burke in 1781, "[is] unprepared for defence—without discipline, without arrangements—even the habits of Civil order and obedience to Laws changed into a licentious Contempt for Authority and a disorderly indulgence of violent propensities."[54] On the other hand, it is highly likely that whig measures did help to speed the loyalists' steady decline in strength. Certainly patriot backing would have suffered had state authorities taken more severe steps.

[53] Burke to Greene, Mar. 28, 1782, Clark, ed., *State Records*, 16:565.

[54] House of Commons Journals, June 29, 1781, ibid., 17:910.

Whatever the impact of whig policies during the war's last years, they probably spurred popular allegiance to state authority once hostilities ended. The backcountry, to be sure, continued to generate political discontent, but later controversies generally arose from sectional differences between east and west. Open opposition to government authority, as in the Regulator riots, or political neutrality, as during much of the Revolution, lay largely in the past. Having attempted to preserve a semblance of order in the midst of war, whigs achieved unprecedented popular acceptance during the welcome years of peace.

JEFFREY J. CROW

Liberty Men and Loyalists

Disorder and Disaffection in the North Carolina Backcountry

ON THEIR WAY to the Anson County Courthouse the morning of May 30, 1778, Capt. George Wilson's militia company
stopped to consider the unpleasant task before them. By act
of the General Assembly each county militia was to muster at
the courthouse to furnish men for the North Carolina Continental Line then serving in the north. With the war seemingly so far removed, the possibility of being drafted must
have been particularly odious to small, often subsistence
farmers who, unlike the slaveholding gentry, could not afford substitutes or time away from their farms and families.
However, the legislative act, which exempted only the governor, did permit each company to elect its draftees. With
cunning simplicity James Terry determined a way to thwart
the repugnant draft. He distributed among his fellow militiamen tickets with the names of some of the county's most
prominent gentlemen. When several of his compatriots protested, Terry retorted that if they objected to any names they
could substitute their own because it was in their "Power to
Elect Whom they Pleased." Thus, when the county militia officers later collected the ballots, they made an alarming dis-

The author wishes to thank the following historians who gave an earlier
version of this essay a thorough critique: Robert M. Calhoon, Paul D. Es-
cott, Don Higginbotham, Marvin L. Michael Kay, and William S. Price, Jr.

125

covery. George Wilson's company had, in effect, drafted David Love, lieutenant colonel of the militia; William Love, a deputy sheriff in the county; John Childs, a justice of the peace; John Hardy, a planter; and Samuel Spencer, one of the state's leading jurists and a judge on the superior court. Shocked by such a display of unrestrained democracy, the officers could do only one thing: overturn the results and rule them "contrary to Law." Spencer, they argued, was away from the county on judicial business and could not be recalled in time, William Love and John Hardy had submitted their names for consideration in another militia district, David Love did not live in Wilson's militia district, and John Childs had already supplied a substitute. The county officers, therefore, arbitrarily named five other men to meet the obstreperous militia company's quota.[1] The formalities of democracy had been observed, but class rule had prevailed.

Such clever opposition to the draft symptomized the class resentment and disenchantment with the Revolutionary cause that led to widespread and persistent disaffection in the North Carolina backcountry during the American Revolution. At first it took many forms, a smoldering resentment that occasionally flared into violence but generally remained unorganized and unsupported as the whigs attempted to impose their will on an ethnically and culturally heterogeneous population. Once the seat of war moved south in late 1778, however, pent-up hostilities burst forth and disaffection hardened into loyalism with a fury that astonished leaders on both sides of the conflict. By 1780 civil war was raging in North Carolina, and in 1781 and 1782 the state was so con-

---

[1] Depositions Regarding Drafting of Troops, Anson County, 1778–79, Military Collection, Revolutionary War, Miscellaneous Papers, 1776–89, Box 5, Archives, North Carolina Division of Archives and History, Raleigh; Laws of North Carolina, 1778, Walter Clark, ed., *The State Records of North Carolina*, 16 vols., numbered 11–26 (Winston and Goldsboro, 1895–1907), 24:154–57. Gov. Richard Caswell chastised Col. Charles Medlock for abrogating the election results, which Caswell deemed "strickly agreeable to the law." He urged the colonel to send on the people elected or their substitutes, though "this is mere matter of advice." Caswell admitted that the people had acted "ungenerously," but "the power of judging was by the law left with them" (Caswell to Medlock, June 6, 1778, Clark, ed., *State Records*, 13:150–51).

vulsed by killing and disorder that vast areas were ungovern-
able and unsafe for whig and tory alike.

To associate such disaffection and loyalism with stout roy-
alist convictions, however, is to make the same mistake the
British ministry did in basing its southern strategy on the
supposed strength of the "Friends of Government." Loyalism
was not necessarily ideological in the sense that some people
loved the crown, upheld its rule, and abhorred the threat to
good order and government posed by the Revolutionaries,
though loyalists of that stripe could be found throughout the
colonies.[2] Loyalism also grew out of a particular set of political, economic, and social circumstances that caused people to
ignore, accommodate themselves to, or resist the onerous demands of an aggressive Revolutionary government that was
dominated by and conducted in the interests of an upper
class consisting of planters, merchants, and lawyers.[3] The relentless and ruthless sacrifices called for by the whigs alienated some people and fomented insurrection, but the
conflicts between whig and disaffected, and whig and tory,
often reflected deep-seated class tensions as well, tensions
which had erupted dramatically in the Regulator movement
of 1766-71 and which pitted backcountry farmers against the

[2] See Paul H. Smith, *Loyalists and Redcoats: A Study in British Revolutionary
Policy* (Chapel Hill, 1964); John Shy, "British Strategy for Pacifying the
Southern Colonies, 1778–1781," in Jeffrey J. Crow and Larry E. Tise, eds.,
The Southern Experience in the American Revolution (Chapel Hill, 1978), pp.
155–73; William H. Nelson, *The American Tory* (New York, 1961); Robert
M. Calhoon, *The Loyalists in Revolutionary America, 1760–1781* (New York,
1973); idem, "Civil, Revolutionary, or Partisan: The Loyalists and the Na-
ture of the War for Independence," in Stanley J. Underdal, ed., *Military
History of the American Revolution . . .* (Washington, D.C., 1976), pp. 93–108;
Adele Hast, *Loyalism in Revolutionary Virginia: The Norfolk Area and the Eastern Shore* (Ann Arbor, 1982); and Sung Bok Kim, "The Impact of Class
Relations and Warfare in the American Revolution: The New York Experience," *Journal of American History* 69 (1982):326–46.

[3] Charles G. Sellers, Jr., "Making a Revolution: The North Carolina
Whigs, 1765–1775," in J. Carlyle Sitterson, ed., *Studies in Southern History*,
James Sprunt Studies in History and Political Science, vol. 39 (Chapel Hill,
1957), pp. 23–46; A. Roger Ekirch, *"Poor Carolina": Politics and Society in
Colonial North Carolina, 1729–1776* (Chapel Hill, 1981), especially pp. 45–
47, 82–83, 156–60, 168–74, 198–200. See also Lindley S. Butler, *North
Carolina and the Coming of the Revolution, 1763–1776* (Raleigh, 1976).

provincial elite in a protest against corrupt and undemocratic government. That elite not only crushed the Regulation at the battle of Alamance in 1771 but it also fostered and carried on the Revolution in North Carolina.[4]

The whig elite recognized from the outset of the war that social fragmentation threatened its rule, and it attempted to unify the colony first with moral suasion and then with stringent political and military discipline. Already possessed of tremendous economic, political, and social advantages, the elite found the deferential patterns of colonial society insufficient to maintain order and to build a cultural hegemony in which ruler and ruled shared similar assumptions, values, and understandings about sources of authority and the exercise of power in society. A deferential society requires a firmly structured social order and harmony of interests between leaders and led, one in which the general populace accepts the elite's rule as beneficial to the interests of all. The residue of class tensions from the Regulation and a restive, ethnically diverse backcountry population made such a harmonizing of interests impossible to achieve. The resistance of poor and middling farmers who preferred neutrality and disliked central authority, whether promulgated by an imperial official or a provincial oligarch, was only temporarily forestalled. As the conditions of war shifted, so did the strategies of these yeoman farmers whose political allegiances were not firmly fixed on one side or the other. The escalation of the war, increased pressure from the whigs, and the opportunity to rise when the British army drew near ignited a ferocious civil war that cannot be explained by simple political and ideological categorizations. Disaffection turned into a retributive loyalism, and the war became a contest for local authority and control of highly prized resources—grain, livestock, horses, arms, and ultimately the land itself.

The rebellious backwoods farmers who challenged the whig gentry's hegemony were not, with a few exceptions, simple "banditti," or freebooters, despite that characteriza-

[4] Marvin L. Michael Kay, "The North Carolina Regulation, 1766–1776: A Class Conflict," in Alfred F. Young, ed., *The American Revolution: Explorations in the History of American Radicalism* (DeKalb, Ill., 1976), pp. 71–123.

tion by the Revolutionaries. The wartime excesses of whig governance that summoned these agrarian rebels to action in many respects also transformed them into social bandits. David Fanning, undoubtedly North Carolina's most notorious tory partisan leader, regarded himself as a staunch supporter of the crown, but in his "narrative" of the war years, published in 1790, he also styled himself a fighter for justice, vengeful guardian of the wronged and oppressed, even a leader of liberation.[5] While indiscriminate plundering and atrocities committed by the contending parties undercut both sides' claims to moral superiority, the equation of loyalist pillaging with banditry distorted the grievances suffered by many small farmers and producers. Loyalist pillaging avenged the expropriating and confiscatory policies of the whig government, retaliated against local oligarchs who controlled the militia, constabulary, and collection of taxes, and replaced loyalist property losses with the property of whigs. While loyalism and disaffection existed virtually everywhere in North Carolina, the backcountry seemed to harbor a disproportionate share of loyalists who were labeled bandits. Geography provided conditions favorable to resistance. Areas that were relatively remote and frontierlike furnished cover for former soldiers and deserters as well as for the poorer and middling elements of agrarian society. These small subsistence farmers and herdsmen practiced a largely independent life-style that removed them in seasons other than harvest and the time of rounding up livestock from centers of social and commercial intercourse and thus the hierarchical constraints of society. Fully capable of brutality, and having been subjected to such violence from the whigs, these loyalists achieved autonomy for a brief period, matched the whigs cruelty for cruelty, and sought to impose their own sense of justice and standards of fairness between rich and poor, weak and strong.[6]

[5] "Narrative of Col'o David Fanning, Written by Himself, Detailing Astonishing Events in No. Ca., from 1775 to 1783," in Clark, ed., *State Records*, 22:180–239. See also Lindley S. Butler, ed., *The Narrative of Col. David Fanning* (Davidson, N.C., and Charleston, 1981).

[6] Regarding social banditry see E. J. Hobsbawm, *Bandits* (New York,

That the North Carolina backcountry was a haven of disaffection and a potential loyalist stronghold was well understood by British strategists and Revolutionaries alike.
Republican governor Abner Nash succinctly commented on
this fact in 1780: "The country below the Yadkin [River], to
within twenty miles of Hillsborough, is chiefly disaffected,
and has been so from the beginning of the war."[7] Royal governor Josiah Martin asserted as early as 1775 that "people in
the Western Counties of this Province, which are by far the
most populous, will generally unite in support of Government . . . with the aid of a considerable Body of Highlanders
in the midland counties."[8] Regulators, Martin believed,
would also support the crown because of the "solemn Oath
of Allegiance" they swore after Alamance, though he may
have remained blind to the intense hostility the Regulators
felt toward the whig oligarchy.[9] Pockets of loyalism also dot-
ted the foothills and valleys of the Blue Ridge. Henry Stuart,
Britain's deputy superintendent for Indian affairs, reported
from Pensacola, in 1776: "One Capt York and some others
of the Loyal Inhabitants of the back Settlements of Carolina
paid us visits to know if there were hopes of assistance com-

1969), pp. 13–17, 21–22, 55, and idem, *Primitive Rebels: Studies in Archaic
Forms of Social Movement in the Nineteenth and Twentieth Centuries* (New York,
1959), p. 5. The use of criminality to redistribute wealth is the theme of
two recent studies on the poor and enslaved in eighteenth-century Anglo-
American culture: see Douglas Hay et al., *Albion's Fatal Tree: Crime and
Society in Eighteenth-Century England* (New York, 1975), and Marvin L. Mi-
chael Kay and Lorin Lee Cary, "Albion's Fatal Tree Transplanted: Crime,
Society, and Slavery in North Carolina" (Paper presented at the Forty-
fourth Annual Meeting of the Southern Historical Association, St. Louis,
November 1978).

[7] Gov. Abner Nash to Samuel Huntington, Oct. 6, 1780, Clark, ed., *State
Records*, 15:99.

[8] Gov. Josiah Martin to General Gage, Mar. 16, 1775, William L. Saunders, ed., *The Colonial Records of North Carolina*, 10 vols. (Raleigh, 1886–
90), 9:1167.

[9] Martin to the earl of Dartmouth, Apr. 20, 1775, ibid., p. 1228. See also
three petitions from backcountry loyalists to Martin, 1775, Martin to Dartmouth, May 18, 1775, and Martin to Dartmouth, Jan. 12, 1776, ibid., pp.
1160–64, 1256, 10:406–7.

ing to them through the Cherokees from St Augustine or
Pensacola. They complained much of the distressed situation
to which the Friends of Government were already reduced."[10] Whig general Griffith Rutherford described the
"unhappy situation of the Frontiers of this State" because of
marauding tories and the British agitation of Indians. The
tories were especially active in Surry County.[11] At the behest
of the state's delegates the Continental Congress even sent
"Ministers of the Gospel . . . to the Western parts of North
Carolina" in 1776 to persuade the inhabitants to "support . . .
those rights & privileges which belong to them in common
with the rest of America."[12]

Whig overtures to the backcountry inhabitants proved un-
persuasive and unavailing. By 1780 Col. Thomas Wade, Anson County's most prominent and ruthless Revolutionary,
urged Governor Nash to establish courts in Anson, Richmond, Montgomery, Rowan, Surry, Rutherford, Burke, and
Lincoln counties to deal with festering toryism.[13] Within a
year vast areas of the upper Cape Fear valley had become a
veritable no-man's-land for whigs. Col. Thomas Robeson informed republican governor Thomas Burke that Bladen
County had become a "Frontier County to the Enemy now at
Wilmington and to the State of South Carolina." Bands of
"Tories and Robbers" were ranging through Bladen along
Drowning Creek and the Little Pee Dee River, as far west as
Richmond County, and along the southern border of the
state all the way to the Cape Fear River, "which is near about
100 miles in Length and about Fifty across, which this part
of the Country is much incumbered with very large Swamps
and other Thick Places." The tories robbed patriots and carried on trade with the British at Wilmington "both by Land

[10] Henry Stuart's Account of Proceedings with Cherokees about Going
against Whites, Aug. 25, 1776, ibid., 10:771–72.

[11] Gen. Griffith Rutherford to Caswell, Feb. 1, 1777, Clark, ed., *State
Records*, 11:372. See also Thomas Sumter to Baron de Kalb, July 17, 1780,
and William Davidson to Horatio Gates, Sept. 14, 1780, ibid., 14:507, 616.

[12] Joseph Hewes to Samuel Johnston, Jan. 6, 1776, ibid., 22:515.

[13] Col. Thomas Wade to Nash, June 28, 1780, ibid., 14:865.

and Water." The inhabitants of Bladen were "obliged to leave their Habitation every Night to take their rest"; no more than seventy or eighty men in the county would "dare move in behalf of their Country," Robeson despaired, whereas the tories were said to number four hundred to five hundred.[14]

Guilford Dudley of Halifax County left a vivid description of the perils facing whigs in the backcountry in the spring of 1781. Discharged from the Continental army, he had to make his way from South Carolina to Hillsborough. He planned to take the road from the Pee Dee River to Deep River and then from there the road to Chatham Courthouse. "But when I got upon Little River of Pee Dee," he related, "I found the country in my front all the way to Haw River and Chatham Courthouse (on my right down along Drowning Creek and the Raft Swamp to Wilmington, and my left to Uharie [Uwharrie] Creek and the Yadkin River) in a state of insurrection and parties of armed Tories spreading themselves in every direction before me and on either flank." Finding himself hemmed in on all sides and unable to retreat "for want of correct intelligence from some person upon whom I could rely, for they were all Tories and in arms," Dudley abandoned his wagon and struck for Randolph Courthouse, though it was far out of his way. After arriving there with David Fanning allegedly in close pursuit, he turned east on the old Hillsborough-Salisbury trading road and hid along the banks of the Deep River that night. Still surrounded by tories, he turned north the next morning toward the Quaker settlement of New Garden. He finally reached Hillsborough after going more than a hundred miles out of his way. In May 1781 he accepted command of a volunteer band to pursue Fanning.[15]

[14] Col. Thomas Robeson to Gov. Thomas Burke, July 10, 1781, ibid., 22:543–44. See also Wade et al. to Caswell, July 26, 1777, ibid., 11:534; Medlock and Will Picket to Council of Safety, July 22, 1776, Saunders et al., *Colonial Records*, 10:669–70; Pension Claim of Pleasant Henderson, Sept. 1832, Burke to Gates, Sept. 15, 1780, Clark, ed., *State Records*, 22:131, 14:620.

[15] John C. Dann, ed., *The Revolution Remembered: Eyewitness Accounts of the War for Independence* (Chicago, 1980), pp. 225–27.

As indicated by these whig and British observers, the areas in which loyalism became most strident and the struggles bloodiest offered terrain conducive to resistance and guerrilla warfare. These areas also tended to be less mature economically than the maritime counties. The backcountry, to be sure, had enjoyed tremendous economic growth in the 1760s and 1770s with a huge influx of new settlers, but its social and economic institutions still lacked full articulation when the Revolution erupted. Loyalism and disaffection abounded in the rolling, sometimes steep lands of the piedmont like Chatham and Randolph counties, in Blue Ridge counties such as Surry, Rowan, and Burke, and in the pocosins, swamps (referred to as "Carolina Bays"), and piney woods of the upper Cape Fear country, especially Bladen and Cumberland counties. Moreover, these areas had not been settled to an appreciable degree by people of English extraction. Between 1750 and 1770 North Carolina's population doubled as settlers poured into the backcountry from northern colonies, principally Pennsylvania and Maryland. They were mostly Scotch-Irish and Germans, with the one important exception being Scottish Highlanders who came directly from Scotland to settle the upper Cape Fear valley.[16]

Why some backcountry counties were hotbeds of organized resistance to the whig regime while others were not yields no simple explanation. North-central counties in the backcountry like Orange, Caswell, and, to a lesser extent, Guilford generally escaped the ravages of civil war if not the marches of British and American armies. But these counties were striding toward economic maturity at a more accelerated rate than their southern and western neighbors, and whig oligarchs may have had firmer control there. Ethnocultural heterogeneity points to another possible cause. The loyalist proclivities of the Highland Scots were well known. Pietist and pacifist German settlers like the Moravians and

---

[16] Harry Roy Merrens, *Colonial North Carolina in the Eighteenth Century: A Study in Historical Geography* (Chapel Hill, 1964), pp. 44, 53–74; Marvin L. Michael Kay and Lorin Lee Cary, "A Demographic Analysis of Colonial North Carolina with Special Emphasis upon the Slave and Black Populations," in Jeffrey J. Crow and Flora J. Hatley, eds., *Black Americans in North Carolina and the South* (Chapel Hill, 1984), pp. 71–121.

Dunkards were generally neutral, as were English Quakers. At least some German settlers, however, took the loyalist side. It is impossible to state with precision the political behavior of the Scotch-Irish, though if one were to judge by Mecklenburg County, many seem to have been whigs.

While the cacophony of English, Gaelic, and German voices and the mélange of cultural mores, religious views and practices, and ethnic stocks are suggestive, the significant differences in economic development that contrasted the southern and western piedmont and foothills of the Blue Ridge with the northern piedmont and maritime counties reveal more. The nascent economy characteristic of the rebellious areas of the backcountry relied less on slavery and on labor-intensive commercial crops such as tobacco, rice, indigo, and naval stores. Only 11.4 percent of the households in Anson County in 1763, for instance, owned slaves, and only 1.8 percent of them owned as many as five. Slaves everywhere were concentrated in the hands of the wealthy. The percentage of blacks in the western counties of Orange, Rowan, Anson, and Mecklenburg in 1767 was only 7.69 percent, whereas in the remainder of the colony blacks constituted from 19 percent to just below 63 percent of the population.[17] Most of these backcountry settlers, excluding those in Orange, Caswell, and Guilford counties, where tobacco production played an increasingly important role, were farmers who raised corn, wheat, and livestock. Many raised no more than fifteen acres of corn, but it formed an important part of their diet and that of their animals.[18]

[17] Marvin L. Michael Kay and Lorin Lee Cary, "Class, Mobility, and Conflict in North Carolina on the Eve of the Revolution," in Crow and Tise, eds., *Southern Experience*, pp. 109–51, especially table 1, pp. 112–13; Marvin L. Michael Kay and William S. Price, Jr., "'To Ride the Wood Mare': Road Building and Militia Service in Colonial North Carolina, 1740–1775," *North Carolina Historical Review* 57 (1980):395–96.

[18] Merrens, *Colonial North Carolina*, pp. 110–11, 114–16; Ekirch, *"Poor Carolina,"* pp. 19–47. Ekirch sees an acquisitive spirit among the backcountry settlers of North Carolina, but James A. Henretta suggests that the small subsistence farmers of eighteenth-century America were largely indifferent to entrepreneurship ("Families and Farms: *Mentalité* in Pre-Industrial America," *William and Mary Quarterly*, 3d ser. 35 [1978]:3–32).

For settlers throughout the colony livestock comprised perhaps their most important economic asset. Almost every holding had domesticated animals—cattle, swine, oxen, horses, sheep, and fowl—and the animals formed a crucial element in the colonial economy. Hog drives to Virginia began as early as 1728, and by the 1750s and 1760s swine were being driven as far north as New Jersey and Pennsylvania. Cattle assumed equal importance, with cattle drives beginning each fall after harvest and lasting into November. Scotsmen in particular emphasized cattle raising, and the wetlands of the Carolina Bays in such areas as the upper Cape Fear country proved well suited for raising livestock. There the animals roamed freely and lived off the fat of the land. The number of animals a settler could raise was limited only by the physical ability to find them and round them up.[19] For more than a hundred years the rhythm of life in the wetlands and piney woods changed little. The backwoods agrarians raised a few crops, drove cattle and swine, lived in relative isolation, and resisted the impositions of the planter class, exacted by a rebel government, whether in 1776 or in 1861.[20]

Despite the economic and ethnocultural differences evidenced in these newly settled counties, the social and political configurations remained the same as those of the older, more economically mature areas. An oligarchy of slaveholders monopolized wealth, power, and status. This hierarchical structure ensured that political roles reflected one's wealth, social status, and class position. Members of the upper class held major offices, middling property holders held middle-rung positions with some discretionary power and authority, and the poor performed menial and low-status political tasks.[21] When the gentry swept North Carolina into the Revolution,

[19] Merrens, *Colonial North Carolina*, pp. 134–40, 248 n. 146; Forrest McDonald and Grady McWhiney, "The Antebellum Southern Herdsman: A Reinterpretation," *Journal of Southern History* 41 (1975):147–66; idem, "The South from Self-Sufficiency to Peonage: An Interpretation," *American Historical Review* 85 (1980):1095–1118.

[20] W. McKee Evans, *Ballots and Fence Rails: Reconstruction on the Lower Cape Fear* (Chapel Hill, 1966), pp. 12–15, 26–27.

[21] The best statements on the class arrangements of colonial North Car-

they continued their well-established pattern of exploitation with a regressive tax system and onerous, not to say compulsory, militia service that now carried increased perils: the potential of having to confront and fight the British army. Such demands, whigs quickly discovered, exacerbated class tensions between whig oligarchs and yeoman farmers, at least as long-standing as the Regulation, and heightened suspicions about the allegiances of Scottish Highlanders and the close-knit, communal German settlements of Wachovia.

The battle of Moore's Creek Bridge in February 1776 confirmed the whigs' worst fears about disaffection among the former Regulators and Scottish Highlanders. British agents and Governor Martin wooed the Highlanders with promises of land, the remission of arrears in quitrents, and twenty years' tax exemption. Many of them had emigrated only as recently as 1770, and Martin had forced them to swear allegiance to the crown before issuing land grants. The Regulators, perhaps, were less concerned about oaths and more interested in settling old scores with the colonial elite. In addition, Martin had shown a marked sympathy for and leniency toward the Regulators and their grievances since early in his governorship. Whatever the exact chemistry of motives that caused an estimated 700 Highland Scots and 200 Regulators to march toward the coast to meet the expected arrival of British forces, the whig regime successfully interdicted them.[22]

---

olina are Kay and Price, "'To Ride the Wood Mare'"; and Kay and Cary, "Class, Mobility, and Conflict." Betty Linney Waugh demonstrates that a "frontier gentry" in the foothills of the Blue Ridge governed before and after the Revolution, brutally crushed loyalism, and preserved the same social and political structure. She concentrates principally on Surry and Wilkes counties ("The Upper Yadkin Valley in the American Revolution: Benjamin Cleveland, Symbol of Continuity," Ph.D. diss., University of New Mexico, 1971, pp. 58–59, 77–78, 81–82, 115).

[22] Col. William Purviance to the Provincial Council, Feb. 23, 1776, Saunders, ed., *Colonial Records*, 10:468; Kay, "North Carolina Regulation," pp. 103–7. On North Carolina loyalism in general see also Carole Watterson Troxler, *The Loyalist Experience in North Carolina* (Raleigh, 1976); Robert O. DeMond, *The Loyalists in North Carolina during the Revolution* (1940; reprint ed., Hamden, Conn., 1964); and Duane Meyer, *The Highland Scots of North Carolina, 1732–1776* (Chapel Hill, 1961).

Discontent with the whigs' policies, however, extended far beyond the Regulator and Highland Scots' communities and far past Moore's Creek. From the opening days of the Revolution, backcountry settlers expressed alarm at the economic impact of the movement for independence. Economic boycotts and embargoes crossed class lines, especially injuring small-time producers who traded in such basic commodities as grain and dairy products but who required some finished products and essentials like salt. As early as 1775 one British observer, who had recently left Cape Fear, reported:

> A Messenger had arrived from the Back Settlers to acquaint the People of the Coast, that they (the back Inhabitants) would not Submit to any Stoppage of their Trade, and that if Their ships were not suffered to proceed with the Produce of the Country, they would come down and burn all the Houses on the Coast, and put the People to the Sword: that they could not live except they had a free Trade, and would not obey any Orders to the Contrary. . . . that the Back Settlers had stopped all Kinds of Provisions from coming down the Country for the Supply of the People on the Coast, which had prevented them from assembling in a Body to exercise and train themselves as they had Orders to do: I enquired if these Back Settlers had any disposition to the King's Service, he said not, but that they wished not to be under the Restrictions of their Trade, and were as People impatient of Rule as the others.[23]

Wary of both sides, bitter towards the whigs' embargo of trade with Great Britain yet unwilling to be identified as loyalists, the inhabitants of the backcountry resented the arbitrary rule of either party.

As the war drove the cost of necessities higher, demands for a just price and moral economy surfaced in the backcountry as well as in counties to the east. In particular the settlers objected to the high price of salt and the profits of the middlemen in Cross Creek, the town located at the head of navigation on the Cape Fear River. In July 1777 discon-

---

[23] Ld. Lt. Harcourt to Lord ———, Oct. 4, 1775, State Papers of Ireland, P.R.O. SP 63/449, British Records Collection, N.C. Div. Arch. and Hist.

tented farmers, gathered at Chatham Courthouse to discuss the price of salt, determined to prevent the shipment of provisions to Cross Creek until they obtained salt at "reasonable terms," and they sent emissaries to Orange and Guilford counties to seek the same commitment.[24] Reports reached Cross Creek "of the Guilford and Chatham people's intention of mobbing us for salt," and, in fact, a band of protesters did march there. Whig leader Robert Rowan reported that he and a "small company of volunteers . . . quelled about 140 persons collected from the Counties of Duplin and Johnston. They came here with a design, as they acknowledged themselves, of taking the salt by force, and paying what price they thought proper, from ten shillings to two dollars pr bushel, and did not expect to meet with the least opposition." When confronted by Rowan, the crowd scattered; those who did not escape took the oath of allegiance to the state. Because they appeared "very penitent" and abandoned their insubordinate posture, Rowan "allowed them what salt they wanted, at the market price, which is 5 dollars, and discharged them."[25]

Rowan's simple show of force maintained social discipline in this instance, but the whigs understood well that harsher measures were needed to enforce compliance with the Revolutionary regime's rule. The whig victory at Moore's Creek effectively forestalled a major tory rising for the next four years, but conspiracy and disaffection made the whigs' control of the colony tenuous.[26] To maintain social discipline and ensure the oligarchy's prerogatives in protecting its interests and property required the Revolutionary regime to enact in-

[24] David Smith to Caswell, July 29, 1777, Clark ed., *State Records*, 11:548–49.

[25] Robert Rowan to Brig. Gen. John Ashe, July 30, 1777, Ashe to Caswell, Aug. 4, 1777, ibid., pp. 560–61, 558. Various manifestations of lower-class dissent and the ways in which the upper class controlled such dissidence are analyzed in an eighteenth-century European context by E. P. Thompson in "Patrician Society, Plebian Culture," *Journal of Social History* 7 (1974):382–405.

[26] See, for example, Jeffrey J. Crow, "Tory Plots and Anglican Loyalty: The Llewelyn Conspiracy of 1777," *North Carolina Historical Review* 55 (1978):1–17; Ronald Hoffman, "The 'Disaffected' in the Revolutionary South," in Young, ed., *American Revolution*, pp. 273–316.

creasingly severe penalties for disobedience (rapidly equated with treason) and to administer such measures through the courts and militia. Test oaths, confiscation of property, three-fold taxation for religious neutrals like the Quakers and Moravians, the draft, and eventually a specific tax or tax-in-kind became the instruments of whig control. How these measures were implemented reveals much about the underlying tensions that afflicted society and the consequent challenge to whig authority mounted by society's powerless and dispossessed.

The test oath in particular came to symbolize public acceptance of the whig gentry's hegemony, but the manner in which it was administered concerned some patriots. From Cumberland County in 1777, Robert Rowan complained of "the grievances that many of the Inhabitants . . . labour under, from the tyranny, oppression and ignorance of those men who were appointed to rule over us." He accused the courts and militia of "evil conduct" toward "poor ignorant Scotch people" who were plundered after the battle of Moore's Creek Bridge and asserted that the actions of the county court had been "truly arbitrary." "One infirm man, seventy years of age, that many years had laid by the profits of a few potatoes, Turnips, Greens, &c.," he wrote, "was compelled to take this oath or go to jail, another poor man, from one of the back counties had his loaded wagon carrying home salt to relieve his family, brought back a dozen miles and the owner thrown in jail for saying he would not take the oath here, but in his own County." Rowan singled out Philip Alston, a prominent whig planter along the Deep River, as a "hectoring, domineering" tyrant.[27]

Even more than the courts, the whig militia became the undisputed local arm of social and political control.[28] Ironically, it created more disorder than insurrectionary tories did

---

[27] Rowan to Caswell, Sept. 18, 1777, Clark, ed., *State Records*, 11:626–31. For similar complaints about Cumberland County authorities see Archibald Maclaine to Caswell, Oct. 31, 1778, ibid., 22:769–70.

[28] See Clyde R. Ferguson, "Carolina and Georgia Patriot and Loyalist Militia in Action, 1778–1783," in Crow and Tise, eds., *Southern Experience*, pp. 174–99.

before the spread of internecine war in 1780. The Moravian settlement of Wachovia on the fringes of the frontier proved an accurate index of whig intimidation of neutral inhabitants. As noncombatants the German settlers had reason to fear both sides, but it was the whig militia that most tormented them. In 1776 the whigs seized the arms of "Non-Associators" among the Brethren. That same year suspected tories along the Yadkin River were "driven from house and home by persecution" and compelled to hide "in the woods . . . (the first *Outlyers*, as they were later called)." Surry and Wilkes county militiamen under Benjamin Cleveland were especially belligerent and abusive. They went into Moravian stores and workshops, took what they wanted, and charged it to "the public account."[29] In September 1780 the whig militia broke into the house of one Brother and began pillaging. When the Brother asked the captain "whether he and his men robbed and plundered like Tories, and that from people whom they should protect," the captain, thoroughly rebuked, ordered an end to the "disorderly conduct" and returned the stolen items.[30] Others were not so fortunate. By October 1780 "the woods were full of Liberty Men on horseback, looking for Tories. . . . From all sides come reports of the bad behaviour of the Liberty Men, especially those from Wilkes County." Another report stated: "Joseph Holder and his family passed on their way to Schemel's farm. The Liberty soldiers have taken everything from them, and beat him and his wife."[31] Although some whigs decried the violence, the Moravians knew that such "barbarous and unjust treatment" had "driven many to the Tories who would gladly have remained peaceful."[32] Just north of Wachovia, Col. Gideon Wright, long suspected of loyalist sympathies, gathered a force of a hundred men to pursue the "Liberty Men" with the intent "to take back the things of which they had been

[29] Adelaide L. Fries et al., eds., *Records of the Moravians in North Carolina*, 11 vols. (Raleigh, 1922–69), 3:1024–26, 1028.

[30] Ibid., 4:1565.

[31] Ibid., pp. 1644–45.

[32] Ibid., p. 1572.

robbed." As one Moravian observer commented: "For a considerable time all those who were more or less suspected as Tories had been sought out, whipped and beaten, houses had been burned, cattle driven away, and farms ruined." Many neutrals fearing similar treatment had openly declared themselves converts to loyalism and joined Wright's band.[33] In February 1781 the whig militia from Lincoln, Rowan, and Mecklenburg counties threatened to destroy Salem, tried to break into stores, and impressed horses and provisions. Although the officers tried to quiet "the vicious men . . . , hardly one house remained unrobbed."[34] In Rowan County the whig militia "unlawfully and feloniously plundered and robbed sundry peaceable people of this State of their property under the pretence of their being Tories and Enemies to their Country, and converted the same to their own use in open violation of the Laws." At least one "barbarous and cruel Murder" had been committed.[35]

This pattern of whig lawlessness persisted throughout the backcountry and particularly in places where disaffection was suspected. Moravians and Quakers, however, escaped relatively unscathed because of their patent and pacifistic neutrality. In other areas the whigs conducted a reign of terror as a matter of policy. From the first days of the war whig militiamen engaged in "Tory hunting," making sweeps through Randolph, Chatham, Anson, Montgomery, and Rowan counties.[36] In Surry and Wilkes counties the militia that once protected settlements from the Indians became an instrument of terror in the hands of Benjamin Cleveland. Beginning in 1778 and regularly thereafter Cleveland routinely made forays through the Blue Ridge Mountains and down the New River, allegedly to restore "tranquility and apparent

[33] Ibid., pp. 1644, 1906.

[34] Ibid., pp. 1677–78, 1679. See also residents of Salem to Nathanael Greene, Feb. 8, 1781, ibid., pp. 1907–8.

[35] Proceedings of the Board of War, Nov. 25, 1780, Clark, ed., *State Records*, 14:468–69; Alexander Martin to Gen. John Butler, Nov. 25, 1780, Military Coll., Revolutionary War, Box 1.

[36] Pension Claim of James McBride, Oct. 1832, Clark, ed., *State Records*, 22:144–45.

security to the settlements." He administered the test oath to suspected tories and retaliated for real and imagined loyalist depredations. In one instance he captured a tory and hanged him by the neck to obtain information, but the torture failed to produce the "desired effect." After the battle of King's Mountain in October 1780, thirty-two "obnoxious" tories were chosen for hanging; nine were subsequently executed.[37]

In the summer of 1777 William Gipson joined the Rowan County militia that campaigned through Guilford, Chatham, and adjoining counties along the Deep and Pee Dee rivers to disperse the tories under Eli Branson. In the sandhills the whigs captured several Scottish tories and hanged one of them. Another escaped, however, when "some disaffected persons in the detachment" set him free one night. Two years later Gipson joined a small band of whigs "who had been more or less harassed and inspired by the disaffected" on another sweep through Guilford, Randolph, and Surry counties. They captured two "notorious" tories, tried and shot one, and "*spicketed*" the other by driving a sharp "pin . . . through his foot." Although admitting the punishment was "cruel," Gipson felt "no little satisfaction" after the "unrelenting cruelties of the Tories of that day," who had, in fact, plundered and beaten his mother.[38]

Moses Hall, another Rowan County militiaman, offered a revealing insight into the ways in which people were radicalized by and made insensitive to the inhumanity of the war. On the evening after the massacre of Dr. John Pyle's tory brigade near Guilford Courthouse in 1781, Hall was horrified by the grisly execution of six loyalist prisoners who were "hewed to pieces with broadswords" in purported retaliation for tory atrocities. The following day, however, he and his compatriots happened upon a youth of sixteen whom the British, fearing he was a spy, "had run through . . . with a bayonet and left . . . for dead." Though "mortally wounded,"

[37] Pension Claim of William Lenoir, May 1833, ibid., pp. 138, 139. Regarding the execution of tories at King's Mountain see also Col. Isaac Shelby's account and Ens. Robert Campbell's account, ibid., 15:110, 103–4.

[38] Dann, ed., *Revolution Remembered*, pp. 186–91.

the boy could speak. "The sight of this unoffending boy, butchered," confessed Hall, "relieved me of my distressful feelings for the slaughter of the Tories, and I desired nothing so much as the opportunity of participating in their destruction."[39]

As atrocities and bloodshed escalated on both sides, the whig government sought to turn such hatreds to its advantage. In October 1781 Alexander Martin, speaker of the state senate and acting governor in the wake of Governor Burke's capture by David Fanning, told the Council of State that the militia must take the field to "chastise the present disaffection, long prevailing in some of the Counties of this State, by destroying, dispersing and capturing the ring-leaders." The Revolutionary regime could not "finally subdue and extirpate" toryism "from the Country while the families of these armed villains are suffered to remain among us uninterrupted, thereby nursing up serpents in our own bosoms for our own destruction." He admitted that "humanity ... pleads the cause of poor women and children, yet does not policy suggest and point out this measure, tho' rigorous, that they be banished from among us into the British lines which thereby will draw away from us a set of men who so long have eluded Justice, and disturb the public Peace with impunity?"[40]

The assault on loyalist families proved especially loathsome. In August 1780 the Moravians recorded: "Several women passed. Their husbands joined those in favor of the king, and now the women have been driven from their farms and told to go to their husbands."[41] Even Francis Marion, South Carolina's famed "Swamp Fox," deplored the terrorization of inoffensive people. At Drowning Creek in October 1780 he wrote in disgust that the whig militia was burning "a Great Number of houses on Little Peedee" and intended "to go on in that Abominable work." Some tories had fled to Georgia while "others are rund into Swamps." Marion de-

[39] Ibid., pp. 202–3.

[40] Meeting of Council of State, Clark, ed., *State Records*, 19:871.

[41] Fries et al., eds., *Records of Moravians*, 4:1642.

nied that he had ordered such a campaign: "It is what I detest to Distress poor Women & Children."[42]

A number of loyalists who submitted claims to the British government after the war commented on this whig tactic. Neil Colbreath, who had settled near Cross Creek in 1768 and owned around 200 acres, fought at Moore's Creek and later joined Cornwallis. As a result, all of his property was confiscated, and in 1781 the whigs "expelled" his wife from Cumberland County and sent her to join him in Wilmington. She was in "great distress, plundered of all her Effects, destitute of Cloathing & Means to support Nature."[43] Kenneth Stewart of Bladen County, also a veteran of Moore's Creek, was forced to conceal "himself in the woods and Swamps contiguous to his house for a space of time little short of four years." He regarded the whig militia as little more than "Banditti ... traversing the Country." Embittered, Stewart described "the distress of his wife and Children, whose cries often call'd him from his lurking places at the most imminent hazard of his life, to defend them from the outrage and barbarity of their persecutors, who taking advantage of his situation, plundered them of their effects."[44] One whig veteran recalled that after the British evacuation of Wilmington in November 1781 he "was ordered with a few soldiers to collect wives and children of the tories and carry them to Wilmington; that he found the execution of this duty so disagreeable that he resolved to desist from it at all hazards, and would choose rather to be cashiered than to perform a duty so repulsive to his feelings."[45] Plainly stunned by such a policy, whig partisan William R. Davie reported in February 1782: "Several poor Wretches have been here [Wilmington] in search after their Children which were kidnapped and car-

---

[42] Francis Marion to Gates, Oct. 4, 1780, Clark, ed., *State Records*, 14:666.

[43] Loyalist Claim of Neil Colbreath, AO 13/118, English Records Collection, Box 4, N.C. Div. Arch. and Hist.

[44] Loyalist Claim of Kenneth Stewart, AO 13/124, English Records Coll., Box 11.

[45] Testimony of James Devane before New Hanover County Superior Court, Oct. 31, 1832, Clark, ed., *State Records*, 15:786.

ried off by the Militia of General Rutherford's Brigade from Bladen and other Counties in the Neighborhood of Wilmington—This is truly shocking to humanity and a Stigma on our Character as a people."[46]

In short, this campaign of terror transformed neutrals into loyalists and deepened the resentments of the disaffected. Gen. Herndon Ramsey, who was captured at Chatham Courthouse by David Fanning in the summer of 1781, outlined the loyalists' grievances while a prisoner at McFall's Mill in Raft Swamp. Fanning's party, he said, "consisted of persons who complained of the greatest cruelties, either to their persons or property. Some had been unlawfully Drafted, Others had been whipped and ill-treated, without tryal; Others had their houses burned, and all their property plundered and Barbarous and cruel Murders had been committed in their Neighborhoods." The loyalists pointed in particular to militia leaders like Thomas Robeson of Bladen County, Thomas Wade of Anson County, and Philip Alston of Cumberland County. A few days earlier, according to Ramsey, Alston "took a man on the road and put him to instant Death, which has much incensed the Highlanders in this part of the County. A Scotch Gentleman the same day was taken at one MacAfee's Mill and ill treated. He is said to be a peaceable and inoffensive man. . . . He lives in the Raft Swamp." Fanning's men demanded "an immediate stop . . . to such inhuman practices" or else "the whole country will be deluged in Blood, and the innocent will suffer for the guilty."[47]

British military leaders, who were hardly blameless themselves, denounced the atrocities of the whig militia in letters to American commanders and to leading Revolutionaries. Cornwallis shuddered at "the Shocking Tortures and inhuman murders which are everyday committed by the Enemy, not only on those who have taken part with us, but on many who refuse to join them." He warned that the war in the

[46] As quoted in John S. Watterson, *Thomas Burke: Restless Revolutionary* (Washington, D.C., 1980), p. 195.

[47] Gen. Herndon Ramsey et al. to Burke, July 22, 1781, Clark, ed., *State Records*, 22:550–51.

Carolinas might become "truly Savage."[48] Maj. James H. Craig, commander of the British forces at Wilmington in 1781, complained to William Hooper, one of North Carolina's signers of the Declaration of Independence, that people were "being put to death often without trial or examination . . . by order of Militia officers commanding parties and acting under the authority of your present Government."[49]

What the British and a few discerning whigs recognized was the breakdown of their society's hierarchical structure, the erosion of deference, and the consequent disappearance of good order and stability. If cultural hegemony offered greater security to a hierarchical society than physical hegemony, that is, the use of armed might, then the whigs miscalculated badly in an effort to impose a harsh peace. Their arrant employment of arms and terror backfired: these tactics, the war's dislocations, and suppressed resentments combined to undermine the upper class's paternalistic authority and control of the means of social discipline. Each man had become judge, jury, and executioner in the name of revolution. The resulting anarchy invited the disaffected and loyalists to impose social justice as they saw it without recourse to the traditional sources of local authority in the community. Thus, how to restore the credibility and legitimacy of the gentry presented a knotty problem when the gentry themselves were acting the part of banditti.[50]

Gen. Stephen Drayton clearly understood this dilemma. Writing to Governor Burke from near Cross Creek in July 1781, he lamented the manner and method "respecting the convicting reclaiming or punishing of Tories; . . . we have by

[48] Lord Cornwallis to Sir Henry Clinton, Dec. 4, 1780, CO 5/397, British Records Coll.

[49] Maj. James H. Craig to William Hooper, July 20, 1781, Clark, ed., *State Records*, 15:554. For similar statements see also Craig to Nash, June 20, 1781, and Cornwallis to Clinton, Dec. 3, 1780, ibid., 22:1023–25, 15:306–7.

[50] For a discussion of the strength of cultural hegemony in a paternalistic society see Thompson, "Patrician Society, Plebian Culture," especially pp. 403–5.

our own imprudencies & irregular proceedings made more Enemies than have become so from mere inclination. . . . Civil wars are always attended with something horrid. The bare Idea of Friend against Friend & nearest Relatives in armed opposition shocks human nature! But good God! Sir, let us not countenance barbarities that would disgrace the Savage! if we cannot totally stop, yet we may check wanton exercise of cruelty." He cited a case in Cumberland County where an Andrew Beard had murdered "one McLeod." Such executions, said Drayton, should not rest in "private hands. . . . I am for wresting that *usurped* power out of the hands of soldiers, & by no means allow them individually to be Judges." Governor Nash had "applauded the *Action*" and wanted more men like Beard in every county. But, argued Drayton, if such evils are sanctioned by high officials, "who is safe where prejudice, envy or Malice may prevail in the breast of a bad man; are not the best liable to be called an Enemy & treated as such?" Not only had McLeod been murdered, but his family had been plundered of every article of clothing and means of subsistence. Those who wished to aid the stricken widow and her children were intimidated by "Beard's adherents & . . . obliged in Consequence to keep out of the way." Drayton cautioned further: "The people cannot place confidence when a proper degree of dignity is wanting, they cannot put their Lives to Stake, when they know *Chance* & not worth guides the whole, & thus for want of a Leader they become indifferent to everything but personal safety & thus, have many been driven to join the Enemy because they have been by *Some* thought to be no friend to their Country."[51]

[51] Gen. Stephen Drayton to Burke, July 6, 1781, Clark, ed., *State Records*, 15:511–13. A similar accusation was made against Andrew Beard by Thomas Cabune, a tanner in Cross Creek since 1774. Cabune was accused of being a tory and reported that Beard, whom he described as "a person in the Practice of Shooting down peoples whom he is pleased to suppose disaffected to the . . . Government," had threatened to kill him. Beard had recently "committed crimes of this Nature on the Bodys of McDonald McLoud & others, without any trial or form of Law whatever, & even without any inquiry being made" (Petition of Thomas Cabune, July 4, 1781, Legislative Papers, Box 39, N.C. Div. Arch. and Hist.). Burke genuinely

Unrestrained violence, as Drayton recognized, had besmirched the symbols of local power and authority, but building anger, frustration, and discontent with other measures adopted by the Revolutionary regime had undermined the growth of cultural hegemony and general obedience to the political and social order. The elite's self-serving paternalism fooled few, but it took a hardy breed to protest openly. Yet grumblers and malcontents had, from the outset, voiced their opposition to whig governance, the oath, militia service, the draft, paper currency, and taxes. Even the peace-loving Moravians, who tried to appease both sides, complained about the paper money spewing forth from whig printing presses and admitted that the "better class of people had no fondness for it. . . . But as it was in circulation it had to be accepted, though each man passed it on as quickly as possible."[52]

The Moravians' civility was in sharp contrast to the more blunt pronouncements of others like Jacob Sides of Tryon County who declared, "God Dam the Liberty money and them that made it for it was good for nothing."[53] Archibald McCoy of Guilford County was accused of inflaming the people against the Revolution because he had been heard to say, "Huzza for King George."[54] James Douthet had been brought before the Salisbury District Superior Court in 1777 and charged with treason for "Drinking Damnation to the States & good Health to George over the Water & Success to General How[e]."[55] Isaac Yates of Anson County likewise was accused of saying "God damn the State," threatening to kill

---

deplored the arbitrary authority of local officials (Burke to Craig, June 27, 1781, to Major Hogg, Mar. 13, 1782, to Major Mountflorence, Mar. 17, 1782, Clark, ed., *State Records*, 22:1026–29, 16:229–31, 235).

[52] Fries et al., eds., *Records of Moravians*, 4:1591–92, 2:850; Thompson, "Patrician Society, Plebian Culture," p. 400.

[53] Examination of George Rutledge, Aug. 29, 1778, Salisbury District Superior Court, Criminal Action Papers, N.C. Div. Arch. and Hist.

[54] Examination of Archibald McCoy, Mar. 5, 1778, ibid.

[55] Examination of James Douthet, Oct. 4, 1777, ibid.

George Washington, and declaring his intent to fight for the king.[56] Henry Daniel doubtless represented a class of marginal men in society who resisted any form of authority from whatever source. In 1778 he was brought before the Salisbury District Superior Court "as a vagerant person" who refused to acknowledge the whigs as "Rulers." He had not taken the oath of allegiance to the state because in his own words he "hoped god would keep him from the marke of the Beast." Daniel insisted that the Revolution had no binds on him, "for he never had justice Done him from the States . . . and [that] he was free from them and the Devil might join them Before he would." If forced to join the Continental army, he warned "he would Shoot the first officer that would offer to Command him and as many as would offer to Do it." If subjected to any "arbetary power," he would kill all who tried to enforce it, "and they might Depend on it" because "he was not a Subject of the united States nor under its Laws nor ought its Laws to have any Concern With him."[57]

This mixture of antagonism toward the Revolution and vague religious scruples about taking the oath apparently troubled many consciences. In Rowan County alone in August 1778 there were 577 persons listed in the court minutes who had refused to take the oath. So many people were incarcerated that court term "for Treason and other Offences against the Government of this State" that the militia had to be summoned to guard the jail, while those who "neglected to appear" before the court to offer an excuse for not taking the oath were ordered to be banished to "the West Indies or Europe."[58] James Glen of Surry County had taken the oath "Contrary to his Concience which he had Violated & that a time would soon come when the sons of Liberty woud be obliged to take as many Black oaths." Glen "did positively refuse paying his Taxes by assesment" until forced to do so, but he had demanded a "Receipt of his own Dictating in or-

---

[56] Bill of Indictment against Isaac Yates, Mar. 1779, ibid.

[57] Examination of Henry Daniel, Aug. 14, 1778, ibid.

[58] Rowan County, Minutes of the Court of Pleas and Quarter Sessions, 1773–86, August term, 1778, N.C. Div. Arch. and Hist.

der to shew General Howe that he Disapproved of the measures carried on by America."[59]

Disaffection among some religious dissenters was also infused with class resentment. In Anson County in 1776 James Childs, a New Light Baptist preacher, warned his communicants not to bear arms, "either Offensively or defensively," and threatened to excommunicate those who did. Childs declared: "Shew him a great man with half moon in his hatt and Liberty Rote on it and his hatt full of feather [and] he would Shew you a devil and the poor men was bowing and Sc[r]aping to them[;] they Lead them down to hell & that he did not value the Congress nor Commityer no more than a passell of Rackoon Dogs for he got his [commission?] from the king and the field offessers got their Commision from Hell or the Devil." Childs believed the British attack on Charleston would have "a good Effe[c]t" because it augured God's "Righteousness." He especially ridiculed the pretensions of those who aspired to be members of the ruling class: "When some upstarts got a Commission they were sweld up as a turkey Cock."[60]

Such forms of verbal insolence and threats soon gave way to more serious types of resistance. Interference with civil officers marked the first appearance of a kind of social banditry. The legislature debated a resolution in August 1778 regarding "divers disorderly persons in the Counties of Guilford, Anson, Cumberland and Bladen" who refused to pay taxes and harassed civil officers in the execution of their

[59] Complaint against James Glen, Mar. 22, 1778, Salisbury Dist. Superior Court, Criminal Action Papers. See also Deposition of Abraham Collins, Mar. 8, 1782, ibid., which reported that "old Perigreen Magness" hoped to persuade British Col. Patrick Ferguson to send forty dragoons in pursuit of Col. William Graham, who "was so troublesome among us the Neighbours could not get any peace."

[60] Deposition of Burlin Hamrod, July 8, 1776; Deposition of William Bennett et al., July 9, 1776; Deposition of Burwell Lanier et al., July 19, 1776, Military Coll., Revolutionary War, Box 5; Saunders, ed., *Colonial Records*, 10:699–700. An excellent discussion of class consciousness among religious dissenters is Rhys Isaac, "Evangelical Revolt: The Nature of the Baptists' Challenge to the Traditional Order in Virginia, 1765–1775," *William and Mary Quarterly*, 3d ser. 31 (1974):345–68.

duty.[61] In July 1779 Gov. Richard Caswell laid before the Council of State information concerning an association of loyalists in Edgecombe, Nash, Johnston, and Dobbs counties intent on resisting the draft and freeing draftees. The insurgents, moreover, treated warrants issued by civil magistrates with the "utmost contempt, and the officers or justices [were] grossly insulted or abused; that they had lately shot at and wounded several persons who were apprehending and Conveying to justice Deserters & Harbourers of Deserters from the Continental Army."[62] In 1781 Robert Rowan reported to Governor Burke that Cumberland County was plagued by "a set of Fellows that bid Defiance to the Civil Law, several horrid Murders and robberies having been committed there lately with impunity." But faced with such a dangerous set of men, no justice of the peace was "hardy" enough to issue warrants against the "Villains."[63] As late as February 1782, when David Fanning rampaged through Randolph County, the targets of his attack remained purposive. He and his band surprised a militia captain at his house who was also collector "of the public Tax," robbed him "of his Horses, Arms, Tax list and all the money he had collected, and threatened him with instant death if ever they catched him again in the execution of his duty."[64]

This sense of social injustice and retribution, reminiscent of the Regulation, underscored the fragility of whig authority in the backcountry and the gentry's continuing inability to fashion a cultural hegemony in which a docile "lower order" accepted the purportedly benign rule of the elite. In one area, however, whig acquisitiveness probably triumphed over agrarian rebelliousness. At the center of many backcountry disputes was the land itself, a subject that has been little stud-

[61] Clark, ed., *State Records*, 12:811.

[62] Meeting of Council of State, July 3, 1779, ibid., 14:319.

[63] Rowan to Burke, July 13, 1781, ibid., 22:545. See also Petition of John Crawford, Legislative Papers, Box 76. Crawford was sheriff of Anson County in 1779 but was not "able to Compleat the Collection of the Taxes for the year . . . by reason of the Troubles in the Late war."

[64] Col. John Collier to Burke, Feb. 25, 1782, Clark, ed., *State Records*, 16:203–4.

ied. While known loyalists or those who refused to take the oath and assume other obligations demanded by the Revolutionary regime suffered the confiscation of their lands and property, more subtle legal and extralegal pressures could also be employed to dispossess the disaffected of the choicest lands. The Revolution set off a land speculation frenzy on the frontier that sent Richard Henderson, Daniel Boone, and the gentry investors of the Transylvania Company into Kentucky and Tennessee and upper-class expansionist Virginians into the Ohio Valley.[65] In North Carolina between 1775 and 1777 unscrupulous whites took possession of lands on the Tuscarora Indian reservation in Bertie County by obtaining long-term leases at a pittance from the defenseless tribe. In the mountains the whigs' merciless retaliation against the British-inspired Cherokee set a precedent for white acquisition of their lands that continued until the final removal of 1838.[66] In the piedmont the Moravians witnessed an unprecedented land-grab. The General Assembly in 1777, as its first act, established a land office in each county wherein a person could enter land to which no proper title had been granted. Just before the Revolution the crown had temporarily suspended the issuance of land grants until the Lords Commissioners for Trade and Plantations promulgated new regulations.[67] To protect squatters but also to

[65] Archibald Henderson, "Richard Henderson and the Occupation of Kentucky, 1775," *Mississippi Valley Historical Review* 1 (1914):341–63; Marc Egnal, "The Origins of the Revolution in Virginia: A Reinterpretation," *William and Mary Quarterly*, 3d ser. 37 (1980):401–28.

[66] Laws of North Carolina, 1778, Clark, ed., *State Records*, 24:171–73; Robert L. Ganyard, "Threat from the West: North Carolina and the Cherokee, 1776–1778," *North Carolina Historical Review* 45 (1968):47–66; James H. O'Donnell III, *The Cherokees of North Carolina in the American Revolution* (Raleigh, 1976).

[67] Proclamation by Josiah Martin, June 28, 1773, Josiah Martin to Dartmouth, May 5, 1774, Saunders, ed., *Colonial Records*, 9:667–68, 989–94; King's Most Excellent Majesty in Council, Feb. 2, 1774, Clark, ed., *State Records*, 11:243–44. In Anson County one of the Regulators' principal grievances concerned land, especially court suits over delinquent quitrents and the engrossing of the best lands by the royal governor and his council's

make land available to "industrious People," the whigs moved quickly to reopen a land office.[68] Only citizens in good standing might apply, however. The Moravians noted that a "person who had not sworn allegiance to the country dared not enter land, not even that on which he lived; but one who had taken the Oath might enter the farm of a non-juror, of which some availed themselves and turned the rightful owner out of house and home, and he had no redress. Soon the Land Office in each County become a veritable Inquisition. If a man came to enter land he was asked whether he had taken the State Oath? If the answer was *Yes* he must be able to prove it twice and thrice; if the answer was *No* he was sent away with mockery and abuse." Many "who wished to be considered as belonging to the better class, planned to take advantage of the opportunity and fish in troubled waters, and to possess themselves of land belonging to the Brethren in Wachovia and elsewhere." Some openly entered land in their own names; "others hid behind some of the mob and were to share with them in pieces they had entered in their names."[69]

The whigs' predatory land policy sent a tremor through the backcountry. James Forbes, a blacksmith in Rowan County, learned that his friend Spears was about to lose land to Capt. John Johnston, a justice of the peace. Johnston had entered a claim for Spears's land, but Forbes wondered "what rite Johston had to the land." Johnston had informed Spears that he would not accept £500 for the claim, but Forbes did not think the magistrate entitled to five shillings. Spears wanted to "keep" the land "as it was" but seemed to realize that more powerful forces were at work than he could oppose. Forbes angrily denounced the whigs and admitted

---

favorites. The Anson Regulators asked for a preemption law guaranteeing squatters with improved lands in the Granville District first choice in purchasing their farms (Kay and Cary, "Class, Mobility, and Conflict," p. 143). Regarding the colony's chaotic land system see Ekirch, *"Poor Carolina,"* pp. 177–78.

[68] Laws of North Carolina, 1777, Clark, ed., *State Records*, 24:43–48.

[69] Fries et al., eds., *Records of Moravians*, 3:1204–6.

that "nothing Never Consern'd him so much as takeing that oath." In Forbes's opinion, there "was no way to bring Love and fear like Love an[d] whiping."[70]

Resistance to harsh whig discipline was perhaps nowhere more evident than in opposition to militia service and the draft. Indeed, Forbes gained a certain measure of revenge on Johnston when the Rowan County militia mustered in 1778. Col. Francis Locke and Captain Johnston both knew that with such a large body of disaffected in the county raising a quota for service in the Continental Line would be difficult. Locke resorted to holding musters at "private places" for the "purpose of balloting, instead of one General Muster as the Law requires." When Johnston attempted to administer the oath of allegiance at one muster, a boisterous tory "huzzaed for King George, and called aloud to the rest to follow him, whereupon about one hundred of the company, in a riotous turbulent manner withdrew, and would by no means take the oath." One of the disaffected, John Depoyster, damned "the blackjack which was the nicname they Gave the oath of Aleigence" and swore he would never muster under Johnston.[71]

Over the course of the summer of 1778 Johnston and Locke continued to hold private musters to raise their county's quota. Johnston quickly realized, however, that the majority of the inhabitants were loyalists and disaffected who would elect only their own as officers. He tried to strike a deal with the tories by offering "several fair and equitable proposals, to this effect: that if the Tory Division would send their propo[r]tion of men, he himself would turn out a volunteer and undertake to procure the remainder from among the Whiggs." The tories refused and proceeded to elect every officer, with James Forbes, Johnston's arch-enemy, to superintend. At another muster Locke denied the vote to several known tories, who were then promptly elected officers by the

[70] Examination of John Haggen, July 27, 1778, Salisbury Dist. Superior Court, Criminal Action Papers.

[71] Report of Joint Legislative Committee, Aug. 19, 1778, Clark, ed., *State Records*, 12:861–63; Examination of George Redman, July 27, 1778, Salisbury Dist. Superior Court, Criminal Action Papers.

rest of the company. The whigs declared the "balloting . . . irregular and illegal and . . . void." Locke and Johnston had tried to obtain their quota "by drawing . . .[draftees] as well from the Whiggs as from the Tories," but instead they found themselves "subject to the arbitrary determination" of the state's "inveterate enemies."[72]

Throughout the backcountry, opposition to the draft remained intense and bitter throughout the war. James Cheetwood of Tryon County chastised one militia officer for rounding up draftees: "It was a Damd purty Story that you are going about in this manner Disturbing your Neiborers."[73] The Salisbury district never did meet its quota for the draft. In 1781 Maj. John Armstrong reported that "a number of Toreys" had been forced into service but had deserted as soon as they received the bounty offered by the Revolutionary government. Half the men in Rowan County, Armstrong estimated, remained at home "without molestation."[74] "Tumults" were reported in Duplin County in 1781 as a result of the draft. There were so many "cursed Tories" or others who were "disaffected" in the county that only twenty-four men had shown up for the muster.[75]

If the oath did not offend a man's sensibilities and provoke open resistance to the Revolution, the draft did. "Fear of being called into the militia," the Moravians recorded in 1781, "has driven many to hide in the woods, and as they have nothing on which to live they resort to highway robbery, which is bringing the country into a pitiable condition."[76] Loyalists who submitted claims to the British government after the war complained acridly about the draft. Peter Blewer of Mecklenburg County "was molested by the Rebels" and "fined for not serving in the Militia." A veteran of

[72] Clark, ed., *State Records*, 12:861–63.

[73] Deposition of Richard Singleton, Feb. 15, 1779, Salisbury Dist. Superior Court, Criminal Action Papers.

[74] Maj. John Armstrong to Gen. Jethro Sumner, July 1, 1781, Clark, ed., *State Records*, 15:504–5.

[75] George Doherty to Sumner, June 22, 1781, ibid., pp. 490–91.

[76] Fries et al., eds., *Records of Moravians*, 4:1669.

Moore's Creek, Eli Branson "from March 1776 to October 1776 . . . never slept in any House—he was constantly in the Woods." He refused to take the oath in 1777, but a friendly justice in Chatham County gave him a certificate anyway; "he remained quiet for some time and then he was drafted to serve & refusing they [the whigs] sold 200 Acres of his Land to pay the Fine." Donald McDonald of Cumberland and Anson counties "was obliged to secrete himself early in the Dispute or he should have been obliged to take up Arms for the Americans." When he was drafted in 1780, he fled to South Carolina and joined Tarleton's Legion. Donald Shaw of Cumberland County was taken prisoner at Moore's Creek but allowed to return home. In 1777 he was drafted; "his none complyance to that or any of their Laws, render'd him so Obnoxious, that he was from that time in prison or sculking in Swamps &c untill the Arrival [of] Lord Cornwallis in March 1781."[77]

Years of frustration with whig rule also bred conspiracy. By 1779 William Holley of Anson County could no longer conceal his sympathies "for the king" or his contempt for the whigs, whom he regarded as "jackases." Holley's ill-fated plan was for the tories to attend the militia muster and seize control from the Liberty Men before they "ruin[ed] the Sittlement."[78]

The foothills of the Blue Ridge seemed particularly fertile for cabals, and the British in anticipation of their invasion of the South may have even encouraged this form of disaffection. Joseph Johnson of Burke County in 1778 tried to persuade his neighbors that he had a proclamation from the king to raise troops and to offer 150 acres of land, one-half crown per day, a $100 bounty upon reaching the British army, and a twenty-year exemption from paying taxes or

[77] Loyalist Claim of Peter Blewer, AO 13/138, English Records Coll., Box 3; of Eli Branson, AO 13/117, ibid.; of Donald McDonald, AO 12/99, ibid., Box 7; of Donald Shaw, AO 13/123, ibid., Box 11. See also Loyalist Claim of Andrew Hamm, AO 12/65, ibid., Box 6.

[78] Examination of Henry Harget, Nov. 3, 1779; Wade to Col. John Duncan, Nov. 13, 1779, Salisbury Dist. Superior Court, Criminal Action Papers.

rent for those who agreed to follow him to the Savannah River to link up with British troops. Johnson had reputedly sworn some eighty adherents to a secret oath. Part of his plan was to "disarm all those that would not join them" and to release prisoners held at Tryon Courthouse.[79] Two other Burke County conspirators were Ambrose Mills and John Perkins. Born in England, Mills settled in South Carolina and then moved to North Carolina around 1765. He joined the whig militia in the campaign against the Cherokee in 1776, but his fierce loyalism had grown to such proportions by 1780 that he was one of the nine tories executed at King's Mountain. Mills and Perkins planned to raise loyalist troops in 1778, punish the gentry, but treat the yeoman farmers mercifully: "Common Men of the Country party [were] to return to their former duty and obtain free pardon."[80] Perkins's role in the plot was evidently known as far east as Anson County, where Nathaniel Biven sought tory recruits in the conspiracy. Biven asserted: "The whole Unightet States was Rising in places to fight for the king of Grate Britan," but his recruits were "to Ly Nutral" until he signaled them. Biven kept a roster of tories disguised as a book of accounts, listing one person for a pound of tobacco, another for indigo, and so on. A yellow hat band identified the plotters to one another. According to Biven, John Perkins had enlisted 4,000 men who would rise "to Subdue the Liberty" on or around November 1, 1779.[81]

Undoubtedly the most bloodthirsty conspirators had confided their plans to Maj. John Walker, a deserter from the Sixth Regiment of South Carolina troops. Walker had lived with various tory sympathizers in the backcountry until he was apprehended in 1778. These cryptoloyalists had promised to secret him if he assisted "in killing & Destroying the Liberty Men in the frontiers of North & So Carolina." Walker

[79] Examinations of Conrad Reignhart, July 29, and Andrew Bolser, July 30, 1778, ibid. Compare with Crow, "Llewelyn Conspiracy."

[80] Examination of Thomas Crayton, July 28, 1778, Salisbury Dist. Superior Court, Criminal Action Papers.

[81] Examination of John Numan, Nov. 7, 1779, ibid.

was to recruit men and arms. Elias Brock, Sr., told Walker that "we hope to see the day that we shall ride to Our horses knees in Liberty Mens Blood & Guts." John French, Sr., believed "since we have beatten them so to the No ward we need not fear doing it here." He had laid up three or four months' supply of corn, flour, and provisions for the coming carnage, and he "hoped to be at the Scalping of the liberty Men, for taking his land from him tho' the Indians had Scalp'd some of the Scofelites." Charles Brock said that "he wou'd be damn'd if he didn't hope to kill some hundreds himself; for the liberty party were all turning Romans." Others in the conspiracy admitted to being "Scofelite" at heart, although they "passed" as "Liberty Men."[82]

Not all loyalists were content merely to make plans for revenge. From time to time the legislature had to send light horse troops into rebellious areas to "Seize and Secure and even . . . remove to places at a distance from their places of residence, all disaffected persons, who not satisfied with entertaining Sentiments inimical to the Country may be justly suspected of a disposition of carrying those Sentiments into execution." The lawmakers enjoined sheriffs to summon posses "to disarm all persons from where any Injury to the publick safety is to be apprehended." In 1779 Gen. Griffith Rutherford reported to Governor Caswell that "our Frontiers are greatly distressed with Tories and Robbers in Burke. There is a Band that rob publicly all the friends of the common cause, and openly declare they will not injure the subjects of his Majesty. They have committed many depredations and continue in the practice." With so many sympa-

[82] Examination of Maj. John Walker, Aug. 4, 1778, ibid. The Scoffelites were a group of tories under Joseph Scoffel in the South Carolina backcountry who had risen in late 1775. Scoffel was a key figure in the complex interplay of social groups along the South Carolina frontier during the 1760s and 1770s. He had led anti-Regulator forces in the 1760s in an attempt to quell Regulator excesses against hunters, vagrants, and bandits. He also had good relations with Indians. In the Revolution his followers were regarded as "white Indians," that is, hunters and banditti (Rachel N. Klein, "Choosing Sides: Americans and Loyalists in the South Carolina Backcountry, 1775–79" [Paper presented at the Forty-sixth Annual Meeting of the Southern Historical Association, Atlanta, November 1980]).

thizers in the mountain counties, Rutherford confessed, it was impossible to apprehend them. Some had been jailed, but by "some means or other every person confined in Gaol are set at liberty; a most notorious horse thief and person guilty of high treason lately made his escape from the Gaol of the District. It must be that they have friends convenient who give them aid. . . . In what manner to proceed against these Robbers and Tories I know not."[83]

The arrival of the British in the South upset the uneasy equilibrium in the backcountry. Whig authority, which had never been unchallenged, crumbled. With the British army poised on the North Carolina border in 1780, loyalist insurgency rose dramatically. Wearied by years of whiggish oppression, disaffected North Carolinians looked to the British for protection and the restoration of order and stability. Longtime loyalists and angry new converts saw in the movements of the British army the means of revenge. Others, like Robert Weir of Lincoln County, who had once been considered "a good Liberty Man," simply switched sides. As Weir, who traded horses with the British and plundered whigs, cynically explained: "Let who wood Rain King he would be subject, [by] which . . . he meant he'd be with the Strongest party." Cornwallis, aware of soaring loyalist hopes, tried to delay a premature rising. He sent emissaries into the backcountry who told the tories "in the strongest Terms that they should attend to their Harvest, prepare Provisions, & remain quiet until the King's Troops were ready to enter the province." Instead, "a considerable Number of loyal Inhabitants of Tryon County, encouraged & headed by a Coll. Moore, whom I know nothing of, & excited by the sanguine Emissaries of the very sanguine & imprudent [loyalist] Lieut. Colo. [John] Hamilton, rose . . . without Order or Caution, and were in a few days defeated by General Rutherford with some Loss." Similarly, Col. Samuel Bryan, "altho' he had promised to wait for my orders, lost all patience, and rose

[83] Resolution by House of Commons, Feb. 12, 1779, Legislative Papers, Box 24; Rutherford to Caswell, June 28, 1779, Clark, ed., *State Records*, 14:132–33.

with about 800 Men on the Yadkin, and by a difficult and dangerous March joined Major M'Arthur on the borders of Anson County."[84]

The loyalist infection rapidly spread to other counties. Tory insurgents were reported in Bladen, Cumberland, Anson, Chatham, Randolph, Surry, Rowan, Mecklenburg, and Lincoln counties by 1781. In Surry County the tories killed the sheriff, surely a symbolic as well as vengeful act. As they "passed they plundered, disarmed and paroled many of the Inhabitants, and determined to imprison and carry off others who had been more obnoxious." Though characterized as "Banditts and Plunderers," these tories included men of property and local standing such as Samuel Bryan of Rowan County and Gideon Wright of Surry.[85]

One Revolutionary veteran from Lincoln County recalled that after the American defeat at Camden in August 1780, the loyalists gained "more confidence and they became more bold, more daring, and more numerous." Supported by detached British units, the tories committed various crimes "almost with impunity." He admitted: "They established posts in various places and for a while seemed to have subjugated the country." In his own militia company only eight members remained "good and true" whigs; "the rest had joined the Tories." This situation persisted into 1781, when Cornwallis's

---

[84] Deposition of Ann Beatty, Sept. 8, 1781, Salisbury Dist. Superior Court, Criminal Action Papers; Cornwallis to Clinton, June 30, 1780, P.R.O. CO 5/100, British Records Coll.; Cornwallis to Clinton, July 14, 1780, Clark, ed., *State Records*, 14:867–68. See also Josiah Martin to Secretary of State, Aug. 18, 1780, Clark, ed., *State Records*, 15:55.

[85] Sumner to Gates, Oct. 4, 1780, Maj. Mark Armstrong to Sumner, Oct. 7, 1780, Gen. William Smallwood to Gates, Oct. 16, 1780, Clark, ed., *State Records*, 14:667, 675–76, 698–99. See also Petition of Charles McLean (Feb. 1780), William R. Davie to Caswell, Aug. 29, 1780, Proceedings of the Board of War, Sept. 18, 1780, Col. Francis Locke to Sumner, Sept. 23, 1780, Sumner to Gates, Oct. 13, 1780, Proceedings of the Board of War, Oct. 17, Nov. 15, 1780, John Ramsey to Burke, Apr. 13, 1781, Senate Journal, July 8, 1781, William Loftin to Sumner, July 20, 1781, Butler to Burke, Sept. 1, 1781, ibid., 15:213, 22:776, 14:381–82, 775, 692, 427, 464, 15:437, 17:849–50, 15:555, 22:584.

capture "disheartened" the tories.[86] Whig partisan William Davidson agreed with that assessment and the impact of Horatio Gates's retreat from Camden: "The effects of it are, in my opinion, worse than those of his defeat. It has frightened the ignorant into despair, being left without cover or support to defend themselves against the whole force of the enemy."[87]

Throughout the backcountry people who had been neutral suddenly had to choose sides with the British army on the march and loyalists in arms. Some deserted their farms and fled to the British "with all their baggage & cattle," leaving behind large fields of corn and wheat. Others, who in past years might have joined the whig militia, stayed home because they were "very Loth to go Against the British and Leive their Families Exposed to a set of Villains, who Dayley threattains their Destruction."[88] Governor Burke in a message to the General Assembly described the "peculiar distress from the internal war which is raging with intemperate fury in some parts of the State between the well affected and the ill affected Citizens and which has produced enormities dangerous in their example to all good Government, and cruelly fatal to Individuals." The Moravians commented on how the war made the "spirit of men . . . more and more debased. Many a lad in his native simplicity, went into the field with the Militia, and a few months later came back a thorough scamp. This made life harder and harder, for men became more and more brutal. This also applied to the Tories." Renegade bands of highwaymen, unconnected "with any party, but . . . independent . . . for the Special purpose of stealing and plundering," appeared.[89]

[86] Pension Claim of William Armstrong, May 20, 1833, ibid., 22:108.

[87] Davidson to Sumner, Sept. 18, 1780, ibid., 14:773.

[88] Lt. Col. C. Porterfield to Gates, Aug. 3, 1780, Col. Thomas Brown to Gen. Alexander Lillington, Feb. 19, 1781, ibid., 14:528–29, 15:423. See also John Rutledge to Nash, May 24, 1780, ibid., 14:823.

[89] Message of Burke to General Assembly, June 29, 1781, ibid., 15:498; Fries et al., eds., *Records of Moravians*, 3:1035–36; Andrew Armstrong to Burke, Aug. 28, 1781, Clark, ed., *State Records*, 22:1047–48. See also Fries et al., eds., *Records of Moravians*, 4:1536, 1564–65.

The ferocious backcountry war waged in North Carolina involved complexities often distant from the struggle between Great Britain and the courthouse and statehouse Revolutionaries. What was at stake fundamentally was "home rule." In its attempts to wring order out of indiscipline and hegemony out of rebelliousness, the whig oligarchy faced the intricate interplay of cultural, ethnic, and class tensions in which agrarian rebels fought for family, farm, and political autonomy. Because the loyalists adopted guerrilla tactics to resist, whigs labeled them thieves, but even the Moravians could distinguish between loyalists and freebooters. Loyalists contested whigs for mastery of local resources such as arms, grain, and livestock. Whigs had the purported sanction of government; loyalists only the sanctity of self-defense. Whereas the whigs were insatiable in their demands for supplies and arms, the loyalists, though not above reproach, frequently tried to discriminate between friend and foe in retaliating against whig expropriations. In the eyes of the state, of course, such resistance constituted banditry and disorder that had to be quashed. For loyalists, however, their insurgency carried genuine social import and only concomitantly reflected larger questions of political partisanship. They were attempting to protect their homes and property from theft by the state, to avenge past whig offenses, and to deny the Revolutionary government and its army the means to assure their ultimate suppression. In this struggle for control of local resources the loyalists achieved a measure of credibility and a political and military power which the whigs could not afford to ignore and which the British army carelessly squandered.

Provisioning the British and American armies was both a military and a civil problem. In North Carolina the two sides competed for increasingly scarce resources. Nathanael Greene preferred "fresh Provisions" to allow his army to move freely without "the great inconvenience of a multitude of Carriages, which are necessary for transportation when an Army is subsisted upon salted Provisions." Consequently, he wanted cattle rounded up, penned, and then forwarded weekly "in droves." Cornwallis faced similar problems and employed a commissary of captures, a commissioner of sequestered estates, and black camp followers to supply his army.[90] These systems did not work well for either side. British officers frequently found areas of "the country . . . So barren that it is impossible to find provisions for a Sufficient number of men." Whig general Jethro Sumner complained to Governor Nash that he had to employ one third of his troops "in beating out wheat, at different farms for the subsistence of the Camp, not a beef secured, the sole dependence is taken from the wood or farms near Camp." At one point he had collected 300 cattle, "Tory Property," but they had been driven from his brigade without his permission. William R. Davie, Greene's commissary, explained how the two opposing forces finally resolved their mutual problem: "The troops of both armies took what they wanted without ceremony or accountability, and used it without measure or economy; an indifference common to all armies in similar situations, produced by the impression, that perhaps the next day these resources may be in the hands of the Enemy."[91]

The Revolutionary government as a matter of policy attempted to punish loyalists and neutralists by seizing their grain, arms, and livestock. In September 1780 one Moravian reported that after "the so-called Tories" rose to commit "deeds of violence to those by whom they had formerly suffered," the whigs called out the militia, "who scoured all the country, pressing horses, arms and provisions and living *at discretion* in various places. We had frequent visits from them, but no pay." Produce from the tories' farms was assigned "to wandering bands of militia for their free use. As these were scattered in rather large parties, and the leader of each was

[90]Greene to Burke, Aug. 12, 1781, Clark, ed., *State Records*, 15:607; Franklin and Mary Wickwire, *Cornwallis: The American Adventure* (Boston, 1970); Jeffrey J. Crow, "What Price Loyalism? The Case of John Cruden, Commissioner of Sequestered Estates," *North Carolina Historical Review* 58 (1981):215–33; idem, *The Black Experience in Revolutionary North Carolina* (Raleigh, 1977), pp. 73–76.

[91]Lt. Col. Robert Gray to Cornwallis, Sept. 30, 1780, P.R.O. 30 11/64, British Records Coll.; Sumner to Nash, Sept. 3, 1780, Clark, ed., *State Records*, 15:410–11; Blackwell P. Robinson, ed., *The Revolutionary War Sketches of William R. Davie* (Raleigh, 1976), pp. 37–38.

the judge, acts of violence occurred in many places."[92]

Throughout the fall of 1780 the whigs ordered military foragers to gather provisions from disaffected communities. One Continental colonel reported to General Gates "that there is the greatest plenty of grain and Cattle on Hogan's Creek; But, as the people in that Settlement are disaffected," the Guilford County commissioner dared "not venture among them without an armed force to protect and assist him, and that no provisions have ever been brought from that quarter." The North Carolina Board of War ordered troops into the upper Cape Fear valley counties to confiscate loyalist property. Alexander Martin, member of the board, noted: "We are informed there are great Quantities of Corn belonging to the Tories now, or late in arms against us especially those on the Yadkin Pee dee & Rocky rivers—which by forfeiture belong to the State." Gen. William Smallwood admitted to General Gates, "Our principal Subsistence has been brought in by Detachments, which they took from the disaffected who have gone over to the Enemy." He continued: "Plundering prevails to an amazing degree, by Persons who go under the denomination of Volunteers." Smallwood wanted to deploy troops along the Pee Dee River, the Waxhaws, and Lynch's Creek "for [the] purpose of . . . suppressing Tories or Covering such supplies as might be Necessarily drawn from the Settlements below and on the Peedee." His idea was to secure supplies "from a fertile and disaffected part of the Country" while depriving the British of the same "resources." Whigs approaching these areas of the backcountry wisely treated them as enemy territory. A light horse officer in the Pee Dee region reported that his band had swept "through the Tory Settlements" in Cumberland County all the way to the Montgomery County line, "made Some Tory Prisoners and obliged a Gang of 45 Tory Thieves, under

[92] Frederic W. Marshall to Joachim H. Andresen, Sept. 1780, Fries et al., eds., *Records of Moravians*, 4:1901–2. The confiscation laws passed by the General Assembly in 1777, 1778, and 1779 were sufficiently vague to allow a broad interpretation of what was subject to seizure: lands, tenements, and "moveable property" (Clark, ed., *State Records*, 24:123–24, 209–14, 263–68).

command of a Tim Guard of Deep River (Said to have been one of Burgoynes Horse) to disperse, they had that day crossed the River with intentions to plunder all before them." The officer stated that the tories would have been captured "but for the disaffection of the Inhabitants who gave to them . . . wrong information as to the Road they had taken." He proposed to establish posts on the Pee Dee River to harass the enemy and to "collect Beeve & Hogs from the South Side the River." In November 1780 Alexander Martin ordered county commissioners to confiscate all grain and livestock from plantations whose owners had fled either to join or escape the British, "leaving a Sufficiency where Women and Children are left for their Support." Gen. William Caswell, wishing to continue the retributive policies of Governor Nash, eagerly informed Governor Burke in August 1781 that "500 to 1000 Head of Cattle & 200 or 300 Sheep may be had from those in actual service against us if your Excellency should think proper to order them off."[93]

In the face of the whig government's rapaciousness, controlling the balance of arms in a locality proved crucial. As early as 1776 Guilford County whigs seized the arms of the disaffected and "gave them to the honest Whig party that had none." Following one tory insurrection in Surry County the whigs commanded all "deluded people" to "deliver up all their Arms, Ammunition, Shot pouches, Horses, Saddles, Bridles, &c." that had been seized from the "good people of the . . . County" or that had been used against them. Military officers who bemoaned the lack of arms for their troops discovered that the "inhabitants secrete them, either owing to their being disaffected or their fearfuln[e]ss of their not

[93] Col. Ralph Falkner to Gates, Sept, 25, 1780, Clark, ed., *State Records*, 14:648; Alexander Martin to Col. Thomas Polk, Nov. 4, 1780, Military Coll., Revolutionary War, Box 11; Smallwood to Gates, Oct. 31, and Nov. 16, 1780, Clark, ed., *State Records*, 14:720, 741–42; Gen. H. W. Harrington to Board of War, Oct. 24, 1780, Order by Alexander Martin, Military Coll., Revolutionary War, Box 1; Caswell to Burke, Aug. 27, 1781, Clark, ed., *State Records*, 15:627. See also Alexander Martin to Harrington, Oct. 11, 1780, John Penn to Thomas Taylor, Sept. 21, 1780, Samuel Spencer to Board of War, Oct. 12, 1780, Military Coll., Revolutionary War, Box 1.

being returned, tho' every assurance is given them." When the tories rebelled, one of the first measures they took was to disarm the whigs. In the summer of 1781 David Fanning gathered about 130 loyalists near the Haw River. According to one report, "They are not so much charged with Plundering as disarming, and, as they say, informing the People. And what is somewhat Strange, altho' the General Complaint is that there is no Arms to oppose them, they seldom fail of finding Arms in every House they go to. They have at present an uninterrupted Command between Deep and Haw River."[94]

The whig impressment of provisions, which often amounted to little more than state-sanctioned plundering, also ensured a stinging response. The Moravians carefully contrasted the behavior of tories who "came . . . during the night to get bread to eat, but were very mannerly" with the whig militiamen who "ate and drank as they pleased" and seized oats, pottery, corn, and whatever came to hand.[95] Gen. Stephen Drayton decried the "unjust, impolitical, & unlawful" procedures of commissary officers who, "under the pretence of being on duty . . . capriciously" selected farms to quarter their men and horses and to collect supplies. Such evils undermined confidence in the whig government, wasted much-needed provisions, and squandered the "Labor of the Farmer . . . in the *name* of the Public, without recompensation to the *One* or benefit to the *Other*," thereby encouraging and keeping "alive that Maroding Spirit, already too prevalent." William R. Davie echoed a similar concern when he admitted that "our *money* and promissory *notes* are called *state tricks* and will be no longer receiv'd, so that I have been obliged to procure the necessary supplies by impressment and contribution." So-called tory banditry thus became an effort to recover impressed provisions. One military officer

[94] Pension Claim of James Martin, Council of Militia Officers, Surry County, Oct. 19, 1780, Gen. William Caswell to Burke, Aug. 20, 1781, Armand Armstrong to Burke, Aug. 20, 1781, Clark, ed., *State Records*, 22:147, 15:123–24, 22:568–69, 567–68. See also John Luttrell to Burke, Sept. 1, 1781, ibid., 22:585.

[95] Fries et al., eds., *Records of Moravians*, 4:1674, 1629. See also ibid., pp. 1561–62, 1676.

in Hillsborough feared sending public stores to General Greene without "a proper guard . . . as there will be the greatest danger on the road from the Tories, who are frequently doing mischief to the Westward."[96]

Above all the tories were protective of their livestock, which constituted such an important part of their property. The Carolina Bays, in which cattle and hogs flourished, were precisely the areas where the contest to safeguard or confiscate the valuable animals became the fiercest. Daniel McNeil of Cumberland County, making a loyalist claim after the war, recalled that "almost all his Cattle (84 Head) were taken by a Commissary of the Rebels for . . . the use of his army." Matthew Ramsey, a Chatham County militia captain and then Continental captain, was sent into the Scottish settlements in 1780 to collect provisions, but he found that the Scots were "all lying out. . . . I have been at fifty houses & not found one Man at home." Ramsey wanted them to help round up cattle for the American army and win General Gates's leniency, "which is more than the Rascalls Deserves." Instead, whenever Ramsey collected steers, the tories came and released them. "I think they are the worst enemy that we have at this present," declared Ramsey. "All their Studey Seems to be is to prevent the army from being Supply'd with provisions. They are a Lawless Gang. it is impossible to catch them among so many Swamps." He had collected fifty more steers but dared not start them for Gates's army because the tories were sure to rescue the animals. Outraged and frustrated, Ramsey urged whigs to lay the Scots' "cottages waste, as they are only a harbour for theives & Tories. A party of Mollatous & Negrous almost kill'd a man." In the spring of 1782 another Continental officer attempting to collect cattle for the army found "that the South Tories threaten taken the Cattle from him in case he offered to drive them." The tories, however, proved willing to supply the British army with beef when it was encamped at Wilmington in 1781. Ramsey, who

[96] Drayton to Burke, July 6, 1781, Clark, ed., *State Records*, 15:511–13; Robinson, *William R. Davie*, pp. 90–136, quotation on p. 124; Maj. A. Tatum to Sumner, May 10, 1781, Clark, ed., *State Records*, 15:457. See also Harrington to Gates, Oct. 10, 1780, Richard Caswell to Gates, June 20, 1780, Clark, ed., *State Records*, 14:683–84, 856.

was briefly captured by the loyalists, warned "them they should answer for their conduct at a future day. Their answer was they would, but not to Rebels."[97] Even the Moravians tried to resist the whigs' onerous demands for horses and cattle: "We hear that horses are to be pressed, therefore our horses shall be put out of sight so far as possible." The Moravians resented such "forcible collections." Later they sent away their cattle because "men were shooting and killing them in the woods."[98]

Dubbed banditti and thieves by the whigs, loyalist insurgents merely retaliated in kind and employed the same tactics that whigs had directed toward them for more than four years. Buoyed by the presence of the British army, the loyalists rode through the countryside seizing guns, saddles, swords, and horses and boasting that they would be "masters of the Country Soon."[99] But even as infamous a plunderer as David Fanning, whose exploits included the capture of Governor Burke, his council, members of the legislature, and Continental officers at Hillsborough in September 1781, practiced a rudimentary discrimination in choosing victims. The loyalists' avenging angel, Fanning sought to punish whigs who had shown special violence toward "Friends of Government." He burned whig plantations, plundered whig

[97] Loyalist Claim of Daniel McNeil, AO 12/35, English Records Coll., Box 9; Matthew Ramsey to Gates, Aug. 9, 1780, Lt. Col. J. Leonard to Col. Henry Young, Mar. 21, 1782, Col. Joseph Hawkins to Nash, June 17, 1781, Clark, ed., *State Records*, 14:543–45, 16:553, 15:487. See also Lt. Col. John Ervin to Gates, Aug. 2, 1780; Harrington to Gates, Sept. 25, 1780, Clark, ed., *State Records*, 14:552, 652–53.

[98] Fries et al., eds., *Records of Moravians*, 4:1541–42, 1551, 1553, 1578, 1622, 1650.

[99] McLean to the General Assembly, Feb. 6, 1779, J. Rand to Burke, July 30, 1781, Brown and Robeson to Burke, July 30, 1781, Burke to Gen. Allen Jones, Mar. 23, 1782, Brown to Lillington, Mar. 24, 1782, Col. Thomas Kenan to Lillington, Mar. 27, 1782, Clark, ed., *State Records*, 14:261–62, 22:1044–46, 1043–44, 16:558, 245–46, 250. Regarding the backcountry civil war see Don Higginbotham, *The War of American Independence: Military Attitudes, Policies, and Practice, 1763–1789* (New York, 1971), pp. 360–64.

families, and hanged or shot those most "assiduous in assisting the rebels." Though undeniably callous and ruthless, Fanning singled out the whig gentry for revenge, men who had led the militia or exercised political power against loyalists. Fanning's contempt for this class of tory oppressors was evident when, after a rampage through Randolph County in March 1782, he boldly, even triumphantly, appeared at the Randolph County Courthouse on the "election day to appoint Assembly men . . . in order to see the gentlemen representatives; On their getting intelligence of my coming they immediately scattered; I prevented their doing any thing that day." Of the cruelty of Fanning's band one whig wrote: "It would make you almost shed tears to see the barbarity of them wherever they go." Though outnumbered, he vowed "to lose" his "life in the attempt" to stop Fanning. Claimed another, "They are not satisfied with the lives of men but fall to cutting and barbarously murdering women."[100]

Confronted with such massive resistance and disorder, the Revolutionary government searched for a means to quell the rebellion and restore its sovereignty in the backcountry. The whig gentry adopted the simple expedient of drafting the disaffected at gunpoint. This method of pacification accomplished several purposes. First, it allowed the whig oligarchy to reassert its power and position of preeminence in the locality. Second, by reaffirming deferential patterns of authority and obeisance, it provided a thin veneer of cultural hegemony in which the elite defined acceptable types of behavior and set minimum standards for political toleration. Third, it safeguarded the loyalists against further violence. Fidelity to the Revolutionary cause impinged little, if any, on the decision.

Col. Thomas Wade of Anson County perhaps best exem-

[100] "Narrative of Fanning," 1790, Capt. Joseph Rosser to Maj. Roger Griffith, Feb. 28, 1782, Griffith to Butler, Mar. 2, 1782, Clark, ed., *State Records*, 22:205, 212–13, 217, 220–21, 16:212–13. Fanning's later difficulties in Canada are detailed in Carole Watterson Troxler, "'To Git out of a Troublesome Neighborhood': David Fanning in New Brunswick," *North Carolina Historical Review* 56 (1979):343–65.

plified this approach to pacification. In late 1780 Wade undertook his own rehabilitation program to discipline the disaffected. He pursued "outlying torys" and offered them a three-month parole if they agreed to serve three months with his "Voluntiars." Obtaining promises of "Good Behavior During the War" from the "common men," Wade asserted he had "upwards of one hundred of those deluded peoples now under arms, and Some of them I have tryed in my Regment and think they will make Good Soldiers." Many of them were "pore and [had] Large familys to maintain." He believed they would become "useful members" of the community. Besides, he mused, it was "better then to Kill them." The affairs of the region had been "very Gloomy" before Wade's program. His method of persuasion had proved compelling: "They are Some of as good melitia as any in the State, but before I could bring the Inhabitents of those Countys to what I now have them we had to Kill in a few Outliers, which Ansured a good End." Variants of Wade's pacification program were repeated elsewhere in the backcountry. After the battle of King's Mountain, when the whig officers threatened to kill every tory prisoner, the anxious loyalists showed "their fidelity by act of Service to their Country," that is, they agreed to join the Continental army. The Moravians recorded: "We hear that most of the captured Tories who live in this section have been released, on condition that they serve six months in the American army. Before beginning service they were allowed to go home and wash their clothes." Shifting allegiance and accommodation often proved the only means of survival for the disaffected. Finally, on December 25, 1781, acting governor Alexander Martin officially sanctioned the policy by offering clemency to "deluded" citizens who revolted and took up arms against the state and found "themselves at last deserted by our feeble and despairing enemies—left unprotected to the vengeance of the State, ready to inflict those punishments due to their crimes." To prevent an "unnecessary effusion of the blood of Citizens," he set March 10, 1782, as the date for tories to surrender and enlist in Continental battalions for twelve months. To be excluded, however, were all "officers, leading men, and persons of this class guilty of murder, robbery, and house burning."[101]

Martin's Christmas proclamation showed more whig vindictiveness than Christian charity, for neither side could cleanse its hands of the atrocities perpetrated on people and property. David Fanning chided the whigs for such disingenuousness: "There never was a man who has been in Arms on either side but what is guilty of some of the above mentioned crimes, especially on the rebel side."[102]

Other whigs and tories, less truculent and more desperate for peace, sought grounds for conciliation and negotiation. In July 1781 loyalist leaders in Cumberland and Bladen counties approached whig militia officers about negotiating a truce, to which one replied with promises of "amicable Terms." The loyalists sought "a cessation of Arms" and pledged to "remain quiet" if a "Treaty" were concluded. Local whigs, surveying "the situation of the Counties, surrounded on all sides with Enemies, . . . thought it to the interest of the friends of the Country to endeavour by some instrument of writing to tie their hands, and in some Measure trust to their Honor for our safety."[103]

Renewed hostilities, Cornwallis's surrender at Yorktown,

[101] Wade to Gates, Nov. 23, 1780, Mark Armstrong to Gates, Nov. 19, 1780, Clark, ed., *State Records*, 14:750–51, 744–45; Fries et al., eds., *Records of Moravians*, 4:1576; Proclamation of Alexander Martin, Dec. 25, 1781, Clark, ed., *State Records*, 17:1049. See also Richard Caswell to Nash, July 31, 1780, Davidson to Nash, Oct. 22, 1780, Butler to the Board of War, Nov. 4, 1782, Petition of John Kimbrough, Feb. 4, 1782, Clark, ed., *State Records*, 15:11, 127, 16:663, 22:612; Bill of Indictment against Kimbrough, Mar. 1782, Salisbury Dist. Superior Court, Criminal Action Papers; John Williams to Alexander Martin, June 27, 1782, Clark, ed., *State Records*, 16:345–47, 19:914–15. Regarding problems of recruitment of Continental soldiers in the South and reliance even on British deserters, see Higginbotham, *War of American Independence*, p. 394; Charles Royster, *A Revolutionary People at War: The Continental Army and American Character, 1775–1783* (Chapel Hill, 1979), pp. 320–27, 373–78.

[102] David Fanning to Burke, Feb. 29, 1782, Clark, ed., *State Records*, 16:205.

[103] James Emmett to Burke, July 19, 1781, Capt. Edward Winston to Burke, July 20, 1781, ibid., 22:548, 549–50.

and the British withdrawal from Wilmington decisively shifted the balance of power in favor of the whigs and doomed such conciliatory initiatives as those in the upper Cape Fear valley. By early 1782 David Fanning recognized that he could not succeed as a solitary agent of the crown's interests, denied the support and succor of the British army. Fanning, who later claimed he "subdued the greatest part of the Province" and returned it to the "protection" of the crown, therefore proposed the establishment of an independent loyalist state in North Carolina. Noting that "it has been daily the case that we have been distroying, one another's property to support and uphold our opinions," he sought amnesty for tories and a free zone or district into which whig forces could not enter: "Our request is from Cumberland twenty miles N. & S.; and thirty miles E. & W.: to be totally clear of your light Horse." Loyalists would withdraw into this district and retain their arms and property. If tories broke the peace, they would be apprehended and turned over to whig authorities. "If any of your party shall be catched plundering, stealing or murdering, or going private paths, with arms signifying as if they were for mischief," the tories might deal with them as they saw fit. "All public roads," Fanning proposed, were "to be travelled by any person, or company unmolested, if he behave himself as becomes an honest man." The guerrilla leader further insisted, "All back plundering shall be void; as it is impossible to replace or restore all the plunder on either side." His loyalist province within the state would also enjoy "free trade with any port with wagons, or horseback without arms." Fanning chose Philip Alston, whom he had defeated and captured in August 1781, to deliver the proposal to civil and military authorities in Hillsborough.[104]

The whigs never seriously entertained Fanning's audacious peace plan and proposal for dual sovereignty. South Carolina had attempted to reach a similar agreement with its disaffected, with disturbing consequences for North Carolina. Francis Marion granted neutrality to the loyalist settle-

[104] "Narrative of Fanning," 1790, ibid., pp. 218–19. See also Loyalist Claim of Archibald McDugald, AO 13/121, English Records Coll., Box 8.

ments along the Pee Dee River and its tributaries. In January 1782 a Bladen County whig reported that the "worst" of the tories still continued to "stand out and not surrender and . . . won't till they can be beaten or killed." About thirty had "gone over the South Line" into a settlement "under what they call a Truce of peace with General Marian, and there they are protected among the south Tories, and is constant[ly] coming over the line into Bladen, and does mischief such as robbing and stealing, and has shot at some men and cut and abused some with their swords." There were said to be 100 tories from different parts of North Carolina in Marion's truce settlement. In true guerrilla fashion, the tories took sanctuary in the South Carolina "neutral zone." Governor Burke vehemently protested the disastrous policy to Gov. John Mathews of South Carolina: "The predatory habits of the people here referred to, being originally outlaws, and since the War remorseless plunderers and murderers, make them an object of terror in their vicinity." Such people, Burke contended, were not entitled to "protection."[105]

Years of civil strife, Burke knew, had brought untidy complexities for the whigs. At the beginning of the war they could easily define loyalism as political opposition. But their policies of punitive military and social discipline, outright terror, and the expropriation of property had provoked an equally violent response from neutral and disaffected settlers, effectively converting them into loyalists. The loyalists, who resisted whig encroachments on land, crops, arms, and livestock and were regarded as banditti, robbers, and thieves by the whigs, fundamentally challenged certain assumptions about the nature of society's polity. Loyalists were no longer perceived simply as dissidents who were firmly located in society's hierarchical structure. They were, rather, an insidious force destructive of that structure and incapable of admission into the polity. Burke, an introspective political philosopher, reasoned that loyalists could not be citizens. Civil government, he believed, must be "Composed entirely of Citizens who own allegiance." In particular the governor ob-

---

[105] Robeson to Alexander Martin, Jan. 24, 1782, Burke to Mathews, Mar. 6, 1782, Clark, ed., *State Records*, 22:608, 16:218–19.

jected to General Greene's plans to treat the loyalist militia as parties subject to exchange with whig militia or Continental prisoners. Loyalists who had been "deceived by false presentations and misled by false hopes," had borne arms for the British, but had acted "agreeably to the Character of Soldiers," Burke asserted, might expect "mercy" from the state by surrendering to civil magistrates. Loyalist "criminals," on the other hand, could expect no such pardon. "It is our Misfortune," the governor explained to the general, "to have amongst us a large Settlement of People who have never thoroughly united with us, and who have always become very dangerous Instruments in the hands of the Enemy." The result had been "blood and Anarchy," Burke said; "numbers of Outlaws of every State have Collected into this, and even many deserters from both Armies. These under pretence of bearing Arms in British Interest Commit the most inhuman Barbarities and the most Attrocious Crimes. The Injured People are provoked by these Outrages into acts of desperate revenge and the Country is in many places filled with assassinations." No man, Burke argued, should "be deemed Militia of the Enemy." He continued: "Every Criminal will have that protection, be his Crime what may, and every bad member of Society will find an Impunity in taking arms with the Enemy and of Course will not be restrained from Crimes by the Laws or their Sanction." If there were any tories still devoted to the British, Burke insisted, they must be "discovered, Secured and finally removed." They must not remain in "peace in the heart of the Country and ready to attack" whenever the British gained a "peculiar advantage."[106]

---

[106] Burke to Greene, Mar. 28, 1782, ibid., 16:565–69. Under the 1783 "Act of Pardon and Oblivion" loyalists who had not accepted commissions from the king, been named in the confiscation acts, or committed murder, robbery, rape, or house burning were pardoned. As the victors, however, the whigs could apply a double standard to lawbreakers. Under another 1783 act whigs who had "committed sundry acts . . . not strictly agreeable to law, yet were requisite, and so much for the service of the public" were exempted from prosecution. Acts passed in 1782, 1785, and 1787 secured land titles for whigs who had purchased confiscated property and protected them from recovery suits by the former owners. Similarly, Governor Caswell in 1787 pardoned the slayers of Alexander Shannon, one of Fan-

Despite Burke's vision and hope for cultural hegemony, severe tensions continued to strain North Carolina society in the wake of the Revolution.[107] Hundreds of loyalists followed the British army into exile. Those who remained became the objects of violence, social ostracism, and political discrimination. The Moravians noted the sad fate of a backcountry settlement at Deep Creek in present-day Yadkin County: "The greater part of these German people have ruined themselves by hiding out or by going to the English, and although they are all at home now, and have surrendered themselves, they are very poor." At the meeting of the Bladen County court in the fall of 1782 a Continental officer "led a Mob of about thirty armed persons" into the courthouse and "furiously attacked" Archibald Maclaine, a conservative whig lawyer who was defending a tory. With the court totally disrupted, the "rioters" proceeded to march "about the Country armed under the color of apprehending Tories . . . to the great Terror of the Good Citizens of that part of the State." Gov. Alexander Martin reluctantly ordered the arrest of the Bladen rioters, among whom were several prominent whigs who had already "suffered too much." "However unpopular the decisions of our Courts may be for the present," Martin commented, "yet they must be supported or our boasted Liberty and government will be no more, and we shall sink into a worse Tyranny than that, which we have lately escaped."[108]

---

ning's "Banditti," who had been executed in 1781 after surrendering to the sheriff of Guilford County. Shannon's father as late as 1796 tried to bring charges against his son's murderers (see Laws of North Carolina, 1782, 1783, 1785, 1787, ibid., 24:424–29, 488–90, 730–31, 794–95; Salisbury Dist. Superior Court, Criminal Action Papers). E. P. Thompson discusses the ways in which English whigs used the law to mediate class relations to the advantage of the rulers and to extinguish lower-class agrarian rebelliousness in *Whigs and Hunters: The Origin of the Black Act* (New York, 1975).

[107] See Jeffrey J. Crow, "Slave Rebelliousness and Social Conflict in North Carolina, 1775 to 1802," *William and Mary Quarterly*, 3d ser. 37 (1980):79–102; Robert M. Calhoon, "A Troubled Culture: North Carolina in the New Nation, 1790–1834," in Jeffrey J. Crow and Larry E. Tise, eds., *Writing North Carolina History* (Chapel Hill, 1979), pp. 76–110.

[108] Fries et al., eds., *Records of Moravians*, 4:1812; Alexander Martin to

In 1785 paticularly rancorous election disputes centering on "whether the Disaffected Should have a free vote or not" inflamed the backcountry. Under a 1781 act all who had borne arms against the state were barred from voting. The disaffected along Drowning Creek in Bladen County, however, were determined to divide the county and form their own to escape the voracious tax demands of the whig merchants and planters along the Cape Fear River and in Elizabethtown. Several days before the August 1785 election Sheriff William McRee declared "that if they could keep the back Inhabitants from Electing their members . . . , the court would lay another tax for building the Court house & Jail, he said then he did not care much if they had a county so that the Court house & Jail was built." On the day of the election nearly 400 backwoods farmers assembled a mile from Elizabethtown and "drew their tickets in Order to Vote as soon as they went into town." When they arrived, however, the sheriff and one of the inspectors of the polls "determined not to receive any Vots from any people from the back part of the County," an area noted for its disaffection during the war. A violent quarrel ensued in which swords were brandished and threats exchanged. On account of such "outrages all the back people went away"; the "river party" had scared them off, though one observer maintained that "men who he knew to be good men that Never raised Arms Against the Country and some of them worthy Characters" had been denied the vote. Though one of the inspectors of the polls characterized the election as one "much Invested with prejudice," conducted with the "greatest Partiality," and undoubtedly "elegal and disagreeable to Law," the General Assembly upheld it.[109]

Similarly, in Anson and Richmond counties erstwhile loyalists were elected to the General Assembly in 1785. Under a 1784 act no person who had aided the British during the war

---

Captain Gillespie, Oct. 24, 1782, Alexander Martin to Greene, Nov. 1782, Maclaine to George Hooper, Dec. 16, 1783, Clark, ed., *State Records*, 16:716–17, 720, 991.

[109] House Journal, Dec. 21, 1785; Laws of North Carolina, 1784, ibid., 17:374–75, 683–84, 732–33; Depositions Regarding Election Disorders in Bladen County, Aug. 1785, Legislative Papers, Box 58.

could qualify for public office. A petition from Mecklenburg County excoriated the loyalists for their "usual Impudence" and "great Thirst for legislative & executive Authority." Declaring them "Enemies both from Principle and Practice," the Mecklenburg whigs said they had seen no "remarkable Proof" of the tories' "friendship as yet—but it rather appears from their continued oppositions to whiggish Measures, that they still view themselves as enemies, or as People whose Interest is something different from that of the Whigs." This lack of cohesion and integration into a homogeneous polity concerned the "Whig-citizens" of Anson County too. They had been willing to forgive "intestine Foes" who had assisted "British Tyrants," but "because we endeavour'd to Suppress the just resentment of the Whiggs against the Loyalists, to promote harmony and union in our country, . . . our moderation has been construed as a tacet acknowledgement that the men so lately in arms against us, were restored to the full rights and priviledges of citizens." They asked the House of Commons to deny a seat to the tory who had won "by a Small majority of Votes"—James Terry. Among the signers of the Anson petition was Thomas Wade. In a separate deposition Wade noted that Terry had sworn an oath in 1776 "against Taking up arms . . . for Religious Scruples." Another Anson whig, however, asserted that the newly elected assemblyman had come to his farm in the fall of 1782 "armed with a Gun Shotbagg and powderhorn, and that he used very warm language and said it was true that he . . . had been with the British, and had taken protection with and carried part of his property to them, and would do so again, if it was to do over again, and always seemed to [be] disaffected to the American Cause from the first of our Contest with the Court of Great Britain." The House Committee on Privileges and Elections agreed, for it declared Terry "unworthy of a Seat in the General Assembly" under a 1784 act disqualifying certain persons.[110]

---

[110] Petitions from Anson and Mecklenburg Counties, Depositions Regarding Election of James Terry. Legislative Papers, Boxes 59 and 60. Solomon Gross, who was elected from Richmond County, apparently was also not seated. According to Wade, Gross had been a tory captain at Moore's

Terry, with whom this essay began, was of course no stranger to electoral defeats. It was he who had rigged the election for the draft at Anson County Courthouse in 1778. The whigs had not forgotten his disaffection, but then neither had his friends and neighbors who after a decade of war and civil strife chose him to represent their interests in the General Assembly. Terry's strange odyssey, from putative religious neutral to disaffected militiaman, loyalist defector, and postwar assemblyman, symbolized the confused wartime experience of North Carolinians as well as the bitter internal conflicts that divided them. The whig oligarchy, no matter how tenuous its grip during the Revolution, had triumphed. But its triumph in one respect appeared incomplete. After nearly two decades of tensions and discord the ruling elite still had failed to extinguish lower-class resistance to its impositions and dominance. Cultural hegemony, as Governor Burke seemed to sense, remained as elusive in the 1780s as it had been in the 1760s.

Creek in 1776, yet Gross represented Montgomery County in the General Assembly of 1779. Terry had a curious political career. During the Regulator troubles he had been a deputy sheriff and had given testimony about those difficulties in 1770. Six years later he was called before the provincial congress and accused of loyalism, but he agreed to take the state oath. He seems to have been elected to the General Assembly in 1784 but does not appear to have taken his seat (Saunders, ed., *Colonial Records*, 10:930, 932; Clark, ed., *State Records*, 15:762–63, 17:290, 293, 307, 413–14, 19:717, 22:411).

EMORY G. EVANS

Trouble in the Backcountry

Disaffection in Southwest Virginia during the American Revolution

HISTORIANS HAVE LONG regarded Virginia, like Massachusetts, as a state in which support for the American Revolution was virtually unanimous. Though they concede that small pockets of loyalists existed in a few areas, a recent scholar expresses the prevailing view in finding that "the supporters of the Crown in Virginia possessed neither the numbers nor the leadership to jeopardize the existence of the Revolutionary movement there."[1] This position, while essentially correct, has nonetheless obscured the fact that the Revolutionary movement created considerable unrest in Virginia between 1776 and 1781, some of it far more serious than simple protests against draft laws, military service, and taxes. Most occurred in peripheral areas of the state—on the entire western frontier, in the Northern Neck, on the Eastern

A version of this paper was presented in December 1981 at the University of Maryland before the Washington Area Seminar on Early American History. Professor William Stanton of the University of Pittsburgh made helpful stylistic comments.

[1] Robert M. Calhoon, *The Loyalists in Revolutionary America, 1760–1781* (New York, 1973), p. 458. See also William H. Nelson, *The American Tory* (Oxford, 1961), pp. 110–18, Isaac S. Harrell, *Loyalism in Virginia: Chapters in the Economic History of the Revolution* (Durham, N.C., 1926), ch. 2, and, most recently, Adele Hast, *Loyalism in Revolutionary Virginia: The Norfolk Area and the Eastern Shore* (Ann Arbor, 1982).

Shore, and in the southeast.[2] In the far southwest in 1779 and 1780, it was clearly insurrectionary.

Virginians had always been closemouthed about public or private problems,[3] and their unwillingness to wash their dirty linen in public has long plagued historians. Yet during the war there was dirty linen in plenty as witness the laws passed during the war to prevent or control disaffection, disloyalty, and treason. Before the Declaration of Independence, legislation was already in force to deal with persons who attempted "to subvert the rights and liberties of the inhabitants" of Virginia. Offenders could be imprisoned and their estates seized. In the fall of 1776, after independence was declared, the assembly enacted further legislation, relating to lesser offenses. Treason, defined as levying war "against this commonwealth" or adhering "to the enemies of the commonwealth by open deed," was punishable by death. Laws dealing with nontreasonable crimes stated that any person who by "word, open deed, or act" maintained and defended "the authority, jurisdiction, or power, of the king or Parliament of Great Britain" or who "maliciously and advisedly" endeavored to "excite" citizens to resist the state government could be imprisoned up to five years or fined as much as £20,000. The next spring the legislature required an oath of allegiance of "all freeborn male inhabitants . . . above the age of 16 years." At the same time the governor, with the advice of the council, was empowered to call out the militia to "oppose . . . invasion or insurrection." After an invasion scare in the fall of 1777 the governor, council, and other officials were indemnified for removing or confining persons suspected of disloyalty.[4]

[2] Harrell, *Loyalism in Virginia*, pp. 50–65; Emory G. Evans, "Executive Leadership in Virginia, 1776–1781: Henry, Jefferson, and Nelson," in Ronald Hoffman and Peter J. Albert, eds., *Sovereign States in an Age of Uncertainty* (Charlottesville, Va., 1981); H. J. Eckenrode, *The Revolution in Virginia* (Boston, 1916), still remains the best overall account, both of loyalism and of the Revolution in the state.

[3] For example see William Nelson to John Norton, Sept. 6, 1766, Frances Norton Mason, ed., *John Norton & Sons, Merchants of London and Virginia . . . 1750 to 1795* (Richmond, 1937), p. 16.

[4] William Waller Hening, ed., *The Statutes at Large: Being a Collection of*

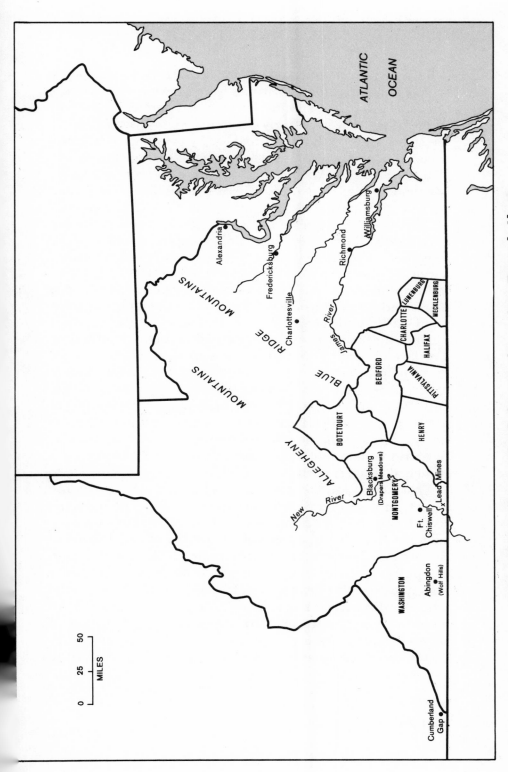

Southwestern Virginia during the Revolution

Because unrest increased in 1780, this legislation had to be replaced. Nontreasonable crimes were now more clearly defined, and the law specifically included women. The language of the new law clearly suggested what was going on in the state. Those "who by writing, or by printing, or by open preaching or by express words, shall" maintain that the "United States of America," or any state thereof, should be "dependent on the crown of Great Britain or on the British parliament" faced fines of up to £100,000 and imprisonment of up to five years. The law also covered persons who acknowledged themselves to be subjects of George III or who suggested that the king had "power or jurisdiction" within Virginia, as well as those who attempted to persuade others to "withdraw" their allegiance to that state or the United States and instead promise "allegiance to the king or parliament." Even endeavoring to "dissuade or discourage" enlistment in the army or service in the militia could be punished. The law went on to proscribe Virginians who, in the event of invasion, did "not attempt to withdraw" from British authority or advised anyone "to entertain . . . one or more of the British enemy." Wishing "health, prosperity, or success," in any way, to George III was a crime. And to make certain that no one escaped the net, "every counsellor, aider, abettor, or procurer of any offender against this act" was "adjudged a principal" subject to the same punishment as the offender.[5]

That same year the governor and council were given the power, in case of invasion or insurrection, to hold "disaffected persons" in "close confinement" or remove them to such places as "may best guard against the effect of their influence and arts to injure this community." Martial law was to be applied to those who, among other things, acted as guides and spies for the British or furnished them with supplies. The executive could also call out "troops of horse" to control "mutiny or riot" instigated "by the arts of the enemy joined by disaffected persons," a provision that was ordinarily directed toward resistance against recruitment efforts for the

---

All the Laws of Virginia . . . , 13 vols. (Richmond, etc., 1809–23), 9:101–6, 130–32, 168, 170–71, 281–83, 291–97, 373–74.

[5] Ibid., 10:268–70.

army. Further, the law provided that any three judges of the General Court could meet at any place in the state to hear and determine all "treasons and misprisions of treason," as well as lesser crimes that were "injurious to the independence of America." If the problems were "west of the Blue Ridge mountains," the governor and council could appoint a "commission" of "three or more persons learned in the law" to hear the cases. These special courts were to have the same authority as the General Court.[6]

In 1781 the powers of the executive to control such activity were extended even further. A British army was in the state, and the number of petitions from patriots suggests a rising impatience with disaffection. The 340 signers of one from Caroline County in June stated that they had been "silent spectators of a toleration of Toryism," but to remain so longer was "insanity," and they asked that the "pernicious vermin" be "driven out of the state." In July of the previous year the House of Delegates and the Senate had required that all their members take an oath stating "unequivocal" support of the American cause. Such action was certainly not taken lightly, and the fact that a number of Virginia's leaders were suspected of being less than enthusiastic about the Revolution is reflected by George Mason's comment to Thomas Jefferson in October 1780 that some of the "principal men" in various counties were at the "bottom" of draft resistance.[7]

"Disaffection" was not confined to the prominent nor did it only occur in the later years of the war. It persistently plagued southwest Virginia. This region in 1777 included six counties—Bedford, Botetourt, Henry, Montgomery, Pittsylvania, and Washington. Four lay along the boundary with western North Carolina and the other two, Bedford and Botetourt, were very near it. Except for the rolling, hilly area of

---

[6] Ibid., pp. 310–11, 386–87.

[7] Ibid., pp. 413–16; Petition of the People of Caroline County, June 2, 1781, David J. Mays, ed., *The Letters and Papers of Edmund Pendleton, 1734–1803*, 2 vols. (Charlottesville, Va., 1967), 1:363–64; Affadavit of Benjamin Harrison's Oath as Speaker, July 7, 1780, Mason to Jefferson, Oct. 6, 1780, Julian P. Boyd et al., eds., *The Papers of Thomas Jefferson*, 21 vols. to date (Princeton, 1950–), 3:482, 4:18–19.

Pittsylvania and Henry counties to the east, it was a region of mountains pierced by frequent valleys. The whole area was "well watered" and its usable land, by and large, fertile. Settlement had begun west of what is now Roanoke in the late 1740s and early 1750s, was checked by the French and Indian War, then resumed in the late 1760s when people began to establish themselves in the valleys of the New and Holston rivers. By the outbreak of the Revolution settlers had advanced to the Powell River, not far from Cumberland Gap. The ethnic composition of these early pioneers was predominantly Celtic, with English and German following in that order. Class structure at this early stage of settlement is less clear, but certainly there were a few substantial persons who pursued a livelihood based on mixed farming and stock raising. Already a small elite had developed whose presence was felt in political life.[8]

This region was far removed from the capital at Williamsburg. Drapers Meadows (present day Blacksburg), where William Preston, the leading figure in Montgomery County, lived, was 250 miles distant; Wolf Hills (present day Abingdon) in Washington County, where the Campbell clan had

[8] Lewis Preston Summers, *History of Southwest Virginia 1746–1786, Washington County 1777–1870* (1903; reprint ed., Baltimore, 1966), chs. 3–6; Thomas Perkins Abernethy, *Western Lands and the American Revolution* (New York, 1937), pp. 5, 79–81; Jack M. Sosin, *The Revolutionary Frontier, 1763–1783* (New York, 1967), pp. 18, 72–75; Klaus Wust, *The Virginia Germans* (Charlottesville, Va., 1969), pp. 39–42, 72–73; Paula Hathaway Anderson-Green, "The New River Frontier Settlement on the Virginia–North Carolina Border, 1760–1820," *Virginia Magazine of History and Biography* 86 (1978):413–31; American Council of Learned Societies, "Report of Committee on Linguistic and National Stocks in the Population of the United States," *Annual Report of the American Historical Association for the Year 1931*, 3 vols. (Washington, D.C., 1932–37), 1:103–452; Forrest McDonald and Ellen Shapiro McDonald, "The Ethnic Origins of the American People," *William and Mary Quarterly*, 3d ser. 37 (1980):180–99; Louis C. Gray, *History of Agriculture in the Southern United States to 1860*, 2 vols. (1933; reprint ed., Gloucester, Mass., 1958), 1:120–26; Mary B. Kegley and Frederick B. Kegley, *Early Adventurers on Western Waters: The New River of Virginia in Pioneer Days, 1745–1800* (Orange, Va., 1980), chs. 12–13. For ethnic composition I have compared the names of 247 persons charged with disaffection or treason with the name lists in the McDonalds' article and the "Report of the Committee on Linguistic and National Stocks."

settled, lay almost a hundred miles beyond that. Charlotte, North Carolina, by contrast, was only 130 miles from Fort Chiswell in Montgomery County. The area had a substantial population—estimated at 33,240 in 1781, with 22,872 in the four westernmost counties. In the mid-1780s the percentage of landholders exceeded that found in any other part of the state. Only 10 percent of the adult males "had no or almost no property." The speculative energies of the Loyal and Greenbrier land companies, with the help of a number of the region's leading citizens, had been focused on this area but had not deterred large numbers of people from acquiring land. Jackson Turner Main has estimated that about half the adult males held between 100 and 500 acres. Distance from Williamsburg, and later Richmond, the high incidence of ownership of land, and the continual struggle with the rigors of a frontier existence (not least of them the continual threat of Indian attack) must have created a certain independence of mind in these people. Many were recent arrivals in Virginia and felt no great allegiance to the state or its leadership. Yet they needed its government to help defend them from the Indians, and the state needed them as well, especially during the war years, because located on the New River near the present town of Wytheville were productive lead mines.[9]

It was in the southwest that the most violent opposition to independence occurred. Signs of unrest appeared as early as 1776, and from 1777 on matters grew progressively worse,

[9] Abernethy, *Western Lands*, pp. 79–81, 84–90, 218–20, 224–25; Sosin, *Revolutionary Frontier*, pp. 5–19, 82–92; Jackson Turner Main, "The Distribution of Property in Post-Revolutionary Virginia," *Mississippi Valley Historical Review* 41 (1954):255; Hening, ed., *Statutes*, 10:35–60. I am basing population figures on the militia rolls because I could not find reliable tithable figures for all counties in any one year. In Virginia the ratio of militia to the whole population was 1 to 6. See U.S. Bureau of the Census, *Historical Statistics of the United States from Colonial Times to 1970*, 2 vols. (Washington, D.C., 1975), 2:1152; H. R. McIlwaine, ed., *Official Letters of the Governors of the State of Virginia*, 3 vols. (Richmond, 1926–29), 2:346, 441. See also U.S. Bureau of the Census, *Heads of Families at the First Census . . . State Enumeration of Virginia; From 1782 to 1785* (1908; reprint ed., Baltimore, 1979), p. 9. For William Preston see Bruce D. Tuttle, "Colonel William Preston, 1727–1783," M.A. thesis, Virginia Polytechnic Institute and State University, 1971.

exploding into insurrectionary activity during the spring and summer of both 1779 and 1780. Perhaps as many as half the inhabitants in one or two counties opposed the patriot cause. This essay will explore this opposition, giving special attention to Montgomery County where much of the difficulty took place.

In 1775 the entire far southwestern area of Virginia east of the Cumberland Gap had been a part of Fincastle County. Then, in 1777, Fincastle was divided and replaced by Washington and Montgomery counties. Fincastle had been one of the earliest counties in Virginia to follow the instructions of the Continental Congress to elect a committee of safety to enforce the provisions of the Continental Association, promulgated in the fall of 1774. The committee had been formed on January 20, 1775, and its members had proceeded, from what they described as "these remote regions," to express their "unpolished sentiments." While not desiring "to shake off our duty or allegiance to our lawful sovereign," they wrote, yet if "our enemies . . . attempt to dragoon us out of those inestimable privileges which we are entitled to as subjects, and to reduce us to a state of slavery, we declare, that we are deliberately and resolutely determined never to surrender them to any power upon earth, but at the expense of our lives." From the very first, however, it is clear that these sentiments were not shared by all the inhabitants of Fincastle, perhaps not even by all the members of the committee of safety.[10]

In January 1776 the committee learned that one John Spratt had "dammd" them, stating that "he could raise one hundred men for the King" and that he had "fifteen loads of Powder for the Comm[itt]ee & Two of them for Colonel Preston." A member of the committee reported that John Hill had told him that he and his neighbors were "for the King"

[10] Hening, ed., *Statutes*, 9:257–61; Richard B. Harwell, ed., *The Committees of Safety of Westmoreland and Fincastle: Proceedings of the County Committees, 1774–1776* (Richmond, 1956), pp. 61–64; Thad W. Tate, "The Fincastle Resolutions: Southwest Virginia's Commitment," *Journal of the Roanoke Valley Historical Society* 4 (1975):19–31. William Ingles, a member of the committee, was later charged with treason.

as were, with two exceptions, "all of the people up and down the [New?] river." Hill had told a "servant man" of William Sayers that in about a month "he and all the Negroes would get there freedom." Both men were summoned to appear before the committee, but only Spratt appeared and was "proven guilty." He promised "good behavior," took an oath to "be faithful & true to the Colony and Dominion of Virginia," and was "restored to the Friendship and Confidence of his Countrymen." Hill does not appear in the public records again.[11] The following June, however, the committee dealt with eight "disaffected" citizens charged with everything from maintaining "an unfriendly disposition to the American Cause" and attempting to "degrade the Characters" of committee members, to offering "forty half Joes" to Thomas Alley "to enlist in the Kings Service," refusing to serve in the militia, and corresponding "with Tories in the Cherokee Nation."[12] There is no indication as to how these cases were resolved but clearly all was not well in the southwest.

In the year following the Declaration of Independence the court records of the southwestern counties reveal little action against tories or the disaffected. British merchants were ordered to leave Virginia. Robert Conan of Bedford County was removed as a justice of the peace for manifesting "an unfriendly disposition towards the American colonies." In Botetourt County William Davis and John Van [Obber?] were forced to post bonds for £1,000 and £500, respectively, that would be forfeited if they left the state or corresponded with the Indians "or other enemies" of Virginia within one year. But, by and large, things appear to have been quiet.[13]

In the summer of 1777 the state law requiring an oath of allegiance from all free white males over the age of sixteen

[11] Harwell, *Committees of Safety*, pp. 70–80.

[12] Ibid., pp. 90–93.

[13] For example see Henry County Order Book 1, 1771–78, Jan. 21, 30, Mar. 16, 1777, Pittsylvania County Court Records 3, 1776–91, Jan. 24, Feb. 5, 27, 1777, Bedford County Order Book 6, 1774–82, Jan. 28, 1777, Botetourt County Order Book, 1776–86, Feb. 11, Mar. 11, 1777, microfilm, Virginia State Library, Richmond.

took effect. When the southwestern counties began to try to enforce the law, it quickly became clear that substantial numbers were not committed to independence. Reports in Montgomery County in January 1778 noted that about one hundred men had refused to take the oath. Both Montgomery and Botetourt counties called out state troops or militia against groups described as tories. The troops guarding the lead mines in Montgomery County "marched up the New River," encountered "a company of Tories" at Round Meadow and fired upon them, but they were able to take only a single prisoner. At Peaked Mountain in Botetourt, where a "body of Tories" had gathered, soldiers commanded by Patrick Buchannan and Thomas Smith captured their leaders and dispersed the rest. In Washington County, William Campbell and a few friends captured a British spy who had been sent to incite the Cherokee Indians against frontier settlements. After wringing a confession from him they hanged him on the spot.[14]

It was reported that during the summer bands of tories roamed the western counties "stealing horses and robbing . . . Whig sympathizers." In Montgomery in December, William Preston, the county lieutenant, bemoaned that "Captain Burke & his whole [militia] Company except four or five & near forty of my Neighbors have Positively refused the Oath of Allegiance." Preston had argued with them until he was "wearied out" and even given them a week's grace, but to no avail. Now he would have to disarm them, an action, he feared, that would bring "much Trouble and perhaps Resistance." Aimed at people like these, Preston complained, the law missed its target. Disarming the "recusants" and depriving them of their rights to vote, serve on juries, sue for debt, buy land, and hold public office had little effect. The law had

[14] Pittsylvania County Court Orders 4, 1777–83, July 26, 1777, Botetourt County Order Book, 1776–86, Aug. 13, 1777, Henry County Order Book 1, 1777–78, Aug. 18, 1777, microfilm, VSL; John C. Dann, ed., *The Revolution Remembered: Eyewitness Accounts of the War for Independence* (Chicago, 1980), pp. 277–80; Frederick B. Kegley, *Kegley's Virginia Frontier: The Beginning of the Southwest* . . . (Roanoke, Va., 1938), pp. 664–65; Summers, *History of Southwest Virginia*, pp. 273–78; William Preston to the governor of Virginia, Jan. 16, 1778, *John P. Branch Historical Papers* 4 (1915):292.

to be made more effective since the "ringleaders," he explained in a revealing comment, "bring no Suits, they never Elect, they don't attend Court, they can dispose of Their arms and they don't want to purchase Land."[15]

Some of the disaffected did resist the attempt to disarm them. Early in the new year Preston swore out a warrant for the arrest of Thomas Heavin, described as one of the "Ringleaders," who refused to surrender his arms and persuaded others in "Captain Taylor's" company to do likewise. The disaffected, in fact, outnumbered the party sent to disarm them. Heavin, evidently a tory, was then charged with threatening the "life of an officer of the state, & in public company [he had] drunk health to King George and success to General Howe." Capt. Thomas Burk, another of the nonjurors, argued that his own refusal to take the oath was a matter of conscience. He stated that he was a "rail friend to my Country" and had no thought of rebelling. But he had a "god to fear . . . who is able to Destroy both soul and body in Hell." Perhaps Burk was a nonjuring Presbyterian, but it should be noted that three years later he was brought before the court and placed on £50,000 bond for good behavior.[16]

Montgomery County remained the center of unrest in southwest Virginia through 1778, but most of the other counties in the region had their troubles too. Evidently there was militia action against persons described as tories in Montgomery and Botetourt. Sixteen disaffected were brought into the various county courts; fourteen were placed on bond for good behavior for one year and two sentenced to jail terms

[15] Summers, *History of Southwest Virginia*, pp. 272–73, Preston to William Fleming, Dec. 2, 1777, Reuben Gold Thwaites and Louise Phelps Kellogg, eds., *Frontier Defense on the Upper Ohio, 1777–1778* (Madison, 1912), pp. 169–70; Fleming to Preston, Dec. 15, 1777, Papers of the Preston Family of Virginia, 1729–1896, Virginia Historical Society, Richmond. The court records do not give much evidence of resistance, but it is likely that at this early stage in the war patriots, ignorant of the law and fearful of retribution, did not bring charges against their neighbors.

[16] Warrant for Thomas Heavin to Constable Bryan McDonald, Feb. 23, 1778, Preston Papers, Lyman C. Draper Collection, State Historical Society of Wisconsin, Madison; Capt. Thomas Burk to Preston, Feb. 18, 1778, Thwaites and Kellogg, eds., *Frontier Defense*, pp. 203–4; Loyalists bound for good behavior, July 29, 1780, Preston Papers, Draper Coll., 5QQ47.

of one and two years, respectively. Beneath the surface more serious trouble was in the making. In the spring of 1779 an informer stated that early the previous year plans had been made to form a combination of tories, British, and Indians with the intent of "destroying the Country." William Preston evidently had some sense of what was going on, for late in the year he had warned Gov. Patrick Henry that in addition to resistance to the draft and militia service he feared "a general mutiny and defiance of the law" in Montgomery and a "neighbouring" county.[17]

In late March 1779 groups of disaffected began to meet in the valley of the New River, a stream that rises in western North Carolina, flows north and west through Montgomery County into what is now West Virginia, and eventually empties into the Ohio.[18] Virginians described as tories gathered on Walker's and Reed's creeks, tributaries of the New River, and probably elsewhere. They were in contact with like-minded people—some living around William Preston's residence, "Smithfield," to the north, others farther west on the South Fork of the Holston River, and still others to the south on the Yadkin River in North Carolina. At least one British agent was in the area, spreading news that "the country" was "sold to the French and that they may as well fight under the King of Britain, as to be subjects to France." He was also trying to enlist the disaffected "for the King," by offering two shillings sixpence per day and 450 acres of land quitrent-free for twenty-one years. They planned to do some disarming themselves, and one reportedly said that he intended to scalp

[17] Lewis Preston Summers, *Annals of Southwest Virginia 1769–1800* (Abingdon, 1929), pp. 684–85; Kegley, *Kegley's Virginia Frontier*, p. 665; Washington County Minute Book 1, 1777–84, Mar. 18, 1778, Montgomery County Order Book 3, 1778–80, Apr. 8, 1778, Bedford County Order Book 6, 1774–82, July 27, Oct. 27, 1778, Pittsylvania County Court Orders, 1777–83, Sept. 27, 1778, microfilm, VSL; Preston to Patrick Henry, Nov. 25, 1778, Deposition of Michael Kenninger [Heninger?], Apr. 18, 1779, *John P. Branch Historical Papers* 4 (1915):298, 304–5.

[18] Various terms are used in contemporary accounts of disaffected people. *Tory* is frequently used, as are *nonjuror* and *recusant*—that is, those who had refused to take the oath of allegiance to the state of Virginia or to submit to authority.

William Preston and James McGavock. Because he had a supply of state arms at his house, Preston was an especially important target. When an informer reported this activity to local militia officers, they immediately sent out troops. Preston himself may have been the first to hear of the plans to attack his house. He called on several "Heads of Families" of the disaffected to meet with him at the home of Jacob Shull. There they discussed the entire matter, as he reported, "in the most neighborly manner." They assured him that they had no intention of disturbing the tranquility of the state or injuring his "Family or Reputation." Preston accepted their disavowal, but word that there was a person in the neighborhood urging people to take the oath of allegiance to the king disturbed him. Shortly after the meeting he was outraged to learn that he had been duped. A "Bloody and Murderous Conspiracy . . . almost ripe for execution" had been discovered in another part of the county, a conspiracy that threatened his life as well as the lives of his whole family. Some of his neighbors were involved, men who had assured him at Shull's house of their desire to remove all obstacles to "our good neighborhood and social intercourse" and had promised to keep him informed. Still Preston made a final attempt to reason with his neighbors, but his efforts failed. In one instance local militia, probably with the help of Col. William Campbell and mounted militia from Washington County, seized the British agent and fourteen of the leaders. Nine were released on bail and two "put into irons," all to await trial. Three others, against whom there was no evidence, were sent to work in the state's lead mines. Reports coming from other parts of the county showed that the trouble was widespread. On Wilkes Creek "a great combination" of tories was threatening patriots with the loss of their land, and fear that they would "execute their Devilege Designs" pervaded the entire area. James McGavock, who participated in the capture of one party of "Tories," believed that they intended to commit murder. When witnesses presented testimony against three of the leaders, he reported that "every Bystander was alarmed and Expected themselves to be in great danger." His own feelings were similar: "We seem to be but a handfull in the Middle, and Surrounded By a Multitude."

Michael Heninger, the informer, suggested that his name not be made public until those "principally concern'd" were brought to trial because he feared "his life would be in danger."[19]

There was great concern that the Montgomery County court would not be able to handle the situation since the "business" was "new," and William Preston, its senior member, could not be present. But when it met on May 5, 1779, the justices tried nineteen disaffected persons who, judged by their landholdings, appear to have been a cross section of the community, owning an average of 203 acres. The jury found Duncan O'Gullion guilty of treason and sent him on to Williamsburg to be tried by the General Court. When he escaped on the way to the capital, the court ordered his property sold. O'Gullion's "sidekick," Nicholas Wyrick, was fined £500 and sentenced to eighteen months in jail. Both stood accused of "maintaining the authority of the King of Great Britain and levying war against the people of this State." John Atter [Etter?] faced the same charge but only had to give security of £1,000 for good behavior for "twelve months and a day." Others charged with "certain offenses committed against the Commonwealth" were forced to pay fines or give security for good behavior varying from £250 to £10,000 for the same period of time; one man won acquittal. The nineteen who were tried probably did not include all who had been charged in April with various crimes against the state, since a number apparently escaped.[20]

In late May an eastern friend wrote William Preston, "The Tories I imagine, were only a little perplexing as I should

[19] Walter Crockett to Preston, Apr. 7, 1779, *Virginia Magazine of History and Biography* 26 (1918):371–72; James McGavock to Preston, Apr. 15, 25, 1779, William Campbell to Preston, Apr. 19, 1779, Preston to Neighbors, n.d. [Apr. 1779?], typescripts, Papers of the Preston Family; Deposition of William Preston, Apr. 24, 1779, Preston Papers, Draper Coll., 5QQ2; Summers, *History of Southwest Virginia*, pp. 292–94.

[20] McGavock to Preston, Apr. 15, 1779, typescript, Papers of the Preston Family; Deposition of Michael Kenninger [Heninger?], Apr. 18, 1779, Crocket to Preston, Apr. 24, 1779, *John P. Branch Historical Papers* 4 (1915):304–6; Montgomery County Order Book, 1774–82, May 5, 1779, Montgomery County Land Tax Books, 1782–1806A, microfilm, VSL.

suppose your courts have long since put it out of their power to be dangerous." Preston must have been amused, for the unrest continued virtually unabated. Tory bands roamed the county. On June 5 one group, led by Nicholas Wyrick, who was supposed to be in jail, fired through the door and roof of William Phip's house and tried to set it on fire. Soon afterward another band, evidently led by the escaped Duncan O'Gullion, killed seven of James McGavock's sheep. McGavock's sons surprised the group, which had camped four hundred yards from the house, but the tories escaped, taking four of the slaughtered animals. McGavock, frightened, placed "four senturies" around his house because the tories reportedly intended to kill him. James Montgomery, who described these incidents, observed that the militia had been on duty for three days in an effort to deal with the "alarming" situation. He believed that unless "speedy measures" were taken things could only get worse "in this Quarter." Suspicion, fear, and anger were rampant. Neighbor informed on neighbor, and William Preston, that man of sweet reason, now spoke of "disorderly Deluded" and "stupid Wretches." County leaders did their utmost but it was the end of July before things calmed down.[21]

The court appears to have dealt reasonably with cases within its jurisdiction involving disaffected. Perhaps it had no choice, for jail facilities were nonexistent. Some of the accused were acquitted, but most were bound, for varying sums, for a year and a day and required to take the oath of allegiance. Perplexed that their neighbors would resort to violence in opposing the patriot cause, the justices asked themselves why. Their official stance was one of moderation, as they tried to find explanations for the problem that did not include disloyalty. Some of the disaffected they found to

[21] Edward Johnson to Preston, May 29, 1779, John Miller to Preston, n.d. [June 1779?], Papers of the Preston Family; James Montgomery to Preston, June 11, 1779, Campbell to Preston, July 16, 1779, Preston to Campbell, July 19, 1779, typescripts, ibid.; Deposition of John Cox before William Campbell, July 16, 1779, *Virginia Magazine of History and Biography* 26 (1918):373–74; Col. William Christian to Fleming, July 23, 1779, Louise Phelps Kellogg, ed., *Frontier Advance on the Upper Ohio, 1778–1779* (Madison, 1916), pp. 404–5.

be "proper objects of Mercy," suggesting, perhaps, that they might be poor and ignorant. Others came from "Remote and Scattered situations" and had been "deluded" by artful villains and emissarys sent from our Enemies." These were assured of leniency if they would inform the court, at the October session, that they were "sorry for their past crimes" and give security for good behavior.[22] The actions in the courts in the other five counties in the region were similar although, as far as it is known, these areas did not experience insurrection.[23]

Not all patriots resorted to the courts. In Montgomery County and probably elsewhere they responded with a variety of illegal activities. They seized the property of the disaffected, conducted forced sales of their estates, and even executed some offenders after trial by drumhead courts. Patriots in Montgomery County had called on William Campbell and his Washington County militia for help. Campbell had earlier hanged at least one person in his own county, and when in the summer of 1779 he and Maj. Walter Crockett, with militia from Washington and Montgomery counties, seized a group of tories, they "shot one, Hanged one and whipt several." It was said that in another instance Campbell hanged twelve tories from two white oak trees in Black Lick Valley. Campbell's and Crockett's activities were extensive enough that the legislature, in October 1779, indemnified and exonerated "William Campbell, Walter Crockett, and other liege subjects of the commonwealth" from prosecution for measures they took, "not . . . strictly warranted by law," to suppress "conspiracy and insurrection."[24]

But neither judicial moderation nor extralegal violence

[22] Montgomery County Order Book, 1774–82, Aug. 3, 4, 5, Sept. 7, 9, 1779; List of suspected tories, n.d. [summer 1779?], typescript, Papers of the Preston Family.

[23] For example see Botetourt County Order Book, 1776–86, May 13, 1779, Washington County Minute Book 1, 1777–84, July 3, June 16, 1779, Bedford County Order Book 6, 1774–82, June 28, 1779, Henry County Order Book 6, 1774–82, June 28, Aug. 26, 1779, microfilm, VSL.

[24] Campbell to Preston, July 16, 1779, Preston to Campbell, July 19, 1779, typescripts, Papers of the Preston Family; Montgomery County Or-

seemed to have much effect. News of the British landing near Charleston on February 8, 1780, reached southwest Virginia within two weeks—perhaps brought by British agents. In early March, William Preston informed Governor Jefferson that he had just learned of a combination of disaffected who planned, once the British had firmly established themselves in South Carolina, "to disturb the Peace of this unhappy Frontier as soon as the season will permit." There were now some fifteen British agents in Montgomery and Washington counties, Preston continued, pressing people to take the oath of allegiance to George III; in "one neighborhood" alone they had succeeded with some seventy-five. Their intention was "to perpetuate the most horrid murders [on] individuals in Authority . . . and many other Things of like Nature." Preston had dispatched four companies of militia to seize and disarm suspects, to collect evidence, and to bring those seized before justices of the peace. He was not quite sure how he would proceed until after "the storm clears," but since there was no jail in Montgomery County, he supposed he would send the worst "villains" to the Augusta County jail. Jefferson responded promptly, approving Preston's actions, advising him how to handle cases in which treason could not be proved, and urging him to protect the lead mines. What took place in the remainder of the spring and early summer is unclear (as the Montgomery County court did not meet between April 5 and November 7, there are no court records for the period), but it was reported in April that the enemy plans involved attacks on "the frontiers from Georgia to Virginia." The initial design, similar to that of the previous year, was to raise an army of loyalists, destroy the lead mines, and then join with Indians "to burn Destroy and cut their way to the English Army and assist them in reducing the Country." As before, substantial pay and quitrent-free land was promised to those who "signed up." But the resident agent from Montgomery County, John Griffith, was not able to produce

der Book, 1774–82, Aug. 5, 1779; Christian to Fleming, July 23, 1779, Virginia Papers, Draper Coll., 2ZZ81; Hening, ed., *Statutes*, 10:195; Summers, *History of Southwest Virginia*, pp. 292–94; *Virginia Gazette* (Clarkson), Nov. 27, 1779 (supplement).

a "Colonel Robinson from the British army" and, as a result, people did not believe that Griffith was properly "authorized" to receive their pledge of loyalty. This circumstance as well as the patriot leaders' awareness of what was going on, forestalled the execution of the tory plan.[25]

Charleston fell to the British army in May, and the news encouraged the disaffected in southwest Virginia and their friends of like mind in North Carolina. John Griffith continued to play a key role in Montgomery County, one report maintaining that he had gone to Ramsour's Mill in North Carolina and would return shortly "with a contingent of Tories to join with those in the county and attack Fort Chiswell and seize the principal Men." Disturbances were commonplace now in all of the six southwestern Virginia counties. In Montgomery County two hundred tories were thought to have gathered at a place called the Glades during the third week in June with the intention of taking the lead mines. They had killed "nine Men" and committed various other "outrages." Militia were called out under Maj. William Edmiston. Throughout late June and early July militia under the command of Colonels Arthur and William Campbell, sometimes with the help of North Carolina militia, pursued groups of tories. Intending to "disarm, distress and terrify," they hanged, shot, and whipped "insurgents" and seized their horses and cattle.[26]

By July 12 William Preston, encouraged by news of the

[25] Preston to Jefferson, Mar. 1780, [Deposition of William Preston?], n.d. [spring 1780?], Preston Papers, Draper Coll., 5QQ27, 28; Jefferson to Preston, Mar. 21, 1780, Boyd et al., eds., *Jefferson Papers*, 3:325; Martin Armstrong to [?], Apr. 10, 1780, Crockett to Preston, Apr. 15, 1780, *Virginia Magazine of History and Biography* 26 (1918):376–78. See also Montgomery County Order Book, 1774–82, Apr. to Nov. 1780. On John Griffith see Kegley and Kegley, *Early Adventurers*, p. 146.

[26] Col. Arthur Campbell to Maj. William Edmiston, June 24, 25, 1780, Arthur Campbell to William Campbell, July 12, [1780?], William Campbell to Arthur Campbell, July [25?], 1780, King's Mountain Papers, Draper Coll., 9DD21, 22, 8DD3, 4; McGavock to Preston, June 30, 1780, Arthur Campbell to Preston, July 3, 1780, *John P. Branch Historical Papers* 4 (1915):315–16; Prospective Friend to [?], June 29, 1780, Christian to Preston, n.d. [summer 1780], Preston Papers, Draper Coll., 5QQ35, 37.

defeat of thirteen hundred tories at Ramsour's Mill in North Carolina in late June, thought things were under control. He had proceeded on two fronts. He dispatched troops of mounted militia to those areas known to contain pockets of disaffected to disarm them. Those who resisted or concealed their weapons were to be held at the lead mines until they could be tried. Preston urged his men to avoid "violence . . . to Women or Children, or the old and helpless," or to anyone who peaceably delivered up their arms and ammunition. But tory property could be seized and held until trial. Secondly, being William Preston, he continued to try to reason with his neighbors. Notwithstanding his unsuccessful efforts the previous summer, he dispatched Michael Price with a second letter to the disaffected. In the face of their continued "offensive" conduct he had restrained himself, he assured them, "not from any love to your Political sentiments, but from a regard for you as Neighbours." But restraint was not universally esteemed, and they could not be "insensible" that the opinion of the "well affected . . . runs very high against you." The "Enraged Multitude" could not long be contained. He then invited his "neighbours" to gather at his house on Saturday morning, July 22, to "consult in a neighbourly way" about their own protection. Preston even prepared notes for the speech he would deliver. Some had conducted themselves in a shameless manner, distributing arms and ammunition, forfeiting their bonds for good behavior, intercepting the express rider whom they had "made drunk" and "King George Huzz[a]ed for," cheering the king at social gatherings and "all Publick Occasions." All had listened to "false reports" and "made Preparations for [extending?] the Trouble." But worst of all they had put a price (a "purse of Guineas") on his own head—and this at the behest of masters to whom they were no more than "draught horses" or "beasts of burden." It could go on no longer. He planned to warn them that William Campbell had been appointed and instructed by the executive and that, unless they ceased their activity, he could not restrain Campbell. Finally, he was going to ask them to consider whether "a few dispersed people . . .[could] fly in the face of a [continent?]. It is true some secret [jobs?] may be given to some murder committees but will it not end in the destruction of the perpetrators & their Adherents[?]"[27]

Preston was not given the opportunity to deliver his speech, for his neighbors did not accept his invitation. John Heavin responded in a dignified and restrained manner, saying that he had read the letter "concerning the Destroying our Small Estates" but it was out of his power to respond satisfactorily since neither he nor his children had "given any offense." He had talked to "several of the Neighbors that all say they only want peace. My Disappearing shall be no token of my gilt and for to sattisfy the Internal peas of this State I know not how to do that, I have no way [to] satisfy you I can find by your riteing unless it is to sweare and that I cannot do for my part for I never meddled with war from the first moment and Cant think of Intangling myselfe with it now." Heavin hoped that "theire may be Compassion Used with our wives and Innocent Children" and he reaffirmed that "no one means to Rais arms against you."[28]

The sweep of mounted militia through disaffected areas had results that were probably more satisfactory to Preston. A number of persons suspected of treason or lesser crimes evidently stood trial in late July or early August in extraordinary sessions of the Montgomery County court, which placed a substantial number on bond for amounts varying from £5,000 to £20,000. Whether it meted out other punishments is uncertain.[29]

[27] Preston to Capt. James Bynn, July 5, 1780, Preston to Captain Taylor, July 12, 1780, Preston to Michael Price, William, John and Howard Heavin, James [?], Jacob Shull, John Wall, Mr. Harlin & [?], July 20, 1780, Warrant for Arrest of John McDonald, July 24, 1780, Preston Papers, Draper Coll., 5QQ40, 41, 43; Paul H. Smith, *Loyalists and Redcoats: A Study in British Revolutionary Policy* (1964; reprint ed., New York, 1972), pp. 142–43; Jefferson to James Callaway, Aug. 1, 1780, Jefferson to Charles Lynch, Aug. 1, 1780, Boyd et al., eds., *Jefferson Papers*, 3:519–20, 523. See also Botetourt County Order Book, 1780–84, July 13, 1780, Bedford County Order Book 6, 1774–82, June 26, July 24, 25, 1780, microfilm, VSL.

[28] John Heavin to Preston, July 22, 1780, Preston Papers, Draper Coll., 5QQ42.

[29] The Montgomery County court did not meet in regular session during the summer of 1780. The evidence for this paragraph comes from

William Preston had hoped that the militia raids would deter any further tory activity, but he was to be disappointed. Sometime in late July, Preston, Col. Hugh Crockett, and other patriot leaders persuaded John Wyatt of Botetourt County and another man to go among the tories on the New River and pose as British officers in an attempt to learn their plans. Wyatt had been captured by the British at Charleston, but he had subsequently exchanged a quart of rum for a pass and escaped. Back in Botetourt County the patriot leaders promised that they would get him excused from army service if he would help them. He agreed and, armed with his pass, a doctored British army commission (from pre-Revolutionary days), and some newspapers from Charleston, successfully made contact with the tories, who revealed their plans to seize the lead mines on July 28 then join with British troops to march on Charlottesville to free and arm the Saratoga prisoners. With such a force they would subdue the entire state. Wyatt later was to claim that he had persuaded the tory leadership to delay their attack on the mines until British troops arrived. But, whatever the case, he returned to Preston and the others with the plans and a "written list of their force." Five hundred militia, apparently under the command of Col. William Campbell, were called out from Montgomery, Washington, and Botetourt counties. Aided by Col. Charles Lynch and Bedford County militia they proceeded to put an end to the immediate threat.[30]

William Preston reported on August 8 that "near sixty" of these "deluded wretches" were in "confinement" with more being brought in "every hour." Justice was swift. Preston's de-

---

bonds for July 26, 29, and August 8 [1780?] in the Preston Papers, Draper Coll., 5QQ44–47, 49, 51, 52.

[30] Narrative of John Wyatt in Dann, ed., *Revolution Remembered*, pp. 351–53; Crockett to Preston, Aug. 6, 1780, Preston to Jefferson, Aug. 8, 1780, Preston Papers, Draper Coll., 5QQ48, 50; Preston to Gen. J. P. G. Muhlenberg, Sept. 1780, Kegley, *Kegley's Virginia Frontier*, pp. 655–56; William Campbell to Preston and others, [Aug. 1780], King's Mountain Papers, 8DD6. Preston's letter to Jefferson of Aug. 8, 1780, as printed in Boyd et al., eds., *Jefferson Papers*, 3:533–34, lists the number of militia as four hundred, but the original in the Draper Collection says five hundred and I use that figure.

scription was brief but graphic. Some "have been whipped & others, against whom little can be made appear, have been enlisted to serve in the Continental Army." Another group, who appeared to be guilty of treason, were sent to the "best prisons in Neighbouring Counties" until they could be tried. Finally, although some of the "Capital Offenders" had escaped capture, they had not escaped punishment for their personal property "has been removed by the Soldiers," who insisted that it be "sold and divided as Plunder to which the officers have submitted, otherwise it would be impossible to get men on these pressing occasions." Preston asked Jefferson's opinion concerning the plundering. Jefferson was out of town when Preston's letter arrived, but Lt. Gov. Dudley Digges replied that it was a "judicial matter" on "which it behoves us to be perfectly silent." Jefferson, writing Arthur Campbell of Washington County earlier, had been more explicit. The executive had no power to allow plundering, but if the seizure "is made by the people themselves and nothing said about it," he doubted "that the former proprietors" would trouble them, for "they will hardly hazard their lives" by raising questions. If, of course, they were "really innocent," their property should be restored.[31] The governor was certainly not suggesting restraint.

The Montgomery and Botetourt county courts meeting together in a special session in August tried fifty-three men accused of treason. The court believed that most of these men were guilty of treason. It acquitted only two and failed to hold the large majority for trial by the General Court as the law prescribed. In fact, it held for trial in Richmond only eight, considered the most serious offenders, while punishing the remainder who had committed lesser crimes. Eighteen, after taking the oath of allegiance, were sent to serve in the Continental army—most of them for eighteen months. Another five, three of whom were described as old, were allowed to remain at home when their sons agreed to serve in

[31] Preston to Jefferson, Aug. 8, 1780, Preston Papers, Draper Coll., 5QQ50; Jefferson to Arthur Campbell, Aug. 9, 1780, Boyd et al., eds., *Jefferson Papers*, 3:534–35; Dudley Digges to Preston, Aug. 17, 1780, McIlwaine, ed., *Official Letters*, 2:168.

the Continental army for eighteen months. Three suffered thirty-nine lashes and three were placed on bonds ranging from £20,000 to £100,000. Two were released after taking the oath of allegiance, one was paroled until December, and the punishment of another two who were convicted of assaulting and beating an officer is not known. There is a final group of nine who were believed to have committed treason; for them the punishment is also unknown. One wonders if they were treated in a more summary fashion.[32]

Other special court sessions must have taken place, but the only other remaining evidence is a record of fifteen men being placed on bond for good behavior. Much that took place on the New River and its tributaries in the summer of 1781 will never be known, but certainly there was great confusion, violence, and terror. In the middle of it all was Col. William Preston trying to bring order and sanity to the scene. Clearly he tried to provide trials for those accused of disloyal behavior, and apparently the court, of which he was the most prominent member, dealt with the accused compassionately and fairly. Through proclamations promising lenient treatment, he continued to try to persuade offenders who were still at large to give themselves up.[33] But the situation grew beyond the control of the compassionate and fair-minded. Even friends, such as Col. Charles Lynch, who came to help bringing a hundred men from Bedford County, became themselves a problem, until Preston found himself between two fires. Lynch evidently marched into Montgomery County in late July or early August seizing those suspected of disloyalty along the way. He ultimately arrived at the lead mines, where he appears to have extracted confessions and dispensed his own brand of justice. Nine of the confessions—apparently taken down in haste on scraps of paper—have

[32] Courts of Montgomery and Botetourt counties meeting to try Col. William Ingles and others, Aug. 1780, Preston Papers, Draper Coll., 5QQ73–79.

[33] Records of Individuals Being Placed on Bond, July 26, 29, and Aug. 8, [1780?], Proclamations concerning Thomas Heavin and Others, Aug. 14, 1780, and Philip Lambert, Aug. 21, 1780, ibid., 44–47, 49, 51, 52, 55, 61.

survived. One can easily imagine a scene with exhausted, frightened men, a musket pointed at their heads, trying to respond to shouted questions. Nonetheless some remained intransigent. John Clifton said "he was forst to take the State Oath, that his wish is still to be with the english and would go if he could." One refused to say anything, but the remainder divulged a variety of information and so implicated others.[34]

It is not known what happened to these men. Lynch himself claimed that those whom he believed "not very Criminal" were set free; others were held "for a proper tryal," some were "Kept for Soldiers" or witnesses, and some "may require they should be made Exampels of." The meaning of Lynch's last comment was perhaps ominous, and there were protests against his behavior. Nancy Davereux wrote Preston that Lynch had her husband in custody at the lead mines. She was certain of his innocence, "but as there is a misunderstanding between Col. Lynch and the Welsh in General I am very uneasy . . . least my Husband should not have the Strictest Justice." She begged Preston to send for her husband and try him properly. If he were then found guilty, "I only wish he get a punishment Suitable to his deserts." Complaints such as this impelled Preston to write and request that Lynch "desist in Trying Tory people." Lynch responded at length agreeing that it might appear odd at "first View" that he should be in Montgomery "apprehending some of those you have had before you" but he had begun by suppressing the "conspiracy" in Bedford County and events had carried him into the neighboring county. He was sure everything would be clear when he talked with Preston. In the meantime, he concluded, "let these Broken hints apologize for my Conduct until I have the pleasure of seeing you. I wou'd tho Request the favor to you Let me have sight of Letters you received relative to my Conduct." It cannot be proved that Charles Lynch arbitrarily hanged suspected persons without trial, but posterity has attached the phrase "lynch law" to such activity, probably with some reason.[35]

[34] Various Confessions, Lynch to Preston, Aug. 17, 1780, ibid., 54, 59, 60, 68, 71, 58.

[35] Nancy Davereux to Preston, n.d., Lynch to Preston, Aug. 17, 1780,

Even Preston may have been implicated in excesses. Two years later the legislature "indemnified and exonerated" both him and Lynch as well as Robert Adams, Jr., James Callaway, and other men of measures they had taken during the summer of 1780 that may not have been "strictly warranted by law." The act of indemnification stated that their acts were "justifiable from the imminence of danger," and there can be no doubt that conditions were hazardous. Even friends of long standing proved unreliable. William Preston must have been shocked when Col. William Ingles, a leading citizen and longtime resident of the area, was implicated in the conspiracy. Charges of treason were not "fully proven," but Ingles was placed on £100,000 bond. Perhaps only his standing in the community saved him.[36]

Although Montgomery County experienced the most difficulty, other counties also had problems. During the fall of 1780 Bedford County held seventeen men in jail to await trial for treason by the General Court. A substantial number of others were convicted of lesser crimes and dealt with in various ways—placed on bond, jailed for varying terms, fined, or whipped. The courts of Botetourt and Henry were also active in trying tories, but in neither county did the court hold suspected persons for trial by the General Court on charges of treason. Heavy bond, fines, and jail sentences were the chief means of punishment. Botetourt County had the distinction of trying the only woman, Sarah Summerfield, charged with activities indicating that she was not "attached to the interest of the United States." The court found her guilty and fined her husband £300. There also appears

---

ibid., 58. For lynch law see, for example, *Webster's New International Dictionary of the English Language*, 2d ed.

[36] Hening, ed., *Statutes*, 11:134–35; Kegley and Kegley, *Early Adventurers*, pp. 352–59. William Ingles, sheriff and militia officer, was commanding militia as late as the summer of 1779 in putting down disaffection, and Preston had ordered another officer on July 5, 1780, not to seize the arms belonging to Ingles's son Thomas. See Montgomery County Order Book, 1774–82, Jan. 7, 1777; Preston to William Campbell, July 19, 1779, Papers of the Preston Family, typescript; Preston to Bynn, July 5, 1780, Preston Papers, Draper Coll., 5QQ37. See also Confessions of James Duggless, Aug. 18, 1780, and Confession of (Morison?) Lovell, ibid., 5QQ59, 68.

to have been substantial seizure of tory property in Botetourt County. In Pittsylvania in late October, Thomas Jefferson reported that "a very dangerous Insurrection . . . was prevented a few days ago" when the "Ring-leaders were seized in their Beds." The court records contain no reference to the incident. In the far southwest county of Washington tory activity seems to have been infrequent in the summer of 1780, owing perhaps to the harsh response that Arthur and William Campbell had made earlier. Such was the opinion of a nineteenth-century historian of Washington County who observed that "the mode of procedure of our Revolutionary fathers, in dealing with this matter, may not meet the approval of some at this day, but it is evident . . . that the methods used were most effective." He favorably contrasted the "stern justice meted out speedily" there with the "persuasion and good treatment" attempted in Montgomery County, which only encouraged "insurrection." Washington's major problem may, in fact, have been external. Arthur Campbell, for example, wrote William Campbell in August 1780 that "a body of 700 tories and Indians had . . . set out against the frontiers of this state" and he asked his cousin to "speedily return with the men from this county."[37]

News of the trouble in southwest Virginia spread quickly to the rest of the state. A Hanover County doctor wrote in his diary of the "dangerous conspiracy" and of "many thousands enlisting in the Kings service." Governor Jefferson was more restrained but he spoke of a "spirit of disaffection, which had never been expected," and reported that "many hundreds had actually enlisted to serve his Britannic Majesty." He even began to worry about the Convention army at

[37] Bedford County Order Book 6, 1774–82, June 26, July 24, 25, Aug. 29, Sept. 25, 26, 27, 29, 30, Oct. 2, 23, 1780, Botetourt County Order Book, 1780–84, July 13, Aug. 10, Sept. 15, 1780, Henry County Order Book 2, 1778–82, Aug. 24, 25, Sept. 28, 1780, microfilm, VSL; Patrick Lockhard to Preston, Aug. 12, 1780, Preston Papers, Draper Coll., 5QQ53; Jefferson to the Virginia Delegates in Congress, Oct. 27, 1780, Boyd et al., eds., *Jefferson Papers*, 4:76–77; Washington County Minute Book 1, 1777–84, Aug. 15, 1780; Summers, *History of Southwest Virginia*, pp. 277–78; Arthur Campbell to William Campbell, Aug. 13, 1780, King's Mountain Papers, 8DD5.

Charlottesville. The legislature responded by offering to pardon those in the six counties who had taken the oath of "fidelity" to the king or who had enlisted "for or into his service" but who had not committed "any overt act by criminal law" if they would take the oath of allegiance to the state before February 28, 1781. The members reasoned, much as the Montgomery County court had earlier, that most of those concerned were either "credulous, ignorant," or "unwary," and had been "deluded and misled by emissaries of the common enemy." They extended the law to sixteen men, fourteen of whom were from Bedford County, who were either in the Henrico County jail, or had recently been released on bail. In this action the legislature, in a sense, mirrored what seems to have been the prevailing view of most of the political leaders in the southwest, namely, that conciliatory treatment was most likely to lessen the threat of loyalism. In November, for example, three men evidently asked the Montgomery County court to overlook the fact they had been involved in "open Rebellion" or "insurrections." The court agreed that they should "be received as members of the Community so long as they behave as good citizens," although the court emphasized that it could not pardon them for offenses against individuals such as "Murder, Robbery, or Feloniously taking away the property of any person." The court went on to say that it did not believe the petitioners had altered "their principles," but that it was a change "of prospect and necessity" that induced them to petition "in the manner they have done." In any event circumstances decreed a policy of conciliation and leniency since the pressure on Virginia for men and supplies to support the American army in the Carolinas was so great that the state lacked the resources to deal forcefully with the problem of disaffection.[38]

The offer of pardon found little acceptance, testimony

[38] Robert Honyman, Diary and Journal, 1776–82, Aug. 31, 1780, Library of Congress; Jefferson to James Wood, Oct. 5, 1780, Jefferson to the Virginia Delegates in Congress, Oct. 27, 1780, Boyd et al., eds., *Jefferson Papers*, 4:14–15, 76–77; Hening, ed., *Statutes*, 10:324–26; Montgomery County Order Book, 1774–82, Nov. 8, 1780. For Bedford County prisoners see Bedford County Order Book 6, 1774–82, Aug. 29, Sept. 30, Oct. 2, 1780.

perhaps that four years of war had only hardened the position of loyalists. James Callaway wrote the governor from Bedford County in March 1781 that most of the "late Conspirators . . . have Refused to accept the Benefit of the Act of Pardon." And even those who had "complyed . . . discover a Disposition to become Hostile whenever it may be in their Powers." The numbers of disaffected persons brought before the county courts in 1781 were about the same as in the previous two years. Certainly William Preston did not think there had been any change. Although insurrection had been temporarily suppressed, he believed there were still more tories in his county "than any other . . . in Virginia." As half the county militia was disaffected, in his estimation, he predicted he would be unable to raise the county's militia quota when the call came from the state. If he tried to punish offenders "according to Law, they would either withdraw to the mountains, or embody and disturb the peace of the county." By the summer of 1781 Preston thought things had gotten worse, bluntly stating that he had "many reasons to believe" there would be further insurrectionary activity "before the end of the Campaign." In the end there was no insurrection, but only the defeat of the British at Yorktown brought some measure of peace to a troubled southwest Virginia.[39]

What is readily apparent about the unrest in southwest

[39] Callaway to Jefferson, Mar. 23, 1781, Boyd et al., eds., *Jefferson Papers*, 5:212–13; Bedford County Order Book 6, 1774–82, Nov. 26, Dec. 25, 1780, May 29, 1781, Botetourt County Order Book, 1780–84, Nov. 9, 1780, Jan. 11, Feb. 8, Apr. 13, Dec. 13, 1781, Henry County Order Book, 1778–82, Mar. 22, July 26, 1781, Montgomery County Order Book, 1774–82, Nov. 7, 8, 1780, Feb. 6, 7, 8, Apr. 4, 1781, Pittsylvania County Court Records 4, 1777–83, July 3, Nov. 20, 1781, Washington County Minute Book 1, 1777–84, Nov. 23, 1780, microfilm, VSL; Preston to Horatio Gates, Oct. 27, 1780, Preston Papers, Draper Coll., 5QQ84; Preston to Jefferson, Apr. 13, 1781, Boyd et al., eds., *Jefferson Papers*, 5:436–38; Crockett to Preston, May 17, 1781, Papers of the Preston Family. Crockett told Preston of his problems in raising militia but said, philosophically, that he was in good health and he was "where there is whiskey plenty to drink and a full bottle standing on the table" (Preston to Thomas Nelson, July 28, 1781, Executive Papers, June 18–July 31, 1781, VSL). No county court was held in Botetourt County from July 12 until Dec. 13, 1781, or in Montgomery County from May 2 until Nov. 6, 1781.

Virginia is that the disaffected were numerous and that they remained obdurate. I have found 247 persons who were brought into the county courts on charges of breaking state laws designed to curb disaffection, the majority of them in 1779 and 1780. Montgomery County tried 168 individuals and Bedford and Botetourt 37 and 17, respectively. Pittsylvania tried 11, Henry 6, and Washington 5. The accused in Montgomery County, most of whom appear to have been eligible for militia service, constituted 22 percent of the militia roll for that county in 1781. The percentage is significant, but there must have been an equally large group that escaped detection. William Preston repeatedly stated that around 50 percent of the militia in Montgomery were disaffected. Writing Gov. Thomas Nelson in July 1781 of his inability to put militia into the field, he not only observed that more than half the people were disaffected but added that this disaffection appeared to him "to be gaining ground everyday." The previous summer, he explained, loyal militia had suppressed "an insurrection that fully appeared to be impending," but he did not believe "one Prospect had been gained," and he feared similar trouble "before the end of the Campaign." It is safe to estimate that more than 40 percent of both the militia and the population of Montgomery County did not support the patriot cause. The percentages of disaffected appear to have been lower in neighboring counties, but opposition was significant in Bedford and Botetourt and probably in the others as well.[40]

The persistence of the disaffected is as striking as their numbers. A large percentage of them simply opposed independence on political grounds. More than once, when attempting to deal leniently with these people, William Preston and other members of the Montgomery County court stated their belief that the political principles of the accused had not changed. As John Clifton told the court, "His wish [was] still to be with the english." Twenty-five or more individuals ac-

---

[40] For the numbers on the militia rolls in Montgomery County see McIlwaine, ed., *Official Letters*, 2:346. Preston to Jefferson, Apr. 13, 1781, Boyd et al., eds., *Jefferson Papers*, 5:436–38; Preston to Thomas Nelson, July 28, 1781, Executive Papers.

cused of disaffection appeared before Preston's court on two or more occasions or were mentioned as being in opposition over a two- or three-year period.[41]

In economic status the disaffected appear to differ little from the Revolution's supporters, as is indicated by the land tax and personal property records for Montgomery County for 1782 and 1787. Further, the opponents were not grouped in any one area but were distributed evenly throughout the county. One hundred and seven of the 168 persons brought into court in Montgomery County appear in the records as holding land or personal property. Eighty-five of them were landholders, and another 20 were listed as holding only personal property. But it cannot be assumed that all the latter were tenants—6 may have been the sons of men with land, and in a few cases the tax assessors may have failed to list landholdings, for 3 or 4 held substantial amounts of personal property. One, for example, had 2 slaves, 8 horses, and 7 cattle.[42]

Of the 85 landholders in the group of 107, 47 owned less than 200 acres, averaging 110 acres. Another 31 owned 200 to 499 acres with an average of 287 acres. Six held 500 to 999 acres with an average of 642 acres. One person owned 1,368 acres. The 20 who held only personal property each had, on the average, about 4 horses and 7 cattle. Two were clearly very poor, one possessed only a cow and the other only 2 horses.

Of the 60 individuals for whom there exist landholding, land valuation, and personal property records, the 30 who owned under 200 acres held an average of 113 acres valued at 5 shillings an acre. They owned about 4 horses and 10 cattle each. Four of the 30 held a total of 10 slaves. Twenty-

[41] Montgomery County Order Book, 1774–82, Nov. 8, 1780; Preston to Price and others, July 20, 1780; Tory Confessions, Aug. 1780, Preston Papers, Draper Coll., 5QQ41, 68.

[42] All information concerning land and personal property is taken from the Montgomery County Land Tax Books, 1782–1806A, VSL. Bound with this volume is the Personal Property Book for 1782. See also Montgomery County Personal Property Books, 1787, VSL. The slaves listed are age sixteen or above. Geographic location is also based on these records as well as reports as to where outbreaks of disaffection occurred.

four held from 200 to 499 acres, averaging 287 acres (valued at 4 shillings an acre), and, on the average, nearly 10 horses and 14 cattle. Four of them held a total of 15 slaves. Another 5 possessed from 500 to 999 acres, an average holding of 659 acres valued at 10 shillings per acre. Each held nearly 20 horses and 35 cattle. One held 12 slaves, one 10, and the other three owned 1 each. Finally, one person owned 1,368 acres valued at 3 shillings an acre. He held no slaves but had 13 horses and 13 cattle.

It is instructive to compare this group of 60 persons with the 17 (of 19) Montgomery County justices serving between 1777 and 1781 who appear on the tax lists. Though presumably the justices represented the political, economic, and social leadership of the county, their holdings differed little from those of the disaffected. Four possessed fewer than 200 acres; the average was 121 acres valued at 6 shillings an acre (as compared to 113 and 5 for the disaffected). Another 4 held from 200 to 499 acres, with an average 335 acres valued at 8 shillings (286 and 4 for the disaffected). Six held 500 to 999 acres, with an average of 671 acres valued at nearly 4 shillings an acre (659 and 10 for the disaffected). Three owned over 1,000 acres—James McGavock with 1,304 acres valued at 7 shillings, William Christian with 1,900 acres, 900 of which were valued at 2 shillings 4 pence, and, finally, William Preston, the wealthiest man in the county, with 7,022 acres valued at 3 shillings 5 pence an acre. If the land valuation seems low, it should be noted that 900 of his acres were valued at 7 shillings an acre and another 310 at 5 shillings. He owned 34 slaves, 36 horses, and 86 cattle. No one among the disaffected equaled Preston in wealth, but William Ingles, with 907 acres valued at over 7 shillings an acre, 10 slaves, 51 horses, and 67 cattle was also a wealthy man.

Thus it is reasonable to assume that those charged with treason or lesser crimes differed little in economic terms from the rest of Montgomery County's population. Class conflict—if wealth can be seen as an adequate index to class—does not appear to have fueled this opposition to the Revolution. Nor does religious belief. One hundred and thirty of the 168 persons who were brought into court refused to take the oath of allegiance as required in 1777.

There is a record of only 10 of these 130 declaring that they refused for reasons of conscience. In an area such as southwest Virginia, where there was a substantial German population, there were inevitably some who for reasons of religious belief would not take oaths of allegiance, but this group was small.[43]

What then distinguished the disaffected from their patriot neighbors? A descendant of the Campbells, writing in 1843, suggested that tories were more recent arrivals in the southwestern counties and had come from outside Virginia. Most people in the area had, of course, arrived within the past fifteen years, but it may be that the disaffected were even more recent newcomers. The fact that, despite similar economic status, only William Ingles, who was not a newcomer, served on the Fincastle County court would suggest that many of the disaffected were recent arrivals. Ingles was not subsequently a member of the Montgomery County court, although he was appointed colonel of the militia and sheriff in 1777; James McCorkle, another of the disaffected, served on the court only during 1777. Consequently, it can be argued that these people, arriving in the area in the middle years of the decade, found themselves not only disagreeing with the political position of the local leadership but also unable to influence that position. They may have continued to feel that they were outsiders.[44]

The close proximity of southwest Virginia to central and western North Carolina, where disaffection was also prevalent, did not in itself foment resistance but it did permit mutual support among the disaffected. John Griffith, for example, the acknowledged leader of tories in Montgomery

[43] Lists of militia who took the oath of allegiance, as well as those who refused on grounds of conscience, can be found in Kegley and Kegley, *Early Adventurers*, pp. 146–51. See also Loyalists Bound for Good Behavior, July 29, 1780, and County Courts of Montgomery and Botetourt Counties Meeting to Examine Col. William Ingles and Others, Aug. 1780, Preston Papers, Draper Coll., 5QQ47, 73–79; Wust, *Virginia Germans*, p. 144.

[44] Kegley and Kegley, *Early Adventurers*, p. 146; Montgomery County Order Book, 1774–82, Jan. 7, 1777.

County, seems to have moved between the Carolinas and Virginia with relative ease.[45]

Finally resistance was also made easier by the fact that in this frontier community government authority was tenuous at best. Montgomery County had been recently formed (1777) and was far removed from the center of power, as its court justices were well aware. Walter Crockett urged William Preston to attend the trial of tories in the spring of 1779 because "the greatest part of our Court is young Justices and not very well versed in the Law and in my opinion would not be the worse of a Good Steady old Gentleman as Your Self to Seat at their head." James McGavock had earlier suggested to Preston that "the Business is new" and without "you it may be very difficult." Citizens held the court in no awe and showed no hesitation in expressing themselves. One John McDonald, the court reported, declared in July 1780 that he would pay "no taxes & if they were Inforced Col. Preston might take care of himself & if any harm followed he might blame himself." And "he would lose his Life before he would give up his arms & that there would soon . . . be a King in every County." McDonald said "he thought We had been fighting for Liberty but slavery was a consequence." It should be added that McDonald was a man of some substance, for he owned 200 acres as well as seven horses and eight cattle. Unlike the courts of the counties to the east, there was not much difference in property holding between the justices and the accused. Preston was one of the very few persons of wealth and status in the area, and his presence on the court was important. But even he recognized the limitations under which the court functioned. Montgomery was a "frontier county," he observed, and so had "many disorderly People." On more than one occasion he did not leave his home because he feared that his "neighbours" might harm his family. And in explaining to Thomas Jefferson his inability to get disaffected militia to answer a call for service, he said that

[45] On John Griffith's movements see, for example, McGavock to Preston, June 30, 1780, *John P. Branch Historical Papers* 4 (1915):315–16. For ethnic composition see footnote 8.

"should they be punished according to Law, they would either withdraw to the mountains, or embody and disturb the peace of the county."[46]

A new community, if that is not too strong a term, peopled by large numbers of recent arrivals who opposed independence and existing under a government whose powers remained shaky, it is not surprising that southwest Virginia had its troubles. On occasion they assumed the proportions of insurrection. Still, the wounds seem to have healed quickly. Perceiving that the disaffected among them were solid, respectable men who differed from the rest in little but their disaffection, the patriot leadership wielded its admittedly weak authority with great moderation. (The still weaker county governments in the Carolinas and Georgia showed less restraint.) After, and even during the war, the Virginians showed themselves openhandedly willing to accept the wayward as neighbors once more. The Montgomery County court put it well when it ruled that three loyalists, who were petitioning for pardon, should be "received as members of the community so long as they behave as good citizens" despite the fact that it was only "a Change of prospect and necessity rather than any alteration in their principles that induces them to petition in the manner they have done."[47]

[46] McGavock to Preston, Apr. 15, 1779, Crockett to Preston, Apr. 24, 1779, Preston to Thomas Nelson [Benjamin Harrison?], Mar. 15, 1782, *John P. Branch Historical Papers* 4 (1915):302–4, 308, 333–34; Warrant for John McDonald, July 24, 1780, Preston Papers, Draper Coll., 5QQ43; Montgomery County Land Tax Books, 1782–1806A, and Personal Property Books, 1782 and 1787, microfilm, VSL; Preston to Jefferson, Apr. 15, 1781, Boyd et al., eds., *Jefferson Papers*, 5:436–38.

[47] Montgomery County Order Book, 1774–82, Nov. 8, 1780, July 2, 1782; Proclamation concerning Thomas Heavin and Others, Aug. 14, 1780, Preston Papers, Draper Coll., 5QQ55; Petition of Resisters to Militia Service to William Preston, n.d. [Dec. 1780?], Papers of the Preston Family, typescript; Calhoon, *Loyalists*, ch. 48.

RICHARD R. BEEMAN

The Political Response to Social Conflict in the Southern Backcountry

A Comparative View of
Virginia and the Carolinas
during the Revolution

SOME THIRTY YEARS ago Carl Bridenbaugh, in his book *Myths and Realities*, reminded his readers that "in 1776 there was no South; there never had been a South. . . . In the four and a half decades before the Revolution the vast domain of the King lying between Mason's and Dixon's line and East Florida was the scene of three . . . different modes of existence. There was the already old Chesapeake Society, erected on a tobacco base; there was the youthful Carolina Society, burgeoning on profits from rice and indigo; and there was the lusty Back Country, as yet unformed but prospering in several stages from hunting to mixed farming."[1]

Having rejected the stereotype of a self-conscious, monolithic South in pre-Revolutionary America, Bridenbaugh

[1] Carl Bridenbaugh, *Myths and Realities: Societies of the Colonial South* (Baton Rouge, 1952), p. vii. The book was the product of Bridenbaugh's Walter Lynwood Fleming Lectures in Southern History, Nov. 5–6, 1951. After delivering the lectures Bridenbaugh speculated that there might have been a fourth society in the colonial South—that covering coastal North Carolina—but he did not elaborate on the characteristics of that region.

then proceeded, with forceful argument and engaging prose, to fashion his own stereotypes of those three subregions within the South. The stable, mature Chesapeake, where *Englishmen* created a responsive and responsible political system based solidly on the principle of noblesse oblige—this was clearly Bridenbaugh's favorite. Carolina, with its quick profits and its more heterogeneous population, was a society not fully formed, displaying extremes of wealth and poverty and lacking much of the gentility and civic responsibility of the Anglo-American society of the Chesapeake. And, finally, the backcountry—still more heterogeneous and less well-formed—seemed to Bridenbaugh a rude and nasty place. It was a region in which "mutual dislike and mutual suspicion more often than not triumphed over brotherhood and charity" and in which "ignorance and rural isolation created a meanness of spirit and a laxity of morals."[2]

There were, in Bridenbaugh's view, a few Englishmen who immigrated south and west from the Chesapeake who were capable of providing some leadership for the backcountry, and the German settlers, "pacific, law abiding, stolid, deeply pious, and temperate," were at least likely to contribute to the economic development of the region even if they lacked the independence of mind and libertarian spirit appropriate to political leadership. But the rest—in particular the hordes of Scotch-Irish who began to move southward into the backcountry from Pennsylvania in the 1730s—seemed to him a brutish lot. "Undisciplined, emotional, courageous, aggressive, pugnacious, fiercely intolerant, and hard drinking, with a tendency to indolence," the Scotch-Irish more than any other cultural group gave to the backcountry its distinctive and not altogether savory flavor. Indeed, Bridenbaugh's depiction of that aspect of backcountry life is often difficult to distinguish from that of his principal primary source, that anguished and vituperative Anglican itinerant minister Charles Woodmason, whose fervent denunciations of the "low, lazy, sluttish, heathenish, hellish life" of the South Carolina backcountry residents provided such a colorful but fundamentally misleading commentary on backcountry cul-

---

[2] Ibid.

ture. Making social relations still more uncertain, the Indian inhabitants of the backcountry continued to constitute even more of an impediment to "civilization." Never one to be caught up with romantic notions of the aboriginal inhabitants of any part of America, Bridenbaugh quoted with approval the "realistic" view of John Bartram that "unless we bang the Indians stoutly, and make them fear us, they will never love us, nor keep the peace long with us."[3]

Most historians of the backcountry, while they may still assign Bridenbaugh's book to their survey courses, have tended not to follow his research strategy in their own work. They have, for good reasons, rejected the ethnocentrism inherent in so many of his cultural judgments. And, working in an interpretive framework that has tended to conceive of each of the backcountry settlements as discrete fragments of individual colonies, they have tended to describe the problems and prospects of the settlers in terms of the political decisions made by members of the dominant culture in the colonial capitals of Williamsburg, New Bern, or Charleston. As a consequence, the prevailing conception of the southern backcountry suggests a fairly sharp distinction between the social orders of North and South Carolina on the one hand and that of Virginia on the other. The dominant image of the Carolina backcountry, fashioned both by the hysteria of the good Reverend Charles Woodmason and by conflict-oriented historians from John Spencer Bassett to Marvin Michael Kay, is of social *disorder*. It is a picture of ethnic diversity leading to ethnic conflict, religious diversity leading to religious conflict, inequality of wealth leading to violent class conflict, and of inequality of political power leading to a governmental system that was at best inefficient and at worst corrupt. The Virginia story, by contrast, seems to be that of the steady westward movement of both the economy and culture of the tidewater, with the younger sons of Virginia gentrymen bringing to the backcountry not only their money and their slaves but their cultural values as well. As a consequence, the

[3] Ibid., pp. 119, 133; Richard J. Hooker, ed., *The Carolina Backcountry on the Eve of the Revolution: The Journal and Other Writings of Charles Woodmason, Anglican Itinerant* (Chapel Hill, 1953), p. 52.

Virginia backcountry supposedly acquired an orderliness that, if it was not an exact replication of eastern gentry culture, nevertheless stood in sharp distinction to the Regulator riots and civil turmoil in the Carolinas. And, looking toward the Revolution, those same perceived differences between the social orders of the Carolinas and Virginia have provided historians with their primary explanation for the apparent unity of support for the whig-patriot effort in Virginia and the confusion of loyalties in North and South Carolina.[4]

[4]The literature on the backcountry of the Virginia, North Carolina, and South Carolina colonies varies considerably in quantity and quality. Surprisingly, that on Virginia is probably the most sparse on both scores. The best single work is Robert D. Mitchell, *Commercialism and Frontier: Perspectives on the Early Shenandoah Valley* (Charlottesville, Va., 1977). Other works are: Thomas Perkins Abernethy, *Three Virginia Frontiers* (Baton Rouge, 1940); Freeman H. Hart, *The Valley of Virginia in the Revolution, 1763–1789* (Chapel Hill, 1942); Charles Henry Ambler, *Sectionalism in Virginia from 1776 to 1861* (Chicago, 1910). There is also one excellent unpublished work, Michael L. Nicholls, "Origins of the Virginia Southside, 1705–1753: A Social and Economic Study," Ph.D. diss., College of William and Mary, 1972. The literature on North Carolina is quite rich. See A. Roger Ekirch, *"Poor Carolina": Politics and Society in Colonial North Carolina, 1729–1776* (Chapel Hill, 1981); Harry Roy Merrens, *Colonial North Carolina in the Eighteenth Century: A Study in Historical Geography* (Chapel Hill, 1964); Hugh T. Lefler and William S. Powell, *Colonial North Carolina: A History* (New York, 1973); Alice Elaine Mathews, *Society in Revolutionary North Carolina* (Raleigh, 1976); Robert W. Ramsey, *Carolina Cradle: Settlement of the Northwest Carolina Frontier, 1747–1762* (Chapel Hill, 1964); John Spencer Bassett, "The Regulators of North Carolina, 1765–1771," *Annual Report of the American Historical Association for the Year 1894* (Washington, D.C., 1895), pp. 141–212; Marvin L. Michael Kay, "The North Carolina Regulation, 1766–1776: A Class Conflict," in Alfred F. Young, ed., *The American Revolution: Explorations in the History of American Radicalism* (De Kalb, Ill., 1976), pp. 84–103; James P. Whittenburg, "Planters, Merchants, and Lawyers: Social Change and the Origins of the North Carolina Regulation," *William and Mary Quarterly*, 3d ser. 34 (1977):215–38; idem, "God's Chosen in the Backcountry" (Paper presented at the Forty-fifth Annual Meeting of the Southern Historical Association, Atlanta, November 1979); Elisha P. Douglass, *Rebels and Democrats: The Struggle for Equal Rights and Majority Rule during the American Revolution* (Chapel Hill, 1955), esp. pp. 71–135. For South Carolina, see especially Richard Maxwell Brown, *The South Carolina Regulators* (Cambridge, Mass., 1963); Rachel N. Klein, "Ordering the Backcountry: The South Carolina Regulation," *William and Mary Quarterly*,

Bridenbaugh's conception of the southern backcountry, while indeed badly flawed by its prejudices, may nevertheless be more useful, at least as a starting point, than these more rigidly segmented approaches. Its great strength rests in its ability to comprehend the history of the whole of the back-country—from Frederick County, Maryland, down through the Great Valley, central piedmont and southside of Virginia, and into those parts of North and South Carolina lying between the fall line and the Great Smokies—as part of a common process involving rapid population increase, phe-nomenal geographic and economic mobility, the intermix-ture of a nearly unprecedented variety of ethnic and religious groups, and a general commitment on the part of that varied lot of citizens to subsistence agriculture. Viewed from that perspective, it seems that, whatever the difference in the outcomes of the Revolutionary movements in Virginia and the Carolinas, the essential character of the social order of backcountry Virginia was not radically dissimilar from that of either North or South Carolina. And, following from that discovery, it seems as well that the most satisfying expla-nation for the varying responses of the backcountry areas to the experience of the Revolution is to be found not in any set of fundamental differences within the social fabric of those regions but rather in politics and, in particular, in drastically different traditions of political leadership.

The starting point for understanding the essential similar-ities in the conditions of life in the southern backcountry is the fact that most of the settlers in that region were part of the same, extraordinary wave of immigration, beginning in the 1730s, but reaching epic proportions in the period from

3d ser. 38 (1981):661–80; idem, "Choosing Sides: Americans and Loyalists in the South Carolina Backcountry, 1775–79" (Paper presented at the Forty-sixth Annual Meeting of the Southern Historical Association, At-lanta, November 1980); D. Huger Bacot, "The South Carolina Upcountry at the End of the Eighteenth Century," *American Historical Review* 28 (1923):682–98; and Robert L. Meriwether, *The Expansion of South Carolina, 1729–1765* (Kingsport, Tenn., 1940). One can also glean useful bits of information from the older work by Edward McCrady, *History of South Carolina in the Revolution, 1775–1780* (New York, 1901).

1750 to 1770.[5] In Virginia the greatest increase in the pre-Revolutionary period was in the southside and great south-west, with the population rising at the rate of about 15 percent every year during the 1750s and then maintaining a steady upward momentum of about 8 to 10 percent each

[5] In arguing for a common social and economic history for the southern backcountry I am not ignoring completely the considerable body of evidence suggesting that long-term patterns of economic development differed in various parts of the region. It is plainly true, for example, that the tobacco culture of the Virginia tidewater and Northern Neck steadily expanded westward, involving at least some of the citizens of the central piedmont and southside in an extensive and expansive economy. By contrast, the rice and indigo planters of coastal South Carolina may have generated profits far in excess of those enjoyed by their Virginia counterparts, but for much of the pre-Revolutionary period that economy did not extend into the backcountry. North Carolina never generated the wealth of her northern or southern neighbors and thus could not spread it to the backcountry.

There is no satisfactory economic history of any of the three colonies, let alone an adequate synthesis of the economic development of the whole of the colonial South. A useful starting point for the early history of the Carolinas and Georgia is Clarence L. Ver Steeg, *Origins of a Southern Mosaic: Studies of Early Carolina and Georgia* (Athens, Ga., 1975). Ekirch, *"Poor Carolina,"* esp. pp. 3–51, and Merrens, *Colonial North Carolina*, are probably the best treatments of North Carolina. Alan Kulikoff, "The Colonial Chesapeake: Seedbed of Antebellum Southern Culture," *Journal of Southern History* 65 (1979), is a useful overview of the unfolding of Virginia's tobacco economy in the seventeenth and eighteenth centuries; Nicholls, "Origins of the Virginia Southside," and Mitchell, *Commercialism and Frontier*, deal with aspects of the economic history of the Virginia backcountry. For South Carolina, Converse Clowse, *Economic Beginnings of Colonial South Carolina, 1670–1730* (Columbia, S.C., 1971), deals with the early economic development of the colony. See also Meriwether, *Expansion of South Carolina*, and Joseph A. Ernst and Harry Roy Merrens, "The South Carolina Economy of the Middle-Eighteenth Century: The View from Philadelphia," *West Georgia College Studies in the Social Sciences* 12 (1973).

Given the dearth of precise information on patterns of economic activity among large and small farmers in the backcountry regions, the best index of economic activity is probably the differing patterns of slave ownership. In parts of the Virginia backcountry, most notably the central piedmont and southside, slaves accounted for about 40 percent of the total population; in a few counties—Amelia, Cumberland, and Goochland, for example—they amounted to as much as 50 or 60 percent. In the rest of the Virginia backcountry, however—the Valley of Virginia and the south-west—slaves probably never constituted more than 15 percent of the pop-

year until the Revolution.[6] In North Carolina the backcountry population more than doubled during the years from 1750 to 1770, with the number of inhabitants of Anson, Orange, and Rowan counties—the center of subsequent Regulator activities—actually tripling in just five years between 1760 and 1765. Similarly, the South Carolina backcountry, though it remained virtually unsettled through the mid-1730s, had by the 1760s increased to between 30,000 and 35,000, comprising nearly three-fourths of the colony's total white population.[7]

There is no denying the compelling evidence that life on the southern frontier was at times arduous for many of the people who had uprooted themselves from their former homes in Pennsylvania, Scotland, Ireland, or Germany. But it strains credulity to argue—as some have done—that only the myth and not the substance of economic opportunity

---

ulation. In the North Carolina backcountry whites probably outnumbered slaves by an average of four to one, with significant regional variations, and in South Carolina by about five to one. The only areas where there was a heavy investment in commercial, single-crop agriculture would seem, therefore, to be the Virginia piedmont and southside, but even there the scale of investment in slaves was but a shadow of that in either the Virginia tidewater or the coastal plain of South Carolina.

[6] The figures cited in the text are based on Nicholls, "Origins of the Virginia Southside," pp. 28–55, and on an analysis of the Lunenburg County tithable lists printed in Landon C. Bell, *Sunlight on the Southside: Lists of Tithes, Lunenburg County, Virginia, 1748–1783* (Philadelphia, 1931). Hart, *Valley of Virginia*, p. 7, estimates that the population of the Valley increased from 21,000 in 1763 to 53,000 in 1776, a roughly similar rate of increase.

Although both the southside and southwestern regions of Virginia experienced their greatest increase in population at about the same time— between roughly 1740 and 1776—the sources of that population differed somewhat. In the southwest the flow of population was overwhelmingly from north to south and included a preponderance of Scotch-Irish and Germans. In the southside it was both from north to south and east to west, and its composition was a mixture of Scotch-Irish and Virginia-born English.

[7] Lester J. Cappon, ed., *Atlas of Early American History: The Revolutionary Era, 1760–1790* (Princeton, 1976), p. 25; Ekirch, *"Poor Carolina,"* p. 6; Whittenburg, "God's Chosen in the Backcountry"; Klein, "Ordering the Backcountry," p. 663; Brown, *South Carolina Regulators*, pp. 18–19.

awaited those tens of thousands of settlers. Those who have argued that overt class conflict was the principal cause of both Regulator disturbances in the 1760s and 1770s and civil disorder within the backcountry at the time of the Revolution have pointed to the fact of increasing differentiation within the region. While it is possible to identify in some statistical sense an emerging "economic elite" in the western areas of all three colonies, the material endowments of that elite were pitifully meager by the standards of their counterparts in Virginia's Northern Neck or in the South Carolina lowcountry. The members of the economic elite in the southern backcountry were people like the wealthiest citizen in Virginia's Lunenburg County, Henry Blagrave, who—though he had invested heavily in tobacco cultivation, amassing some two thousand acres and twelve tithable slaves by the time of the Revolution—was only a slightly more successful than average planter. His estate, probated at his death in 1781, had a full inventory of slaves, horses, cattle, sheep, hogs, pails, tubs, saws, hoes, plows, harnesses, reap hooks, and jugs, as well as a hogshead of rum, a fiddle, and one wine glass, but missing altogether are those items—silver, plate, china, crystal, or a portrait or even a picture—that might suggest the life of a more refined Virginia gentleman.[8]

[8] Lunenburg County Will Book 3, Oct. 11, 1781, p. 99, microfilm, Virginia State Library, Richmond. For a more extensive treatment of Blagrave's economic and social attainments and of the southside "elite" generally, see Richard R. Beeman, "The Creation of an Elite Ruling Tradition in the Virginia Southside: Lunenburg as a Case Study" (Paper presented at the Seventy-third Annual Meeting of the Organization of American Historians, San Francisco, April 1980). For further negative evidence on the relatively modest attainments of the backcountry "gentry" see Jackson Turner Main, "The One Hundred," *William and Mary Quarterly*, 3d ser. 11 (1954):354–84. Main's index of the hundred wealthiest men in Virginia is badly skewed because it depends on land, not slave holdings, as the primary criterion for inclusion within the group, but few backcountry residents appear on his list anyway. Significantly, those who do—men like Wilson Cary Nicholas of Albemarle County—are a part of that atypical group of individuals who were successful in transplanting wealth acquired in the east to the west. In this respect both the economic and demographic histories of Albemarle and Orange counties—the "backcountry" homes of Thomas Jefferson and James Madison respectively—are notable exceptions to my general analysis here.

Far more striking than the modest attainments of those who rose to the statistical top of the economic order was the extraordinary expansiveness of the middling ranks. In the Virginia and North Carolina backcountry the number of households owning their own land exceeded 70 percent, with the great majority of those householders owning between 100 and 400 acres; in South Carolina's Ninety-Six District over 90 percent of the adult male population owned land.[9] While there is no dearth of testimony attesting to some of the rude aspects of life in the region, observers were often struck by the relative ease with which the inhabitants could support themselves. The Virginia gentryman William Byrd, on one of his trips to inspect his speculative holdings in the backcountry, commented: "Surely there is no place in the world where the inhabitants live with less labor than in North Carolina. It approaches nearer the description of lubberland than any other, by the great felicity of the climate, the easiness of raising provisions, and the slothfulness of the people." Byrd's observations betray, it should be noted, the incomprehension of a gentryman who had never bothered to ponder the daily hardships of people living on the frontier. Nevertheless, he recognized, like so many others, that this was "the Best Poor Man's Cuntry," a description that had once been applied to parts of Pennsylvania and Virginia.[10]

Most of the members of the middle ranks who inhabited the backcountries of Virginia, North, and South Carolina

[9] The figures for North Carolina are taken from Ekirch, *"Poor Carolina,"* pp. 19–47. The Virginia figures are based both on my intensive analysis of the Lunenburg County tithable lists in Bell, *Sunlight on the Southside*, pp. 58–161, and on the more general findings of Jackson Turner Main, *The Social Structure of Revolutionary America* (Princeton, 1965), pp. 46–54. Main was inclined to exaggerate the amount of inequality in Revolutionary America, but his calculations on the southern backcountry bear out the contention of rough equality in the middling ranks.

[10] Louis B. Wright, ed., *The Prose Works of William Byrd of Westover: Narratives of a Colonial Virginian* (Cambridge, Mass., 1966), p. 204. The phrase "Best Poor Man's Cuntry," which we most often associate with New York and Pennsylvania, was also used to describe Virginia and North Carolina (S. Johnson, Jr., to Robert Cathcart, Nov. 28, 1774, quoted in Ekirch, *"Poor Carolina,"* p. 26).

were less dependent than their lowcountry neighbors on labor-intensive crops like tobacco, rice, and indigo and more
reliant on the cultivation of foodstuffs such as wheat and
corn and—of particular and overlooked importance—on
the grazing of cattle, one of the easiest and cheapest ways of
gaining a subsistence in a land-plentiful but labor-scarce
economy.[11] To be sure, there were variations in the profit-
ability of this sort of agriculture from Virginia's central piedmont to the Saluda River in western South Carolina, but on
the whole the daily rhythms of what I would term *expansive-
subsistence* agriculture dictated a common style of life.[12]

This picture of a generally uniform pattern of rapid population increase, enhanced economic opportunity, and a relatively fluid and unstratified economic order admittedly
looks a bit whiggish, yet it is important to stress that the egalitarianism of the backcountry often meant equality of hardship as well. Though the middling ranks may have enjoyed
unprecedented opportunity to purchase inexpensive land,
that commodity did not allow them to accumulate the surplus capital that might enable them to participate in the consumer revolution that seems to have been occurring
elsewhere in America. In Lunenburg County, for example,
the median estate during the 1760s was valued at only about
£75, with the typical estate containing a few horses, some
livestock, simple carpenter's tools, the basic complement of
farm implements, a bed (usually of straw, and without a bed-
stand), and a few plates and pots (but only rarely earthen-

[11] For informative treatments of the grazing economy see Nicholls, "Origins of the Virginia Southside," pp. 210–13, and David O. Percy, "Of Fast
Horses, Black Cattle, Woods Hogs, and Rat-Tailed Sheep: Animal Hus-
bandry along the Colonial Potomac," *National Colonial Farm Research Report
No. 4* (Accokeek, Md., 1979).

[12] Perhaps by the early nineteenth century the increasing number of
settlers in the backcountry may have placed a strain on the land resources
of the region, but in the period before the Revolution population growth,
more than being merely an indicator of economic opportunity, was in itself
a cause of heightened opportunity. As new settlers poured into the region,
local merchants and traders with a modest store of goods, or farmers with
surplus livestock or a little extra land, were able to take advantage of the
burgeoning internal economy created by the needs of the newcomers.

ware) for the kitchen. All of this was plainly enough for an "independent" existence, but hardly sufficient for a luxurious one.[13] Moreover, only good fortune—or the avoidance of misfortune—separated the great mass of middling farmers from a return to dependence. Lacking surplus capital, most backcountry planters knew well that a serious illness or a fire—phenomena that touched all too many of their friends and relatives—could destroy the material basis of their independence.[14]

If the extraordinary mobility of the backcountry settlers served to enhance economic opportunity, it worked at the same time to create chronic instability. The settlers who came to the backcountry brought with them an unprecedented variety of cultural preferences and only the vaguest loyalties to the government or traditions of a single colony. Indeed, it is clear that many of the citizens of Virginia's southside had less identification with their colony than they did with that backcountry subregion which included parts of north-central North Carolina. In Lunenburg, for example, marriage patterns were just as likely to cross colonial boundaries into North Carolina as they were to move either to the north or east, and even church congregations—at least for dissenting religions—drew members from outside the colony as well as from within.

Perhaps the most dramatic sign of the impermanence of colonial or even regional attachments was the phenomenal

[13] Lunenburg County Will Book 2, 1760–65, microfilm, VSL.

[14] There did exist in the southern backcountry an underclass—probably no larger than existed anywhere else in America but by most reports a good deal meaner—of individuals who did not cultivate the land and instead tried to derive a subsistence from hunting, peddling, or plundering. This itinerant class of men was plainly one of the sources of the Regulator movements in both North and South Carolina, but it existed as well in the Virginia backcountry. Indeed, the sorts of men who made up the itinerant hunters and peddlers of the region were precisely those who did not confine their activities to any one county or colony. For the life-style of the peddling class in Virginia see Richard R. Beeman, "Trade and Travel in Post-Revolutionary Virginia: A Diary of an Itinerant Peddler," *Virginia Magazine of History and Biography* 84 (1976):174–88. See also Mitchell, *Commercialism and Frontier*, pp. 134–35.

movement of citizens *out* of the backcountry counties. During the 1750s, when Lunenburg's total population was increasing at the rate of 16 percent annually, it was also losing its existing population at the rate of 17 percent per year, a migration pattern that assured that over 30 percent of the county's population would consist of individuals who had arrived only within the past year.[15] This extraordinary mobility in and out of the county made the Virginia backcountry—no less than that of North and South Carolina—a "moving frontier" in the fullest sense of that phrase, with an uncertainty of kin and social relations that affected community stability in countless ways.

The cultural diversity of the people who were moving in and out of virtually all parts of the southern backcountry has been well known to every historian who has studied the region, but few have explored the effects of that diversity on the social order of the backcountry. Charles Woodmason's English and Anglican sensibilities were obviously overwrought when he described the Scotch-Irish settlers of South Carolina as "the Scum of the Earth and the Refuse of Mankind," but his denunciations of their "gross licentiousness, Wantoness, Lasciviousness, Rudeness, Lewdness and Profligacy" serve as a powerful indicator of the kind of tension that cultural diversity created in a world wholly unused to that diversity and where ethnocentrism and provincialism were the norm rather than the exception.[16]

That ethnic diversity, in combination with the structural and spiritual frailty of the established Church of England, led to an unprecedented diversity of religious life as well. Rhys Isaac has portrayed in vivid fashion the character of the "evangelical revolt" in Virginia, but in depicting that movement as a response to "internal disorder"—to inherent weaknesses within the Anglican-gentry culture throughout the whole colony—he has underestimated the extent to which the rise of the evangelicals, a movement plainly most apparent in the western counties, was a function both of the partic-

[15] These calculations are based on an analysis of the tithable lists printed in Bell, *Sunlight on the Southside*, pp. 58–161.

[16] Hooker, ed., *South Carolina Backcountry*, pp. 52, 60.

ular weaknesses of the established church in the backcountry and of the entirely different sorts of people—most of whom had never had any connection with the religious culture of the gentry in the first place—who had settled there.[17]

The evangelicals, particularly the Baptists, faced an essentially similar experience in both the Carolina and Virginia backcountries. It was in their conflict not only with the representatives of the established church but also with the great mass of the unchurched who were most prominent in scorning and disrupting their religious observances that the diversity and the instability of the social order were displayed most fully. The intensity of opposition to the Baptists may have varied from group to group within the backcountry (it seems possible, for example, that the Anglicans were more outspoken in their scorn for the Baptists in Virginia while it was the unchurched who were largely responsible for harassment in parts of the Carolinas), but the Baptist church records in both Virginia and the Carolinas testify forcefully to a religious experience that was common to evangelical adherents everywhere in the backcountry.

It was, first and foremost, a profoundly emotional experience in which the exhortations of the ministers "kindled the flame of the Christians," provoked "the devil, a raging and blaspheming," and set "the sinners trembling and falling down convulsed." And it was a profoundly communitarian experience. When scores, sometimes hundreds, of converts walked into the rivers of Virginia and the Carolinas to bind themselves together through the ritual of adult baptism, they were both setting themselves apart from those who gathered on the river banks to scoff and scorn them and at the same time seeking to create the kind of community that was lacking in virtually any other institutional form in the spacious and often isolated backcountry. And those same individuals, by submitting themselves to the rigorous disciplinary code of the church meeting, were both affirming their intention to create some kind of order in their lives on the frontier and

[17] Rhys Isaac, "Evangelical Revolt: The Nature of the Baptists' Challenge to the Traditional Order in Virginia, 1765 to 1775," *William and Mary Quarterly*, 3d ser. 31 (1974):345–68.

issuing an implicit rebuke to those many around them who chose to live their lives differently.[18] In this sense poor Charles Woodmason, though he never recognized it, shared a common objective with those Baptists whose practices he found so offensive. Woodmason's more genteel mission to bring order to the backcountry (one might almost call it an "evangelical" mission) was constantly being interrupted by "lawless Ruffians" telling him that "they wanted no damned Black Gown Sons of Bitches among them," threatening his very safety in much the same way that Baptists were intimidated by Anglicans who urged their suppression and by nonbelievers who scorned their pious rituals. Like Woodmason, however, the Baptists persisted. Indeed, as one Virginia Anglican minister observed, "they [the evangelicals] pray for Persecutions, and therefore if you fall upon any severe method of suppressing them, it will tend to strengthen their cause."[19] The kind of disorder that these conflicts represented—worrisome to pious Anglicans as well as to their evangelical rivals in the southern backcountry—was not confined to the political boundaries of Virginia, North Carolina, or South Carolina.

While the economic and social conditions of life in the Virginia and Carolina backcountries displayed striking similarities, the operation of the political institutions designed to govern those regions was decidedly different. There is, of course, hardly anything novel about that assertion, for most historians who have written about politics in Virginia and the Carolinas have emphasized the persistence of deferential, consensual styles in the former and of a high degree of conflict in the latter. There was, it seems clear, a dramatic difference in the way in which the political systems of the Virginia and Carolina colonies operated. Given the independence,

[18] For a fuller discussion of this see Richard R. Beeman, "Social Change and Cultural Conflict in Virginia: Lunenburg County, 1746–1774," *William and Mary Quarterly*, 3d ser. 35 (1978).

[19] Hooker, ed., *South Carolina Backcountry*, pp. 16–17; Rev. James Craig to Thomas Dawson, Sept. 8, 1759, William Dawson Papers, II, 218, Library of Congress.

impermanence, cultural and religious dissidence, and general obstreperousness of the citizens in all of those colonies, however, it is wholly implausible to assume that Virginia frontiersmen were any more intrinsically deferential than their Carolina counterparts.

Nowhere is the absence of deference in politics more clearly seen than in the record of contested elections in the Virginia backcountry, a record displaying a consistent pattern of rowdiness, drunkenness, and occasional outright intimidation. For example, the Committee of Privileges and Elections of the House of Burgesses was moved to set aside a 1758 election in Lunenburg because of "the behavior of one John Hobson, which was very illegal and tumultous, in offering to lay Wagers the Poll was closed, when it was not; in proclaiming at the Courthouse that the poll was going to be closed, and desiring the Freeholders to come in and vote, and then, violently, and by striking and kicking them, preventing them from doing so, by which Means many Freeholders did not vote at said election." In neighboring Halifax County the sheriff charged that Nathaniel Terry, one of the candidates for the Burgesses, "came to me, his Coat and Waistcoat being stripped off, and his Collar open, and holding up a large Stick, threatened to cane me, and declared, if I attempted to read the Writ [of election] he would split me down, and did aim and endeavour several times to Strike me . . . with his Stick. . . . Immediately after this such a Tumult ensued, and the Electors were in such a Temper, and so disorderly, and some of them drank of spiritous liquors to such excess, that I was convinced a fair Election could not have been made afterwards on that Day."[20]

When Charles Sydnor analyzed the meaning of those scenes in his classic book *Gentlemen Freeholders*, he depicted them as an amusing deviation from the prevailing deferential code of the Old Dominion, but in fact those scenes, occurring as consistently as they did in the Virginia back-

---

[20] H. R. McIlwaine, ed., *Journals of the House of Burgesses of Virginia, 1752–1755, 1756–1758*, Mar. 8, 1758 (Richmond, 1909), pp. 83–84; John P. Kennedy, ed., *Journals of the House of Burgesses of Virginia, 1766–1769*, Nov. 8, 1769 (Richmond, 1906), p. 231.

country, suggested a system in which claims by political candidates to traditional deference were far less secure and in which the inclination of an independent and mobile citizenry to give deference was far more grudging at the very outset.[21] Yet in spite of the collapse of traditional, deferential ways and in spite of the occasional tumult at election time, the political system of the Virginia backcountry counties was, on balance, strikingly more successful than that in the Carolinas, both in its ability to represent the interests of the western counties in the politics of the colony as a whole and in its ability to serve the particular legal needs of nearly all the citizenry at the local level.

By contrast, the institutional machinery of both the North and South Carolina backcountry was woefully inadequate to the needs of the burgeoning population of those areas. Most obviously, the Carolina backcountry counties lacked adequate representation. In North Carolina the ratio of representatives to constituents in the northeastern counties was about 1:150, as compared with about 1:1500 in parts of the west.[22] On most occasions the attitude of the assembly toward the west was not one of aggressive oppression but of simple indifference. When that inattention was perceived to be a part of the cause for the closing of the government land office for nearly the entire northern half of the colony in 1763—at precisely the time when demand for land by newcomers was peaking—the settlers could no longer afford to be content with benign neglect.[23] Far more serious, however, than the inefficiency and inattention of the colonial assembly was the utter inadequacy of local government in backcountry North Carolina. Scholars have disagreed on the precise extent of deliberate political corruption at the county level, but there is no disputing the fact that local officials in backcountry North Carolina were as feckless, venal, and larcenous a

[21] Charles Sydnor, *Gentlemen Freeholders: Political Practices in Washington's Virginia* (Chapel Hill, 1952). For a more extended discussion of this subject see Richard R. Beeman, "Robert Munford and the Political Culture of Frontier Virginia," *Journal of American Studies* 12 (1978):169–83.

[22] Douglass, *Rebels and Democrats*, p. 75.

[23] Ekirch, *"Poor Carolina,"* pp. 177–78.

lot as existed anywhere in America. Sheriffs embezzled public tax moneys and illegally seized property from those unable to pay inflated tax assessments, and justices of the peace, most of them lacking any significant previous political experience, sought to use their offices improperly in pursuit of private gain. Some of this behavior was the result of pure, calculated avarice, but the principal blame must be placed on a colonywide political system that had never given serious consideration to the question of how best to govern a rapidly expanding, multiethnic society. As James P. Whittenburg has observed, "Even if the Regulation had not brought local government to a standstill in the late 1760s, the impossibility of administering—with only the meager tools provided by the assembly—an area larger than most contemporary European nations and containing a population whose diversity was rivalled only by that of Pennsylvania, would probably have done the trick."[24]

In South Carolina the situation was probably worse. Backcountry residents in that colony comprised some three-fourths of the colony's white population, yet were granted only three of the colony's thirty representatives in the assembly. And while North Carolinians had at least some of the formal machinery if not the actual substance of local government, South Carolina's assembly systematically refused to es-

[24] The most convincing accounts of the underlying sources of the Regulator disturbances in North Carolina are those by Ekirch in *"Poor Carolina,"* pp. 161–211, and in "The North Carolina Regulators on Liberty and Corruption, 1766–1771," *Perspectives in American History* 11 (1977–78): 199–256, and by Whittenburg in "God's Chosen in the Backcountry," p. 5. Both Ekirch and Whittenburg agree that Marvin L. Michael Kay overstates the extent of class differences between Regulators and non-Regulators, but differ somewhat on the underlying causes of the conflict. Ekirch views the movement in almost purely political terms, as a protest by a reasonably prosperous group of backcountry settlers whose "country ideology" sensibilities were outraged by the extent of political corruption in their society. Whittenburg finds that members of evangelical religious sects were particularly drawn to the Regulator movement and that, while corruption in the backcountry was a significant source of discontent, it was not any greater in the west than in the east. The fact remains, however, that the corruption of the government, together with the meager institutional and financial resources of that government, rendered the political order of the backcountry exceptionally insecure.

tablish any local courts at all in the backcountry until 1772, and even then the justice was meted out by circuit courts rather than county courts staffed by local residents.[25]

The effect of this political inattention, inefficiency, and more-than-occasional corruption in creating a class of individuals who set their faces firmly against the provincial government was far more profound than anything that the cross-cutting mixture of ethnic, economic, and religious jealousies was capable of producing. That intense alienation—often ill-focused and only fuzzily diagnosed—surfaced sporadically in the Ninety-Six District of South Carolina in the 1760s and had a momentary flash point in the Regulator uprising at Alamance Creek, North Carolina, in 1771, but perhaps the most significant consequence of those years of political irresponsibility came when the eastern rulers of North and South Carolina society asked the backcountry's settlers for their support in the common cause of the Revolution.

In both North and South Carolina there were two crisis points during which the members of the provincial elite paid the price for their failure to build a respectable tradition of political leadership. The most obvious of these, of course, occurred during the period between the summer of 1775 and the summer of 1776 when the initial decisions to raise an army and, ultimately, to declare independence were made. Plainly the failure of eastern provincial leaders either to build a following for themselves among westerners or to admit into their ranks western leaders capable of winning the confidence of their neighbors created disastrous problems for the unity of the Revolutionary movement in those two states. Thus far there seems to be little agreement among historians about the specific considerations that caused some social groups to ally with the patriots, others with the loyalists, and, perhaps most commonly, to cause still others to withhold any commitment whatever. The one thing that is certain is that deference to established leaders in either the provincial or royal elite had absolutely nothing to do with those decisions. In some cases the deciding factor was prob-

---

[25] Brown, *South Carolina Regulators,* pp. 13–37.

ably a sort of negative-reference group-behavior that signi-
fied a simultaneous rejection not only of deferential behavior
but also of any strong ideological attachment to the cause for
which the whig leaders supposedly stood. Thus, in North
Carolina it is not wholly surprising that the one to two
hundred former Regulators who threw themselves into
battle on the side of the British at the battle of Moore's Creek
Bridge in February 1775 were, as John Adams suggested,
motivated by "such a hatred toward the rest of their fellow
citizens that in 1775, when war broke out, they would not
join them."[26] Conversely, many South Carolina backcountry
residents may have made their decision to support the whigs
when they saw such traditional enemies as the Cherokee Indians and backcountry banditti like Joseph Scoffel join the
loyalist armies. Whatever the case, the allegiances of each of
those backcountry groups can hardly be regarded as a victory either for traditional notions of deferential politics or
for the unifying power of American republican ideology.[27]

It is also clear that whig leaders in the east, recognizing the
potentially disastrous consequences of backcountry disaffection, made belated but nevertheless meaningful efforts to
meet the real interests of western settlers for the first time.
Neither the North nor the South Carolina constitutions completely redressed backcountry political grievances, but in
each case the framers touched upon the most obvious complaints of backcountry citizens. In South Carolina representation in the lower house was increased from 3 of 30 to 72 of
202, and in North Carolina underrepresentation of the west

[26] Kay, "North Carolina Regulation," pp. 104–8, argues that the Regulator movement was a class conflict, but his discussion of the behavior of
former Regulators at the time of independence supports this notion of
negative reference groups. Charles Francis Adams, ed., *The Works of John
Adams*, 10 vols. (Boston, 1850–56), 7:284.

[27] Klein, "Choosing Sides," has an excellent description of the reasons
why backcountry settlers would feel considerable hostility toward both the
Indians and the hunters, itinerants, and bandits—the "white Indians"—
who allied themselves with the British during the Revolution. Her contention, however, that backcountry political leaders were able to command
deference from their neighbors and thus bring their support to the whig
cause is without empirical foundation.

was eased somewhat and, more importantly, some of the principal demands of the Regulators—prohibition against plural officeholding and stricter controls on the activities of receivers of tax moneys—were explicitly written into the constitution. Finally, in both North and South Carolina the Anglican Church was immediately disestablished, a move generally seen only as a sign of the preexisting weakness of the established church everywhere in those colonies, but one that was likely to find particularly active and positive support from the west.[28]

The power of ethnic, economic, and purely personal animosities and of specific political concessions appears to have initially swung the balance of the backcountry populace in South Carolina toward the patriot cause and to have left the North Carolina backcountry severely divided and confused at the outbreak of hostilities. As the war persisted, however, and as it became clear that the personal sacrifices involved in the commitment to independence extended far beyond that of a dramatic moment of affirmation or even of a few moments of danger in a single battle, the full consequences of the lack of a firm political connection between east and west became more apparent. Ronald Hoffman's portrait of "The 'Disaffected' in the Revolutionary South" demonstrates most clearly the ways in which the strains of war finally began to tear apart the political fabric of the Carolinas. Hoffman's description, based in large measure on the anguished reports of Gen. Nathanael Greene, gives compelling evidence of a society altogether lacking a sense of civic polity. It was a country in which, Greene observed, "the whigs and the tories pursue one another with the most relentless fury, killing and destroying each other whenever they meet. Indeed, a great

[28] Douglass, *Rebels and Democrats*, pp. 33–44, 115–35. See also Lindley S. Butler, *North Carolina and the Coming of the Revolution, 1763–1776* (Raleigh, 1976); Marvin L. Michael Kay and Lorin Lee Cary, "Class, Mobility, and Conflict in North Carolina on the Eve of the Revolution," in Jeffrey J. Crow and Larry E. Tise, eds., *The Southern Experience in the American Revolution* (Chapel Hill, 1978), pp. 109–51. For more detailed, though not necessarily more satisfactory, discussions of the divisions within North and South Carolina see Robert O. De Mond, *The Loyalists in North Carolina during the Revolution* (1940; reprint ed., Hamden, Conn., 1964).

part of this country is already laid waste and in the utmost danger of becoming a desert. The great bodies of militia that have been in service this year employed against the enemy and in quelling the tories have almost laid waste the country and so corrupted the principles of the people that they think of nothing but plundering one another." Even after York-town, Greene reported that the South Carolina backcountry was "still torn to pieces by little parties of disaffected who elude all search and conceal themselves in the thickets and swamps from the most diligent pursuit and issue forth from these hidden recesses committing the most horrid murders and plunder and lay waste the country."[29]

The economic hardship and personal grief occasioned by the war was no less in the Virginia backcountry than in the Carolinas, but Virginia's response, both in the months pre-ceding independence and in the dark aftermath of Corn-wallis's southern invasion, was fundamentally different. Nonetheless, that response was most assuredly not the result of time-honored practices of unquestioning deference. Rather, the great majority of the citizens of the Virginia back-country (and here it may be useful to think of Emory Evans's people in Montgomery County as the exceptions who truly do prove the rule) supported the patriot cause because the whig leaders of Virginia were able to demonstrate in tangible ways that it was clearly in the real interests of the backcoun-try settlers to give their support. The makeup of the social order itself in the Virginia backcountry was not significantly more or less consensual than that of other parts of the back-country, but in the still relatively limited sphere of activity in which the operation of the provincial government had any relevance or immediacy to backcountry settlers, those agencies of local and provincial government had done a re-spectable job. Virginia's legislators, unlike their Carolina counterparts, had regularly created new counties, thus in-creasing the number of Burgesses from the west whenever the population warranted it. And local justices of the peace, sworn by the king's commission "to do equal right to the Poor

[29] Hoffman, "The 'Disaffected' in the Revolutionary South," in Young, ed., *American Revolution*, pp. 273–318, esp. pp. 294–95.

and to the Rich . . . according to law," had by the 1760s managed to lodge an impressive claim to legitimacy among the citizens of the region. In Lunenburg County, for example, while the radical Separate Baptists were the one group in the county that self-consciously placed itself in firm opposition to the values and practices of the Anglican culture and while the Baptist adherents were generally excluded from effective power on the local county court, their essential legal interests were nevertheless served by that court. Although it is difficult to make judgments on the merits of individual cases on the basis of the brief notations made in the court records, it is apparent that Baptist complainants and defendants got their way in court-adjudicated matters as often as their Anglican counterparts.[30]

The only area in which the evangelicals did have persistent—and persistently voiced—complaints, was that of religious persecution, yet such persecution was generally carried out on an extralegal basis by nonbelievers as well as by the more zealous supporters of established religion. And perhaps the most important point to be made about this one area of significant discontent is that the evangelicals were, by the time of the Revolution, ready and able to enter the political fray in order to guarantee that their interests on that important question were more appropriately served.

In the early years of the constitutional conflict with Britain most of the western counties of Virginia, in common with most areas in America, were much less caught up in the dispute than either the commercially oriented residents of port towns or political leaders in provincial capitals. Yet by 1775 Virginia's political leadership had scored a remarkable suc-

[30] The division of power between Anglicans and Baptists on the Lunenburg court is discussed in Beeman, "Social Change and Cultural Conflict," pp. 464–66. The statement on the representation of Baptist and Anglican legal interests in the county court is based on an analysis of Lunenburg County Order Book 13, 1769–77, microfilm, VSL, which indicates that although Baptists involved in legal disputes with one another tended to settle them within the confines of their own religious gatherings, they were upheld in court in their legal disputes with Anglicans as often as they were ruled against.

cess in spreading whig institutions of protest and resistance to the backcountry. The first county committees in Virginia, originally modeled on the colonial Committees of Correspondence, began to spring up in the eastern counties in the early summer of 1774, but by mid-1775 those committees— by that time charged with the task of enforcing a boycott of all British goods through the agency of a Continental Association—had spread to virtually every county in Virginia. The committees were supposedly elected by the freeholders of their respective counties in much the same way Burgesses were chosen, although in some counties it appears that the sitting members of the county court routinely assumed the position of county committeemen along with their regular duties. Whether the committees were appointed or elected, however, the fact that emerges about their composition in the Virginia backcountry is that the same, moderately wealthy, principally Anglican planters who controlled institutions of local government before the Revolution also controlled them during that struggle.[31]

Those county committees were remarkably successful in both creating and enforcing unity within the population at large, proceeding swiftly against those guilty of violating the nonimportation agreements of the Continental Association and moving forcefully against those who were suspected of disloyalty to the patriot movement.[32] Even those historians who have been most aggressive in looking for internal division within Virginia's Revolutionary movement—from H. J. Eckenrode to Ronald Hoffman—have been hard pressed to

[31] Astonishingly, no one has attempted to write a full-scale history of the Revolution in Virginia since H. J. Eckenrode, *The Revolution in Virginia* (Boston, 1916). Dale Benson, "Wealth and Power in Virginia, 1774–1776: A Study of the Organization of Revolt," Ph.D. diss., University of Maine, Orono, 1972, discusses the unchanging—and in his view, oligarchical— character of the county committees.

[32] It is now much easier to chart the course of resistance in the individual counties of Virginia due to the continuing progress of the documentary series *Revolutionary Virginia: The Road to Independence*, compiled and edited by William J. Van Schreeven, Robert L. Scribner, and Brent Tarter, 7 vols. (Charlottesville, 1973–83).

find many signs of it during the critical years between 1774 and 1776. The only easily identifiable group of loyalists in Virginia seems to have been the Scottish merchants and factors who operated in Norfolk, on the Eastern Shore, and throughout the Virginia southside; it is plain that backcountry residents united with their eastern brethren in a policy of thoroughgoing repression and persecution of these loyalists. In December 1775 Lunenburg's citizens petitioned the Virginia Convention to affirm their determination "with their lives and fortunes, to defend the liberties of America, and to stand or fall with their Country." At the same time they asked for the introduction of a test oath, aimed obviously at the Scottish merchants and factors living in the area, by which "the Friends of America may be distinguished from those who are inimical to the glorious cause to which this Country is engaged."[33]

At least one backcountry resident, Robert Munford, was deeply disturbed about the authoritarianism implicit in the systematic repression of the Scots. In his play *The Patriots* the prevailing attitude of the backcountry leaders was expressed by Colonel Strut (a character probably modeled after Mecklenburg County's Col. William Goode). When Strut brought a group of Scotsmen before the county committee he proclaimed: "The nature of their offense, gentlemen, is that they are Scotchmen; every Scotchman being an enemy and these ones being Scotchmen, they are under an ordinance which directs an oath to be tendered to all those against whom there is just cause to suspect they are enemies." When one of the Scots protested that there was no proof of his disloyalty, another committee member, Brazen, retorted: "Proof Sir! We have proof enough. We suspect every Scotchman. Suspicion is proof Sir."

When Courtlandt Canby edited *The Patriots* in 1949, he noted the disturbing parallels with the Communist witch-hunts of the postwar era; indeed, what is most striking about the repression of the Scots merchants is that there was sufficiently overwhelming unity of sentiment in the Virginia

[33] Van Schreeven, Scribner, and Tarter, eds., *Revolutionary Virginia*, 5:157.

backcountry to allow that kind of totalitarian orthodoxy to be imposed.[34] Given the temper of the citizens, it is no doubt a good thing that even potential targets of suspicion were so few. In Lunenburg, for example, only four men were ordered to leave the state on grounds of disloyalty to the patriot cause; three of those were Scotsmen.[35]

One might expect that the one area of visible discontent in the Virginia backcountry before the Revolution—the conflict between the evangelicals and the established church—would have caused divisions in the politics of the Revolutionary movement, but in many respects the immediate effect of the Revolution was to submerge—and ultimately, to arbitrate—that conflict. The Baptists, no less than their Anglican neighbors, supported the resistance against Great Britain wholeheartedly. The Virginia Baptist Association, acting on a set of resolutions proposed by Lunenburg's Meherrin Church, denounced "the violent usurpations of a corrupted ministry" and asked "every Christian Patriot to enlist himself in the struggle." The rhetoric of American republicanism, the calls for the defense of virtue against corruption and the representation of the struggle against Britain as an important opportunity for purging American society of luxury and vice, was in close accordance with the austere doctrines and lifestyles of the insurgent evangelical movement.[36] That shared belief in the ideological abstractions of republicanism, however, is certainly not a sufficient explanation for the unity of allegiance within the Virginia backcountry, for Baptists and Anglicans seem to have shared the principles of republican-

[34] Courtlandt Canby, ed., "Robert Munford's *The Patriots*," *William and Mary Quarterly*, 3d ser. 6 (1949):437–503. For an analysis of the play see Rodney M. Baine, *Robert Munford: America's First Comic Dramatist* (Athens, Ga., 1967).

[35] Lunenburg County Order Books 13 and 14, 1777–81, microfilm, VSL; see esp. Jan. 9, 1777, for the indictments of the four.

[36] Meherrin Baptist Church Minute Books, Sept. 2, 1774, Virginia Baptist Historical Society, Richmond; Gordon S. Wood, *The Creation of the American Republic, 1776–1787* (Chapel Hill, 1969), pp. 91–124, makes a convincing case for the tendency among Americans to link their Revolution with the "moral reformation" of society.

ism in the Carolina backcountry as well, yet unity obviously did not automatically follow.

The principal difference in Virginia was that the republican ideas of the Revolution were given expression by leaders who actually spoke the language of the backcountry and who were then capable of welding east and west, Anglican and Baptist, into a unified movement. The most prominent and influential of these leaders was undoubtedly Patrick Henry, who had plainly developed an oratorical style—much closer in its form to an evangelical exhortation than to classical oratory—that enabled him to communicate the ideology of republicanism in a vastly more popular mode than had ever been achieved before.[37] Nor was it simply empty rhetoric. Henry was the leading member of an influential group in the assembly that actively sought to advance the interests of the backcountry, arguing for such vital concerns as the commutation of taxes in that region during the most financially trying times of the Revolutionary and post-Revolutionary periods.[38]

Ironically, it was not Henry but two of his foremost rivals—Thomas Jefferson and James Madison—who helped their "fellow" backcountry residents win their most striking victory of the Revolutionary era. As Rhys Isaac and I have argued in greater detail elsewhere, Jefferson supplied the lapidary philosophic phrases and Madison played the role of legislative pilot in the battle for disestablishment of the Anglican Church, but that contest—from its inception in 1776 to its culmination in 1785—was initially prompted and consistently propelled by backcountry dissenters. And perhaps most remarkably, the Episcopalian-dominated assemblies responsible for passing the religious reforms of 1776–85 differed little in composition from those assemblies that had moved to restrict the rights of dissenters just a few years be-

[37] The most persuasive argument for this proposition is by Rhys Isaac, "Preachers and Patriots: Popular Culture and the Revolution in Virginia," in Young, ed., *American Revolution*, pp. 151–54.

[38] Richard R. Beeman, *Patrick Henry: A Biography* (New York, 1975), pp. 117–34; Jackson Turner Main, *The Antifederalists: Critics of the Constitution, 1781–1788* (Chapel Hill, 1961), pp. 92–94.

fore the Revolution. Faced, however, with a determined political mobilization by the backcountry evangelicals, the assemblymen of the Revolutionary period—from both east and west—acknowledged the reality that the common cause of the Revolution demanded a religious accommodation with the dissenters. Indeed, in a clear display of the recognition of the constituent power, those very Anglican assemblymen who had placed their names at the top of petitions supporting the church establishment were equally prominent in abandoning their personal preferences and supporting the wishes of the dissenters on the final vote on the question.[39]

The political accommodation between Anglicans and dissenters achieved in Jefferson's famed Bill for Religious Freedom hardly eliminated all of the sources of antagonism that existed both within the Virginia backcountry and between the backcountry and the east, but it was dramatic proof of the vitality of a tradition of political responsiveness that had been established well before the Revolution commenced. Charles Sydnor may have been correct in linking the responsiveness of that system to traditional notions of deference and noblesse oblige in the tidewater and Northern Neck counties of the Old Dominion, but the legitimacy of the political system in the Virginia backcountry rested on a concept far more durable. Few Anglicans or evangelicals in the backcountry would have been comfortable with the label of "democrat," but each side had embraced a form of egalitarian, voluntary contractualism that presaged the acceptance of an explicitly democratic ideology.

[39] Rhys Isaac and Richard R. Beeman, "Cultural Conflict and Social Change in the Revolutionary South: Lunenburg County, Virginia," *Journal of Southern History* 46 (1980):538–50.

EDWARD J. CASHIN

"But Brothers, It Is Our Land We Are Talking About"

Winners and Losers in the Georgia Backcountry

DURING THE AMERICAN Revolution both Great Britain and the United States solicited the help of Indians. One Cherokee chief weary of such importunities cut to the heart of the matter: Whites of both sides ignored the fact that the land they were fighting for belonged to the Indians. "But Brothers," said the chief, "do you remember that the difference is about our land. . . . It is this very land which we stand on which is ours."[1] He was right, of course. Regardless of which side won the war, the Indians were sure to be the losers.

[1] Talk of the Tassel, Apr. 21, 1777, Preston Papers, Lyman C. Draper Collection, 4QQ14, State Historical Society of Wisconsin, Madison. Another copy of the talk identified the chief as Old Tassel (4QQ95). The Cherokee inhabited the southern Appalachian highlands, now western North Carolina, eastern Tennessee, and northeastern Georgia. The Lower Creeks occupied the region of the Chattahoochee River, today's boundary between Georgia and Alabama. The Upper Creeks lived in the area that today is northern Alabama. The Choctaws were west of the Lower Creeks, and the Chickasaws west of the Upper Creeks. In 1768 Gov. James Wright estimated the strength of the tribes in the number of gunmen: Creeks 3,400, Cherokee 2,000, Choctaws 2,200, Chickasaws 400 (Wright to the earl of Hillsborough, Oct. 5, 1768, Allen D. Candler, Lucian L. Knight, Kenneth Coleman, and Milton Ready, eds., *The Colonial Records of the State of Georgia*, 28 vols. [Atlanta, 1904–16, 1979–82]; additional volumes [29–39] are in manuscript at the Georgia Department of Archives and History, Atlanta; the quotation is in vol. 37, pt. 2, p. 369).

Other losers in the Revolution can be recognized by their degree of affiliation with the Indians, from those who fought alongside them to those who did business with them. The winners are easily identified as those who finally possessed the land. Since in Georgia these winners included whigs of all factions, this essay will avoid any attempt to identify radicals or conservatives.

The American Revolution in the Georgia backcountry was a powerful instrument in the transfer of land. The essential features of the process were these: the great land cessions of 1763 and 1773 opened the Georgia backcountry to a wave of immigrants, newcomers who were not all alike but whom older Georgians tended to despise uniformly. The new settlers feared and dreaded the Indians, their nearest neighbors, and because they believed that royal policy favored the Indians they turned against the government. An Indian uprising triggered the initial violence of the Revolution in Georgia, but what began as a backcountry brawl escalated in ways the original participants could not have imagined; specifically, the amorphous mass of settlers became structured under leaders who emerged into history, and the century-old British policy of trading with the Indians ended and a century-long policy of Indian removal began.

The conventional opinion among historians who have studied the backcountry is that the people there were generally loyal and would have remained so had not Georgia been dragged into the war by her sister states. The opinion is based on the published protestations of loyalty by backcountry people in 1774. Why did these very real declarations of loyalty turn sour within a year? When James Wright became governor in 1760, he reported that there were about six thousand whites and half that number of blacks in all of Georgia. After the Treaty of Augusta in 1763 opened new lands above Augusta as far as the Little River and west to the Ogeechee, settlers immediately began to stream into the colony, many of them coming from the Carolina and Virginia backcountry. By 1773 the governor reported a total population of eighteen thousand whites and fifteen thousand blacks. To his chagrin, many of those who settled in the backcountry were drifters—"Crackers" as he called them. He would have preferred at least "the Middling Sort of People, such as have Families and a few negroes."[2] Worse still, the Crackers infiltrated the Indian territory above the Little River. By 1772 there were an estimated three thousand people living on Indian land.[3] Governor Wright agreed with James Habersham of Savannah that the Crackers "were by no means the sort of people" that should settle the desirable lands.[4] Wright was so anxious to put some of the better sort on these lands that he cheated on his own treaty of 1763 and signed grants above the Little River.[5] The Creek chieftain Emistisiguo complained to John Stuart, British Indian superintendent in the South, that one man had brought forty slaves across the boundary. "I am now far advanced in life," he said, "and this is the first time I ever saw plantations settled in my nation." The chief hoped that such incidents would not lead to war and interrupt the trade in skins and furs; he reminded Stuart of their treaty pledge to preserve the path "that leads to the sun-rising always white and clean."[6]

When Governor Wright engineered the second Treaty of Augusta in 1773, by which over a million acres above the Little River were opened to settlement, he intended that only those who could afford to purchase land should move there, confident that "they will, of course, be something better than

[2] "Colonial Records," vol. 38, pt. 1A, p. 120; Wright to the earl of Halifax, Dec. 23, 1763, ibid., vol. 37, pt. 1, pp. 69–71.

[3] Kenneth Coleman, *Colonial Georgia: A History* (New York, 1976), pp. 226–27.

[4] James Habersham to Wright, Aug. 22, 1772, Georgia Historical Society *Collections* 6 (1904):203.

[5] John Richard Alden, *John Stuart and the Southern Colonial Frontier* (1944; reprint ed., New York, 1966), p. 296.

[6] Philemon Kemp to the governor of Georgia, with Talks from Emistisiguo and Gun Merchant, June 6, 1771, Proceedings of the Congress with Upper Creeks, Oct. 29–Nov. 2, 1771, K. G. Davies, ed., *Documents of the American Revolution*, 21 vols. (Shannon, Ireland, 1973), 3:118–21, 224; Governor Wright referred to Emistisiguo as "a man of by far the greatest consequence, weight and influence of any in the Creek country" (Wright to Hillsborough, Sept. 17, 1768, "Colonial Records," vol. 37, pt. 2, p. 371).

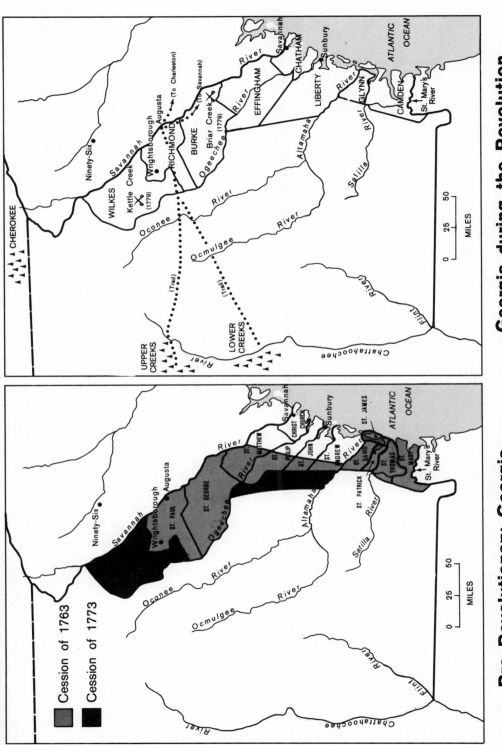

Georgia during the Revolution

Pre-Revolutionary Georgia

the common sort of backcountry people."[7] Given a choice between Indians and Crackers, Wright and other royal officials seemed to prefer the Indians. The British military commander in America, Gen. Thomas Gage, said as much when he heard that Indians had attacked trespassers upon their lands: it "might save us trouble by preventing our vagabonds from strolling in the manner they do."[8]

Two backcountry petitions provide an insight into the attitudes of the generally voiceless settlers. The first of these was prompted by a meeting held in Savannah on August 10, 1774, at which delegates had adopted resolutions objecting to the punitive measures known popularly as the Intolerable Acts.[9] Petitions condemning the Savannah action were immediately circulated throughout the backcountry, and over six hundred persons signed the various statements that bore a common theme: the people of Savannah did not speak for those in the backcountry. The great difference between them was the proximity of the Indians and the danger of an Indian war. In such an event, "the back settlements of this Province . . . would most certainly be laid waste and depopulated, unless we receive such powerful aid and assistance as none but Great Britain can give."[10] The possibility of an Indian war was a consideration of highest priority and took precedence over arguments about taxation without representation. A petition of 1776 revealed that the settlers on the frontier disliked those who traded with the Indians as much as the Indians themselves: "Whilst an Indian trade is carried

[7] Wright to Hillsborough, Dec. 12, 1771, Candler et al., eds., *Colonial Records*, vol. 28, pt. 2, p. 356; Davies, ed., *Documents of the Revolution*, 3:274; Governor Wright put the total acreage of the ceded lands above the Little River at 1,616,298 (Wright to the earl of Dartmouth, Aug. 10, 1773, "Colonial Records," vol. 38, pt. 1A, p. 80).

[8] Lt. Gen. Thomas Gage to Hillsborough, June 4, 1771, Davies, ed., *Documents of the Revolution*, 3:106.

[9] Allen D. Candler, ed., *Revolutionary Records of the State of Georgia*, 3 vols. (Atlanta, 1908), 1:15–17; *Georgia Gazette*, Aug. 17, 1774.

[10] A Protest of Declaration of Dissent of the Inhabitants of St. Paul's Parish, *Georgia Gazette*, Oct. 12, 1774; other backcountry resolutions are in *Georgia Gazette*, Sept. 21 and 28, 1774.

on it tends to bring those savages down into the settlements, and they seldom return without either committing murder or robbery and generally both upon the white people."[11] If the Indian trade were stopped, the argument continued, more people would be willing to settle in the backcountry. Frontier people were acutely aware that the traders put guns and powder into the hands of the Indians. At least on one occasion a group of irate settlers marched into Augusta and forcibly unloaded several packhorses intended for the Indians.[12]

Thus, the backcountry was a tinder box about to explode. The royal government was committed to perpetuating the Indian trade and an Indian presence in the backcountry and to a policy of discriminating against the poorer settlers, or Crackers, who were flocking into the newly ceded lands. These newcomers, on the other hand, harbored strong feelings against their Indian neighbors, a hostility that exploded with the second great land cession, in 1773. The Indian war that then broke out was the opening chapter of the American Revolution in the backcountry. There the Revolution was, from start to finish, an Indian war.

The immediate cause of the outbreak was that the Creek Indians felt betrayed by the second Treaty of Augusta, a scheme whereby the Cherokee's debts to traders would be canceled by the cession of land. The traders would be paid from the proceeds of the land sales. Although the Creek chiefs had been persuaded to agree to the Treaty of Augusta, disgruntled young warriors took up the war hatchet. Attacks on outlying settlements during the winter of 1773–74 threw the frontier into a state of panic. Even in Augusta stockades were thrown around some of the houses. Governor Wright vainly called on the help of British regulars in Boston and then imposed an embargo on the Indian trade on April 13, 1774. No act of his could have pleased the backcountry set-

[11] The Petition of the Inhabitants of the Parish of St. George and St. Paul, including the ceded lands in the Province of Georgia . . . July 31, 1776, in the New-York Historical Society *Collections* 5 (1872):181.

[12] Candler et al., eds., *Colonial Records*, 15:425–26; Alden, *John Stuart*, p. 305.

tlers more. Nor could anything have convinced the settlers of the perfidy of the traders more than the fact that some of the traders ignored the governor's edict and continued business as usual with the Indians. Wright placed himself more firmly on the side of the settlers by ordering rangers stationed on the ceded lands to interdict all commerce with the Indians. There was irony here, because Wright's original intention was that the rangers would drive off settlers who could not pay for their land.[13]

The governor's anti-Indian policy explains why the backcountry was so quick to rally behind him in August 1774 when the Savannah merchants raised their protests. Events had placed the governor and settlers on the same side against the Indians and those who did business with them. This unaccustomed alliance began to break down when a party of nine Indians visited Robert Mackay's trading house in Augusta and offered to make amends. Wright was delighted with the success of his strategy and signed a formal treaty with the Creek chiefs in Savannah on October 20, 1774. He announced that the trade was again open, and at the same time he forbade any "attempt to settle or trespass upon any lands of the Indians . . . or to assault Indians who come into settlements."[14]

Many of the settlers felt betrayed by the governor's failure to obtain better terms from the Indians. They found a spokesman in one George Wells, a "practitioner of physick" in Augusta and a future hotspur of the Revolution. A petition attributed to Wells argued that the Creeks were ready to make major concessions in 1774. The most important of these was to have been the opening of land between the

---

[13]*Georgia Gazette*, Feb. 2, 1774; Wright to Dartmouth, Jan. 31, 1774, "Colonial Records," vol. 38, pt. 1, pp. 163–71; Journal of William Tennent, in Robert Wilson Gibbes, ed., *A Documentary History of the American Revolution*, 3 vols. (Columbia, S.C., and New York, 1853–57), 1:236; Alden, *John Stuart*, pp. 309–10; Candler et al., eds., *Colonial Records*, 12:390, 409.

[14]Candler et al., eds., *Colonial Records*, 12:406–7; Extract of a Letter from Charlestown, Nov. 11, 1774, Letter from Charlestown, June 27, 1774, Proclamation by His Excellency Sir James Wright, Oct. 20, 1774, Peter Force, ed., *American Archives*, 4th ser. 6 vols. (Washington, D.C., 1837–46), 1:974, 451, 1137; Alden, *John Stuart*, p. 311.

Ogeechee and the Oconee for settlement, and access to the Oconee would have provided the backcountry with an outlet for its timber and grain. According to the petition, the Indian traders "from self interested views" prevailed upon Wright not to press for the Oconee cession. There could be but one conclusion. The governor had decided to perpetuate the trade by sacrificing the interests of the settlers. In fact, it was during the aftermath of the Creek crisis that a new political alliance was forged between Wells, representing discontented backcountrymen, and Button Gwinnett, future signer of the Declaration of Independence, who was already emerging as a leader of lowcountry radicals. By year's end Wells and his friends were coming around to the position of the coastal radicals that Georgia should join with her sister colonies in enforcing the Continental Association, the ban on trade with Britain.[15]

Governor Wright managed to parry the efforts of those who wished to join the association until the spring of 1775, when Georgia was galvanized by two reports. The first was the news of fighting in Boston. Savannah's "liberty boys" broke into a powder magazine and threatened royal officials with bodily harm. More alarming from the backcountry viewpoint was a second report that John Stuart had been instructed by the ministry to incite an Indian war. The report, in fact, was false. It grew out of Stuart's attempt to assure his superiors of the loyalty and dependability of Indians. But despite his denials, Stuart was hounded out of Charleston, first to Georgia and then to Florida.[16] The rumor played into the hands of Indian haters like George Wells, who was elected chairman of the Augusta committee that undertook

[15] Petition of the Inhabitants of St. George and St. Paul, p. 181. A Savannah whig expressed the opinion that Georgia would soon join the Continental Association because "two of our back Parishes which made the most noise are now come over to us" (Extract of a Letter from Savannah to a Gentleman in Philadelphia, Dec. 9, 1774, Force, ed., *American Archives*, 1:1033–34; Edward J. Cashin, "'The Famous Colonel Wells': Factionalism in Revolutionary Georgia," *Georgia Historical Quarterly* 58 [1974]:137–56).

[16] *Georgia Gazette*, May 12, 1775; "Colonial Records," vol. 38, pt. 1, pp. 444–45; John Stuart to Committee of Intelligence, July 18, 1775, Force, ed., *American Archives*, 2:1681.

to enforce compliance with the association. The organization of the network of similar committees might be seen as the first step in the political emergence of the anti-Indian faction.[17]

With fears of an Indian war fanning emotions, those who refused to join the association were exposed to insult and worse. Any man who dared to organize opposition to the association—for example, Thomas Brown, who was to become the chief protagonist in the forthcoming struggle for the backcountry—was certain to attract the attention of the committeemen. Brown was typical of the "better sort" of settlers favored by Governor Wright. Brown was a native of Whitby in Yorkshire and a descendant of Sir Anthony Browne, master of the horse to Henry VIII.[18] He had transported 149 indentured servants to Georgia since 1774 and had obtained over five thousand acres near Augusta and on the ceded lands. Brown was not content merely to criticize the committeemen as upstarts, he took an active part in organizing a counterassociation pledged to the king. The Augusta committee decided to make an example of Brown, and a group of liberty boys marched out to his plantation. He faced the mob and shot and wounded one Chesley Bostick before being clubbed down. He was scalped, tarred and feathered, and burning brands were applied to his feet.[19] This small

[17] Candler, ed., *Revolutionary Records*, 1:142; Cashin, "'The Famous Colonel Wells,'" p. 139.

[18] A genealogical chart showing Brown's ancestors and descendants was provided by Mrs. Joan Leggett, a native of St. Vincent and herself a direct descendant. Although the family spelled the name with an *e*, Brown did not. After the war he became a planter, the occupation he originally had in mind, married Esther Farr, and had four children; he died in 1825 at Grand Sable, his plantation on St. Vincent.

[19] State of the Claim of Jonas Brown of Whitby, Col. Thomas Brown and James Gordon . . . , American Loyalists, Audit Office, Transcripts of the Manuscript Books and Papers of the Commission of Enquiry into the Losses and Services of American Loyalists in the Public Record Office, New York Public Library, New York City; Claim of Lt. Col. Thomas Brown, Military Records Collection, Ga. Dept. Arch. and Hist.; *Georgia Gazette*, Aug. 30, 1775; Heard Robertson, "A Revised, or Loyalist Perspective of Augusta during the American Revolution," *Richmond County History* 1 (1969):11; "Colonial Records," vol. 38, pt. 1, p. 564. The best account of

victory for the liberty boys would have fateful consequences, for Brown would rouse up allies in the backcountry as few men could. He would enlist the help of the Indians, convince the British ministry to send royal troops to support his efforts, and return to Augusta as its master.

Thomas Brown joined Moses Kirkland, a wealthy Carolina planter, in whipping up loyalist sentiment in the Ninety-Six District of South Carolina. Brown's appeals to patriotism and tradition, however, were not as effective as the propaganda about a Stuart-inspired Indian war that was spread by ardent Carolina whigs like William Henry Drayton and William Tennent. In Drayton's opinion, Brown was too formidable an opponent to be left alone; "his bitterness and violence are intolerable," he reported to the Revolutionary council in Charleston.[20] Brown managed to escape capture and find sanctuary in East Florida.

Meanwhile, rumor was becoming fact. General Gage decided to use the assistance of Indians on the frontiers of America and instructed John Stuart accordingly. Stuart passed the word to his deputies to support "such of His Majesty's faithful subjects as may have already taken or shall hereafter take arms."[21] Just how the Indians might tell the difference between a loyal and a disloyal subject was a fatal flaw in Stuart's instructions. The attempts of Stuart's agents to obtain the signatures of loyalists were ridiculous on the face of it and certainly more alarming than reassuring to people in the backcountry.[22] The decision to use Indians was

---

the episode is by Thomas Brown himself in a letter to Lord Cornwallis, July 16, 1780, Cornwallis Papers, P.R.O. 30/11/2, microfilm, South Carolina Department of Archives and History, Columbia.

[20] Brown to Lord William Campbell, Oct. 18, 1775, Clinton Papers, Clements Library, University of Michigan, Ann Arbor; William Henry Drayton to the Council of Safety of South Carolina, Aug. 21, 1775, Force, ed., *American Archives*, 3:214; extract of a letter from Savannah to Mr. Morrison, Dec. 26, 1775, Margaret Wheeler Willard, ed., *Letters on the American Revolution 1774–1776* (Boston and New York, 1925), pp. 245–46.

[21] James H. O'Donnell III, *Southern Indians in the American Revolution* (Knoxville, 1973), p. 33.

[22] Henry Stuart to a Gentleman (undated). Nathaniel Reed testified that

a major miscalculation by the British high command. The strategy might explain why many of those who understood the Indians and wanted to continue to do business with them remained loyal. It also explains why those land-hungry Indian haters on the frontier saw the rebellion as an opportunity for improvement.

If Indians were to be used against Georgia in the backcountry, Thomas Brown was determined to lead them. Gov. Patrick Tonyn of East Florida was won over by Brown's enthusiasm and became the leading exponent of the plan to coordinate an Indian offensive with the landing of British regulars. The particular target of Brown's strategy was the town of Augusta, which lay "quite exposed" to an Indian attack. According to Brown, its capture would distress the rebels beyond measure and gain control of the navigation of the Savannah River for the British.[23] With Governor Tonyn's approval, the intrepid young Yorkshireman, with no previous experience among Indians, plunged into the forests with a train of ammunition intended for backcountry loyalists. The Lower Creeks were delighted to see Brown and his gunpowder. Fearful that they would take it anyhow, Brown told them that it was a present from the king. At least Brown could "fire their imagination," in Governor Tonyn's words, with news that Gen. Henry Clinton was on his way with an army.[24] Meanwhile Tonyn wrote to Clinton, an old comrade in arms, that "the Americans are a thousand times more in dread of the Savages than of any European troops." Tonyn "warmly requested" that Brown be permitted to bring the Indians down upon the frontier in concert with Clinton's attack upon Charleston.[25]

While Brown was attempting to recruit the Creeks,

---

he had received the document before John Carter; Carter then transmitted it to the Virginia convention, from which it was forwarded to Gen. Charles Lee (N.Y. Hist. Soc. *Collections*, 5:28–30).

[23] Brown to John Stuart, Feb. 24, 1776, to Patrick Tonyn, Feb. 24, 1776, Clinton Papers.

[24] Brown to Tonyn, May 2, 1776, Tonyn to David Taitt, Apr. 20, 1776, ibid.

[25] Tonyn to Gen. Henry Clinton, June 8, 1776, ibid.

thereby alienating many potential allies in the backcountry, the whig leaders displayed a shrewder understanding of the backcountry mentality. Their strategy was to persuade the Indians to remain neutral and to stay as far away as possible. A major problem for the whigs was to pose as the friends of the Indians when the opposite was actually the case. That they achieved a limited success in the Georgia backcountry was due almost entirely to the efforts of George Galphin. Galphin was a veteran Indian trader with blood relations among the Creeks. One of the few great traders who enlisted in the whig cause, he was the object of suspicion by most settlers and he, in turn, despised the settlers. Galphin complained that his task was nearly impossible. "I think I could keep them peaceable," he said of the Creeks, "if it was not for the people upon the ceded land."[26] Those people were determined to provoke an Indian war.

When Gen. Charles Lee was appointed by Congress to take command in the southern department, he was already aware of the British plan to coordinate an attack by sea with frontier warfare. As Lee took personal charge of the defense of Charleston, he directed Virginia and the Carolinas to send their militia against the Cherokee.[27] In his instructions to the Carolina officers, Drayton made the object of the attack clear: "And now a word to the wise. It is expected you make smooth work as you go—that is you cut up every Indian cornfield and burn every Indian town and every Indian taken shall be the slave and property of the taker and that

[26] Commissioners John Walker, Willie Jones, George Galphin, and Robert Rae, meeting with the Head Men of the Creeks, May 16, 1776, Secretary of State, Continental Congress, 1774–79, Archives, North Carolina Division of Archives and History, Raleigh; Galphin to Jones, Oct. 26, 1776, Peter Force, ed., *American Archives*, 5th ser., 3 vols. (Washington, D.C., 1848–53), 3:648–50. William Gilmore Simms advanced the theory that Scots Highlanders were the backbone of loyalism (see George C. Rogers, Jr., "The South Carolina Backcountry on the Eve of the Revolution," *Richmond County History* 6 [1974]). Many of the fur traders were Scots; very likely their loyalty was rooted in economic rather than ethnic reasons. The royal government was partial to the fur trade.

[27] Lee to Archibald Bulloch, July 18, 1776, N.Y. Hist. Soc. *Collections*, 5:144.

the nation be extirpated and the lands become the property of the public."[28] It was exactly the kind of rhetoric that the backcountry wanted to hear.

For the Georgia settlers the invitation was their golden opportunity to expand the war to include the Creeks, especially if others could be induced to do the fighting. General Lee received a petition from those "living on the frontiers of the Western parts of the Province of Georgia exposed to the barbarous attacks of the Creek Indians." In it they urged the general "to exterminate and rout those savages out of their nation." In a heroic vein the petitioners pledged to hazard their lives and fortunes for "so desirable a purpose."[29] The Georgians soon had their chance. Galphin urged Capt. Leonard Marbury to intercept Brown, then among the Creeks with fifty horses laden with ammunition. According to Galphin, Marbury "could not get one of those people to go with him that wants to declare war."[30] Nor did the Georgians heed South Carolina's request to attack the Cherokee town of Chote—Gen. Andrew Williamson's Carolinians had to do that job. Georgians knew what they wanted but they were not yet ready to do it themselves.

The Cherokee campaign waged by Virginia and North and South Carolina crushed that proud tribe and doomed the strategy advocated by Brown and Tonyn. Thomas Brown himself, frustrated by the hesitancy of the Lower Creeks to fight, returned to East Florida to work out his plan by another method. Always with the support of Governor Tonyn, if not the regular military, Brown organized the loyalist refugees from the backcountry into a mounted troop under his own command, the East Florida Rangers. Most of them had been in the Indian trade and, according to Brown, were expert woodsmen and guides. Tonyn thought that they were "daring fellows" and admitted that "the love of plunder" mo-

[28] Drayton to Francis Salvadore, July 24, 1776, in Gibbes, ed., *Documentary History*, 2:28–30.

[29] Petition of the Inhabitants of St. George and St. Paul, pp. 181–82.

[30] Galphin to Jones, Oct. 26, 1776, Force, ed., *American Archives*, 5th ser., 3:648.

tivated many of them.[31] The Georgia whigs called them simply tories. Years later veterans remembered this war as one against the "Indians and tories." The adjective "British" was reserved for regular troops and provincials fighting with them.

After declaring independence of Britain, Georgians confessed their dependence upon Congress for protection. General Lee took pity upon the weak and distracted state. Lee told Gov. John Rutledge of South Carolina that he had to "break up" Florida in order to save Georgia.[32] Lee was called to duty in the north before the Florida expedition got underway, but he had committed his successors to a strategy that would become almost a compulsion. Meanwhile, the protection of the Georgia frontier was the responsibility of Georgia's first brigadier general, Lachlan McIntosh. McIntosh attempted to station his light horse in a chain of frontier forts from the ceded lands to the Altamaha. The trouble was that many of the light horse were backcountrymen who would fight in an emergency but did not see the sense of military routine. While McIntosh blamed the insubordinate men from the backcountry for his inability to protect the frontier, the backcountry blamed him. The great petitioner George Wells, on his way up in the world as a member of the select committee drafting a constitution for Georgia, was especially critical. "Wells makes a great noise in Convention of the negligence of the light horse," McIntosh complained to his brother. He implied that Wells and Button Gwinnett encouraged insubordination.[33]

What had happened was that the backcountry brawl was

[31] Brown to Cornwallis, July 16, 1780, Cornwallis Papers; Tonyn to Lord George Germain, Oct. 30, 1776, Edward J. Cashin and Heard Robertson, *Augusta and the American Revolution: Events in the Georgia Back Country, 1773–1783* (Darien, Ga., 1975), p. 15; Martha Condray Searcy, "The Georgia-Florida Campaigns in the American Revolution, 1776, 1777 and 1778," Ph.D. diss., Tulane University, 1979, p. 127.

[32] Lee to Gov. John Rutledge, Aug. 1, 1776, N.Y. Hist. Soc. *Collections*, 5:186–87.

[33] Lachlan McIntosh to William McIntosh, Dec. 19, 1776, Ga. Hist. Soc. *Collections* 12 (1957):25–26.

now a military conflict, the brawlers turned soldiers. Lt. Col. Thomas Brown with his refugees-turned-rangers faced his old tormentor Capt. Chesley Bostick, who commanded Fort Howe on the Altamaha. Also on the borderlands were other backcountry stalwarts, who also bore officers' commissions. Moreover, these men recognized each other: Georgia veterans said that they skirmished with "Burntfoot Brown" in the Florida swamp.[34]

But even in uniform the Georgians liked the Indians no better than before. When Brown decided to take a fort on the Satilla, he had his Indians give a few war whoops. The garrison surrendered. "Poor fellows," said Brown in his report, "they generally associate the idea of Indians with fire and faggot." The British regulars took a dim view of Indian antics. Brown complained to his patron Tonyn that Lt. Col. Lewis V. Fuser treated the Indians like children while his rangers were "insulted with the Epithet of plunderers."[35]

In Georgia the disputes between civilian and military achieved a level of comic farce when Button Gwinnett led the militia in an invasion of Florida and refused to cooperate with Lachlan McIntosh. After the inevitable failure of the invasion, Gwinnett and McIntosh fought a famous duel in which Gwinnett lost his life. The resulting hue and cry of the Gwinnett faction drove McIntosh out of Georgia for service in the North.[36]

Gwinnett's legacy to Georgia was the radically democratic constitution of 1777. Gwinnett was president of the convention and chairman of the committee that drafted the constitution; it provided for a unicameral assembly, a plural executive, virtually universal suffrage, and provisions for compulsory voting.[37] One Savannah conservative scoffed at

[34] Pension Claims of James Hall and Caleb Johnson, Revolutionary War Pension Claims, Record Group 15, National Archives.

[35] Brown to Tonyn, Feb. 20, 1777, Robert S. Davis, Jr., *Georgia Citizens and the Soldiers of the American Revolution* (Easley, S.C., 1979), pp. 148–51.

[36] For the best treatment of McIntosh's career, see Harvey H. Jackson, *Lachlan McIntosh and the Politics of Revolutionary Georgia* (Athens, 1979).

[37] Albert B. Saye, *New Viewpoints in Georgia History* (Athens, 1943), pp. 171–72.

the new constitution as the work of a small clique "at a nightly meeting in a Tavern."[38] If so, the backcountry was well represented because George Wells was a member of the drafting committee and presumably of the clique. The "western members," as the men from the backcountry were called, exerted considerable influence in the first session of the legislature. Two battalions of militia were authorized to defend the frontier. Land was uppermost upon the minds of the legislators and a land office was opened on June 7, 1777.[39] The property of loyalists was subject to confiscation by inquisitorial committees set up in each county. For Wells, who sat on the committee for Wilkes County on the westernmost frontier, the confiscatory legislation represented a new opportunity. He had long coveted the Indians' land, and now he was in a position to covet his neighbors'.[40]

Through George Galphin the Georgians made an effort to coax the Creeks into giving up the Oconee strip. Galphin entertained the Creek chiefs at his Old Town plantation on the Ogeechee and managed to outrage the already suspicious settlers. Not only did he fail to obtain land but he promised a resumption of the hated Indian trade. To cap the climax, he invited the Creeks to take a leisurely stroll to see the sights in Charleston as his guests.[41] If the frontiersmen disliked Galphin's "coddling" of the Creeks, Thomas Brown liked it even less. Brown staged a daring raid to the outskirts of Augusta, creating consternation in the countryside. Creeks allied with Brown burned a fort on the Ogeechee and scalped settlers who had moved across that boundary.[42]

[38] John Wereat to George Walton, Aug. 30, 1777, Ga. Hist. Soc. *Collections*, 12:66–74.

[39] Candler et al., eds., *Colonial Records*, vol. 19, pt. 2, pp. 53–58.

[40] An Act for the Expulsion of the Internal Enemies of This State, Sept. 16, 1777, in the petition of Thomas Young, Loyalist Claims, Military Records Coll.

[41] Lilla M. Hawes, ed., "Collections of the Georgia Historical Society and Other Documents, Minutes of the Executive Council, May 7 through October 14, 1777," *Georgia Historical Quarterly* 34 (1950):110.

[42] Ibid., p. 109; Samuel Elbert to Lachlan McIntosh, Sept. 9, 1777, Ga. Hist. Soc. *Collections* 5, pt. 2 (1902):59; Elbert to Lachlan McIntosh, Aug.

These events provided an excuse for the backcountry delegates in the assembly to clamor for an all-out war. Conservative Georgians were exasperated by the uproar; one
remarked that the war "was principally pushed by the famous Colonel Wells, the principal motive I believe plunder
and Offices."[43] Indeed, land and offices were the most powerful arguments used by the whigs in rallying adherents. Galphin enlisted the intercession of Gen. Robert Howe,
commanding the southern department, to quash the war
rhetoric and to protect the sightseeing Creeks.[44]

General Howe desperately tried to avert a war, but in vain.
Thomas Brown saw to that. In order to prove his point that
the Carolina backcountry was loyal, Brown's agents administered the oath of allegiance to thousands there.[45] In March
1778 he took the offensive in Florida. With his rangers and
Indians he swam the Altamaha and captured Fort Howe. As
though this were a signal, the Carolina loyalists began a mass
migration to St. Augustine and Pensacola. Howe, at least,
seemed to regard it as such. "This plan, by a variety of different ways, we heard of before," he observed, "and the raising
of these people was a part of the story."[46]

Anticipating an attack on Georgia's frontier, Howe reluctantly agreed to try another invasion of Florida. The Georgia
assembly voted Gov. John Houstoun emergency powers and
directed him to lead the militia down to Florida. South Carolina contributed its backcountry militia under the capable
Andrew Williamson. With incredible difficulty and little co-
ordination, this trifurcated expedition managed to reach

16, 1777, Emmet Collection, N.Y. Public Library, New York City; John
Lewis Gervais to Henry Laurens, Aug. 16, 1777, *South Carolina Historical
Magazine* 66 (1965):21–23.

[43] Joseph Clay to Laurens, Oct. 16, 1777, Ga. Hist. Soc. *Collections* 8
(1913):51.

[44] Gen. Robert Howe to "Sir," Sept. 4, 1777, Georgia State Papers 1777–
88, Papers of the Continental Congress, Record Group 360, National Archives.

[45] Searcy, "Georgia-Florida Campaigns," p. 378.

[46] Howe to William Moultrie, Apr. 7, 1778, *South Carolina Historical Magazine* 58 (1957):203.

Fort Howe on the Altamaha. Brown withdrew one step to Fort Tonyn on the St. Mary's. The Americans caught a glimpse of him as Howe's Continentals crossed the St. Mary's: with two others, Brown calmly observed their crossing. He was pursued but escaped into a swamp; after burning Fort Tonyn, he withdrew again. The only real skirmishing took place at Alligator Creek where Elijah Clark's backcountry militia fought Brown's rangers. They would meet again. As Brown retreated he sent a detachment of his rangers to threaten Augusta again.[47] John Stuart liked to think that Indian raids that he instigated along the frontier caused the failure of the Florida invasion. Probably the expedition would have broken down of its own ineptitude, but it is certain that the rangers and the Indian uprisings caused the Georgia Continentals to hurry back to the ceded lands, now Wilkes County. "Galphin's labors have been immense," Governor Houstoun reported, "but Stuart's presents have got the better of them."[48] With Col. Samuel Elbert's light horse on patrol in Georgia and Williamson's militia in Carolina, quiet settled upon the frontier.

Thomas Brown could not be flushed out of Florida, but he could not return to the backcountry, at least not without assistance. Late in December 1778, however, help was on the way. The British ministry had at last decided to act upon Brown's plan, so ardently advocated by Tonyn, and Moses Kirkland in New York repeated the plan in painstaking detail to Gen. Henry Clinton.[49] John Stuart was ordered to coordi-

[47] The most thorough treatment of the invasion is Searcy, "Georgia-Florida Campaigns"; for a detailed contemporary account see John F. Grimké, "Journal of the Campaign to the Southward: May 9th to July 14th, 1778," *South Carolina Historical and Genealogical Magazine* 12 (1911):60–69, 118–34, and 190–206.

[48] Gov. John Houstoun to Laurens, Oct. 1, 1778, Revolutionary Papers, South Caroliniana Library, University of South Carolina, Columbia.

[49] Moses Kirkland to Clinton, Oct. 13, 1778, in Randall M. Miller, ed., "A Backcountry Loyalist Plan to Retake Georgia and the Carolinas, 1778," *South Carolina Historical Magazine* 75 (1974):207–14. Exiled Gov. James Wright kept up the pressure for a coordinated offensive by Indians and British troops (see Wright to Germain, Oct. 8, 1777, "Colonial Records," vol. 38, pt. 2, p. 131).

nate an Indian offensive with the arrival of a British army from New York. What had been a sideshow would now occupy the main arena.

On December 28, 1778, Lt. Col. Archibald Campbell landed his army of three thousand British, loyalists, and Hessians and routed Robert Howe's forces defending Savannah. Howe later expressed the opinion that Campbell made a mistake in not swiftly moving upon Charleston. That, of course, was not Brown's plan nor was it now official policy. Augusta and the backcountry were the object, and Campbell waited only for the arrival in Savannah of Gen. Augustine Prevost's regulars from Florida and Thomas Brown's rangers. The march to the backcountry was led, appropriately enough, by Brown. His glory was dimmed by the low opinion Campbell had of his rangers, "A mere rabble of undisciplined freebooters," Campbell called them.[50] Nor did Campbell approve of Brown's attempt to rescue some of his scouts who were held in the Burke County jail. Brown was repulsed by Georgia militia under Colonels Benjamin Few and John Twiggs, two men who were typical of the emerging leadership. Except for that, Campbell had no trouble taking Augusta. At first it seemed that the predictions of backcountry loyalty were accurate. Campbell reported that over a thousand Georgians had taken the oath of allegiance. In addition, a large body of Carolina loyalists under Col. James Boyd was on the way to Augusta to join Campbell.

The auspicious beginning was frustrated by countermovements ordered by the new American commander in the South, Gen. Benjamin Lincoln. Lincoln sent a North Carolina army under John Ashe to reinforce Andrew Williamson, camped opposite Augusta on the Savannah River. Ashe's arrival caused Campbell to beat a hasty retreat, much to the consternation of the declared loyalists in Augusta. At the same time backcountry militia under Andrew Pickens, John

[50] Colin Campbell, ed., *Journal of an Expedition against the Rebels of Georgia in North America under the Orders of Archibald Campbell Esquire* . . . (Darien, Ga., 1981), p. 48; Campbell to Clinton, Mar. 4, 1779, P.R.O., CO 5/182, microfilm, Library of Congress; *London Gazette*, Feb. 23, July 6–10, 1779; for Howe's criticism see *Proceedings of a General Court Martial . . . for the Trial of Major General Howe*, Dec. 7, 1781, N.Y. Hist. Soc. *Collections* 12 (1880).

Dooly, and Elijah Clark surprised Colonel Boyd's loyalists and defeated them at Kettle Creek in Wilkes County.[51] Pickens, Dooly, and Clark were three more leaders whom the war raised from obscurity to prominence.

Archibald Campbell retreated only to Briar Creek, halfway down river to Savannah. Under a new commander the British dealt a stunning blow to John Ashe and his North Carolinians. Before returning to Britain, Campbell invoked the authority vested in him to declare that Georgia was restored to the king. In July, Governor Wright returned to take up his former duties.[52]

For the British high command, Campbell's expedition was a successful test of Brown's plan. Half a state was better than none. The number of people who pledged loyalty was encouraging. The conspicuous failure was that John Stuart in far off Pensacola could not mobilize the Creeks in time. Campbell had already retreated from Augusta before Creeks led by David Taitt appeared on the Ogeechee. Col. LeRoy Hammond, a backcountry commander, engaged and defeated Taitt's force.[53]

The defects in the plan would be corrected and the British would try again. The death of John Stuart on March 21, 1779, was an opportunity to improve Indian administration. The region of which Stuart was superintendent was divided in two. The eastern part, including the Cherokee and Creeks, was assigned to the plan's foremost champion, Lt. Col. Thomas Brown of the East Florida Rangers, the west to Alexander Cameron. That there might be no mistake about it, the letter of commission from Whitehall spelled out Brown's mission: "The King's Service now requires that the procuring, sending out of leading Parties of the Indians to cooperate with His Majesty's Forces, or otherwise to annoy

---

[51] Robert S. Davis, Jr., and Kenneth H. Thomas, Jr., *Kettle Creek: The Battle of the Cane Brakes, Wilkes County, Georgia* (Atlanta, 1975).

[52] Wright to Germain, July 13, 1779, Ga. Hist. Soc. *Collections* 3 (1873):254–55.

[53] Malcolm Brown to John Bowie, Apr. 3, 1779, Bowie Papers, N.Y. Public Library, New York City; *South Carolina and American General Gazette*, Apr. 9, 1779.

the Enemy, shou'd be the principal Object of your Attention."[54] Meanwhile Henry Clinton prepared to lead an even larger army from New York to carry out his plan.

The American generals were not idle. Benjamin Lincoln was persuaded to move his army from its position guarding the lower Savannah River up to Augusta. Under his protection a whig government might be set up. Lincoln thought the backcountry was worth the gamble and began the ponderous movement, leaving only a skeleton force on the lower river. British General Prevost in Savannah was equally anxious to prevent the establishment of a rival government in Augusta, so he ordered a penetration into South Carolina. He succeeded better than he had planned and almost captured Charleston. Lincoln had to abandon his backcountry project and hurry to the rescue.[55]

George Washington's interest in the Georgia backcountry was increasing in direct proportion to that of his opposite number, Clinton. Washington was surprised and gratified to hear of Campbell's retreat from Augusta and was particularly relieved at the defeat of the Creek Indians. Perhaps that would convince the disaffected in the backcountry that they were "leaning upon a broken reed." Washington directed troops from Virginia to Georgia and sent Lachlan McIntosh to take command. Finally, he suggested that if the French naval commander, comte d'Estaing, could not bring his fleet to New York, it would be helpful if he would take Savannah. There was a new feature. Spain was in the war as of June 21 and began laying plans to take Pensacola.[56] If the ordinary

[54] Germain to Alexander Cameron and Thomas Brown, June 25, 1779, Clinton Papers; Lt. Col. James Prevost blamed the failure of the Indian attack on the poor health of Stuart (Prevost to Germain, Apr. 14, 1779, P.R.O., CO 5/182, microfilm, Library of Congress).

[55] Gen. Augustine Prevost to Germain, June 10, 1779, P.R.O., CO 5/182, microfilm, Library of Congress; same in *London Gazette*, Sept. 25, 1779. *South Carolina and American General Gazette*, Apr. 9, 1779. For an account of Lincoln's movements see his Warrant Book, N.Y. Public Library, New York City, and "Order Book of John Fauchereau Grimké," *South Carolina Historical and Genealogical Magazine* 15 (1914):82–90 and 124–32.

[56] George Washington to Laurens, Mar. 20, 1779, to Conrad Alexandre Gérard, May 1, 1779, to Brig. Gen. Charles Scott, May 5, 1779, to the

Cracker of Wilkes County had known of all this attention from high places, he would have been astounded.

D'Estaing's attempt upon Savannah was spectacular but in the end changed nothing. After a three-week siege and a gallant but futile assault, he sailed away.[57] The incident only delayed for a while the great invasion from New York. Meanwhile the backcountry organized a government in Augusta after the Virginia troops arrived in July. Hot-tempered George Wells did not like the people who served and argued loudly that they were trying to subvert Georgia's democratic constitution.[58] As if in agreement, General Lincoln sent George Walton to Augusta with instructions to hold elections for a constitutional government.[59] The assembly met in the last week of November, elected Walton governor, and turned out a spate of new business. Because of a forged signature, the assembly's letter requesting the second removal of Lachlan McIntosh received so much attention then and later that its contents have gone unnoticed. Congress was reminded of how important Georgia was to the British, especially now that Spain was in the war. Georgia's location between the disaffected in Carolina and the Indians made the possession of the backcountry crucial: "The preservation of this State will destroy the Enemy's designs and form a barrier by land for the other states in the Union." Congress was reminded that "we were scarcely emerged from Infancy when we risqued our lives and rich Territory in the great struggle." The letter ended with an appeal worthy of the notice of posterity. "We combated internal and external foes, and notwithstanding the invasions from Halifax, New York, the Floridas and the

president of Congress, May 11, 1779, to Benjamin Lincoln, Feb. 27, 1780, John C. Fitzpatrick, ed., *The Writings of George Washington*, 39 vols. (Washington, D.C., 1931–44), 14:266, 470, 498, 15:40, 18:55.

[57] For a general account of the siege, see Alexander A. Lawrence, *Storm over Savannah: The Story of Count D'Estaing and the Siege of the Town in 1779* (Athens, 1951).

[58] Affidavit for William Glascock, [n.d.], Ga. Hist. Soc. *Collections*, 12:122–26.

[59] Lincoln to Walton, Oct. 17, 1779, Benjamin Lincoln Letterbook, Boston Public Library.

Indians—which drew on us innumerable hardships—we still preserve free government and a determination of losing the idea in a general wreck of the state."[60] There could be no doubt that these backcountry amateurs in politics understood what was going on. Nor could there be any doubt about their concern about the "rich Territory" around them. One of the framers of the above statement was heard to remark that he had bled in defense of this country and "By G— he meant to have part of it."[61]

When the legislature met again, it made certain that all who wanted land would be satisfied. An act of January 23, 1780, may be regarded as a legislative embodiment of the war aims of the backcountry. The intent of the act was expressed in its title, "for the more speedy and effectually settling and strengthening this State." Two hundred acres of land were offered to each head of a family, with fifty additional acres for each family member. Newcomers to the state were excused from militia duty for two years, except when they needed to defend themselves. The framers of the law showed that they were planners as well as promoters. Anyone who would set up a sawmill or gristmill would be awarded five hundred acres. For a new ironworks, up to six thousand acres was the reward. The act went on to set up a five-man commission to restore the original checkerboard plan for Augusta and to build a courthouse, jail, and a "seminary of learning." A new town for Wilkes County was created and was one of the first in America to bear the name "Washington."[62] It was appropriate that George Wells was given a place on the commission for Augusta and fitting too that he became acting governor of Georgia when Richard Howley was elected to Congress. He had won his particular war. And

[60] Glascock to Samuel Huntington, Nov. 30, 1779, Georgia State Papers, Papers of Cont. Cong. For a treatment of the episode see Edward J. Cashin, "George Walton and the Forged Letter," *Georgia Historical Quarterly* 62 (1978):133–45.

[61] Wereat to Lachlan McIntosh, Jan. 19, 1780, Peter Force Papers, Series VII, 3, Library of Congress.

[62] Candler et al., eds., *Colonial Records*, vol. 19, pt. 2, pp. 130–40; Candler, ed., *Revolutionary Records*, 2:225–26.

even as the land offices opened to a new boom, it was just as well that he was not spared to see the dream undone. The turbulent Wells was killed in a duel with young James Jackson on February 16, 1780.[63]

At the time Clinton was implementing his southern strategy. On March 9 he wrote to the secretary of the colonies, Lord George Germain, that he had occupied James Island, off Charleston. "It will remain to be proved if we have in the interior part of the Country that number of friends there has formerly been such strong cause to believe in."[64] With the fall of Charleston and the loss of Benjamin Lincoln's army on May 12, 1780, the war that seemed won was suddenly lost. Resistance collapsed all over the backcountry. Lord Cornwallis, given command in the south by Clinton, planned to hold the interior by a chain of forts anchored in the west by Augusta. Ordered to Augusta was none other than Lt. Col. Thomas Brown of the King's Carolina Rangers, now superintendent to the Indian nations of the eastern district.[65] The moment was fraught with irony worthy of a Greek drama. Brown, who championed the loyalty of the backcountry from the first, now had to test that loyalty. Striking was the contrast between Brown's ignominious flight of five years before and his triumphant return.

The clock of history was turned back. As Brown had once been banished for refusing to swear an oath, so now those who would not swear allegiance to the king were forced to seek the rugged sanctuary of the North Carolina mountains. The decision to go into exile required sacrifice that not all could make. One old soldier recalled how Joshua Inman

[63] Candler, ed., *Revolutionary Records*, 2:222–23; Ga. Hist. Soc. *Collections* 11 (1955):37–41.

[64] Clinton to Germain, Mar. 9, 1780, Clinton Papers.

[65] Lt. Col. Alured Clarke to Cornwallis, June 23, 1780, Lt. Col. Nisbet Balfour to Cornwallis, June 24, 1780, Cornwallis Papers, P.R.O. 30/11/2, microfilm, Library of Congress. Brown's East Florida Rangers were reorganized as the King's Carolina Rangers for the invasion of Georgia; after the occupation of Augusta in 1780 they were known as the King's Rangers (Heard Robertson, "Notes on the Muster Rolls of Lieutenant Colonel Thomas Brown's Battalion of Loyalist Provincial Rangers [1776–1782] . . .," *Richmond County History* 4 [1972]:5–15).

gathered his neighbors and told them that he was determined to serve his country as long as he could raise an arm. They went with him.[66] So did others under Elijah Clark, John Twiggs, and Benjamin Few. They followed Gov. Stephen Heard to the mountains, keeping up at least a fiction of government. "Things bore a gloomy aspect then," Heard later wrote, "all communication being entirely cut off from our friends."[67]

The clock was turned back in another important way: Augusta was again an Indian town. The trading road that Chief Emistisiguo had described as white and clean was again open to Indians. Even before Thomas Brown marched up to Augusta, he had invited the head men of the Creeks to meet him there.[68] During the summer and fall there was a constant traffic of Creeks and Cherokee to Augusta. Brown promised to bring back the deerskin trade, drive settlers off Indian lands, dismantle the rebel forts, in short, to restore the status quo ante bellum. Under Brown, Augusta became the center of a vast frontier communications network. Brown's Indians carried messages to British Pensacola, to Detroit, and even Quebec. His backcountry was a veritable empire. His charges intercepted rebels on their way down the Ohio and Mississippi to New Orleans. One group of captives, including women and children, survived the long trek from the central rivers to Augusta. The Cherokee, disheartened since 1776, were persuaded to take up the hatchet again. According to Brown, "They have cheerfully agreed to attack the Rebel Plunderers and Banditti who have taken forcible Possession of their hunting Grounds."[69] The Upper Creeks agreed to send out war parties to support the Cherokee; the Lower Creeks promised to punish squatters on

[66] Pension Claim of Israel Eastwood, Revolutionary War Pension Claims.

[67] Gov. Stephen Heard to Richard Howley, Mar. 2, 1781, Special Collections, University of Georgia, Athens.

[68] Thomas Brown to Germain, May 25, 1780, Germain Papers, Clements Library, Univ. of Mich., Ann Arbor; Brown to Cornwallis, June 18, 1780, Cornwallis Papers, S.C. Dept. Arch. and Hist.

[69] Thomas Brown to Cornwallis, Dec. 17, 1780, Clinton Papers.

their lands. Brown hoped that his commissaries would be able to prevent the "wanton outrages" to which the "savage ferocity" of the Indians might incline them.[70] But the frontier warfare he promoted was beyond his control and outside any known law.

The exiled whigs were no better losers than Brown had been in Florida. The presence of Indians and Indian supplies in Augusta acted as a magnet upon Elijah Clark and his militia from the ceded lands. Clark took advantage of the hiatus in the high command of the Southern Department to strike a blow at Brown. Horatio Gates, the hero of Saratoga and the particular hope of the radical wing of Congress, had been named on June 13, 1780, to succeed Benjamin Lincoln.[71] Clark decided not to wait for Gates's permission; he would attack while Brown was holding one of his Indian conferences. Only about seventy of his old regiment had followed Clark to the mountains; the rest had taken parole in Wilkes County. Clark sent word to these men that he expected them to join him on a certain September day at Soap Creek or, as one of his veterans recalled, "he would put every one of them to death."[72] In Clark's opinion Cornwallis's edict that paroled men must bear arms in the king's service had absolved them from their parole. Since Thomas Brown promised to hang anyone who took up arms and Clark threatened to shoot anyone who did not, the lot of a peaceable man was not an easy one. Many of the Quakers of Wrightsborough, harassed from both sides, sought protection in Savannah.[73]

[70] Ibid.; the same letter is to be found in the Cornwallis Papers, S.C. Dept. Arch. and Hist.

[71] Huntington to Horatio Gates, June 13, 1780, Gates Papers, New-York Historical Society, New York City; Gates to Huntington, June 21, 1780, Papers of Cont. Cong. Gates seems to have learned of Clark's raid a month later, and then "unofficially" (Gates to the president of Congress, Oct. 16, 1780, Papers of Cont. Cong.).

[72] Pension claim of Joshua Burnett, Revolutionary War Pension Claims.

[73] Heard to Howley, Mar. 2, 1781, Special Coll., Univ. of Ga.; Memorial to Sir James Wright, Sept. 22, 1781, Joseph Maddock et al. to Wright, May 1782, Telamon Cuyler Collection, Univ. of Ga., Athens.

Elijah Clark's attack upon Augusta was more than a quest for plunder, though it was that, too. It was a deliberate attack upon Indians, a challenge for territorial rights. Above all, it was a signal that the men of the backcountry were ready to assert their independence. The first battle of Augusta lasted four days and involved over a thousand men. Clark's six hundred horsemen fell first upon the Indian camp west of town. Brown marched to the sound of guns and the raiders slipped into town behind him. Realizing that he was surrounded, Brown occupied Robert Mackay's former trading post, a stone building near the river. He hastily dug earthworks around the house and the Indians were placed in them. Clark showed that he too knew something of the science of war. His earthworks completely encircled Brown's, cutting off the tories and Indians from the river and their water supply. Clark hauled two captured cannons from town and blasted the house and outbuildings. This kind of warfare was grim enough by day, but at night it was terrible. The Indians left their lines and crept into the works of the Georgians to scalp the unwary. The British won the battle, but only because Brown was rescued by the regulars under Lt. Col. John Harris Cruger from Ninety-Six.[74]

Clark's attack proved that the backcountry was not restored, much to the exasperation of those on the British side. Even the paternalistic Governor Wright thought that an army ought to march into the ceded lands and "lay waste and Destroy the whole Territory." Cruger wrote to Cornwallis that his patrols were out searching for the "traiterous rebels"; he thought that those caught would be "roughly handled, very probably suspended for their good deeds."[75]

[74] Thomas Brown to Lt. Col. John Harris Cruger, Sept. 15, 1780, Clinton Papers; Pension Claim of Joshua Burnett, Revolutionary War Pension Claims; Heard to Howley, Mar. 2, 1781, Special Coll., Univ. of Ga. Clark said that three hundred men joined him in Wilkes and that Brown had between three and four hundred Indians. Clark claimed to have killed up to 40 of Brown's rangers and up to 60 Indians (Elijah Clark to General Sumter, Oct. 29, 1780, Thomas Sumter Papers, Draper Coll., 7VV75).

[75] Wright to Balfour, Sept. 18, 1780, "Colonial Records," vol. 38, pt. 2, pp. 424–27; Cruger to Balfour, Sept. 19, 1780, Cornwallis Papers, Library

Indeed Thomas Brown, wounded and unable to join in the pursuit of the raiders, did hang thirteen of the captives. All had broken their paroles and, under the Cornwallis edict, paid with their lives. Although Cornwallis, Wright, and Cruger agreed with the policy of hanging, it was Brown the rebels blamed. He was depicted in the first histories as something of a monster taking a fiendish delight in torturing his victims. Brown lived long enough to deny any such thing.[76] The worst cruelties were perpetrated by the Indians in their pursuit of Clark's men, away from Brown's moderating influence. Clark reported that the Indians fell upon the families of his men and loyalist families alike, "Women and Children strip'd, scalped and suffered to welter in their gore. . . . Lads obliged to dance naked between two large fires until they were scorched to death. Man strip'd, dismembered, scalped, afterwards hung up."[77] Members of Clark's own family had been thus treated. Clark was severely criticized by his fellow partisans for having brought down the fury of the Indians upon the frontier.[78]

This bloody autumn of 1780 was a backcountry struggle from start to finish. Clark's raid was only the beginning. As the Georgians made their way to the mountains with their Augusta plunder, Maj. Patrick Ferguson's Carolina loyalists

---

of Congress; Wright to Germain, Oct. 17, 1780, Ga. Hist. Soc. *Collections* 3:321–22; Rutledge to delegates of the state of South Carolina, Nov. 20, 1780, *South Carolina Historical and Genealogical Magazine* 17 (1916):131–46.

[76] Thomas Brown to David Ramsay, Dec. 25, 1786, in George White, *Historical Collections of Georgia* (New York, 1855), pp. 614–19. Apparently Cruger was as much responsible for the Augusta hangings as was Brown. A British officer serving under Maj. Patrick Ferguson reported that Cruger had "hanged several of the inhabitants and has a great many more to hang." He expressed the opinion that such hangings would bring a speedy end to the rebellion (Lt. William Stevenson to Lt. Col. Barton, Sept. 25, 1780, to Mrs. Susannah Kennedy, Sept. 25, 1780, Sumter Papers).

[77] Extract of Col. Clark's letter in William Campbell to William Preston, Dec. 12, 1780, *Virginia Magazine of History and Biography* 27 (1919):313–15.

[78] William Moultrie, *Memoirs of the American Revolution So Far As It Related to the States of North and South Carolina and Georgia*, 2 vols. (New York, 1802), 2:238.

marched to intercept them.[79] Instead it was Ferguson who was caught by Clark's friends from over the mountains. The battle of King's Mountain on October 7, 1780, resulted in Ferguson's death and the complete rout of his men. King's Mountain was a stunning blow to British hopes of holding the backcountry.[80]

Cornwallis fell back upon his Indian allies for support. He instructed Brown to instigate Cherokee attacks on the mountain settlements. By late December, Cornwallis reported to Clinton that the strategy had worked; the rebels were "soon obliged to return to oppose the incursions of the Indians."[81] Unfortunately for them, the fierce mountain men turned their wrath on the Indians. For the second time since 1776 the Cherokee villages were devastated. The Raven of Chote, the most loyal of the Cherokee chiefs, later told Thomas Brown what happened. "They dyed their hands in the Blood of our Women and children, burnt 17 towns, destroyed all our provisions."[82] On the frontier, Indian women and children were no safer than their white counterparts.

Although the Raven and a few others stood fast with Brown, most of the chiefs were discouraged. Their "bad situation" was not their fault; rather it was all "due to the designs of Colonel Brown." Chief Tassel had had enough; he would have no more to do with Brown or his talks since Brown "brought all the troubles upon us."[83] Without the Indians, the British strategy was doomed. Although it was not clear at the time, 1780 was the highwater mark of British hegemony in the backcountry. Brown had been able to dominate the Georgia backcountry and even to send the Creeks

[79] Cornwallis to Clinton, Dec. 2, 1780, P.R.O., CO 5/182, Miscellaneous Military Correspondence, Library of Congress; Ferguson to Cornwallis, Oct. 1, 1780, Cornwallis Papers, P.R.O. 30/11/3, S.C. Dept. Arch. and Hist.

[80] Lord Francis Rawdon to Clinton, Oct. 28, 1780, P.R.O., CO 5/182, Miscellaneous Military Correspondence, Library of Congress.

[81] Cornwallis to Clinton, Dec. 29, 1780, Clinton Papers.

[82] O'Donnell, *Southern Indians*, p. 119.

[83] Clanosee and Ancoo (Cherokee Messengers) to Col. Joseph Martin, Apr. 28, 1781, Talk of the Tassel to Commissioners, July 26, 1781, Tennessee Papers, Draper Coll., 1XX43, 1XX47.

to defend Pensacola against the Spanish. His Indians had roamed from the Gulf to the Great Lakes. After 1780, before Nathanael Greene, Washington's new commander in the south, launched his first campaign, all this had changed. A veteran frontiersman briefed Greene on the Indian situation. The recent Cherokee offensive "was a measure of the British Generals to facilitate their inhuman Projects of ruin and subjugation."[84] In other words, by joining the British the Cherokee forfeited their rights to the land. Therefore the private seizure of Indian land, which was illegal before, now became a patriotic act. Backcountry squatters would not have known the meaning of *uti possidetis*, but they acted upon that principle.

The term was being bandied about in the high chambers of diplomacy in a way the backcountry would not have liked. There had been talk even before the fall of Charleston that the British would offer independence to the eleven northern states if Georgia and South Carolina were retained.[85] Spain was clearly in favor of the cession of occupied territory. In December 1780 Russia offered to mediate the war and agreed to accept Austria as comediator. In February 1781 the powerful French minister Vergennes accepted the principle of a truce on the basis of *uti possidetis*.[86] Georgia's delegates in the Congress were seriously concerned about such talk and made an impassioned pleas to their fellow delegates not to forsake Georgia.[87] Backcountry victories over tories and Indians seemed not to count for much as long as the British held Augusta and Ninety-Six. Therefore, Nathanael Greene set as his first priorities the capture of the backcountry posts. Charleston and Savannah would come later.

[84] Robert Lanier to Nathanael Greene, Apr. 19, 1781, Nathanael Greene Papers, Perkins Library, Duke University, Durham, N.C.; O'Donnell, *Southern Indians*, p. 116.

[85] Edmund Cody Burnett, *The Continental Congress* (New York, 1941), p. 468.

[86] Samuel Flagg Bemis, *The Diplomacy of the American Revolution* (Bloomington, Ind., 1935), p. 181.

[87] Edmund Cody Burnett, *Letters of Members of the Continental Congress*, 8 vols. (Washington, D.C., 1912–36), 5:457–58.

Greene encouraged Benjamin Few and the Georgia partisans to keep up their spirits; help was on the way. He was sending his best fighter, Gen. Daniel Morgan, "to give support to your actions."[88] Cornwallis countered by ordering the celebrated Banastre Tarleton to head off Morgan. The result was the smashing victory at Cowpens: "I have given him a devil of a whipping," reported the jubilant Morgan.[89] Just how important the backcountry posts were to Greene was revealed after the battle of Guilford Courthouse. When Cornwallis moved into Virginia, Greene turned south. Governor Wright in Savannah was dismayed; "the very great Distance Lord Cornwallis and his Army are at Gives every opportunity to the Disaffected to Collect and Murder, Plunder, etc. in a most cruel and shocking manner."[90]

Indeed Thomas Brown was a beleaguered man in Augusta during April. With Nathanael Greene's approval, the Georgia partisans filtered into the countryside until Brown controlled only Augusta. Across the frontier Pensacola was besieged by the Spanish forces. When Pensacola fell on May 8, 1781, western superintendent Alexander Cameron made his way toward Augusta to join Brown.[91] Moses Kirkland, who had been with Brown in 1775, was there already. The drama that began at Augusta with the assault upon the planter Thomas Brown ended there with the siege of Lt. Col. Thomas Brown. After two weeks of determined defense Brown surrendered to Light Horse Harry Lee of Greene's army. Brown's terms included a guarantee of protection for the Indian families who were with him in Augusta. He insisted that the Indians and his rangers be given an escort to Savannah where they would be paroled.[92]

[88]Greene to Benjamin Few, Dec. 16, 1780, Nathanael Greene Papers, Clements Library, Univ. of Mich., Ann Arbor.

[89]Gen. Daniel Morgan to Deal Will, Jan. 26, 1781, Gates Papers.

[90]Wright to Germain, Apr. 24, 1781, Ga. Hist. Soc. *Collections* 3:346–47.

[91]O'Donnell, *Southern Indians*, p. 114.

[92]Capitulation of Augusta, June 5, 1781, Miscellaneous Manuscript Collections, Clements Library, Univ. of Mich., Ann Arbor.

With an eye on the European peace negotiations, Greene urged Georgians to reestablish civil rule. "A Legislature is necessary to give you political existance not only in America but in Europe."[93] With the fall of Augusta, British peace negotiators lost any possible claim to Georgia. Brown's plan had been tested and had failed. The expected numbers of loyal subjects were not there. It was demonstrated that the intrinsic flaw in Brown's plan was the supposition that a large number of backcountry people would accept Indian allies and become loyalists. Another flaw was the assumption that those despised people of no property would be afraid to fight against Indians. The surprising fact was that the Crackers at the critical moment stood up for themselves under leaders who rose out of obscurity and into history. By defeating the Indians they scotched the plan.

There were two more years of the war, one before Savannah fell. During that year unnumbered tories switched sides under Nathanael Greene's generous amnesty policy.[94] Greene's commander in Georgia, the famous Gen. Mad Anthony Wayne, complained that his task was more difficult than that of the children of Israel. They had to make bricks without straw while he had to make whigs out of tories.[95] Thus many of the rank and file escaped becoming losers.

As long as the British held Savannah, they clung to their failed plan. Governor Wright begged for troops and insisted that Thomas Brown, after his exchange, call upon the Indians. Incredibly, Emistisiguo of the Creeks answered. Brown gathered up a motley troop of volunteers and rode to the Ogeechee to meet the Indians. Instead he met Anthony Wayne's cavalry. The result, as Wayne reported, was "the total defeat and dispersion" of Brown's force.[96] General Greene

[93] Greene to Clay, July 24, 1781, Greene Papers, Duke Univ.

[94] Proclamation, Feb. 20, 1782, Cuyler Coll.; John Martin to Greene, Jan. 19, 1782, *Georgia Historical Quarterly* 1 (1917):285; Greene to John Martin, Mar. 12, 1782, Greene Papers, Univ. of Mich.

[95] Quoted in Kenneth Coleman, *The American Revolution in Georgia, 1763–1789* (Athens, 1958), p. 142.

[96] Gen. Anthony Wayne to Greene, May 24, 1782, Greene Papers, Univ. of Mich.

saluted Wayne, "You have disgraced one of the best officers the enemy have."[97] It was a pretty compliment to the Yorkshireman who meant only to be a planter. Three weeks later Emistisiguo arrived. His Creeks had somehow managed to cross the state without being detected and they took Wayne's sleeping infantry by surprise. The Continentals recovered and drove off their attackers. In the melee, Emistisiguo was killed.[98] The road that was to be always white and clean was dark and bloody—and it was closed.

When the British evacuated Savannah the spotlight of history left Georgia, but the war was not quite over. During the last year the backcountrymen celebrated their independence by delivering final blows to the Indians. Elijah Clark led those men who had once been afraid to attack the town of Chote in a devastating winter raid of the Cherokee.[99] John Twiggs, now a general, purged the Ogeechee frontier. As one of his men recalled, "After the war was supposed to be over Indians and Tories would come out into Burke County and plunder. General Twiggs would gather up his old soldiers and drive them off into Florida."[100]

Augusta was still celebrating news of the peace with Britain when, on May 13, 1783, the head men of the Cherokee and Creeks sat down with the Georgia commissioners to make their own peace. The Cherokee agreed to cede land to the Oconee. Among the commissioners were John Twiggs, Elijah Clark, and William Few.[101] Backcountrymen did their own fighting and their own peacemaking. In that respect the contrast with the 1773 congress at Augusta was striking.

The winners, then, were clearly the settlers who moved into Georgia after the cessions of 1763 and 1773 and those

[97] Greene to Wayne, May 28, 1782, ibid.

[98] Henry Lee, *Memoirs of the War in the Southern Department of the United States* (New York, 1869), pp. 556–61; Hugh McCall, *The History of Georgia: Containing Brief Sketches of the Most Remarkable Events, up to the Present Day,* 2 vols. (Savannah, 1811–16), 2:408–10.

[99] Memorial of Thomas Waters, June 2, 1783, Georgia Official Records, Ga. Dept. Arch. and Hist.; McCall, *History of Georgia,* 2:411–14.

[100] Pension Claim of Joel Darsey, Revolutionary War Pension Claims.

[101] "Colonial Records," 39:500–502.

who organized and led them. The losers were the Indians and those associated with Indians. At first the Cherokee and Upper Creeks refused to believe that their father across the waters had given up the struggle, believing the rumor a "Virginia lie." There was reproach as well as pathos in the talk delivered to Thomas Brown in St. Augustine by the Raven: "We never turned our backs on the Enemy but remembered your talks. We subsisted our Women and Children on acorns . . . and were determined to hold the English fast by the arm and like Men stand or fall with our friends. . . . we have heard from the Virginians that the English have smoked the Pipe of Peace with their enemies and have given up our lands and yours to be divided amongst their Enemies. The Peacemakers and our Enemies have talked away our land at a Rum drinking." There was not much that Brown could do as the British prepared to evacuate Florida. He did what he could and transmitted the Cherokee talk with an equally poignant message from the Upper Creeks to the Lords of the Treasury with a request for a final subsidy for supplies for those distressed nations. "I must confess," he wrote, "I feel most sensibly for our poor brave unfortunate allies who have ever given the most distinguished proofs of their fidelity and attachment to us."[102] The supplies were paid for. It was little enough.

Of those associated with the Indians, Thomas Brown was a loser and indeed the prince of losers. A Savannah gentleman informed Brown quite candidly that "there is not salvation for you here," that is, in postwar Georgia. Brown was blamed for all manner of ills: by settlers for the reluctance of the Creeks to cede Oconee and Ocmulgee lands, by mer-

---

[102] Talks from Little Turkey and Headmen of Overhill Cherokees to Lt. Col. Thomas Brown, Nov. 17, 1783. Brown to Hon. Lords Commissioners of the Treasury, Feb. 15, 1785, P.R.O., T1 601/298–306. These documents are in the bundle described by Charles M. Andrews as a "Thick bundle from Brown at Pensacola on Indian affairs and Spanish intrigues" and which he located in box 600 (Charles M. Andrews, *Guide to the Materials for American History to 1783, in the Public Record Office of Great Britain*, 2 vols. [Washington, D.C., 1914], 2:201). Actually the bundle was from St. Augustine and is in box T1 601 and there is nothing about Spanish intrigues in any of the papers.

chants who once supplied the Indian traders for the loss of
the trade. Georgians generally blamed Brown for attaching
the Indians to Spain.[103] Next to Brown in the ranks of losers
were those who had fought alongside the Indians, the tories.
Robert M. Weir has suggested that the South Carolina legislature exhibited a certain vindictiveness in order to establish
credibility and prevent the more violently inclined from taking the law into their own hands. Perhaps that explains why
the Georgia legislature came down particularly hard upon
the tories. A list of twenty-two "hellish and diabolical fiends"
was published and a reward was offered for their capture
dead or alive.[104] In addition the legislature authorized companies under Paddy Carr and James McKay "for the purpose
of suppressing these blood-thirsty and diabolical villains."[105]
Since McKay and Carr were notorious themselves, it was a
classic case of setting thieves to catch thieves. The emphatic
language of the legislation left no doubt in anyone's mind
that tories were losers.

Next on the list of losers were the Indian traders. A number of Augusta traders moved to Pensacola at the outset of
the war.[106] Many of the traders were Scots, and, in a glorious
display of arbitrary legislation, the Georgia assembly barred
all natives of Scotland from entering the state.[107] This edict
served nicely to appease those who demanded a harsh policy,
and it did not prevent the legislature from pardoning individual traders. There is no evidence that anyone in Scotland
took umbrage. Finally, those who protected the Indians were
losers. This category included the royal establishment from

[103] J.H. to Thomas Brown, Aug. 5, 1785, in Thomas Brown to Vincente
Manuel de Zespedes, Aug. 18, 1785, East Florida Papers, LC42C4, microfilm, Florida State University Library, Gainesville.

[104] For a listing of "hellish and diabolical fiends," see Candler, ed., *Revolutionary Records*, 2:384–86.

[105] Ibid., pp. 384, 397.

[106] James Jackson and Andrew McLean to Wright, Mar. 21, 1776, "Colonial Records," vol. 38, pt. 2, pp. 95–99; Searcy, "Georgia-Florida Campaigns," p. 96; J. Leitch Wright, Jr., *Florida in the American Revolution*
(Gainesville, 1975), pp. 86, 105, 139.

[107] Candler et al., eds., *Colonial Records*, vol. 19, pt. 2, pp. 162–66.

Governor Wright down to militia officers who had not taken advantage of the amnesty.

When we contemplate the geographical dimensions of the victory, we are not surprised that the winners became intoxicated with their success. No longer was the Ogeechee their western limit; now it was the Mississippi itself. A Georgian confided to the exiled Thomas Brown, "We are determined to possess ourselves of the territory and priviledge of navigation agreeable to the treaty of peace—and tis an object richly worth contending for."[108] The same correspondent described how Georgians were moving "by shoals to the land of Promise . . . the banks of the Ohio and Mississippi."[109] As Georgia faced toward the west, the backcountry became the forecountry. The capital moved from Savannah to Augusta and frontier politics dominated events. Our backcountry heroes embarked on a decade of unparalleled land speculation climaxed by that astonishing sale of fifty million acres, amounting to the present states of Alabama and Mississippi, known as the Yazoo Fraud. If critics remonstrated with their right to do such a thing, our winners might have reflected upon Kettle Creek, Briar Creek, and the two battles of Augusta and then have replied righteously, "But Brothers, it is our land we are talking about."

[108] J.H. to Thomas Brown, Aug. 5, 1785, in Thomas Brown to Zespedes, Aug. 18, 1785, East Florida Papers.

[109] The remark was quoted by Thomas Brown to Manuel de Zespedes, Dec. 20, 1785, ibid.

HARVEY H. JACKSON

The Rise of the
Western Members

Revolutionary Politics and the

Georgia Backcountry

ON THE EVE of the Revolution, Georgia was a royal colony, governed by a crown-appointed chief executive and his council and by an assembly in which a coalition led by merchants and planters from Savannah and surrounding Christ Church Parish held sway. Less than a decade later Georgia was a free and independent state, governed by a one-house legislature in which the dominant force was a coalition of merchants and planters led by citizens of Augusta and the backcountry counties of Richmond, Burke, and Wilkes. What had occurred was a shift in political power that seemed, at least to some, as revolutionary as separation from Great Britain itself.

Recent attempts to understand this transformation, and what it reveals about Georgia's struggle for independence, have focused on the conflict between whig factions that struggled for control of the state and its government. Evaluations of these competing parties demonstrated that their efforts were as significant in shaping the system of government that emerged as were the debates about the nature of that government and man's relation to it. This analysis, however, has been plagued by problems inherent in identifying impre-

The author would like to thank Edward J. Cashin, Robert S. Davis, Jr., G. Melvin Herndon, and Bradley R. Rice for reading this essay at various stages of its development and offering helpful advice and suggestions.

cise groups with labels implying a firmer ideological base and cohesive composition than actually existed. *City-country, popular-elite,* and *radical-conservative* have all been used to designate the divisions, and because of the fluid nature of whig factionalism, especially above the fall line, all are to some degree correct. Unfortunately, when allowed to stand unqualified, this effort to impose order on what was essentially a disorderly situation can result in the terms becoming part of the confusion rather than a means of ending it.[1]

This essay will identify the factions simply as "conservative" and "radical." Since the groups were distinguishable more by action than ideology, these terms, modifiers in most cases and relative ones at that, serve their purpose well enough. Georgia's conservative whigs, generally the movement's more socially prominent members and initially its most powerful politically, opposed the alteration and democratization of the government that remained after royal officials were expelled, especially when such modifications threatened their own authority. Their opponents, the radi-

---

[1] Early Georgia historians tended to treat political factionalism as an unfortunate, embarrassing, and, if the small amount of attention devoted to it is an indication, an unimportant aspect of the struggle for independence. The real assessment of the whig divisions began in the 1970s with Edward J. Cashin, "'The Famous Colonel Wells': Factionalism in Revolutionary Georgia," *Georgia Historical Quarterly* 58 (1974):137–56, and with Harvey H. Jackson, "Consensus and Conflict: Factional Politics in Revolutionary Georgia, 1774–1777," *Georgia Historical Quarterly* 59 (1975):388–401. Since the appearance of these two articles a number of other works have been published that add to our knowledge of whig factionalism in general and of the backcountry's role in particular. Cashin has written "Augusta's Revolution of 1779," *Richmond County History* 8 (1975):5–13, and "George Walton and the Forged Letter," *Georgia Historical Quarterly* 62 (1978):133–45, while Harvey H. Jackson has published *Lachlan McIntosh and the Politics of Revolutionary Georgia* (Athens, 1979) and "Button Gwinnett and the Rise of the 'Western Members': A Reappraisal of Georgia's 'Whig to Excess,'" *Atlanta Historical Journal* 24 (1980):17–30. Other works contributing to the understanding of the period and region are George R. Lamplugh, "'To Check and Discourage the Wicked and Designing': John Wereat and the Revolution in Georgia," *Georgia Historical Quarterly* 61 (1977):295–307, and Robert S. Davis, Jr., *Thomas Ansley and the American Revolution in Georgia* (Ansley, S.C., 1981).

cals, sought those changes—changes that promised to increase their power at the expense of the conservatives. To define beyond this point only begs exceptions.[2]

Because these factions first appeared in Georgia's coastal region and because it provided their more articulate spokesmen, the role of that area in the struggle to determine "who would rule at home" has traditionally overshadowed that played by inland patriots. Despite eventual backcountry support for both factions, most western members—a term used to identify frontier legislators and upcountry whigs in general—cannot be consistently connected to either party. Instead they moved between the two, allying with whichever position seemed best to address their needs. As they did so, they revealed that equal to their commitment to whiggery was their concern for the safety and security of their families, their property, and themselves. Pragmatic rather than inflexibly partisan, these Revolutionaries often flirted with the extremes, but in the end they usually sought more moderate means to achieve their goals. For those attempting to understand Georgia's Revolution, however, these frontier fluctuations only confused an already complicated situation.

Faced with this apparent inconstancy among backcountry whigs and influenced by the primary role played by coastal patriots in the early stages of the struggle, historians have tended to underestimate or ignore the contributions western members made to the political settlement that emerged from the conflict. Since the west seemed constantly under siege or attack, its citizens were believed too preoccupied with defending the region from Indians, loyalists, and each other to be really effective politicians. Despite the obvious advantages upcountry forces gained when the new government was framed, it was considered to be largely the work of lowcountry partisans. Westerners were treated as little more than extensions of their coastal counterparts.

There is, of course, some truth to this interpretation. Eastern influence on western involvement in the struggle for independence was considerable, and the question of who could

---

[2] See, for example, Merrill Jensen's codification of these terms in his *The Articles of Confederation* (1940; reprint ed., Madison, 1970), p. 10n.

best defend the region was indeed a determining factor in shaping political attitudes and alliances on the frontier. To overemphasize these points, however, obscures the critical role of backcountry politicians and, in turn, limits our knowledge of the Revolution in Georgia. If the significance of Georgia's Revolution is to be understood, and if that Revolution is to be placed within the context of similar conflicts in other colonies, it must be seen from the perspective of those who gained the most from it—the western members.

Georgia's backcountry initially appeared to want no part of a whig movement. In the summer of 1774, when "Liberty People" met in Savannah to denounce British abuses in Massachusetts, few from the frontier attended. Instead, nearly five hundred citizens from the western parishes of St. Paul and St. George signed petitions denouncing such gatherings and any "resolutions, or proceedings in any wise tending to express disloyalty to our most gracious Sovereign, and the Lords and Commons of Great Britain." To these petitioners Parliament's so-called Intolerable Acts were only "intended to reduce the people of Boston to a sense of their duty," and that, they strongly implied, needed to be done.[3]

But more than loyalty to king and constitution was behind this outpouring. During the previous decade, as immigrants from Virginia and the Carolinas crossed the Savannah to claim land that was theirs almost for the asking, these frontier parishes had grown more rapidly than the rest of the colony. The new arrivals swelled the ranks of the region's small-farmer majority and pushed settlement dangerously close to the already alarmed Creeks and Cherokee living on their borders.[4] Adding to this tension was the growing num-

---

[3] "A Protest or Declaration of Dissent of the Inhabitants of St. Paul's Parish . . . ," Aug. 5, 1774. This and the other petitions are in Robert S. Davis, Jr., *Georgia Citizens and Soldiers of the American Revolution* (Easley, S.C., 1979), pp. 11–19. See also Kenneth Coleman, *The American Revolution in Georgia, 1763–1789* (Athens, 1958), pp. 41–43. There was also an anti-whig petition from St. Matthew Parish, just upriver from Savannah, and one from Christ Church Parish.

[4] A good discussion of Georgia-Indian relations during this period is in

ber of landless, hunting, herding "Crackers," looked down on by frontier elites as "a set of Vagabonds often as bad or worse than the Indians themselves."[5] Their disregard both for tribal territorial rights and for the property of white settlers resulted in an unstable, unpredictable situation that made westerners all the more aware of their vulnerability.

And conditions seemed to be growing worse. Although in 1773 royal governor James Wright had negotiated with the tribes a settlement that gave Georgia over a million and a half acres north and west of St. Paul, many Indians refused to accept the treaty and the possibility of war seemed as great as before.[6] Thus, the St. Paul and St. George petitioners feared that if an outbreak occurred, their region "would most certainly be laid waste and depopulated, unless we receive such powerful aid and assistance as none but Great Britain can give." But, they reasoned, if frontiersmen were party to acts "that arraign the conduct of the King and Parliament," they "could not in justice expect any such assistance" from them. To whom, then, could they turn? To the whigs? What help, some signers caustically asked, could they expect from a movement led "chiefly [by] those whose property lies in or near Savannah, and, therefore, are not immediately exposed to the bad effects of an Indian war?"[7] Despite the recent influx of immigrants, the backcounty was still a region of widespread, weakly defended settlements and farms; consequently, frontier leaders were prepared to

---

W. W. Abbot, *The Royal Governors of Georgia, 1754–1775* (Chapel Hill, 1959), pp. 89–94, 158–60.

[5] Allen D. Candler, Lucian L. Knight, Kenneth Coleman, and Milton Ready, eds., *The Colonial Records of the State of Georgia*, 28 vols. (Atlanta, 1904–16, 1979–82), 14:475–76. Additional volumes (29–39) are in manuscript at the Georgia Department of Archives and History, Atlanta.

[6] "Colonial Records," 39:496–99; *Georgia Gazette*, Feb. 2, 16, 1774; James Wright to the earl of Dartmouth, Jan. 31, 1774, "Colonial Records," vol. 38, pt. 1, pp. 163–71; Abbot, *Royal Governors of Georgia*, pp. 158–59, and Edward J. Cashin and Heard Robertson, *Augusta and the American Revolution: Events in the Georgia Back Country, 1773–1783* (Darien, Ga., 1975), pp. 2–6.

[7] "St. Paul Dissent," Davis, *Citizens and Soldiers*, p. 16.

support the British, who seemed most able and willing to protect them in return.

The concerns raised by these western petitions had long been crucial for the region. Since 1736, when Augusta was founded at the falls of the Savannah River, the backcountry's development had depended on relations between settlers and their Indian neighbors and on commercial connections between inland merchants and their Savannah-Charleston counterparts. After the Trustee era ended, the perpetuation of peace and prosperity became the task of Georgia's royal government, the only force in the colony capable of keeping the tribes pacified and trading routes to the backcountry and beyond open and active.[8] For this reason, it should have been no surprise to coastal whigs when the citizens of these "out parishes" rejected their overtures and instead pledged continued loyalty to their governor and their king.

Many *were* surprised, however, for during the previous decade a bond between east and west had formed that tidewater whigs believed would carry over into their new movement. As the backcountry's population grew, Augusta-based merchants became increasingly involved with counterparts on the coast. At the same time rising planters in the west found that their increasing dependence on slave labor made their way of life more like that of planters in the coastal ricelands. Both economic and social bonds came to link the regions, and backcountry elites were soon welcomed not only in the counting houses of the capital but in the homes of Savannah gentry as well. These associations, which lowcountry leaders understood and encouraged, led to a political alliance formed to further the increasingly intertwined interests of each.[9]

[8] For this western development see Kenneth Coleman, gen. ed., *A History of Georgia* (Athens, 1977), pp. 9–67.

[9] The best discussion of colonial Georgia's social and economic associations may be found in Harold E. Davis, *The Fledgling Province: Social and Cultural Life in Colonial Georgia, 1733–1776* (Chapel Hill, 1976). See also, Harvey H. Jackson, "Georgia Whiggery: The Origins and Effects of a Many-Faceted Movement," in Harvey H. Jackson and Phinizy Spalding, eds., *Forty Years of Diversity: Essays on Colonial Georgia* (Athens, 1984), pp. 251–73.

This coalition, led by Christ Church Parish but including western members from St. Paul and St. George, had inspired efforts to force Governor Wright to share with the legislature more responsibility in governing the colony. When attempts to accomplish this through the assembly failed, the coastal faction sought to use the whig movement to bring the governor to terms.[10] Yet in the summer of 1774 these men were hardly revolutionaries. As politically and socially elitist as one could be in a colony as poor and provincial as Georgia, they did not initially propose overturning the existing system; indeed, they were part of it. Later, when the dynamics of the Revolution took hold, they still sought to preserve as much of the old order as would be compatible with the movement's rapidly changing goals. What these conservative whigs wanted was a government in which the legislature was supreme and they, or men like them, were supreme in the legislature. Naturally they supposed their confederates in the west wanted the same thing and would help.[11]

Yet this alliance between backcountry and lowcountry was never complete, for though western prosperity came increasingly to depend on commercial connections with the coast and on the coalition's assembly policies, frontiersmen still believed that the governor was the ultimate source of their security. Therefore, while backcountry legislators might oppose the executive on some issues, they had to remain ready to moderate their positions to avoid incurring the executive's displeasure or the wrath of authorities in London. Although Wright never gave any indication he would "punish" the back parishes by withholding "aid and assistance" needed for their defense, many in the region clearly felt he might—a fear that bound colonists to him for the moment but did not bode well for future relations between the royal

[10] Jack P. Greene, *The Quest for Power: The Lower Houses of Assembly in the Southern Royal Colonies, 1689–1776* (Chapel Hill, 1963), discusses these efforts. See pp. 493–95 for a list of leading legislators in Georgia that reveals the influence of Christ Church and the part played by backcountry parishes.

[11] Jackson, *Lachlan McIntosh*, pp. 20–22, and idem, "Consensus and Conflict," 389–92.

governor and his western constituents.[12] Still, so long as the threat of an Indian war existed, the backcountry's commitment to legislative supremacy, however sincere, remained conditional—an important point to remember and one coastal whigs apparently forgot.

This lack of western support was not the only problem facing the whigs. Hardly had the protests begun when delegates from St. John, a parish located down the coast from Savannah, challenged Christ Church's leadership. St. John had been settled in the 1750s by a Puritan congregation whose search for a new Zion took them from Massachusetts to South Carolina, and from there to Georgia. There they established a plantation economy and a port, Sunbury, to compete with the capital. But when they attempted to translate economic accomplishments into political power through the assembly, as counterparts in other parishes had done, they found their way blocked by the Christ Church clique that controlled the legislature. Frustrated at their inability to advance through traditional channels, St. John's leaders embraced the whig movement as a means of attacking not only the royal governor and his policies but also the conservative whigs whose limited objectives offered them little hope of improving their status.[13]

For these Puritans who, according to Governor Wright, still retained "a strong tincture of Republican or Oliverian principles,"[14] legislative supremacy was of little consequence if others controlled the legislature. Thus they attempted to establish themselves as the leaders of the whig movement by going beyond the passive resolutions proposed by Christ

[12] For Wright's handling of Indian affairs see Abbot, *Royal Governors of Georgia*, pp. 89–94, 158–60.

[13] James Stacy, *History of Midway Congregational Church, Liberty County, Georgia*, 2 vols. (Newman, Ga., 1903), 1:1–46; Charles Colcock Jones, *The Dead Towns of Georgia* (Savannah, 1878), pp. 141–223; and Jackson, *Lachlan McIntosh*, pp. 22–24. The list of leading legislators in Greene, *Quest for Power*, pp. 493–95, shows St. John's power relative to that of Christ Church.

[14] Wright to Dartmouth, Apr. 24, 1775, in George White, *Historical Collections of Georgia* (New York, 1855), p. 523.

Church and calling for delegates to be sent to the forthcoming intercolonial congress in Philadelphia. But Christ Church conservatives, determined to keep the matter localized, were able to defeat the motion, and the province went unrepresented at the first Continental Congress. Thus, Georgia's whigs divided into two tidewater factions, each vying for supremacy and each aware that to succeed it would need the help of an apparently hostile backcountry.[15]

Yet even as out parish petitioners circulated antiwhig protests, some from the region attended meetings held by the competing coastal parties.[16] Then, in late October, Governor Wright concluded "a treaty of peace, friendship, and commerce" with the Creeks, an agreement frontier settlers felt put the interests of the Indians and the Indian traders above their own. Angered at this betrayal, westerners began to abandon the royal governor.[17] Some of these, mostly members of the region's less prosperous, less influential small-farmer and Cracker classes, found a voice for their concerns and hope for improving their status in the more radical stand taken by St. John; others responded to Christ Church's cautious concern for the future of the colony and gravitated to that faction. Among this latter group were many who had been part of earlier east-west alliances inside and outside the assembly. They found old friends and allies ready to welcome them, and soon Savannah whigs were boasting of how the recently reluctant had "come over" to their position.[18]

[15] Letter from St. John Parish, author unidentified, Sept. 2, 1774, Peter Force, ed., *American Archives*, 4th ser. 6 vols. (Washington, D.C., 1837–46), 1:766–67; Coleman, *Revolution in Georgia*, pp. 42–43; and Jackson, "Consensus and Conflict," pp. 391–92.

[16] Letter from St. John, Sept. 2, 1774, extract of a letter from Savannah, Dec. 9, 1774, Force, ed., *American Archives*, 1:766–67, 1033–34; *Georgia Gazette*, Aug. 24, Sept. 7, 1774; Coleman, *Revolution in Georgia*, p. 43.

[17] *Georgia Gazette*, Oct. 26, 1774. For a full account of how Wright's Indian policy and this treaty caused many in the backcountry to join the whigs see Edward J. Cashin, "Sowing the Wind: Governor Wright and the Georgia Backcountry on the Eve of the Revolution," in Jackson and Spalding, eds., *Forty Years of Diversity*, pp. 233–50.

[18] Extract of a letter from Savannah, Dec. 9, 1774, Force, ed., *American Archives*, 1:1033–34.

Savannah's success in reestablishing ties with the west was revealed in January 1775 when Georgia's first provincial congress met in the coastal capital. The congress, called by Christ Church whigs in an attempt to seize the initiative from their rapidly rising rivals, was boycotted by St. John because, its spokesman asserted with revealing logic, "the greatest number of parishes in this Province are not represented therein" and the congress had not adopted the Continental Association, as St. John had done.[19] But just as St. John's absence underscored the division in the whig ranks, the list of those present called attention to the fact that the political alliance that had dominated Georgia's colonial legislature had not disintegrated during the protests. Although only five of the colony's twelve parishes sent delegates, among those five, the most populous in the province, were delegates from St. Paul and St. George. Antiwhig petitions to the contrary, the Christ Church coalition was intact.[20]

Hoping to overcome what opponents claimed was a lack of popular support and give its actions the aura of legality, the provincial congress sought assembly endorsement of its resolutions, which included a conditional acceptance of the Continental Association and the selection of three Christ Church stalwarts to represent the colony at the second Continental Congress. But before the legislature could act, Governor Wright prorogued it. With that, whigs who had hoped to alter the allocation of power with little disruption to the political system were forced to realize that reform was impossible while the governor controlled the means of reformation. If political change was to come, it would have to be accomplished outside the security of normal channels.[21]

In the months of maneuvering that followed, whig factions reluctantly realized they could accomplish little as opponents

[19] White, *Historical Collections*, pp. 521–22.

[20] Ibid., pp. 58–61; and Allen D. Candler, ed., *Revolutionary Records of the State of Georgia*, 3 vols. (Atlanta, 1908), 1:42–43.

[21] Noble W. Jones, Archibald Bulloch, and John Houstoun (Georgia delegates to the Continental Congress) to the president of the Continental Congress, Apr. 6, 1775, and the association entered into by forty-five deputies assembled in provincial congress, Jan. 28, 1775, in White, *Historical Collections*, pp. 58–63.

of one another and united against their first obstacle—royal governor James Wright. The moment was such that there was little time or desire to define goals carefully or calculate results beyond the immediate, so the new alliance concentrated instead on what was to be undone, and not what was to replace it. News of fighting in the north combined with rumors of planned British outrages against Georgia and Carolina to give whigs south of the Savannah popular support that previously eluded them. Meanwhile, on the frontier reports that Indian superintendent John Stuart had "been endeavouring to raise the Cherokee Indians to come down against them" convinced many of the wavering that their former protectors had become enemies. Georgia whigs accordingly set aside their differences and, on July 4, 1775, assembled in the colony's second provincial congress.[22]

This gathering brought Georgia into the mainstream of the whig movement when it passed resolutions supporting the recommendations of the Continental Congress, including the original Continental Association, and elected five delegates to go to Philadelphia. The fact that none of those chosen was from the backcountry seems to have been of little importance, but if it was, another of the congress's actions surely compensated for it. Realizing the newly united movement would stay united only if all elements felt they received even-handed treatment, the provincial congress, under pressure from western delegates, drew on whiggery's republican underpinnings and declared that in future elections "every man contributing towards the general tax, shall be qualified to vote" and that representatives would be allocated in a manner more in line with provincial patterns.[23]

Under the new system delegations from St. Paul and St.

[22] Jackson, "Consensus and Conflict," pp. 393–94; Wright to Dartmouth, June 20, 1775, Georgia Historical Society *Collections* 3 (1873):189–90; Wright to Dartmouth, May 12, 1775, "Colonial Records," vol. 38, pt. 1, p. 439; *Georgia Gazette*, May 17, 1775; White, *Historical Collections*, p. 65; and Abbot, *Royal Governors of Georgia*, pp. 172–77.

[23] White, *Historical Collections*, pp. 65–80, contains the proceedings of the congress. This was not the first time payment of the general tax was a qualification to vote. Savannah whigs used it as a requirement in voting for the first provincial congress (see the *Georgia Gazette*, Dec. 7, 1774).

George were enlarged and representatives were added for the rapidly growing population in the 1773 Indian cession, which increased backcountry membership from 15 percent to 22 percent of the total. It still did not give the region "equal" representation, but it marked a beginning. More significantly, the alteration indicated that western legislators planned to play anything but a passive part in the government being created. St. John also received an additional representative, as did each of the parishes south of the Altamaha River, while Christ Church, along with its sometime ally St. Matthew and the southern cornerstone of the coalition, St. Andrew Parish, had their representation reduced. Still, Christ Church's delegation remained the largest and, if traditional alliances held firm, the increased strength of the west would easily offset other coalition losses—or so coastal conservatives must have thought.[24]

[24] White, *Historical Collections*, pp. 65 and 78. Population figures for Georgia as a whole, and for the backcountry specifically, are difficult to come by. James M. Grant, "Legislative Factions in Georgia, 1754–1789: A Socio-Political Study," Ph.D. diss., University of Georgia, 1975, p. 7, estimated that by the end of the 1770s the western parishes contained nearly half the state's white citizens, while in 1776 Lachlan McIntosh wrote George Washington that the men available to fill his ranks were "chiefly in the back country," an indication Grant's estimate might well be correct. Despite the imprecision, however, it is clear that the backcountry population was growing rapidly and would soon eclipse the coast (McIntosh to Washington, Feb. 16, 1776, ibid., p. 92; see also Davis, *Citizens and Soldiers*, pp. 12–13, for remarks on the size of St. Paul and St. George parishes).

The number of members in the congress was reduced to ninety-six and the 1773 Indian Cession was allowed three delegates. The following table shows the shift in power taking place.

Parish	Delegates elected to the July 1775 congress	Delegates authorized to attend later congresses
Christ Church	41	27
St. Matthew	12	9
St. Philip	7	7
St. George	8	9
St. Paul	8	9
St. John	11	12
St. Andrew	13	9

The provincial congress adjourned in mid-July. In the months that followed, the Christ Church–dominated Council of Safety, which had been created to direct whig activities when the congress was not in session, continued the systematic usurpation of authority that by the end of the year left James Wright governor in name only.[25] Paying particular attention to frontier defensive needs, council members appeared determined the western members would not regret their decision to join the movement and would recognize the whig government and its Christ Church leaders as the authority royal officials once had been. The tactic seemed to work, for an increasingly despondent Governor Wright reported that "the People in the Back Parts of the Province, following the Example of others, [were] forming Cabals, and setting up for themselves," while spreading the word "that there [was] a new Government now, and that no Application [was] to be made to [him], but to the Council of Safety." Led by Augusta's parochial committee, backcountry whigs, with all the zeal of converts, set out to rid the area of anyone considered less than committed to the "common cause" and in so doing made enemies for themselves and their movement like the future loyalist Ranger Lt. Col. Thomas Brown, who

St. David	2	3
St. James	0	2
St. Patrick	0	2
St. Mary	1	2
St. Thomas	1	2
Indian Cession	0	3

Three delegates to the July 1775 congress refused to take their seats. The parishes of St. James and St. Patrick sent no delegates, but there is nothing to indicate they could not have had they wished. The number of Christ Church delegates in the later congresses includes seventeen for Savannah and the rest for districts in the parish.

[25] The minutes of the Council of Safety from Nov. 1775 to Feb. 1777 are in Candler, ed., *Revolutionary Records*, 1:67–227; and in the Ga. Hist. Soc. *Collections* 5, pt. 1 (1901):15–127. See also White, *Historical Collections*, pp. 86–92; and Coleman, *Revolution in Georgia*, pp. 62–66.

would return to plague the frontier.[26] Already the forces that would drive reason from the region and replace it with fanaticism and vendetta were making their presence known—a foreshadowing of what was to come.

Even as Savannah whigs were seeking to confirm the backcountry's role in their new coalition, whigs from St. John, also aware the frontier could well decide which tidewater faction would be victorious, worked to forge a western alliance of their own. Button Gwinnett, a parish planter and politician who had emerged as leader of St. John's "liberty boys," was the key figure in this effort. In the summer of 1775 he organized what opponents claimed was a "nocturnal Cabal" created to convince "members, both to the southward and westward . . . that the views and interests of [Christ Church Parish and] the town of Savannah were different from those of the State" and that whigs from St. John's were their natural allies. The apparent ease with which this was accomplished among some western members indicated, however, that Gwinnett's task was not as great as one might suppose. Traditional ties between coast and backcountry were already crumbling.[27]

Even before the present crisis, frontier elites upon whom the pre-1774 Christ Church coalition depended had found their leadership threatened by the stream of immigration into the region. The events of 1775 added to their anxiety. Despite assurances to the contrary, some remained unconvinced that a whig government could or would defend their property and position as the royal government had done. As the political struggle grew more intense, some of these "principle People . . . through fear of the Consequences . . . withdrew

---

[26] Wright to Dartmouth, Nov. 1, 1775, Ga. Hist. Soc. *Collections* 3:218; *Georgia Gazette*, Aug. 30, 1775; White, *Historical Collections*, pp. 606–7; Coleman, *Revolution in Georgia*, pp. 65–66; Gordon B. Smith, "The Georgia Grenadiers," *Georgia Historical Quarterly* 64 (1980):410; Cashin and Robertson, *Augusta and the Revolution*, pp. 9–10.

[27] Jackson, "Button Gwinnett," pp. 17–30; [Lachlan McIntosh and John Wereat], "Remarks on a Pamphlet, Entitled 'Structures on a Pamphlet, entitled The Case of George McIntosh' . . ." (Savannah, 1777), p. 15.

themselves & . . . by which means they lost that influence they otherways wou'd have had."[28] Not all frontier leaders chose this course, and some who did later returned to the whig fold, but enough held back to open the way for others—rising planters and recent arrivals—to take a more active role. The latter group especially, feeling little loyalty to Georgia's royal government and, never having been important to the earlier Christ Church coalition, knew few of the pressures that made others uncertain what to do. Although rallying to the whig cause, many of these less-established frontiersmen concluded that for them the alliance Gwinnett offered was a better arrangement than the traditional union with Christ Church.[29]

The first indication of what that "nocturnal Cabal" had accomplished came early in 1776 when the more popularly based provincial congress, with its increased western membership, met in Savannah. One of the items on its agenda was the selection of a commander for the recently authorized Continental battalion, an office of political as well as military significance. Christ Church delegates nominated Samuel Elbert, commander of the Georgia Grenadiers. Although the grenadiers were in effect the military arm of the Council of Safety in Savannah, on at least one occasion Elbert had marched his troops to the aid of whigs in Augusta, a show of support expected to garner backcountry votes. The opposition countered with Button Gwinnett. Then, for the first time in nearly two decades, the advantage shifted away from Christ Church. When the votes were counted it was found that enough southern and western members had joined St. John to turn the tide, and Button Gwinnett was declared elected.[30]

[28] Joseph Clay to Messrs. Bright and Pechin, July 2, 1777, "Letters of Joseph Clay," Ga. Hist. Soc. *Collections* 8 (1913):35.

[29] Jackson, "Button Gwinnett," pp. 21–22. For the impact recent arrivals from other colonies had on the Revolution in Georgia see W. W. Abbot, "A Cursory View of Eighteenth Century Georgia," *South Atlantic Quarterly* 61 (1962):339–44.

[30] The most thorough discussion of this election may be found in Jackson, *Lachlan McIntosh*, pp. 29–33. See also Smith, "Georgia Grenadiers," pp. 408–9.

But Christ Church and its supporters, who still included some backcountry leaders, refused to accept the outcome. Threatening to desert the movement if it meant following "Colonel Gwinnett," they prevailed on the congress to accept a compromise candidate—Lachlan McIntosh from the Altamaha River village of Darien. A product of the southern frontier, which implied an appreciation of the problems facing out parishes, McIntosh was also a member of the merchant-planter elite that rose to prominence under royal rule and could be counted on to see to coastal interests as well. On the whole he was acceptable to most and objectionable to none, so the bargain was struck. Lachlan McIntosh was given the Continental command, Elbert became his lieutenant colonel, and Button Gwinnett was sent to the Continental Congress. It appeared to be an arrangement with something for everyone.[31]

Western members willingly accepted the compromise, revealing again the importance placed on regional defenses, but no sooner had the new colonel begun to raise his army than he found recruiting hampered by South Carolina's high enlistment bounty and by "the ease in which the poorest People generally live[d] in the Southern Coloneys, and the prejudice they [had] to any regular service, on account of the restraint that any thing of a strict discipline require[d]."[32] As a result, the task of defending the backcountry fell to short-term, home-based militia and to the men the units chose to lead them. Some of these officers naturally were drawn from prewar leaders who now championed the whig cause; others came from the ranks of those who rose to replace the wavering. The rank and file militiamen often put their faith in men more like themselves, however, members of the region's "middling" and even "meaner" classes. Claiming authority from the trust and approval of the soldiers who elected them, proud (even jealous) of their recently acquired status, these men stood ready to further the common cause as they

[31] Jackson, *Lachlan McIntosh*, pp. 29–33.

[32] McIntosh to Washington, Apr. 28, 1776, in Lilla M. Hawes, ed., "The Papers of Lachlan McIntosh," Ga. Hist. Soc. *Collections* 12 (1957):4–5. Information on the militia may be found in Candler, ed., *Revolutionary Records*, 1:88–100, and Coleman, *Revolution in Georgia*, pp. 63.

saw it, which was from a decidedly western perspective.

Thus, by early 1776 one can begin to identify those back-country whigs who would soon be competing for the leader-ship of the western members. Though a small group made still smaller by its subdivisions, they exercised an influence that far exceeded their number, an influence critical to the transformation of Georgia's political system. On one hand were whigs whose ties were to Savannah and Christ Church Parish and who shared the conservative goals and attitudes of that coastal-led coalition. Prominent in pre-Revolutionary affairs, though their ranks were depleted and their influence diminished by the withdrawal of those "principle people" who earlier concluded whiggery had gone too far, they re-mained a force with which others in the movement had to reckon. At the opposite pole were whigs from the region's small-farmer and Cracker classes, though some from other groups also gravitated in that direction. Emerging to fill civil and military positions created by the emergency, they sought not only to increase their power and prestige but also to guarantee that any gains made would not be lost when the struggle ended. Representing an element that was more a consequence of the Revolution than a cause, these men had little sympathy for the issues and interests that moved con-servative Georgians to join it. Quite to the contrary, they were determined that the system others wished to preserve, a sys-tem that largely excluded them and denied them its benefits, would not survive. With the most to gain and the least to lose, they were potentially the most radical whigs in Georgia.

There was yet another group, one composed of rising backcountry planters and merchants, including some who were about to take their place among the west's most promi-nent citizens when the struggle began. Initially seeing whig-gery as a threat to their future, many of them signed the 1774 petitions denouncing the movement, but reversed themselves when Wright's policies were discredited. Moving quickly to claim their share of the offices available, they ably assumed the responsibilities and exercised the authority that accompanied their new positions. Some apparently wanted less to alter the system than be part of it. Yet many remained skeptical of the role coastal interests intended for them to play in the new government, an attitude that led them to reject Elbert's bid to command the battalion, support Gwinnett's selection with something less than enthusiasm, and finally accept the "southern frontiersman" Lachlan McIntosh because he seemed most sympathetic to the needs of their region. They were, however, equally uneasy over the rise of backcountry radicals, whose growing strength threatened their progress as surely as the resistance of entrenched conservatives. Finding themselves between the two extremes, these western "moderates" avoided as much as possible any permanent association with either and worked to establish themselves as a creditable alternative.

Yet most western members were concerned less with who would lead them than with whether those leaders would be able to bring order and security to a region where crisis seemed to follow crisis. Independent raiding parties had recently attacked nearby Indian settlements, raising the danger of a general Indian war, while at the same time "many disaffected persons [were] possessed of and . . .[were] building and erecting divers forts and fortifications without any leave or authority," further complicating whig efforts to control the frontier. The disaffected presented a particular problem, for throughout the conflict they showed scant commitment to any cause but their own and consistently rallied to whichever side seemed best able to protect them from the ravages of the other. Then, once the threat passed, they wanted only to be left alone. If the backcountry was to be brought under whig military control, a necessary preliminary to political consolidation, some way had to be found either to weld the disaffected to the cause or at least to prevent their disaffection from spreading. It promised to be no easy task.[33]

Still, backcountry disaffection was hardly Georgia's most pressing problem. In March 1776 a British attempt to resup-

[33] Wright to Dartmouth, Nov. 1, 1775, Ga. Hist. Soc. *Collections*, 3:218, and vol. 5, pt. 1, p. 34. Bulloch to Major Walton, May 1, 1776, Candler, ed., *Revolutionary Records*, 1:118. For the best discussion of disaffection and its impact on the Revolution see Ronald Hoffman, "The 'Disaffected' in the Revolutionary South," in Alfred F. Young, ed., *The American Revolution: Explorations in the History of American Radicalism* (DeKalb, Ill., 1976), pp. 275–316.

ply ships at Savannah resulted in an armed confrontation that sent Governor Wright fleeing to a man-of-war and the provincial congress scurrying upriver to Augusta. There, legislators drew up the "Rules and Regulations of 1776," a temporary constitution that did little more than legitimize the status quo and provide Christ Church a framework for reasserting its authority, which it did with surprising ease.[34] For their part western whigs accepted this arrangement and waited to see if McIntosh would be able to raise the "troop of sixty horse . . .[he felt would] protect [the] Western settlements from the insults of Indians," and if Continental commissioners, scheduled to meet the Cherokee and Creeks at Augusta in May, could entice the tribes from their British allies.[35] But by summer the danger of an Indian war had not abated and the "troop of horse" remained a skeleton force at best. To the further dismay of the western members, McIntosh deployed most of his small army along the Georgia-Florida border or stationed them in Savannah. This placed an even heavier burden on the hastily raised, undersupplied militia and on its officers, who often seemed to spend as much energy quarreling among themselves as they did combating the enemy. With the military situation increasingly bleak and with shortages of basic necessities such that "the small remains of goods [had] advanced two or three hundred percent," it was hardly surprising that many in the backcountry began to reassess their support for Lachlan McIntosh and for the Christ Church–led government he served.[36]

Adding to western anxiety were reports that some westerners were carrying on correspondence with the loyalist Alexander Cameron, who was leading Indian raiding parties in

[34] Jackson, *Lachlan McIntosh*, pp. 35–40, 51–52, discusses this episode. See also Candler, ed., *Revolutionary Records*, 1:274; Cashin and Robertson, *Augusta and the Revolution*, p 14; Coleman, *Revolution in Georgia*, pp. 76–78; and White, *Historical Collections*, pp. 96–98.

[35] McIntosh to Washington, Apr. 28, 1776, White, *Historical Collections*, p. 95; Cashin and Robertson, *Augusta and the Revolution*, p. 14.

[36] Jackson, *Lachlan McIntosh*, pp. 35–50, discusses this topic. See also Candler, ed., *Revolutionary Records*, 1:119, 120, 122, 155, 156–57, 161; and McIntosh to Washington, Apr. 28, 1776, White, *Historical Collections*, p. 95.

the region, and that on the coast prominent whigs were secretly trading with the enemy. Already many suspected of treason were being arrested. Although the Council of Safety spent no small part of its time dealing with these accused, the fear that the cause might be betrayed continued to grow. News of the Declaration of Independence was reason for some celebration, as was the reported destruction of the Cherokee lower towns by troops from South Carolina, but no one knew what effect the latter would have on the Creeks, who remained the primary concern of Georgia's frontier. Conditions were so unsettled that some disaffected in the west took what property they could and began to leave, but the council, fearing a reduced population would further weaken regional defenses, ordered the militia to stop the exodus and return the refugees to their homes. This response did little to relieve the conditions causing the migration in the first place, but it did increase the visibility of local troops and their commanders and made frontier whigs all the more aware that it was upon these soldiers that their security depended.[37]

It was amid this growing backcountry dissatisfaction with coastal leadership that instructions arrived from the Continental Congress for each former colony to adopt a government suitable to the present crisis. This moved council president Archibald Bulloch to call for the election of a "convention" to write a permanent constitution for the state, thereby setting the stage for one of Georgia's pivotal political contests.[38] Button Gwinnett, aware of the significance of what was taking place, returned from Philadelphia to rally supporters in St. John and resurrect his earlier coalition. Finding many western members convinced that Georgia's government was dominated by an elitist clique willing to sacrifice frontier interests for those of the coast and fearing that

[37] James H. O'Donnell III, *Southern Indians in the American Revolution* (Knoxville, 1973), pp. 45, 51–52; Charles Lee to John Rutledge, Aug. 28, 1776, New-York Historical Society *Collections* 5 (1872):247–48; White, *Historical Collections*, pp. 200–201; Candler, ed., *Revolutionary Records*, 1:122, 161, 162, 168, 186, 189, 190; Jackson, *Lachlan McIntosh*, p. 56.

[38] Candler, ed., *Revolutionary Records*, 1:280–81.

some lowcountry aristocrats were actually working to subvert the cause they pretended to serve, Gwinnett was able to forge an alliance more powerful than the one that first put him in office. Critical to his success was the fact that some moderate western leaders, now convinced that the government would respond to them only if they were an essential part of it, abandoned their wait-and-see policy and joined the radicals' all-out assault on the Christ Church coalition.[39]

The election that September proved a turning point in backcountry politics. Not only did frontier whigs repudiate the government that for the past months had attempted to lead them but, equally important, they rejected those western leaders who still maintained ties to traditional coastal allies. In their place were selected frontier partisans who saw themselves as part of a movement legitimized by popular support and mandated to rescue the Revolution from enemies without and within. These delegates joined radicals from St. John and, helped by some key legislators from Christ Church—for even there traditional leaders were losing ground—they first gained control of the convention and then of the committee charged to draw up a constitution. More than at any time since the conflict began, western members were in a position to influence the forces that shaped their lives—not only to define the conditions under which future Georgia governments would govern but to determine who would govern Georgia as well.[40]

[39] Jackson, "Button Gwinnett," pp. 23–24; Coleman, *Revolution in Georgia*, p. 103; Jackson, *Lachlan McIntosh*, pp. 52–53. For a good discussion of backcountry attitudes see Cashin's "Augusta's Revolution," pp. 5–13, and "'The Famous Colonel Wells,'" pp. 137–43.

An additional reason for the backcountry being upset with conservative policies was a futile expedition launched against St. Augustine just before the election. This attempt by the government to prove itself able to defeat the enemy only expended men and resources that western members felt could have been better used for their defense (see Jackson, *Lachlan McIntosh*, pp. 43–46).

[40] Jackson, *Lachlan McIntosh*, pp. 52–53; Samuel Elbert to McIntosh, Sept. 23, 1776, *Pennsylvania Magazine of History and Biography* 42 (1918):77–78; Jackson, "Button Gwinnett," pp. 24–25. The only surviving part of the convention's minutes are in Charles Jenkins, *Button Gwinnett* (New York, 1926), pp. 108–10.

By winter the committee's work was well underway, but since the convention was also the legislature, the drafting of the constitution often had to be set aside as members turned to more pressing matters. Still, by year's end a draft was being circulated and discussed. Debate on the document in its final form began on January 29, 1777, and on February 5 it passed without a dissenting vote. Those who opposed it either were absent, abstained, or accepted the inevitable in hopes of turning it to their advantage. The new government, though in many ways a dramatic departure from those preceding it, was a natural consequence of changes that had been set in motion. A one-house assembly, with an executive elected by and responsible to it, made its structure as near a reflection of radical whig philosophy as would come from Revolutionary constitution writing. Yet its provisions for lower qualifications to vote and hold office were simply another step in a process begun as early as 1774, and though some conservatives later expressed dismay at what the alterations accomplished, there is little to indicate that at the outset they seriously opposed the change.[41]

Nor apparently were they disturbed by the fact that, in one of the most thorough acts of reapportionment to occur during the Revolution, the constitution of 1777 swept away the parishes and replaced them with eight counties. Christ Church and lower St. Philip (which were usually allied) were combined to form Chatham County; upper St. Philip and St. Matthew (areas now more western than coastal in outlook) became Effingham, while St. Paul, St. George, and the 1773 Indian Cession became Richmond, Burke, and Wilkes, respectively. The parishes south of the Altamaha were made Camden and Glynn and, in what was the most controversial change, St. Andrew Parish, home of Lachlan McIntosh and his supporters, was combined with St. James and St. John to form Liberty County. Effingham, Burke, Richmond, and

[41] McIntosh to George Walton, Dec. 15, 1776, Ga. Hist. Soc. *Collections*, 12:23–24; Jenkins, *Button Gwinnett*, pp. 108–10. The constitution of 1777 may be found in Candler, ed., *Revolutionary Records*, 1:282–97. See also Albert B. Saye, *A Constitutional History of Georgia* (Athens, 1948), pp. 93–113; Clay to Bright and Pechin, July 2, 1777, Ga. Hist. Soc. *Collections*, 8:35, and *Georgia Gazette*, Dec. 7, 1774.

Wilkes were to have ten representatives each. Chatham was given fourteen (the extra four to Savannah "to represent their trade"), and Liberty got sixteen (two for Sunbury and fourteen, it was explained with some difficulty, because the county contained three parishes). Counties below the Altamaha were given one delegate each and more could be allocated if population increased, yet that provision was not everywhere applied, for with the exception of Liberty and Chatham counties the maximum representation was ten. But confused as it might seem, this combination of equal and proportional representation made one thing clear; if prewar population patterns held true, and there is no reason to believe whigs expected otherwise, the constitution of 1777 guaranteed that western members would shape Georgia's political future.[42]

Nevertheless, decisions being made on the coast caused frontier politicians to wonder if they would reap the rewards recently won. Newly promoted to the rank of general, McIntosh was convinced that the greatest threat to the state was from the south. He chose to ignore "repeated Complaints from the back [c]ountry [that the] Light Horse [stationed there were] of no kind of Service" and instead concentrated what troops he could spare in forts along the Altamaha.[43] To make matters worse, although Button Gwinnett was elected president of the Council of Safety, giving him some authority to answer backcountry complaints, he chose to expend his energy and the state's meager resources on an invasion of Florida, leaving his frontier friends to fend for themselves. Not surprisingly, when Gwinnett called for militia to man the expedition, only troops from St. John appeared; that forced the president to seek Continental support, which he had hoped to avoid. Meanwhile, personal and political differences between McIntosh and Gwinnett reached a point where cooperation became impossible. The expedition finally ended amid quarreling commanders, leaving the cause of the failure to be determined by the first assembly meeting

[42] Candler, ed., *Revolutionary Records*, 1:284–85.

[43] McIntosh to Leonard Marbury, Nov. 25, 1776, Ga. Hist. Soc. *Collections*, 12:19–20; Jackson, *Lachlan McIntosh*, pp. 35–50.

under the new constitution, a body in which once neglected frontier delegates held the balance of power.[44]

At its May meeting the initial task facing Georgia's legislature was the election of a governor, a post Gwinnett desired and to which he seemed natural heir. But the backcountry had found little to its liking in the St. Augustine expedition and President Gwinnett's determination to carry it through lost him much of that region's support. The office, in which there was as much symbolism as substance, went to John Adam Treutlen from what was formerly St. Matthew Parish, upriver from Savannah and increasingly more western than coastal in outlook. When the blame for the invasion's failure was decided, frontier delegates, who had little to gain from adding to Gwinnett's humiliation, voted with the majority to declare his conduct legal and proper. McIntosh, outraged at the decision, publicly called Gwinnett a *"Scoundrell & lying Rascal,"* and a challenge was issued. The duel followed, both were wounded, and on May 19, Button Gwinnett died. With his passing Georgia lost one of its most aggressive and controversial politicians and the west lost the linchpin in its alliance with St. John.[45]

Reaction to Gwinnett's death was swift and predictable. Pushing aside issues that might divide them, western and coastal radicals, under the auspices of a "Nocturnal Club" christened the "Liberty Society," launched a pamphlet and petition campaign against McIntosh that ultimately drove the general from the state and left his supporters in disarray.[46] Coastal conservatives could do little more than bemoan the fact that "Rule & Government [had gotten] into the Hands of those whose ability or situation in Life [did] not entitle them to it" and that "Gentlemen of ability, whose char-

[44]Lyman Hall to Roger Sherman, May 16, 1777, in Jenkins, *Button Gwinnett,* pp. 226–30; see also Jackson, *Lachlan McIntosh,* pp. 60–64.

[45]Jackson, *Lachlan McIntosh,* pp. 64–68; Hall to Sherman, May 16, 1777, Jenkins, *Button Gwinnett,* pp. 228–29.

[46]Jackson, *Lachlan McIntosh,* pp. 66–70; McIntosh's comments, Aug. 1777, Ga. Hist. Soc. *Collections,* 12:74. The petitions may be found in the Papers of the Continental Congress, Record Group 360, No. 73, pp. 51–58, 67–95, 112–14, National Archives.

acters [were] well established, [were] the only persons objected to." Meanwhile conservatives entrenched themselves as best they could in offices under Continental jurisdiction and waited for the radicals' next move. By the end of the summer the once powerful Christ Church coalition seemed in full retreat and the matter of "who would rule at home" appeared decided.[47]

Leading the backcountry in this campaign was George Wells, an enigmatic Augusta physician and moderately well-to-do planter. Like some in the west, he had signed one of the 1774 antiwhig petitions, but a short time later he joined the cause he previously denounced. His rise began with that decision. He was elected a militia colonel and then appointed justice of the peace, a testament to his growing reputation among the region's propertyless Crackers and more radical small-farmer class. Finding a kindred spirit in Gwinnett, Wells first became his western lieutenant and eventually exercised as much influence in the backcountry as his more famous ally did on the coast. A member of the convention that met in the fall of 1776, he was on the select committee that drew up the new constitution and thus had an extraordinary interest in the document and the system of government it created, an interest that was to shape his career. Wells served as Gwinnett's second in the president's fatal duel with McIntosh, and he never forgave the general and his conservative supporters for the death of his friend. Political differences notwithstanding, George Wells's crusade was a deeply personal one.[48]

Guided by Wells, radical western members began to enjoy the authority granted their region by the new constitution

[47] Clay to Bright and Pechin, July 2, 1777, Ga. Hist. Soc. *Collections*, 8:35; John Coleman to McIntosh, July 31, 1777, Peter Force Transcripts, Library of Congress.

[48] Cashin, "'The Famous Colonel Wells,'" pp. 137–55, describes the career of this leader of the backcountry's meaner sort. For reactions to the work of Wells and his supporters see Clay to Bright and Pechin, July 2, 1777, Wereat to George Walton, Aug. 30, 1777, Ga. Hist. Soc. *Collections*, 8:35, 12:66–73. Apparently Wells had also been a resident of St. John Parish in the early 1770s and may have known Gwinnett then (see Georgia Official Records, Miscellaneous Bonds, Drawer 40, Box 36, Ga. Dept. Arch. and Hist.).

and exerted an influence over the government unknown in previous years. Yet their increased political power proved of little value in reducing tensions on the frontier. Although a treaty with the Cherokee was signed in May at De Witt's Corner in South Carolina, efforts by Continental Indian agent George Galphin to reach a similar agreement with the Creeks were not successful and raids by that tribe continued. The final insult came later in the summer when Thomas Brown's East Florida Rangers, who had been pillaging the backcountry almost at will, attacked Augusta and revealed to all just how exposed the western counties really were.[49] An "Act for the Expulsion of Internal Enemies of the State," passed by the assembly in September, allowed frontier whigs to seek out those believed to be aiding Brown and his men. Under its provisions they vented their frustrations against the suspect as well as the guilty, in the final analysis perhaps doing more harm than good. As a result of their activities, many who might have supported the cause were alienated from it, for in the end these zealots set a standard for loyalty few could meet or maintain.[50]

By fall, however, it was apparent that the summer's excesses had caused many to take stock of their situation and seek less divisive methods to keep the cause alive. The result was a subtle but significant shift in alliances that seems to have left St. John radicals the weaker. Already some in that parish, disturbed at the course of events, were taking a less active role in the movement, and with Gwinnett dead the remainder lacked a leader who could garner popular support outside their immediate area. The Liberty Society remained vocal, but when McIntosh left the state the object of their wrath was absent and tempers began to cool.[51] Coastal conservatives could still accuse the assembly and "the famous

[49] Cashin and Robertson, *Augusta and the Revolution*, p. 18; O'Donnell, *Southern Indians*, pp. 57–58; and Coleman, *Revolution in Georgia*, pp. 113–14.

[50] Heard Robertson, ed., "Georgia's Banishment and Expulsion Act of September 16, 1777," *Georgia Historical Quarterly* 55 (1971):274–82; Cashin and Robertson, *Augusta and the Revolution*, p. 19.

[51] Coleman, *Revolution in Georgia*, pp. 89–94, 105–12, describes political and military activities in Georgia after McIntosh's departure.

Col. Wells" of raising troops "under the pretence of Defending our Western Frontiers" when the "principle motive . . .[was] plunder & Offices," while Governor Treutlen could counter that "wicked and designing Men"—apparently low-country merchants and planters—had purchased land titles given soldiers and thereby threatened to "prevent the increase of inhabitants in the frontier parts of this State." But such exchanges became increasingly rare and should not obscure the fact that beneath the "radicalization" of Georgia's political system, less-partisan whigs from the coast and from the frontier were reestablishing lines of communication and cooperation.[52]

A period of political consolidation began in the winter of 1777 and continued through the following year. It was marked by the election of Chatham County planter John Houstoun as governor and the return of many moderates and even some conservatives to state and local offices. Radicals remained in positions of power, but with the province threatened by loyalist invasions from both north and south, defensive concerns were again given priority over party politics. In the spring of 1778, when "between five and six hundred . . . disaffected People . . . from the back Parts of South Carolina" moved through Georgia on their way to Florida, the Executive Council responded by putting all power over military matters into the hands of the governor. Meanwhile, the assembly decided to meet in Augusta, "where its presence was thought necessary to raise the spirits of the Inhabitants of the back parts and encourage them to oppose any further attempts of the disaffected"—another indication of the influence backcountry delegates were able to exert on the government.[53]

When that threat eased, Governor Houstoun followed the

[52] Clay to Henry Laurens, Oct. 16, 1777, Ga. Hist. Soc. *Collections*, 8:51; Candler, ed., *Revolutionary Records*, 1:318–19.

[53] Edith D. Johnson, *The Houstouns of Georgia* (Athens, 1950), covers Governor Houstoun's career; Candler, ed., *Revolutionary Records*, 1:332–33, 2:6, 13, 24, 48–49, 62–63, 72–73, 75–76; Houstoun to the president of the Continental Congress, Apr. 16, 1778, and James Whitefield to the president of the Continental Congress, May 6, 1778, Papers of Cont. Cong.

example of earlier chief executives and launched yet another invasion of Florida, but now even western members finally had to admit that activities directed from St. Augustine endangered the entire state. Still, the expedition ended as unsuccessfully as its predecessors, and, by late August, Georgia found itself even less secure than before.[54] Rumors of a "rupture" with the Creeks and reports of the "alarming state of Affairs in the back Country" continued to shape the thinking of frontier politicians, although many among them had begun to see that the interests of their region were linked to those of the rest of the province.[55] This less parochial point of view, however, would have an impact only if the whig cause and the state it created were able to survive.

In December the long-feared British assault finally came. Savannah fell with frightening ease and what remained of the whig movement sought sanctuary in the backcountry. A few weeks later fugitive assemblymen met in Augusta and after some initial confusion established an Executive Council "in order to at least keep up a show of Government."[56] Presided over by William Glascock, who had represented St. Paul at the first provincial congress but had not been part of the factional excesses that followed, this rump government directed the defense of what remained of the state and continued the retreat from partisan politics that had begun after McIntosh's departure. Dominated by western members less radical in political leanings than those who had rallied around Gwinnett, this new coalition provided Georgia with at least the illusion of government which, when all is considered, was no small feat.[57]

[54] Coleman, *Revolution in Georgia*, pp. 107–8; Houstoun to the president of the Continental Congress, Aug. 20, 1778, Papers of Cont. Cong.; Candler, ed., *Revolutionary Records*, 2:100, 103–4.

[55] Candler, ed., *Revolutionary Records*, 2:90–95.

[56] William Glascock to the Continental Congress, July 10, 1779, Papers of Cont. Cong.; Affidavit of William Glascock, Ga. Hist. Soc. *Collections*, 12:123; Candler, ed., *Revolutionary Records*, 1:401, 2:129.

[57] For the activities of Glascock's council, see Jackson, *Lachlan McIntosh*, pp. 110–13; Coleman, *Revolution in Georgia*, pp. 155–56, Candler, ed., *Revolutionary Records*, 1:401–2, 2:129–40.

Meanwhile Lt. Col. Archibald Campbell, determined to be "the first British Officer to rend a Stripe and a Star from the Flag of Congress," was not content to control only the coast. Consolidating his position in Savannah, he swiftly struck inland, drove most of the already demoralized whig militia into South Carolina, and on January 31 occupied Augusta.[58] But Campbell's hopes of using the town as a base for conquering the entire state were dashed when whig militia returned to rally the countryside and the dedication of his loyalist forces became questionable. Realizing his precarious position, Colonel Campbell decided that evacuation was the prudent course, and on February 14 the withdrawal began. The defeat of a loyalist force at Kettle Creek in Wilkes County that same day gave frontier whigs yet another reason for optimism, but efforts to capitalize on that victory were set back when, in early March, a patriot army was routed at Briar Creek, midway between Augusta and Savannah. That ended the American advance and left Georgia divided—the British holding the coast and whigs the backcountry.[59]

By late March the Executive Council was again meeting in Augusta, and area residents apparently accepted it for what it claimed to be, an interim government born of necessity. Under Glascock's direction it continued to function until late July, when a group of whigs described as "the Representatives of the people of Wilkes, Richmond, Burke, Effingham, Chatham, Liberty, Glynn and Camden and other free men of the State" gathered in the backcountry capital.[60] Although a more representative body than Glascock's council, its members still felt "inadequate to proceed to business as a House of Assembly," so they selected a nine-man Supreme Executive Council to govern until a legal legislature could be convened. Promising to "tak[e] care in all [their] proceedings to

[58] Archibald Campbell, "Journal of an Expedition against the Rebels of Georgia in North America under the Orders of Archibald Campbell, Esquire, Lieut Colo of His Majesty's 71st Regimt, 1778," Mss., p. 74, Ga. Dept. Arch. and Hist.; Coleman, *Revolution in Georgia*, pp. 122–24.

[59] Coleman, *Revolution in Georgia*, pp. 123–24.

[60] Candler, ed., *Revolutionary Records*, 2:138–45; Coleman, *Revolution in Georgia*, p. 156.

keep as near to the spirit and meaning of the Constitution
. . . as may be," the new government was "recommended . . .
to the inhabitants of the State and [was] adopted by a very
large majority of them."[61] Georgians were, according to William Glascock, "as happy as any people in their Situation
cou'd be under their Government."[62]

But Glascock's assessment was not entirely correct, for
some whigs were far from happy. Radical leader George
Wells, whose political fortunes had waned as the movement
moderated, charged that the Supreme Executive Council
was the instrument of a coastal counterrevolution whose goal
was to overthrow the constitution and restore tidewater aristocracy to power. To some observers, then and now, these
charges were not without foundation. Five of the council's
nine members—John Wereat, who was elected president, Joseph Clay, Seth John Cuthbert, Joseph Habersham, and William Gibbons—were indeed displaced coastal conservatives
who opposed the government created in 1777 and would
gladly have replaced it with one less democratic and more
oriented to their interests. But if Wells was correct, his reve-
lation begs yet a bigger question. Why would Georgia's western members risk their recent gains by turning government
over to men whose commitment to its fundamentals was
questionable at best and who might seize the moment to
undo what had been done? The answer, quite simply, was
that most western whigs, who were surely the better part of
that "very large majority" who accepted the council, did not
see the matter in the same light as Wells. For them the interim government—it never claimed to be anything more—
was not a threat to the constitution and the cause but rather
the salvation of both.[63]

[61] Supreme Executive Council to Gen. Benjamin Lincoln, Aug. 18,
1779, Candler, ed., *Revolutionary Records*, 2:154–55, 142.

[62] Affidavit of Glascock, p. 123.

[63] Cashin, "'The Famous Colonel Wells,'" pp. 145–47, describes the action from Wells's point of view while Jackson, *Lachlan McIntosh*, pp. 112–
15, deals with the same events from the council's perspective. See also Candler, ed., *Revolutionary Records*, 2:140–44, and Coleman, *Revolution in Georgia*, pp. 156–57.

At the time the Supreme Executive Council was created, Georgia's revolution was at yet another critical juncture. Glascock's committee had done its best, but by the summer of 1779 it was obvious Georgia could not overcome the enemy without substantial help from the Continental Congress or from nearby states. It was apparent that such aid would be more easily obtained if government was in the hands of experienced leaders whose voices would be heard north of the Savannah. Given the fact that many of the state's leaders had fled or were prisoners of war, Georgians were fortunate to have able, well-connected patriots like Wereat, Clay, Cuthbert, Habersham, and Gibbons, to whom they could turn. Despite the problems their coastal residence, social status, and previous political positions caused among the zealous, these five were men whose influence extended well beyond the boundaries of the province, and their inclusion signaled a renewed dedication that might, with proper encouragement, rescue the state. To most backcountry whigs, that was far more important than ideological purity.[64]

But frontier Revolutionaries did not sacrifice constitutional gains for conservative support and outside aid, though that was what Wells's charges clearly implied. With the council's remaining seats filled by westerners William Few, John Dooly, Humphrey Wells, and Myrick Davies, the coastal majority could hardly govern unchecked. These four were frontier leaders whose rise to power had begun before the war, was accelerated by the conflict, and was finally confirmed by the constitution. Given their prominence in the government and the seat of the council in the backcountry, any attempt to overturn the popular-based system created in 1777 had little chance of success. Coastal conservatives surely recognized this as did, one suspects, most other whigs.[65]

[64] All the lowcountry members had ties to South Carolina and friends in the Continental Congress. In addition, Joseph Clay was Continental paymaster general for the Southern Department and a close friend of General Lincoln, which made his inclusion in the government all but essential (see Coleman, *Revolution in Georgia*, p. 157, and Lamplugh, "John Wereat," pp. 298–300).

[65] Candler, ed., *Revolutionary Records*, 2:141–44.

But the fear—real or imagined—that the Supreme Executive Council was established to overthrow Georgia's legitimate government was only part of the reason for the opposition of Wells and his followers. Behind their protests was an unspoken conviction that may have been the most important motivation of all. Not only does it help explain why backcountry radicals responded as they did, it also reveals how far western whiggery had come and the direction that it was taking, for in truth Wells and the radicals were losing the west. None of the council's western members can be identified as part of the movement that defeated the Christ Church–led coalition in 1776. They did not sign the anti-McIntosh petitions circulated by Wells's forces in 1777, nor were they associated with the Liberty Society or its activities. Instead, they apparently avoided the factional excesses that engulfed the state, spent their energy on regional matters, and when the retreat from radicalism began, rose in influence as Wells and his supporters declined. Drawing strength from the radicals' greatest accomplishment, the constitution of 1777, these backcountry moderates and others like them offered the region unity instead of division. The Supreme Executive Council sanctioned their ascent and put frontier radicals even farther outside the circle of power. Little wonder George Wells and those like him opposed what was taking place.[66]

Wells believed Wereat's council was not only attempting to undermine the constitution but was also the means by which conservatives and moderates were seeking to reduce radical influence in the state. Although his assessment in the former instance is open to dispute, in the latter he was more accurate. Concerned above all else for the security of the region and the survival of the movement, council leaders felt they needed to do more than enlist aid from outside allies. With the British in Savannah and Governor Wright restored, wavering whigs, of whom there were many, had to be offered a

---

[66] Three of the four council members had signed the antiwhig petitions circulated in 1774, but for that matter so did Wells. Evidence of Wells-Dooly tension may be found in Candler, ed., *Revolutionary Records*, 2:173, 176.

creditable alternative if an independent Georgia was to emerge from the struggle. Yet earlier efforts to weld the apprehensive to the cause had been hampered by radicals seeking to solidify their position and enforce their partisan point of view. Their zeal, which had given the movement so much force, now alienated as many as it converted. It seemed possible that if ardor was not tempered with moderation, those who had created the constitution would now bring about its downfall.[67]

To preserve the government framed by the very group they wished to control and to calm the passions of those to whom the Revolution was a passionate cause, western moderates accepted, perhaps enlisted, the aid of traditional leaders from the coast, men who were dedicated whigs well before factional fissures formed and who might help restrain those "jealousies, natural to a people tenacious of their liberties."[68] The conservatives, seeking their place in a system that reason told them would not soon be undone, accepted the arrangement as easily as it was offered. Thus was forged an alliance of coastal and backcountry interests, created to guarantee that the Revolution would survive, that the government would respond to the needs and wishes of Georgians like themselves, and that radical excesses would be kept in check. It was, however, an alliance guided by its western members. Their influence in the council, which met in Augusta and was surrounded by frontier partisans, far exceeded the four seats they held. The Supreme Executive Council was a glimpse into Georgia's future, a future Wells's radicals found disturbing at best.

Rising to the challenge, Wereat's council agreed to serve gratis, downplayed regional divisions, and stood forth as champions of "virtue"—that is, the willingness to sacrifice all

[67] Council efforts to give Georgians a more safe and stable government can be found in McIntosh to Lincoln, Aug. 4, 1779, Lachlan McIntosh Collection, Clements Library, University of Michigan, Ann Arbor; Supreme Executive Council to the treasurers of Georgia, Aug. 13, 1779, McIntosh to Lincoln, Aug. 18, 1779, and Supreme Executive Council to the governor of South Carolina, Aug. 18, 1779, Candler, ed., *Revolutionary Records*, 2:151–52, 158–59, 163.

[68] Candler, ed., *Revolutionary Records*, 2:147.

in the fight for liberty—and "moderation." At about the same time, Gen. Lachlan McIntosh returned to take command of what remained of the state's Continental forces, raising hopes that Georgia would soon receive the military aid it needed. With the general's encouragement the council cautiously began easing the penalties placed on some who had sworn allegiance to the king when Augusta was taken and who now wished to recant that oath. Concerned more with practical results than with Revolutionary consistency, the Supreme Executive Council pursued a policy of internal tolerance and external vigilance that it hoped would restore a sense of unity and purpose to the whig movement and to the backcountry.[69]

Wells's uncontrolled animosity toward the council, which many of its members returned in kind, was personal as well as political. Wereat, Clay, and Habersham had long been friends and supporters of General McIntosh, whom radicals considered the personification of all that was wrong with upper-class whiggery. Colonel Habersham had even served as the general's second in his duel with Gwinnett. When McIntosh was welcomed home and the government began to show leniency to those whom radicals felt were guilty of treason, Wells concluded that not only was the constitution in danger but that the cause was threatened as well. Ignoring the fact that the government's western members were as committed to the constitution as he, the radical stalwart assumed that if they were willing to associate with men who supported the likes of Lachlan McIntosh they too were surely tainted. Thus convinced, George Wells "raised a Small party against the Council" and embarked on a crusade to set things right.[70]

Elected colonel of the lower battalion of Richmond County

[69] Jackson, *Lachlan McIntosh*, pp. 113–14; Candler, ed., *Revolutionary Records*, 2:171–72; Affidavit of Glascock, p. 123. For backcountry support for the Supreme Executive Council see Candler, ed., *Revolutionary Records*, 2:146, 154, 170, and for opposition to the policy of leniency see Cashin, "George Walton," pp. 136–38.

[70] Cashin, "'The Famous Colonel Wells,'" pp. 144–47; Affidavit of Glascock, pp. 123–24; Cashin, "George Walton," pp. 136–37.

militia, Wells launched an unauthorized purge of those he considered disloyal. Local citizens raised an outcry for his removal, but Wells answered attempts to have him dismissed with a call for the election of a legitimate assembly to replace what he branded a usurping "Tory Council," and on that issue he rallied his followers. But for the moment Colonel Wells was little more than an irritation, for most Georgians apparently appreciated the problems faced by the Supreme Executive Council and seemed to feel it was doing as much as any government could do to overcome them.[71]

Then events played into the radicals' hands. In the fall a Franco-American attack on Savannah, which whigs were sure would succeed, failed miserably, and frontier faith in Wereat's government evaporated. Backcountry patriots began to wonder if the Supreme Executive Council could be expected to defend vigorously a political system so many of its members found faulty. To many, the charges leveled by George Wells were beginning to have the ring of truth. But just as coastal conservatives might have been too extreme for most Georgians had they not been balanced by backcountry moderates, western radicals might not have been able to capitalize on the debacle at Savannah had they not found a moderate ally able to convince Georgians that Wells and his party would not lead them to ruin. Such a man was George Walton.[72]

Perhaps no one better symbolized the sort of leader frontier patriots sought in time of crisis than Walton. Long a prominent whig, and one of national stature, he had served in the Continental Congress, signed the Declaration of Independence, and—it is interesting to note, considering the ease with which Wells accepted him as an ally—had helped secure his friend Lachlan McIntosh an honorable reassignment to escape his radical enemies after the duel. But though

[71] Candler, ed., *Revolutionary Records*, 2:138, 140, 148–50, 153, 160–61, 173.

[72] Jackson, *Lachlan McIntosh*, pp. 96–103, 114–15. See also Alexander A. Lawrence, *Storm over Savannah: The Story of Count D'Estaing and the Siege of the Town in 1779* (Athens, 1951).

a comrade of coastal conservatives, George Walton had equally strong ties with the backcountry. His brother, John Walton, was a leading Augusta planter who had served the west as a delegate to the royal assembly and later to the provincial congress, while George had made his own mark in the region as the Council of Safety's representative to backcountry whig committees during the early days of the Revolution. George Walton knew the rising frontier elites upon whom Wereat and his council depended and they knew him. With the failure to take Savannah, many of these men concluded that new leadership was needed, and it was to Walton they turned.[73]

Had George Walton been in Augusta when the Supreme Executive Council was chosen, he would surely have been on it, but he was captured by the British when Savannah fell in 1778 and not exchanged until October of the next year, at about the time French and American forces made their last futile assault on the city's fortifications. With that disaster on his mind and with a letter from Gen. Benjamin Lincoln "suggest[ing] that it would be for the interest of the State if the Assembly were convened as soon as possible," Walton traveled to Augusta, where he found Wells and Richard Howley, a radical refugee from St. John, trying to raise a legislature while Wereat and his supporters were at Savannah. Concluding that the Supreme Executive Council would now find it difficult, if not impossible, to govern effectively, Walton used Lincoln's letter as his authorization and stepped into the breach. Wells and Howley joined him—an alliance of convenience that disturbs historians to this day—and disillusioned, fearful whigs rallied to the triumvirate.[74]

[73] The most thorough treatment of Walton's career is found in Edwin C. Bridge's "George Walton: A Political Biography," Ph.D. diss., University of Chicago, 1981. Bridges has published a biographical sketch, "George Walton," in *Georgia Signers and the Declaration of Independence* (Covington, Ga., 1981), pp. 59–74.

[74] Lincoln to Walton, Oct. 17, 1779, Benjamin Lincoln Papers, Boston Public Library; Walton to Lincoln, Oct. 28, 1779, Sang Collection (private), Chicago; see also Jackson, *Lachlan McIntosh*, pp. 114–17.

Moving quickly, the new coalition brought together a body of supporters who took the name "Assembly," chose Walton governor, and elected William Glascock Speaker—an effort, it would seem, that assured some that moderation would mark this body as it had its predecessor. But although these choices may have implied a continuation of moderate politics, other factors made it clear such was not the case. The new Executive Council, over which Howley was to preside, drew members from Burke, Richmond, Wilkes, Effingham, and Liberty counties, but ignored Chatham, from which a number of qualified representatives were present. Furthermore, Glascock would later testify that the assembly was a sham, for "every Matter that was brought [up for its consideration] . . . was first Settled, and determined upon, in a private Club held at Geo. Wells's Lodging."[75] Despite the moderating forces at work in the region, there remained those for whom the ultimate expression of Revolutionary ardor was found in radical politics.

Returning to find his western allies abandoning the council, Wereat attempted to regain the initiative by calling upon whigs from the occupied counties "to repair to such place within this State as to them shall appear most safe and convenient" and there elect representatives to a "Legal and Constitutional House of Assembly." But this attempt to offset backcountry defections failed, for the Supreme Executive Council had lost support in every area of the state. The election only gave the council's opponents a chance to legitimize what they had already done. When the new assembly met in

[75] Affidavit of Glascock, pp. 124–25. It was at one such meeting that this triumvirate wrote the Continental Congress of the "repugnance" citizens of Georgia had toward General McIntosh, requested he be transferred, and signed Glascock's name to a supporting letter without the Speaker's knowledge or approval. McIntosh was at the siege of Charleston when he learned Congress had suspended him on the basis of this letter, and his efforts to clear his name became one of post-Revolutionary Georgia's most bitter political conflicts (letter from Glascock, Nov. 30, 1779, and Council Resolution, Ga. Hist. Soc. *Collections*, 12:79–80, 83. For contrasting views of these events and Walton's role in them see Lamplugh, "John Wereat," pp. 295–307, Cashin, "George Walton," pp. 133–45, and Jackson, *Lachlan McIntosh*, pp. 115–27).

January, their victory was sealed by choosing Howley governor, Walton a delegate to the Continental Congress, and George Wells president of the Executive Council.[76]

It was not a complete radical triumph, though conservative critics would later picture it as such and decry what they considered excessive state spending and an unrestrained spoils system. Backcountry moderates, such as Glascock, Davies, Few, Dooly, and Humphrey Wells, remained prominent members of the government, while Walton, who could never be considered an ideological ally of George Wells, also exercised a moderating influence until he left for Philadelphia. The real victors were the western members in general—those frontier whigs whose loyalty to their region transcended factional differences. Finally in the majority, they had achieved what the constitution of 1777 promised, and the future of Georgia and her Revolution was now in their hands.[77]

With the votes at last to do what they wanted, it is hardly surprising that western delegates passed legislation aimed at securing Augusta's position as capital of the west (and perhaps of Georgia), while also acting to entice new settlers into the region with liberal land laws and grants. Coastal conservatives, their numbers severely depleted, could do little but complain, though on the whole their objections seemed to lack the force of earlier protests. This weakness was due in part to the fact that tidewater support for backcountry development was a time-honored policy having little to do with partisan divisions, for if the west flourished then the east, at least that part of it through which western goods traveled, prospered as well. As was the case so often in the past, practical considerations again won out—political divisions might

[76]"Wereat's Proclamation," Nov. 4, 1779, in Charles Colcock Jones, *The History of Georgia*, 2 vols. (Boston, 1883), 2:428; Coleman, *Revolution in Georgia*, p. 157; Lamplugh, "John Wereat," pp. 300–303; and Candler, ed., *Revolutionary Records*, 2:182, 185, 186, 196–97.

[77]Candler, ed., *Revolutionary Records*, 2:196–205; Candler et al., eds., *Colonial Records*, vol. 19, pt. 2, pp. 130–40; Wereat to McIntosh, Jan. 19, 1780, Force Transcripts.

come and go, but economic needs and the alliances formed to meet them had to be maintained.[78]

Then in early February elements of a British fleet appeared at the mouth of the Savannah River and sent a shockwave through the state. Howley issued a call to arms, Heard's Fort in Wilkes County was declared the new seat of government, and whigs prepared for the worst. But it did not come, for the fleet was bound for Charleston, yet in the already nervous backcountry some began to panic. "Outrages" against suspected enemy sympathizers increased as the line between authorized confiscation and illegal plundering was wantonly ignored; the undercurrent of disaffection and violence that had plagued the frontier from the start now came to the surface as Georgia's Revolution became a civil war.[79]

Later that month Governor Howley was chosen to serve with Walton in the Congress and it fell to his successor, George Wells, to attempt to bring order to the growing chaos. But the violence and vendetta that had become Georgia's lot were not confined to rural raiders operating outside the law. Shortly after taking office Governor Wells was killed in a duel by Maj. James Jackson, a Wereat protégé. The cause of their confrontation is not known, in part because their supporters let the matter pass with little or no comment. With half the state occupied by the enemy and the rest feeling increasingly under siege, other concerns were far more pressing. Howley delayed his departure and tried to hold the government together, but the advantage continued to shift to Britain and its allies. On May 12 Charleston surrendered, and later that month a column moved upriver and occupied Augusta. Whig morale crumbled. Howley left for Philadelphia, and the little effective government that remained was conducted on the run. For the next year whig civil authority, where it existed at all, was able to accomplish little. Augusta remained in enemy hands, while bands of loyalists, patriots,

[78] Candler, ed., *Revolutionary Records*, 2:226; Candler et al., eds., *Colonial Records*, vol. 19, pt. 2, pp. 130–40; Coleman, *Revolution in Georgia*, pp. 159–60.

[79] Cashin and Robertson, *Augusta and the Revolution*, pp. 36–37; Candler, ed., *Revolutionary Records*, 2:206–12.

and disaffected roamed the region, plundering and killing almost at will. It was, as one historian aptly noted, "every man for himself in Whig Georgia."[80]

Through this critical period the only vestige of whig resistance came from irregular units who raided the area. In time, however, British operations began to focus farther north and their troops were withdrawn. As that occurred whigs grew bolder and, supported by allies from occupied parts of the state and by South Carolina militia, began to close in on Augusta. Continental aid arrived in May 1781, and in early June the town was taken. Whigs slowly began to reclaim what they had lost. Meanwhile Justice of the Peace John Wilkinson, one of the few civil officers functioning in the backcountry, wrote Nathanael Greene, commander of the Southern Department, asking for assistance in restoring the rule of law to a region that had been without formal government for over a year. Having seen Georgians attempt to cool passions and unite their brethren in the common good, only to fail, those leaders left in the state were unwilling to try again on their own. So they turned to General Greene, a man widely respected and one they hoped fellow citizens would follow.[81]

Greene knew and appreciated their plight. Earlier warned by Henry Lee that Georgians "exceed the Goths & vandals in further[ing] their Schemes of plunder murder & ininqu[i]ty" and urged to "take on [him]self to govern this State till civil government [could] be introduced," the general had already directed Joseph Clay to go to Augusta, to "consult the people of Georgia," and set up a council composed of "persons of good Character in whom the people will comply with a de-

---

[80]Cashin, "'The Famous Colonel Wells,'" pp. 151–52; Cashin and Robertson, *Augusta and the Revolution*, pp. 40–54; Coleman, *Revolution in Georgia*, pp. 160–61; Candler, ed., *Revolutionary Records*, 2:228–47. During this period John Dooly, leader of the backcountry moderates who had kept his military command after the Wells-Walton victory, apparently surrendered and returned to his home on parole. There he was killed by vengeful loyalists.

[81]John Wilkinson to Nathanael Greene, June 8, 1781, Nathanael Greene Papers, Clements Library, Univ. of Mich., Ann Arbor. See also Edward J. Cashin, "Nathanael Greene's Campaign for Georgia in 1781," *Georgia Historical Quarterly* 61 (1977):43–58.

gree of confidence."[82] After Wilkinson's letter arrived, the general apparently reconsidered what he had done, for he soon sent his emissary a note of caution. Realizing that the arrival of Clay, a member of Wereat's deposed council, could raise the expectation that political reorganization might follow, Greene made it clear he would be no party to such a plan. "And as to what some people propose of taking advantage of the present time to reform the Constitution," the commander wrote his friend, "rely upon it, there is nothing more injudicious. It will throw everything into confusion and finally the people will agree to nothing." The council Clay was to raise was not to be the government, but a step toward that end. "A Legislature is necessary," General Greene perceptively advised, "to give you political existence not only in America but in Europe."[83]

Nathanael Greene understood what the constitution had come to mean to backcountry whigs. Early in the war, rising western leaders had concluded that the goals of their Revolution—land, commerce, and a safe, stable society in which to reap the benefits of both—could be realized only if they were able to influence the government and its policies to their advantage. At first they attempted this through a reconstituted Christ Church coalition, but when its tidewater majority chose to concentrate the bulk of Georgia's meager military resources along the coast and to the south, leaving the backcountry to fend for itself, frontiersmen forged an alliance with Gwinnett and his St. John's radicals, hoping through it to protect themselves and their interests. This new coalition sealed its victory with the constitution of 1777. With it the government was established on a democratic base, representation was apportioned so as to reduce the power of Savannah and its allies, and the rise of the western members entered another phase.

The loss of Savannah in 1778, which left the whig movement in the hands of its western wing, only accelerated the

---

[82] Henry Lee to Greene, June 4, 1781, Nathanael Greene Papers, Perkins Library, Duke University, Durham, N.C.; Greene to Wilkinson, June 13, 1781, ibid.

[83] Greene to Clay, July 24, 1781, Greene Papers, Duke Univ.

inevitable shift in power begun the year before, for with migration and settlement patterns already established, it was only a matter of time before the region above the fall line became the dominant force in state politics. But the invasion also brought home the fact that if the Revolutionary movement was crushed, constitutional gains would count for naught. Therefore backcountry leaders did what all but their most extreme colleagues consistently did in time of crisis— they sought a practical political arrangement capable of keeping the Revolution alive. Rather than establish a partisan, sectional government, as they easily could have done, backcountry moderates allied with respected coastal conservatives and gave whigs reason to believe their cause and their constitution would survive.

When that coalition failed to retake Savannah, another more radical than the first replaced it; yet, as with its predecessor, moderate whigs influenced its policies and the practical matter of survival remained paramount. It is important to note, however, that regardless of their critics' charges, neither the Supreme Executive Council nor Walton's assembly attempted to alter or overthrow the constitution of 1777. Nor could they had they tried. After 1778 the survival of Georgia's Revolution depended on the dedication of backcountry whigs to the cause; to the western members, radical, conservative, or moderate, the cause was the constitution— they had become inseparable.

Even the complete breakdown of civil authority in 1780–81 could not sway western whigs from this conviction, and so Greene's note to Clay was no idle warning. To reward their sacrifice with any government other than that sanctioned by the constitution of 1777 might well set off another round of partisan fighting and lead to a British resurgence. Although the document had suffered as much from defenders as detractors, from conservative criticism as radical excess, the principles upon which it was based and the balance of power it created were sacrosanct in the backcountry. Greene was correct to warn Clay to avoid any action that might make it seem he felt otherwise. The constitution of 1777 let western members lead where once they had followed, made them responsible for their future, and convinced them that under its auspices they could reach the goals they sought. For back-country whigs the constitution of 1777 was what the Revolution was all about.

Joseph Clay heeded the warning. The council of "persons of good Character" was organized, an election held, and on August 17 the new assembly met in Augusta, where it put together a government that was moderate in its politics. Every important region of the state, including those still in British hands, was represented; positions of power and trust were divided so as to reward many, alienate few, and avoid extremes. For the next year this coalition, in which western delegates naturally played an important role, administered the state as it came increasingly under whig control. Augusta served as the seat of government until May 1782 when the governor and council, anticipating Savannah's surrender, moved to Ebenezer, some thirty miles upriver from the colonial capital. At last the British withdrew, and on July 14 the state Executive Council met in the city for the first time since 1778. Except for a few scattered pockets of resistance Georgia's war for independence was over.[84]

The government's return to the coast did not signal a restoration of either the Christ Church conservatives or the St. John radicals. With peace it was apparent to all, but especially to those in the east, that Georgia's recovery depended heavily on parceling out and populating the backcountry and on the revival of trade expected to follow. That process would guarantee that the rise of the western members would continue well past 1782. Tidewater leaders faced the choice of economic stagnation or western political expansion, which was really no choice at all. Thus lowcountry whigs, radical and conservative, who had hoped the American Revolution would either preserve or enhance their power and prestige, found their ambitions thwarted, not by each other as they had feared but by those western members both courted.

Yet even before the conflict closed, an alliance began to

[84]Candler, ed., *Revolutionary Records*, 2:250, 255–61, 291, 294, 296–97, 318–19, 339–41, 3:8, 25, 34, 44–46, 58, 78, 80, 118–22, 187; John Brickell to McIntosh, Oct. 11, 1781, Ga. Hist. Soc. *Collections*, 12:100–101.

form that made it possible for one coastal faction to achieve part of its original goal and also provided a glimpse of what the future held for a Georgia governed from above the fall line. Frontier merchants and planters, the rising and the established, found as the war dragged on that they had little in common with and much to fear from Revolutionary radicals who denounced those who "possess[ed] too much property in this place" and who vowed they "by G— must have part of it."[85] Instead these western leaders concluded that their interests lay with their tidewater counterparts, men whose values—acquisition and expansion—they shared, and not with the followers, and later the heirs, of Button Gwinnett and George Wells. Coastal conservatives, seeing this as their chance to be part of the new order and also preserve some semblance of the old, chose to cooperate with backcountry leaders and try to influence their course. The arrangement did not mark the end of sectional conflict, for the growing power of the west would keep such rivalries prominent in state affairs for years to come. Nevertheless, beneath these controversies remained the realization that lowcountry-upcountry interests were so intertwined that one section might pursue policies detrimental to the other only at its own risk.

But despite their alliance with conservatives, western moderates never subscribed to the political elitism associated with the coast. Instead they embraced the democratic innovations framed in 1777, undercut the radicals' support among the state's small farmers, and established a popular base for their authority. Rejecting the socioeconomic alterations espoused by George Wells and his supporters, moderates made the left wing of Georgia's whig movement appear negative and divisive at that critical time when others were seeking a positive, unified solution to Revolutionary problems, and in the end emerged victorious in the conflict to determine who would rule at home. The losers were the Georgia radicals, those political visionaries led by Gwinnett and Wells who early understood the power of the people and the promise of the west and who sought to reorganize the state to take advan-

---

[85] Wereat to McIntosh, Jan. 19, 1780, Force Transcripts.

tage of both. Their success in this laid the foundation for their own defeat, but it also left Georgia their legacy. Although the victors rejected much their opponents stood for, backcountry moderates were and would remain the chief defenders of the radicals' greatest accomplishment—the constitution of 1777.

Thus the Revolution ushered in a new era for Georgia, one dominated by an east-west alliance whose composition was not too different from the prewar Christ Church coalition but whose source of strength now lay with the backcountry. Yet western members did not exploit their advantage to its fullest. With an economy in shambles, a frontier still threatened by hostile Indians, and a social structure straining under increased immigration, ambitious westerners, seeking land, labor, and commercial connections that would turn farms into plantations and trading posts into towns and cities, were not anxious to alienate any potential source of support. Nevertheless, their recognition of the role eastern interests had to play if an independent Georgia was to succeed did not hide the fact that eastern Georgia was, and would remain, the subordinate section. With few exceptions postwar Georgians sought inspiration and leadership in the region where the state's future seemed to lie—they looked to the west.[86]

[86] For information on post-Revolutionary Georgia and its problems see George R. Lamplugh, "Politics on the Periphery: Factions and Parties in Georgia, 1776–1806," Ph.D. diss., Emory University, 1973; W. W. Abbot, "The Structure of Politics in Georgia, 1782–1789," *William and Mary Quarterly*, 3d ser. 14 (1957):47–65; Harvey H. Jackson, "The Road to the Constitution, 1783–1787: Georgia's First Secession," *Atlanta Historical Journal*, 20 (1976):43–52; and George R. Lamplugh, "George Walton, Chief Justice of Georgia, 1783–1785," *Georgia Historical Quarterly* 65 (1981):82–91.

W. W. ABBOT

Lowcountry, Backcountry

A View of Georgia in the American Revolution

DEPENDING ON WHAT is attempted and what demanded, historians of Revolutionary Georgia have an easy time of it or face peculiar difficulties. The relative manageability of its records invites broadly comprehensive treatment. About every half century since the event a new history of Georgia's Revolution has appeared; Virginia still awaits someone with the temerity to claim title to historian of its Revolution. The small number of people, slave and free, living in eighteenth-century Georgia—probably little more than 5,000 in 1754, 35,000 or so in 1775, and 100,000 in 1789—suggests also both the practicality and the particular utility of studying in detail various aspects of this society between 1763 and 1789. The historian coming fresh to Georgia's Revolutionary past might reasonably expect to find a large accumulation of books and articles, rich in data, dealing with towns and counties, families, church congregations, houses, roads, business and cultural organizations, individuals. He would hope to have at his disposal, too, a growing number of studies analyzing one or another characteristic of this society. And he certainly would assume that he could easily identify any number of promising topics for full investigation. He would be disappointed on every count.

The records of Georgia in its Revolutionary era are manageable because they are relatively sparse and very thin. Nearly all the surviving papers have to do with goings on at the top. This was a new, frontier society, its population more or less transient and largely illiterate. As a royal colony and a newly independent state Georgia generated and preserved few records unconnected with the overall management of affairs at Savannah and for a time at Augusta. Town and county records, local court records, church records, plantation and mercantile records, even land records and personal correspondence—never very extensive—are few in number or virtually nonexistent.

The dearth of research materials not directly related to war and politics in Revolutionary Georgia is not quite so severe as it once seemed, however. Harold E. Davis's *The Fledgling Province* made us aware of the many bits and pieces of information lying about in the records of colonial Georgia, unnoted and unused.[1] The official papers of Georgia's political and military leaders and the journals and enactments of its legislative bodies are, of course, full of all sorts of things not political or military. Recent studies—those in particular of seventeenth-century Virginia and the Chesapeake region and of early South Carolina—show how rewarding it can be to root about for evidence of social arrangements and social change in such materials as those surviving from life in Georgia in the second half of the eighteenth century.[2] But detailed treatments of specifics in the life of Revolutionary Georgia remain hard to come by. Just how hard is revealed by a survey of pertinent articles and book reviews published in the *Georgia Historical Quarterly* during the past half century and more. Students of the American Revolution still must turn to one or more of the four general histories of the period in Georgia not only for the sequence of events but also for clues to what was happening beneath the surface and away from the center.

Among the works that treat the Revolution in Georgia at

[1] Davis, *The Fledgling Province: Social and Cultural Life in Colonial Georgia, 1733–1776* (Chapel Hill, 1976).

[2] See, for example, Thad W. Tate and David L. Ammerman, eds., *The Chesapeake in the Seventeenth Century: Essays on Anglo-American Society* (Chapel Hill, 1979), and Peter H. Wood, *Black Majority: Negroes in Colonial South Carolina from 1670 through the Stono Rebellion* (New York, 1974).

length, that of Hugh McCall, published in 1816, stands apart. McCall, as a participant in Georgia's war, was able to add to what he drew from the public record things he himself had heard and seen of the raids and counterraids and skirmishes between rebels and Indians and tories. In the telling he also reveals something of the Georgia Revolutionists' view of their Revolution. Bishop William Bacon Stevens, whose boast it was that he used only the original documents to write his history in the 1850s, recounts the political story in far greater detail than McCall does, and in the 1880s the Rev. Charles Colcock Jones published a new history of Georgia with an even fuller and more balanced political narrative of the 1760s, 1770s, and 1780s while also making good use of McCall's superior account of fighting during the war years. In the 1950s Kenneth Coleman went back to the sources to prepare a straightforward, succinct history of the Revolution in Georgia, which is now the standard account.[3]

These four works, based almost exclusively on the public or official records of the colony and state, are chronicles of political and military events. Each seeks to record the struggle by the friends of liberty against its foes, evil or only misguided, and of liberty's triumph. Coleman also makes allusions to—and seems to assume the existence of—political motives and political rivalries of a more complex sort. At one point he writes that "from the time of the Stamp Act, it was obvious that there was a party in Georgia in essential agreement with the more radical parties in the other colonies." Elsewhere he refers in passing to the existence of conservative and radical parties in Georgia in the spring of 1775, to the "two main Whig groups [in 1776 and 1777] which may be called the radical or popular or country party on one side, and the conservative or city or merchant party on the other,"

---

[3] Hugh McCall, *The History of Georgia, Containing Brief Sketches of the Most Remarkable Events, up to the Present Day,* 2 vols. (Savannah, 1811–16), vol. 2; William Bacon Stevens, *A History of Georgia from its First Discovery by Europeans to the Adoption of the Present Constitution in MDCCXCVIII,* 2 vols. (New York and Philadelphia, 1847–59), vol. 2; Charles Colcock Jones, *The History of Georgia,* 2 vols. (Boston, 1883), vol. 1; and Kenneth Coleman, *The American Revolution in Georgia, 1763–1789* (Athens, 1958).

and to "a political split between the radical or country group
. . . and the more conservative group" in the political infight-
ing at Augusta in 1779.[4] But that is about it. At no point does
his political narrative become, either implicitly or explicitly,
the story of competition for power between parties of divergent economic interests or ideological biases.

Both before and since the appearance of Coleman's history, there have been historians writing about the period who
seem to take for granted that as the Revolution approached
and independence came, Georgia, like Carl Becker's New
York and Merrill Jensen's America, in some way or another
divided itself into radical and conservative factions that persisted through the war and into the 1780s and beyond. It
remained, however, for a young student of Kenneth Coleman's to begin assembling a bit of detailed evidence to support such a view. In 1975 Harvey H. Jackson published in the
Georgia Historical Quarterly a brief argument for looking upon
Georgia politics from 1774 through 1777—and by clear im-
plication well beyond that—in terms of conflict between radical colonial and state leaders on the one side and
conservative ones on the other. Jackson's strategy was to show
that Georgia's slowness in aligning herself with her sister colonies in 1774 and 1775 was the consequence as well as the
cause of a radical-conservative split in the ranks of the whig,
or patriot, leaders of the colony. In 1774 rice planters in lowcountry St. John Parish and merchants at the parish's little
port of Sunbury, being of New England stock and Puritan
principles, wished to have Georgia join the other British colonies in the meeting of a continental congress in New York.
Up the coast, in and around Savannah, in Christ Church Parish, other lowcountry men, who were similarly engaged in
trade and in the cultivation of rice and indigo, were opposed
to this. These Christ Church merchants and planters and
their associates had since its beginning dominated the colonial assembly, and from the passage of the Stamp Act onward
had led the opposition to unpopular British measures. Now,
in 1774 and until the summer of 1775, the Christ Church
men used their influence in the assembly and provincial con-

---

[4] Coleman, *Revolution in Georgia*, pp. 75, 87, 159.

gresses to prevent the adoption of any measures that might lead to a final break with Britain.[5]

Given the state of the historiography of Revolutionary Georgia, to establish firmly and with precision that this division among Georgia's resistance leaders in 1774–75 represented a deeply rooted radical-conservative split in that society might even at this late date have important consequences. For one thing, it could open the way to adding a new dimension to an old tale told by everyone from James Wright in the eighteenth century, to McCall, Stevens, and Jones in the nineteenth, down to Coleman, this writer, and Jack P. Greene in this century: the history of the struggle for dominance between the Georgia assembly and Governor Wright from the repeal of the Stamp Act to the overthrow of royal government in 1775.[6] Better yet, once the political squabbles of the war years are taken to be projections of a long-term radical-conservative division rather than simply manifestations of factional politics of a random sort, then the hunt is on for the wellsprings of political action, something which the nineteenth-century chroniclers and their twentieth-century successors have been little concerned with and which the skimpy sources for Georgia's Revolutionary history will not easily yield.

There is no doubt that from the calling of the Continental Congress until after the fighting at Lexington and Concord in 1775, most of Georgia's leading men outside St. John Parish, and probably most people generally, favored or at least went along with a wait-and-see policy for the colony. But what has been and remains uncertain is the extent to which the hesitancy of the resistance leaders arose from a lack of sympathy with the American cause and from a fear of the loss of political control to other elements of the local population—that is, from conservative impulses as the term is

---

[5] Harvey H. Jackson, "Consensus and Conflict: Factional Politics in Revolutionary Georgia, 1774–1777," *Georgia Historical Quarterly* 59 (1975): 388–401.

[6] See W. W. Abbot, *The Royal Governors of Georgia, 1754–1775* (Chapel Hill, 1959), and Jack P. Greene, *The Quest for Power: The Lower Houses of Assembly in the Southern Royal Colonies, 1689–1776* (Chapel Hill, 1963).

used in reference to the American Revolution. It should be noted at the outset that whatever else may or may not have given rise to and then prolonged rivalry between the low-countrymen of Christ Church and the lowcountrymen of St. John, the public issue that brought it to the fore in the summer of 1774 was resolved by the summer of 1775. At that juncture the leaders of the two parishes joined forces in the provincial congress to drive out Governor Wright and his followers and then saw to it that Georgia kept pace with the other colonies as they moved toward independence and war.

The explanation produced at the time and advanced ever since for Georgia's delay in making common cause with Britain's other mainland colonies is not easily set aside. To defend Georgians from charges of faint-heartedness made in 1774–75 by South Carolinians and others, the historian McCall wrote early in the nineteenth century:

> The situation of Georgia was inauspicious. It was but thinly inhabited on a territory about one hundred and fifty miles from north to south; and about thirty miles from east to west. It presented a western frontier of two hundred and fifty miles. It had on the north-west the Cherokees; on the west, the Creeks; on the south, a refugee banditti in Florida; and on the east the influence of governor Wright, who controled the king's ships on the sea-coast. The population of the eastern district of the province, was composed of white people and negro slaves; the latter, the most numerous, the former but few in number.

In other words, common prudence demanded that the Georgians proceed with caution. Or, as McCall put it, "from surrounding dangers, their measures were to be adopted with cautious circumspection."[7]

The urgent need of this weak and exposed colony for British protection from "surrounding dangers" was not the only reason for the general reluctance of the inhabitants, upcountry and low, to follow St. John's lead until after May 1775. The reluctant rebel leaders of Savannah described themselves in early 1775 quite accurately as "mostly in their first advance towards wealth and independence, destitute of even

[7] McCall, *History of Georgia*, 2:48.

the necessaries of life within themselves."[8] During the two preceding decades, as these men well knew, the steady flow of British capital in the form of government subsidies and especially of credit advances from British merchants had been financing the initiation and steady expansion of agriculture in Georgia—and of trade. To risk now an abrupt and permanent stoppage of British investments would be to court ruin for planters and merchants just beginning to enjoy the first fruits of prosperity, and seemingly the death of hope for the far more numerous who only dreamed of prosperity yet to come.

By the same token, the future happiness of the upcountryman, as he saw it in 1775 and as he was to see it for decades to come, depended upon his ability to satisfy his insatiable hunger—his constant need he would call it—for new and more land, for that land stretching before him to the north and west and held by the Cherokee and the Creeks. It was British might and British money that had made it possible initially for him to come and live across the river from Carolina, and as he moved north and west he would long continue to require support of this sort. The large cession of land that Governor Wright had got from the Cherokee in 1773 was for frontiersmen simply the latest proof of the advantages of maintaining ties with Britain. Nor should it be forgotten that until 1775 there was in Georgia an experienced and influential king's governor who knew how to bring home to upcountrymen and lowcountrymen alike how much each had to gain by preserving the British connection and how much to lose by its rupture.

Not why Georgians were late in rebelling but why they rebelled at all is the more difficult question. It is perhaps the more important one as well. Certainly it is the more useful one for the historian to try to answer. As the late Verner Crane once commented, in its situation and condition in 1776 Georgia was far more like Nova Scotia than rebellious South Carolina, to say nothing of Virginia or Massachusetts. Yet Georgia made the difficult decision for independence,

---

[8] Noble W. Jones, Archibald Bulloch, and John Houstoun to Continental Congress, Apr. 6, 1775, in Jones, *History of Georgia*, 2:172–74.

and Nova Scotia did not. Governor Wright attributed the belated rebelliousness of his charges to the proximity of South Carolina, to the "voices and opinions of men of overheated ideas."[9] Given the general recognition of the advantages to the young colony of continuing the British connection, and the lack of disadvantages, Wright concluded that the Georgians were led into folly by the example and machinations of the Charleston liberty boys.

Even if it is true that, by opting for Revolution, Georgia was only responding to the push and pull of the Revolutionary movement in South Carolina, its route to independence would appear to testify in its own way to the force of ideas in bringing on the American Revolution. Those holding that Georgia's revolt was more than a mindless aping of her more powerful neighbor, as Wright would have it, note that the leaders of the new state in 1777 drafted and adopted a constitution embodying republican principles of a more extreme sort and then proceeded to differ vigorously with one another about who should hold office and set public policy in their new republic. Joseph Clay, a Savannah merchant and a leading member of the old Christ Church faction, wrote several letters in 1777 describing the political situation at this juncture. In one letter he spoke of

> a Defect in our New Constitution, which is so very Democratical & has thrown power into such Hands as must ruin the Country if not timely prevented by some alteration in it, this has arose in a great measure from so large a Number of the principal People being either Tories or through fear of the Consequences have withdrew themselves & wou'd not til very late take an Active part in the present contest by which means they lost that influence they otherways wou'd have had & Rule & Government has got into the Hands of those whose ability or situation in Life does not intitle them to it.[10]

[9]George White, *Historical Collections of Georgia* (New York, 1854), pp. 50–51.

[10]To Bright and Pechin, July 2, 1757, "Letters of Joseph Clay, Merchant of Savannah, 1776–1793 . . . ," Georgia Historical Society *Collections* 8 (1913):34–36. See also his letters to Henry Laurens, Oct. 16, 21, 1757, pp. 46–57.

Historians, who accept Clay's analysis, have been largely content to point to the constitution of 1777 itself as sufficient proof of the supremacy of the radicals and of the rapid advance of democracy in the state. Unfortunately, evidence of how and by whom the constitution was made in 1777 is largely lacking. Nevertheless, it is clear that the executive council and the assembly that the constitution created were little different from the then existing committee of safety and provincial congress dominated by those patriots we now label conservative. Thus, while the constitution of 1777 may have given free rein to ideological differences and political conflict, it neither created nor defined them. Clay himself seems to suggest that his conservative political allies who took part in the making of the constitution found it unsatisfactory only after discovering they were unable to control the legislature chosen under its terms. While Clay is certainly right about the profound effect on political life of the removal of Governor Wright from the scene and the consequent increase in power of the locally elected assembly, it remains to be shown how different in its membership or its aims the new assembly was from its colonial counterpart.

Surely the meaning of the American Revolution for these people occupying the southern frontier of the new United States—its impact—was determined in no small part by the peculiarly nasty and prolonged war that they fought there from 1777 to 1783. The effect on the upcountry and its settlers of the general dislocation of people and widespread destruction of property, the cruel violence of Indian raids and counterraids by settlers, savage guerrilla warfare involving friends and neighbors, and simply the years of unremitting insecurity of life and property must be taken into account. Also to be considered is the effect upon people along the coast of bitter internal divisions, frequent destructive raids from the sea and from the south, and, finally, large-scale invasion followed by British occupation. The trauma of Georgia's war, great though it undoubtedly was, was perhaps made less serious and less lasting than it otherwise might have been by certain circumstances. Georgia had climbed not very far up the ladder toward even moderate stability and wealth when the fighting began. For the most part it was a rough frontier, sparsely populated with uprooted people accustomed to violent behavior, to conflict with the Indians, and to eking out a bare living from newly cleared fields and the surrounding woods. The horrors of war were not as different from the hardships of peace as they might have been.

Even so, the savagery and destructiveness of Georgia's war was such that, left to themselves, the embittered and impoverished Georgians of 1783 would have been a generation or more in regaining even the level of harmony and prosperity that the colony had reached by 1776. A great wave of immigration from the Carolinas and Virginia swept into Georgia during the 1780s. Thousands of new people quickly diluted and blurred the old settlers' collective memory of their war, of the bitter feuds and deep personal hatreds engendered by years of internecine strife. Simultaneously, thousands of new farms carved from the wilderness eased the sense of loss and ameliorated the effect of the widespread destruction of property during the war.

As Georgia emerged from its long war and in the 1780s was being transformed by the arrival of tens of thousands of new settlers in the upcountry, there arose a bitter and decisive battle for control of the state legislature. The challengers, and victors, were the representatives of the expanding upcountry; the losers were the lowcountry representatives, the old Christ Church crowd that had dominated the local assembly almost without interruption since its founding in 1754.[11] It was here in the political competition between sectional leaders in the mid-1780s and, earlier, in the conflict between resistance leaders in 1774–75 that the immediate issues were most clear-cut and the sides people took were more nearly ascertainable than at any other time—except when the resistance leaders united in late 1775 to drive Governor Wright from the colony. The two episodes provide points of entry into the functioning of political forces in this society. To get at the roots and trace out the implications of the divergence of lowcountry planting and trading interests

[11]See W. W. Abbot, "The Structure of Politics in Georgia: 1782–1789," *William and Mary Quarterly*, 3d ser. 14 (1957):47–65.

and upcountry expansionist interests as manifested in 1785 may be easier and less telling than following the trail of a St. John radical and Christ Church conservative division in 1775, but the two undertakings require the same sort of detailed studies based upon elusive evidence, for the most part yet to be done. The rewards are likely to be gratifying, perhaps unexpected, and certainly not always identical.

Every historian who has tried to deal with Revolutionary Georgia in any general or comprehensive way has been guilty of distortion. The historian of the American Revolution looking at Georgia in the Revolution and the historian of Georgia looking at the Revolution in Georgia always get things out of scale. Georgia was so young, so remote, so small, poor, and weak—and getting smaller, poorer, and weaker day by day in the war years—that the words we use to talk about the American Revolution do not fit: they conjure up the wrong images, blow things up into something they were not. The fact is, as I once argued and still believe, Georgia's political and social arrangements of the 1750s and 1760s were in many ways far more like the Virginia of the 1640s than the Virginia of the 1760s. Perhaps the historian of seventeenth-century Virginia should take a look at eighteenth-century Georgia and report what he sees. It may be going too far to say that because of what and where Georgia was in 1776, its revolution was not merely different in degree but in fact different in kind, but it is not going too far by much. Historians stand a better chance of getting closer to the truth if they will assume that this is so. The Georgia story must be told in its own terms.

If the Revolutionary leaders at Savannah in 1777 had not rejected William Henry Drayton's proposal that Georgia become a part of South Carolina, we now would be treating the line of settlement across the Savannah River as a part of the South Carolina backcountry. But as the Georgians did not ever think of themselves as South Carolina backcountrymen, or ever function as such, the history of Georgia along the west bank of the Savannah and down the coast in the 1760s, 1770s, and 1780s is not and cannot be the history of South Carolina. On the other hand, in a sense all of Georgia during

331

these decades was a part of the backcountry south. The student of Georgia's Revolution has much to learn from those studying various aspects of life in the Carolina and Virginia backcountry and not so much from historians writing about the goings on of the grandees in Williamsburg, New Bern, and Charleston.

Contributors
Index

Contributors

W. W. ABBOT is editor in chief of the Papers of George Washington and is the James Madison Professor of History at the University of Virginia. His publications include *The Royal Governors of Georgia, 1754–1775* (1959), *The Colonial Origins of the United States, 1607–1763* (1975), and essays in a number of journals. He has served as editor of the *Journal of Southern History* (1961–63) and the *William and Mary Quarterly* (1963–66).

RICHARD R. BEEMAN is professor of history at the University of Pennsylvania and director of the Philadelphia Center for Early American Studies. His publications include: *The Old Dominion and the New Nation, 1788–1801* (1972), *Patrick Henry: A Biography* (1975), *The Evolution of the Southern Backcountry: A Case Study of Lunenburg County, Virginia, 1746–1832* (1984), and numerous articles in a variety of scholarly journals. Professor Beeman is currently working on a full-scale history of the Revolution in Virginia.

EDWARD J. CASHIN became professor of history at Augusta College in 1969; since 1975 he has been chairman of the Department of History, Political Science, and Philosophy there. In 1975 he was awarded the Georgia Historical Society's E. Merton Coulter award for excellence in writing Georgia history, and in 1983 he received Augusta College's Outstanding Faculty Member Award. His books include *Augusta and the American Revolution* (with Heard Robertson, 1975), *A History of Augusta College* (1976), and *The Story of Augusta* (1980).

JEFFREY J. CROW received his Ph.D. from Duke University in 1974, where he was elected a member of Phi Beta Kappa. He is the author or editor of a number of books and articles on the New South and Revolutionary periods, including *The Black Experience in Revolutionary North Carolina* (1977; 2d printing, 1983). His article "Slave Rebelliousness and Social Conflict in North Carolina, 1775 to 1802" was awarded the Daughters of Colonial Wars Prize as the best article published in the *William and Mary Quarterly* in 1980. Currently he is the administrator of the Historical Publications Section, Division of Archives and History, North Carolina Department of Cultural Resources, and editor in chief of the *North Carolina Historical Review.*

A. ROGER EKIRCH is associate professor of history at Virginia Polytechnic Institute and State University. In 1981–82 he was Paul Mellon Research Fellow at Cambridge University and a Fellow Commoner of Peterhouse. Author of *"Poor Carolina": Politics and Society in Colonial North Carolina, 1729–1776* (1981), he is currently completing a book on the transportation of British convicts to eighteenth-century America.

EMORY G. EVANS is professor and chair, Department of History, University of Maryland—College Park. He is the author of, among others, "Planter Indebtedness and the Coming of the Revolution in Virginia" (1962), "Private Indebtedness and the Revolution in Virginia, 1776–1796" (1971), and *Thomas Nelson of Yorktown: Revolutionary Virginian* (1975). He is working on a long-term study of the Virginia elite in the eighteenth century.

JACK P. GREENE is Andrew W. Mellon Professor in the Humanities at The Johns Hopkins University. He is the author of *The Quest for Power: The Lower Houses of Assembly in the Southern Royal Colonies, 1689–1776* (1963) and the editor of *The Diary of Colonel Landon Carter of Sabine Hall, 1752–1778* (1965). He is currently at work on a study of the formation and changing character of collective identity in the plantation colonies of colonial British America from 1660 to 1815.

HARVEY H. JACKSON is professor of history and chairman of the Division of Social Sciences at Clayton Junior College, Morrow, Ga. He is the author of *Lachlan McIntosh and the Politics of Revolutionary Georgia* (1979), and coeditor of *Forty Years of Diversity: Essays on Colonial Georgia* (1984). Among the journals his articles have appeared in are the *William and Mary Quarterly*, the *Georgia Historical Quarterly*, and *Southern Studies*. He is currently preparing an article on the relationship between the Great Awakening in South Carolina and that colony's fear of slave insurrection. His long-range plans include a study of the evolution of political ideas and institutions in early Georgia.

RACHEL N. KLEIN, assistant professor of history at the University of California at San Diego, completed her research on the South Carolina backcountry while she was a fellow at the Institute of Early American History and Culture in Williamsburg. The article included in this volume, together with an earlier article entitled "Ordering the Backcountry: The South Carolina Regulation" (1981), is part of her forthcoming book *Unification of a Slave State: The Rise of the Planters in the South Carolina Backcountry, 1760–1808*.

ROBERT M. WEIR is professor of history at the University of South Carolina. Among his publications are "'The Harmony We Were Famous For': An Interpretation of Pre-Revolutionary South Carolina Politics" (1969), "Who Shall Rule at Home: The American Revolution as a Crisis of Legitimacy for the Colonial Elite" (1976), "The Role of the Newspaper Press in the Southern Colonies on the Eve of the Revolution" (1980), and *Colonial South Carolina—A History* (1983). Professor Weir's current research interests include the American colonists' perceptions of the natural environment as well as the Revolution in South Carolina.

Index

Abbot, W. W., 325
Adams, John, 100, 231
Adams, Robert, Jr., 203
Alamance, battle of, 100, 102, 128, 230
Alley, Thomas, 187
Alston, Philip, 139, 145, 172
American Revolution, historiography of, 7–8; in southern backcountries, 30–36
Ammerman, David, 31
Anglicans, 225–26, 237
Anson Co., N.C., 219
Armstrong, Maj. John, 155
Ashe, John, 258–59
"Assembly" (Ga.), 312
Atter, John, 192
Augusta, battle of (1780), 266; (1781), 270
Authority, 21; in colonial America, 23–27; in southern colonies, 22

Backcountries, southern, 5–6; and American Revolution, 30–36
Backcountry, southern: Bridenbaugh's view of, 214–15, 217; contrast with lowcountry, 9–12; as a cultural region, 3–5; economic structure of, 219–23; ethnic diversity in, 224; as a geographical region, 3; historiography of, 215–16; political institutions in, 226–30; population mobility in, 223–24; religious diversity in, 224–26; settlement of, 217–19; as a socioeconomic region, 3–5; see also Georgia backcountry; North Carolina backcountry; South Carolina backcountry; Virginia, southwest

Bailyn, Bernard, 21
Bandits, 42–43; British and, in South Carolina, 59, 61–62; South Carolina loyalists and, 55–61; South Carolina whigs and, 61
Banning, Lance, 96
Baptists, 225–26, 234, 237
Bartram, John, 215
Bassett, John Spencer, 215
Baxter, Col. John, 95
Beard, Andrew, 147
Becker, Carl, 324
Bedford Co., Va., 183; disaffection in, 207; whig response to disaffection in, 187, 203
Beeman, Richard R., 6, 11, 14, 33, 238
Beverley, Robert, 16
Biven, Nathaniel, 157
Blagrave, Henry, 220
Blewer, Peter, 155
Bloch, Marc, 8
Boone, Daniel, 152
Bostick, Chesley, 248, 254
Botetourt Co., Va., 183; disaffection in, 207; whig response to disaffection in, 187–88, 200–201, 203–4
Boyd, Col. James, 258–59
Branson, Eli, 142, 155–56
Briar Creek, battle of, 259, 304
Bridenbaugh, Carl, 4–6, 213–15, 217
Brock, Charles, 158
Brock, Elias, Sr., 158
Brown, Richard Maxwell, 40
Brown, Thomas, 59–60, 248–50, 252–59, 263–75, 288–89, 301

INDEX

Georgia (*cont.*)
286–88; Supreme Executive
Council, 304–12
Georgia backcountry: disaffection
in, 293; petitions of, 244–45,
279–81; Revolutionary War
in, 329–30; settlement of,
241–42, 262–63, 279–80;
whig response to disaffection
in, 288, 301
Georgia factions: Christ Church,
282–85, 299–301, 308, 310–
11, 313, 324–27, 330; conservatives, 277–78, 323–24;
radicals, 277–78, 299, 307–
10, 313, 319–20, 323–24,
329; St. John, 283–85, 301,
324; western members, 255,
278–79, 284, 289–91, 296,
305–6, 309, 313, 316–20,
327, 330; western moderates,
292–93, 303, 308, 310, 313,
317, 319–20; western radicals, 292, 300–301, 307, 310;
whig, 276–79, 284, 323–25
Germain, Lord George, 263
Gibbes, John Walter, 94
Gibbons, William, 305–6
Gipson, William, 142
Glascock, William, 303–5, 312–13
Glen, James, 149–50
Goode, Col. William, 236
Government, in colonial America,
29
Greene, Jack P., 325
Greene, Gen. Nathanael, 107–10,
115, 121–22, 162, 232–33,
269–72, 315–16; and plun-
dering, 63–64, 75, 88; and
policy toward loyalists, 81–
82, 119–20, 174, 271; and
slaves, 66, 68
Griffith, John, 195–96, 210–11
Gruber, Ira, 109
Guerard, Benjamin, 77, 83, 89
Guilford Courthouse, battle of,
270
Gwinnett, Button, 247, 253–54,
289–91, 293, 295–96, 298–
301, 309

Habersham, James, 242, 305–6,
309
Hall, Moses, 142–43
Hamilton, Lt. Col. John, 159
Hammond, Col. LeRoy, 88, 259
Hampton, Henry, 65
Hanger, George, 74
Hardy, John, 126
Hart, Oliver, 44–45, 50
Hay, Douglas, 97
Hayes's Station, S.C., 72
Heard, Gov. Stephen, 264
Heavin, Thomas, 189, 198
Henderson, Richard, 152
Heninger, Michael, 192
Henry, Gov. Patrick, 190, 238
Henry Co., Va., 183–84; whig re-
sponse to disaffection in, 203
Hewes, Joseph, 100
Hierarchical society, 22
Higginbotham, Don, 71
Hill, John, 186–87
Hobson, John, 227
Hoffman, Ronald, 70–71, 115,
232, 235
Holder, Joseph, 140
Holley, William, 156
Hooper, William, 106, 122, 146
Houstoun, Gov. John, 256–57,
302–3
Howe, Gen. Robert, 59, 256, 258
Howley, Richard, 262, 311–14
Hunt, William, 56
Hunter, James, 102–3
Hunters, 42–43
Hutto, 57

Improvement, social, 15–20
Independence, personal, 12–14
Independents, 12–13
Indians: British and, in Georgia,
249–50, 254, 259–60, 268;
Georgia whigs and, 251–52;
South Carolina loyalists and,
54; South Carolina whigs
and, 51–54; Thomas Brown
and, 254, 264–65, 271–72;
"white," 42, 56
Indian trade, 245–46
Ingles, Col. William, 203, 209–10

INDEX